T0321985

Artificial Intelligence and the Law

This volume presents new research in artificial intelligence (AI) and law, with special reference to criminal justice.

It brings together leading international experts including computer scientists, lawyers, judges and cyberpsychologists. The book examines some of the core problems that technology raises for criminal law ranging from privacy and data protection, to cyberwarfare, through to the theft of virtual property. Focusing on the West and China, the work considers the issue of AI and the law in a comparative context presenting the research from a cross-jurisdictional and cross-disciplinary approach.

As China becomes a global leader in AI and technology, the book provides an essential in-depth understanding of domestic laws in both Western jurisdictions and China on criminal liability for cybercrime. As such, it will be a valuable resource for academics and researchers working in the areas of AI, technology and criminal justice.

Dennis J. Baker, Research Professor, De Montfort University, UK.

Paul H. Robinson, Colin S. Diver Professor of Law, University of Pennsylvania, USA.

Artificial Intelligence and the Law

Cybercrime and Criminal Liability

**Edited by Dennis J. Baker
and Paul H. Robinson**

Routledge
Taylor & Francis Group

LONDON AND NEW YORK

First published 2021
by Routledge
2 Park Square, Milton Park, Abingdon, Oxon OX14 4RN

and by Routledge
52 Vanderbilt Avenue, New York, NY 10017

Routledge is an imprint of the Taylor & Francis Group, an informa business

British Library Cataloguing-in-Publication Data
A catalogue record for this book is available from the British Library

Library of Congress Cataloging-in-Publication Data
Names: Baker, Dennis J, editor. | Robinson, Paul H., 1948– editor.
Title: Artificial intelligence and the law : cybercrime and criminal
    liability / edited by Dennis J Baker and Paul H. Robinson.
Description: Milton Park, Abingdon, Oxon ; New York, NY :
    Routledge, 2021. | Includes bibliographical references and index.
Identifiers: LCCN 2020023089 (print) | LCCN 2020023090
    (ebook) | ISBN 9780367347970 (hardback) | ISBN
    9780429344015 (ebook)
Subjects: LCSH: Artificial intelligence—Law and legislation. |
    Artificial intelligence—Law and legislation—Criminal provisions. |
    Computer crimes—Law and legislation. | Criminal liability. |
    Privacy, Right of. | Data protection—Law and legislation. | Artificial
    intelligence—Law and legislation—China. | Data protection—Law
    and legislation—China.
Classification: LCC K564.C6 A925 2021 (print) | LCC K564.C6
    (ebook) | DDC 345/.0268—dc23
LC record available at https://lccn.loc.gov/2020023089
LC ebook record available at https://lccn.loc.gov/2020023090

ISBN: 978-0-367-34797-0 (hbk)
ISBN: 978-0-429-34401-5 (ebk)

Typeset in Galliard
by Apex CoVantage, LLC

Contents

11   Don't panic: artificial intelligence and Criminal Law 101   247

MARK DSOUZA

Contributors

Dennis J. Baker FRSA, Research Chair in Criminal Law & Penal Theory, School of Law, De Montfort University.

Jonathan Clough, Professor of Criminal Law and Procedure, Faculty of Law, Monash University.

Sadie Creese, Professor of Cybersecurity, Department of Computer Science, University of Oxford.

Mark Dsouza, Lecturer in Law, Faculty of Laws, University College London.

Liang Genlin, Professor of Criminal Law, School of Law, Peking University.

Gabriel Hallevy, Professor of Criminal Law, Faculty of Law, Ono Academic College.

The Right Hon. Lord (Patrick) Hodge, Deputy President of The Supreme Court of the United Kingdom.

Dongyan Lao, Professor of Criminal Law (Changjiang Scholar), School of Law, Tsinghua University.

Li Lifeng, Professor of Law, School of Law, Jilin University.

Jing Lijia, Post Doctorial Fellow, School of Law, Wuhan University.

Zhang Mingkai, Changjiang Distinguished Professor, School of Law, Tsinghua University.

Paul H. Robinson, Colin S. Diver Professor of Law, University of Pennsylvania, Carey Law School.

He Ronggong, Professor of Criminal Law, School of Law, Wuhan University.

Wang Wenjing, Post-Doctoral Fellow, School of Law, Tsinghua University.

Tianhong Zhao, Professor of Criminal Law and Procedure, Chinese University of Political Science and Law.

1 Emerging technologies and the criminal law

Dennis J. Baker and Paul H. Robinson

1. Introduction

In this volume, the contributors explore criminal liability in the context of artificial intelligence and other emerging digital technologies. Some of the chapters focus more on how these technologies are being used by criminals to facilitate crime, while others consider how emerging technologies can assist law enforcement agencies by collecting cogent evidence (such as biometrics) or act as a deterrent (i.e., burglars may be more deterred by a security camera system that can do face recognition, and report them to the police in real time, than they might be by an traditional closed-circuit television [CCTV] camera footage). The key areas covered include are cyberfraud, cybersecurity, data retention laws, digital privacy invasions, liability for intermediaries such as Internet service providers (ISPs) and criminal liability for artificially intelligent entities.

We have included a diverse range of chapters from scholars. We also have a chapter from The Right Hon. Lord Hodge, the Deputy President of the Supreme Court of the United Kingdom. Additionally, we have chapters from some of China's foremost criminal law professors. Some of those chapters draw some comparisons between the common law and Chinese law, but none of them aim to conduct a wholesale comparative study. Their primary aim is to draw out legal and ethical issues concerning emerging technologies and the law. The seven common law chapters cover also artificial intentional and cybersecurity matters. Our contributors aim to tease out some of the core problem areas to provide some sort of platform for thinking about law reform in this area. Some problems relate more to enforcement than to a lack of legal regulation. We briefly discuss a few issues that have arisen as a result of emerging technology in the remainder of this chapter. Hopefully, this will provide some background to some of the problems addressed in the chapters. Some of those issues include artificial intelligence; privacy, surveillance and biometrics; and Internet censorship to prevent online harms.

2. Artificial intelligence and criminal justice

(a) *Artificial intelligence*

Artificial intelligence (AI) is a misnomer since what it refers to is not intelligence at all. When McCarthy coined the term "artificial intelligence," he had machine learning in mind.[1] Algorithms building a mathematical model from a set of data to allow a processor to make predictions is nothing like human reasoning.[2] At this point in time, machines cannot reason and make rational and autonomous choices. Most of what is currently labelled intelligence is computer processing.[3] Emotional intelligence, the capacity for practical reasoning and the capacity for social decision-making are well beyond the capacity of any existing machine.[4] It will not be long before private individuals will be able to purchase a robot that will be equipped to act as a cleaner, security guard, Michelin star chef and so on. A robot equipped with face recognition and gait (walk) recognition capacity might guard a house and instantly recognise a burglary. It might not only be able to report it to the police in real time, but also report that the perpetrator is Joe Bloggs. However, no existing AI-operated robot can cook with the passion and emotion that Rick Stein cooks with. Similarly, a robot security guard might hold down a burglar until the police arrive, but it would not do so this action with any emotion. It would not act with human irrationally as a result of anger or fear, or even human rationally as a result of steadfastness, but would simply be triggered

---

1 See his seminal paper, J. McCarthy, "Recursive Functions of Symbolic Expressions and their Computation by Machine, Part I," (1960) 3(4) *Communications of the ACM* 184; see too J. McCarthy and P. J. Hayes, "Some Philosophical Problems from the Standpoint of Artificial Intelligence," in D. Meltzer and D. Michie (eds.), *Machine Intelligence*, (Edinburgh: Edinburgh University Press, 1969) Vol. 4 at 463.

2 A. Turing, "Computing Machinery and Intelligence," (1950) 49 *Mind* 433; V. Lifschitz, *Artificial and Mathematical Theory of Computation: Papers in Honour of John McCarthy*, (Boston: Academic Press, 1991).

3 There is no doubt machines have tremendous processing capacity. See for example, P. Dockrill, "In Just 4 Hours, Google's AI Mastered All the Chess Knowledge in History," (Science Alert, 7 December 2017); J. Lee, "Deep Learning – assisted Real-time Container Corner Casting Recognition," (2019) 51(1) *International Journal of Distributed Sensor Networks* 1; S. R. Granter *et al.*, "AlphaGo, Deep Learning, and the Future of the Human Microscopist," (2017) 141(5) *Archives of Pathology & Laboratory Medicine* 619 reports that the game:

> Go's much higher complexity and intuitive nature prevents computer scientists from using brute force algorithmic approaches for competing against humans. For this reason, Go is often referred to as the "holy grail of AI research." To beat Se-dol, Google's AlphaGo program used artificial neural networks that simulate mammalian neural architecture to study millions of game positions from expert human – played Go games. But this exercise would, at least theoretically, only teach the computer to be on par with the best human players. To become better than the best humans, AlphaGo then played against itself millions of times, over and over again, learning and improving with each game – an exercise referred to as reinforcement learning. . . . It implements machine-learning algorithms (including neural networks) that are effectively an extension of simple regression fitting. In a simple regression fit, we might determine a line that predicts an outcome y given an input x. With increased computational power, machine learning algorithms are able to fit a huge number of input variables (for example, moves in a game of Go) to determine a desired output (maximizing space gained on the Go board).

4 J. R. Lucas, "Minds and Machines," (1961) 36 *Philosophy* 112; Cf. E. Yudkowsky and N. Soares, *Functional Decision Theory: A New Theory of Instrumental Rationality*, (Machine Intelligence Research Institute, 2018).

on the relevant information being received that the burglar has entered not as a guest, but by breaking in, and, is someone who is not on the database of faces of people who normally visit the property.

Machine learning and computer processing cannot at this stage be compared with human reasoning and emotional intelligence.[5] If AI eventually acquires the faculty for practical reasoning (and it probably will in the distant future) and agency, then the normal rules of criminal responsibility (whatever they are at the given point in time) will apply. There will be no need for new rules if these machines are able to make rational choices, but there will be a need for transitional rules for the long period when these AI machines straddle between being able to make fully autonomous choices and partially autonomous choices. At the moment, they can do neither. Civil law such as manufacture liability rules already apply to AI, because at the moment, it is considered no more than an instrument in the hands of human agents.[6]

We often hear the term "autonomous weapon," but this is an oxymoron.[7] Currently, a machine cannot be criminally liable either directly or through the law of complicity for any harm it causes.[8] There is currently no comparison between "machine learning" and "human understanding." Nonetheless, like all machines, AI has capabilities beyond those of a single human. It is true that AI-equipped machines can do many things that humans cannot, but the same can be said of machines generally. A motorbike can travel from London to Cambridge faster than a human. A bulldozer can clear acres of precious rainforest in an hour whereas a team of humans with axes might not clear even half an acre in a day. Similarly, AI-operated databases can keep accurate records of vast quantities of information and recall and analyse basic information in an instant. It can process volumes of data at speeds beyond the capacity of a single human mind. A human does not have the ability to scan 100,000 faces in a football stadium and pick out a single person in real time. It would be churlish to label it AS (Artificial Stupidity) since its incredible processing abilities can obtain intelligent results.

---

5 Machines are not even close to achieving consciousness, let alone the ability to make ethical decisions based on practical reasoning. Cf. K. B. Korb, "Searle's AI program," (1991) 3(4) *Journal of Experimental & Theoretical Artificial Intelligence* 283; G. Meissner, "Artificial Intelligence: Consciousness and Conscience," (2020) *AI & Society* 225.

6 For a very detailed discussion of civil and regulatory rules concerning AI, see the extensive report by the European Commission, *Liability for Artificial Intelligence and Other Emerging Technologies*, (Brussels: 2019).

7 A robot by definition is an automaton that acts without volition.

8 If killer robots are used in war, then liability has to rest with those using them in the same way it would if they were to use bombs *simpliciter* against the law. International law and humanitarian law violations would rest with the humans misusing such robots. Apparently, Taranis, a flying killer robot, if put into service, will allow the Royal Air Force to programme it to search for targets and take them out without further human input. Suppose Taranis is programmed to strike all people wearing a yellow vest within a combat zone. Its systems would allow it to search and kill such people without further human input. However, the command for it to do so would lie in the hands of the humans who set it in motion, as would any criminal responsibility for the deaths of those wearing yellow vests, if killing them was not justifiable.

If an AI operated robot is developed that has the capacity for "emotional intelligence" and "practical reasoning,"[9] it might be assumed it would have a much longer life span than a human currently has; therefore, sentencing and punishment would need a rethink. How do we punish a machine that might have a 1,000-year or even a 10,000-year lifespan? A machine might have no need for property other than standing space, so economic fines also might be a very outdated concept by the time machines can be criminality liable. If it has emotional intelligence, then jail or something similar might cause it mental distress and thus work as punishment. It is doubtful that jail sentences will last more than another century as an effective form of punishment for humans, let alone for anything else, so new thinking will be required when considering penalties for the criminal offending of AI. It might be as simple as cutting off the machine's energy supply for a period of time to punish it, but if it is not subject to the normal lifespan limits of a human life span, forced hyphenation is hardly likely to act as a deterrent. If a machine is very advanced, it will have dignity equal to that of humans and thus it could not be reprogrammed to make it behave: to do so would be akin to subjecting human criminals to a eugenics programme.

Humans and machines are both made of matter and it is not fanciful to imagine the two evolving into one being or the artificial life form eventually evolving into the natural life form.[10] If someone had explained the idea of a smart-phone to Sir Isaac Newton and told him that within 200 years of his death, almost everyone would be using them, even a visionary mathematician of his standing might have though it total fantasy. Humans have been evolving for more than 85 million years.[11] What happens long into the future is not our concern here. The problems that this sort of advanced future technology might pose will need to be dealt with in the future in accordance with the social context in which it takes place. Our problem here is to deal with emerging technologies and their impact in the current legal context.

Emerging technologies pose threats to privacy and have the potential to help fraudsters and other criminals to perpetrate crime, but they also help to reduce crime. There is great utility in the police and intelligence services having access to surveillance technology, but such technology could be misused more often if made widely available to private individuals.[12] When the former double agent,

---

9   Practical reasoning is the antithesis of machine learning. See generally, M. Bratman, *Intention, Plans, and Practical Reason*, (Cambridge: Harvard University Press, 1987); J. Hampton, *The Authority of Reason*, (Cambridge: Cambridge University Press, 1998); J. Raz, *Engaging Reason*, (Oxford: O.U.P., 1999).

10   J. Lovelock, *Novacene: The Coming Age of Hyperintelligence*, (London: Allen Lane, 2019); N. R. B. Martins *et al.*, "Human Brain/Cloud Interface," (2019) 13(112) *Hypothesis and Theory: Front. Neurosci*. 1; N. Bostrom, *Superintelligence: Paths, Dangers, Strategies*, (Oxford: O.U.P., 2014).

11   A. Clark, "Natural-Born Cyborgs?" in M. Beynon *et al.*, (eds.), *Cognitive Technology: Instruments of Mind*, (Berlin: Springer, 2001) at 17.

12   Targeted surveillance and interception ought always require a warrant. See the discussion in *Capenter v. United States* (2018) 138 S. Ct. 2206.

Sergei Skripal, was poisoned with Novichok (a nerve agent), the police were able to trace every move the suspected perpetrators made through surveillance footage. The many imagines of the alleged perpetrators in London, at Gatwick Airport, and in Salisbury were crystal clear. They were able to bring up their border control moves at Gatwick and the hotels where they stayed. None of this relied on eyewitnesses. Eyewitnesses are no match for the reliability of CCTV, face recognition biometrics and computer programmes that can scan thousands of hours of footage and perform facial recognition matches instantly.[13]

Artificial intelligence was used to process 11,000 hours of film footage[14] from airports and a city such as Salisbury to find matching faces at record speed. Similarly in China, facial recognition technology identified a wanted suspect in a concert crowd of 60,000.[15] Artificial intelligence also can be used to process evidence and help overwhelmed enforcement agencies deal with the wealth of digital evidence produced by emerging technology. It is a necessity in the modern age, since human police are capable of solving only a fraction of the crime that is perpetrated.[16] While it would not be possible to prosecute and imprison all criminals who are likely to be caught due to technological surveillance, the certainty of being caught could act as a deterrent to many criminals. No large-scale empirical study of the deterrent effect of "biometric" evidence has been conducted to date, so it is only possible to speculate about its potential deterrent impact. The ability to capture a crime on camera and use the captured biometrics such as gait or face recognition information to categorically link the crime to a particular perpetrator will have an impact on enforcement and conviction rates if nothing else.[17]

Home security systems now come with face recognition technology, so a homeowner can now give the police biometrical identifying information concerning burglars. This might allow police to trace burglars within hours (arguably because many are recidivists who no doubt are already in police databases) or by doing

---

13 J. P. Vallano *et al.*, "Familiar Eyewitness Identifications: The Current State of Affairs," (2019) 25 *Psychology, Public Policy, and Law* 128.

14 "A London Hotel Room, Counterfeit Perfume and 11,000 hours of CCTV Footage: How Russian Novichok Suspects Were Found," (London: *Independent Newspaper*, 5 September 2018).

15 London: BBC News online, *Chinese Man Caught by Facial Recognition at Pop Concert* (13 April 2018). In the same news story it is reported that: "China has a huge surveillance network of over 170 million CCTV cameras. . . . In August last year, police in Shandong province arrested 25 suspects using a facial recognition system that was set up at the Qingdao International Beer Festival."

16 *R. (Edward Bridges) v. Chief Constable of South Wales Police* [2020] 1 W.L.R. 672 at 678 citing *R. (on the application of S) v Chief Constable of South Yorkshire* [2004] 1 W.L.R. 2196.

17 "Crown Prosecution Service Head: Justice System Can't Cope," (London: Guardian Newspaper, 27 October 2018) where it is reported: "Britain's criminal justice system is 'creaking' and unable to cope with the huge amounts of data being generated by technology, the head of the Crown Prosecution Service has warned in her final interview before stepping down." Artificial intelligence can be used also to process voluminous evidence.

face matches with images on Facebook and other social media.[18] Alternatively, the police might do a match at a later time when a suspect (whose biometrics are on the police database as a result of a burglary victim giving the police a copy of information captured on their home security system) passes through a busy public railway station or High Street where biometric capture cameras are being used. Biometric surveillance cameras can capture more than faces. They can capture gait patterns, as well. Even DNA has been helpful in tracing burglars. "For example, recent Home Office statistics show that while the annual detection rate of domestic burglary is only 14%, when DNA is successfully recovered from a crime scene this rises to 48%."[19] Facial recognition data is likely to be vastly superior for identifying criminals, because unlike DNA, many people post their photographs online in social media accounts and so on. No one can post their DNA online. Similarly, increasing awareness of the fact that a certain crime might not only be caught on camera, but could be biometrically traced back to the perpetrator fairly quickly, could have a significant deterrent effect. It is too soon to prognosticate about the likely deterrent effect of biometric evidence.[20] Criminologists no doubt will conduct large scale empirical surveys to try to ascertain the deterrent effect as biometric capture technology becomes more prevalent.

It has been reported that China is already using gait recognition technology to catch criminals.[21] Gait recognition is useful for when a criminal covers his or her face. There was a famous case in England in 2006 when a male murder suspect got through Heathrow Airport and fled wearing a Muslim niqab. Heathrow now operates on a fully automated face recognition system, but one is not required to give biometrics such as a fingerprint or iris scan[22] to leave the United Kingdom.

---

18 This goes both ways, as better evidence can clear the innocent, too.

> As of April 2017, the federal DNA database [in the United States] has assisted in more than 358,069 investigations. DNA evidence has exonerated 350 innocents who combined had served 4787 years in prison, sometimes on death row.3 DNA also enabled law enforcement to identify 149 of the true perpetrators of those crimes, who 'went on to be convicted of 147 additional violent crimes, including 77 sexual assaults, 35 murders, and 35 other violent crimes while the innocent sat behind bars for their earlier offenses.' A universal DNA database could have prevented those 350 false convictions and 147 later violent crimes.

> Kirsten Dedrickson, "Universal DNA Databases: A Way to Improve Privacy?" (2018) 4(3) *Journal of Law and the Biosciences* 637.

19 Cf. *R. (Edward Bridges) v. Chief Constable of South Wales Police* [2020] 1 W.L.R. 672 at 680.

20 *R. (Edward Bridges) v. Chief Constable of South Wales Police* [2020] 1 W.L.R. 672.

21 Dake Kang, "Chinese 'Gait Recognition' Tech IDs People by How They Walk," (Associated Press, *Business Insider*, 5 November 2018, 9:37 PM), writes:

> Huang Yongzhen, the CEO of Watrix, said its system can identify people from up to 50 meters (165 feet) away, even with their backs turned or faces covered. This can fill a gap in facial recognition, which needs close-up, high-resolution views of a person's face to work.

22 The United Kingdom tried an Iris Recognition Immigration System at Heathrow for frequent flyers for about a decade, but abandoned it for a much less reliable and cheaper face

Obviously, face recognition would not pick up a covered face. Arguably, all faces ought to be shown at all times during the process of passing through immigration, but if this cannot be achieved due to cultural sensitivities, gait recognition could be helpful.[23] Perhaps this sort of biometric will be included in future passport biometrics as the technology advances. It would not be difficult to order people to provide gait data as a condition of obtaining a passport.

More generally, it is not going to be a ubiquitous enforcement tool until enforcement agencies develop an extensive gait information database. It surely will be very little time at all before a home camera will be able to perform gait recognition, because they already do face recognition. One of the cheapest is the Tend Secure Lynx Pro home security camera (other widely available face recognition cameras are Netgear Arlo Pro 2 and the Nest Cam IQ Outdoor camera), which costs not much more than £100 and comes with free cloud storage and detailed HD video. Capturing this sort of biometric information and handing it on to enforcement agencies will allow the information to be stored on a database so that a match might be done when the suspect wanders past a biometric recognition camera in the future. One can also imagine such cameras automatically calling the police if certain activities take place, such as a burglary or a home invasion. Cameras in High Streets will soon be able to alert the police to incidents of criminal damage, and so on. Similarly, pickpockets targeting tourists at distraction points such as the Little Mermaid statue in Demark might soon find it not so easy to disappear, if alerts are given to the police as they move pass other cameras in the city.

3. Privacy, surveillance and biometrics

The collection and use of biometrics without consent or lawful justification could cause grave harm and requires greater deterrence than is provided by the civil sanctions in *Data Protection Act 2018*. Why should a bar or restaurant be allowed to collect biometrics without consent and then create a "social credit" rating system which would result in a person being banned from shops and cafés all over England? Basically, private providers are being allowed to create their own quasi-criminal record on persons which affects their freedom of movement without them having been proven guilty of any wrong in a court of law with the due

---

recognition and e-passport system. Part of the problem with facial recognition as used for passport checks is that is relies on passport photos that have been submitted with a passport application, rather than digitally collected facial dimension information.

23 P. Stokes, "Murder Suspect Fled under Muslim Veil," (London: *The Telegraph*, 20 December 2006), where it was reported:

A Somali asylum seeker wanted for the murder of WPc Sharon Beshenivsky is believed to have fled Britain dressed as a woman wearing a Muslim niqab, which covers the whole face apart from the eyes. . . . His photograph and details were circulated to every police force, port and airport. There are four stages where 'visual checks' can be carried out for departing passengers where the face is matched to a passport photograph.

process that process offers. Private shops and restaurants are using automated face recognition systems such as Facewatch and Stoplift to share CCTV images not only with police, but with other private companies to create a watchlist of those who have been seen stealing or are suspected to have stolen. This allows those using these programmes to identify potential shoplifters and bar them from their shopping mall or café, even though they might have no criminal record and even though the image match might be mistaken. It is worrying when a quasi-criminal record system is used like this to exclude certain people from having equal access to public places. "Facewatch, is being tested by a major U.K. supermarket chain, several major events venues and even a prison. It uses off-the-shelf facial recognition software to match criminals against police watch lists, *and against watch lists compiled by its customers*"[24] (emphasis added).

Media reports report that the owner of a London wine bar was one of the first private operators to embrace automated face recognition surveillance in the United Kingdom.[25] Facewatch was adopted by Gordon's Wine Bar to identify and blackball pickpockets. Gordon's Wine Bar's privacy statement states:

> We also use facial recognition for the prevention of unlawful acts and we are able to fulfil the requirement for this to be in the "substantial public interest" (a requirement of the *Data Protection Act 2018*) by using the Facewatch real time alerting service.[26]

Gordon's Wine Bar is not a public authority that is responsible for policing, and thus is not acting in the public interest, and thus would not be able to use the "public interest" exception to avoid seeking proper consent from its patrons.[27] It is unlikely any of the exemptions to seeking consent for processing data without consent would apply to private firms collecting and sharing biometrics without consent in the context of private security. After all, Gordon's Wine Bar is not merely collecting the biometrics of putative pickpockets, but also all its customers who are acting within the law.

This wine bar does not inform customers that their biometrics are being collected (unless they go to the extraordinary length of searching for a privacy statement on its webpage) and stored on a national database. If the wine bar collected finger prints and DNA from patrons' glasses and put them into a national database, then that might get noticed and cause more of a public outcry. However, it has collected face images without consent to put on a national (private) database that

---

24 "How One London wine bar Helped Brazil to Cut Crime," (London: *The Financial Times*, 8 February 2019).

25 *Ibid.*

26 <https://gordonswinebar.com/cookie-policy/>

27 A private operator might, for example, act in the public interest by processing data without consent that might help to contain a pandemic. However, general security arrangements at a private café or bar would not come within the "public interest" exception found in Section 8 of the *Data Protection Act 2018*.

might be used to blackball the wrong people from shopping malls and restaurants up and down the country. While matches are becoming more accurate, current technology does result in errors.[28] Furthermore, even a person who has a criminal record and has been released from prison has the fundamental right to freedom of movement, which would include access to a public grocery shop. Is it the right balance to let private operators collect biometrics on all those who enter their commercially created public spaces simply because a very small number of those people will steal? Essentially, these private operators are collecting biometrics and using them to make their own "social credit rating" system. Clearly, there needs to be regulation and criminal offences to ensure that the collection of biometrics is done with consent and that any misuse of the data or failure to properly secure it results in criminal punishment. It is doubtful that a private organisation should be allowed to collect such data for the purposes of policing, because that ought to be done by the police and national security agencies.[29]

In *R. (Edward Bridges) v. Chief Constable of South Wales Police*,[30] it was held that a police pilot project using automated facial recognition on certain surveillance cameras was lawful and thus complied with the right to privacy found in Art. 8 of the *Convention for the Protection of Human Rights and Fundamental Freedoms* as recognised in the *Human Rights Act 1998* (U.K.). After also considering Section 4(4) of the *Data Protection Act 1998*, Sections 35 and 64 of the *Data Protection Act* 2018 and Section 149 of the *Equality Act 2010*, it was held that the facial biometric information was retained for only a very short time, if there was no match, and thus was lawful. The surveillance was held to be proportionality deployed. Even when a match was made, it was reviewed by a human eye and the data captured was only retained for either 24 hours or 31 days, depending on its relevance. In that case, live face recognition cameras were taken to the event for the specific purpose of identifying wanted criminals, among others. However, this sort of technology is no longer limited to a few mobile police vans and fixed-point locations, but rather is being used on police body cameras and drone surveillance.[31]

---

28 *R. (Edward Bridges) v. Chief Constable of South Wales Police* [2020] 1 W.L.R. 672.
29 It has been repeatedly reported in the media that it is not just law enforcement agencies using face recognition cameras, but also private operators. All this has been done without proper transparency and sufficient warnings and safeguards being put in place for misuse of such information.
30 *R. (Edward Bridges) v. Chief Constable of South Wales Police* [2020] 1 W.L.R. 672; cf. *Patel v. Facebook, Inc.* (2019) 932 F.3d 1264; *Michael Schwarz v. Stadt Bochum* (2013) ECR I-12971 (concerning biometrics as data).
31 "Coronavirus: Peak District Drone Police Criticised for 'Lockdown Shaming,'" (London: *BBC News*, 27 March 2020); A. Roth *et al.*, "Growth in Surveillance may be Hard to Scale Back After Pandemic, Experts Say," (London: *The Guardian*, 14 April 2020), point out this surveillance technology such as health apps, drones and facial recognition cameras are is being used both in the West and East to enforce not only the lockdowns, but also to trace potentially infected people to ensure they are self-isolating. None of these laws have sunset clauses, meaning that after the lockdown, they might be misused.

AI-operated biometric capture technology raises privacy issues beyond those ever raised by CCTV, because it has the ability not only to capture the information but also to sort and analyse it. CCTV was limited in that humans had to sort through it and resources meant that it would only be viewed and analysed when a crime had been reported. It simply is not possible to employ and army of humans to watch every bit of CCTV footage captured daily in all the public spaces where it operates in Britain. CCTV provides evidence for trials and acts as a deterrent, but does not have the real-time tracing capacity of captured biometrics being processed by artificial intelligence in real time to do matches and provide police with real-time alerts. Algorithms can identify suspects instantaneously and notify police of their current location. Most of the criticism of face recognition surveillance is about the accuracy of the matches that are possible with current technology, but as the technology and the quality of the biometrics captured improve, matches are likely to be exceptionally accurate.

Live face recognition provides real-time automated processing of digital images of individuals whose images are on a wanted list. This technology evaluates facial features to produce a biometric template of each image for the purposes of matching those included on the database with those walking past the real-time cameras. The most significant balance between privacy and crime prevention is that the only people who are identified are people already known to police. No record of any other person walking pass the camera is kept or matched up to information. Hence, the police do not have access to the DVLA driving licence database or to H.M. Passport Office's database and thus are not able to track the location and moves of the entire population going about their business. Social media and messages have end-to-end encryption, but there is nothing preventing police harvesting images that are publicly available on Twitter and other social media profiles, since these are in the public domain. What the police can do lawfully is to locate people already known to them and whose details they have on a watchlist. To be on the watchlist, the person must be someone who is wanted for a warrant or questioning for allegedly engaging in criminal conduct. They might also be on their because they have been reported as missing. The police need probable cause of including any person on its watchlist.

In *R. (Edward Bridges) v. Chief Constable of South Wales Police*,[32] an issue concerned the lawfulness of state surveillance by the police, not private surveillance by private operators running public places for commercial profit. It was important that all matches were double-checked by humans. The concerns raised about the wrong person being identified or that the technology was more likely to bring up a match of minorities or women was not supported by evidence. The reliability of the technology is continuously increasing. Not only are the police using better equipment, but so, too, are those collecting biometrics. Home security cameras are being fitted with advanced face recognition cameras, so it is not

---

32 *R. (Edward Bridges) v. Chief Constable of South Wales Police* [2020] 1 W.L.R. 672.

difficult to image the images being passed onto the police increasing in quality. False matches by the equipment was not likely to see more minorities or women wrongly questioned and asked to prove their identity, because all matches were double-checked by humans. While the collection of the biometrics did involve a privacy invasion, it was done for a lawful purpose and thus complied with the *Data Protection Act 2018* and the right to privacy contained in the *Human Rights Act 1998* (U.K.).

The decision seems to strike the right balance if the police are limited to including only people on its watchlist when it has probable cause for including them. If a person captures a burglar on his or her own security system, this is exactly what they would expect the police to do. There is little doubt this sort of technology, if placed in traffic bottlenecks such as busy train stations, airports, shopping malls, sporting events and busy High Streets, will help the police and other agencies such as the Border Force track down criminal suspects and those who have entered Britain illegally. The idea that a person can be tracked while going about their lawful business will cause great consternation to many, but the technology is not used in this way. It is being used to track down wanted people, and as long as the wanted list is constructed in a transparent and lawful manner, there is no risk of a unwanted person being tracked. However, one issue not addressed is what happens when a rogue police officer or employee of a private organisation misuses data to the great detriment of others. Any misuse of biometric data collected in this way "is not currently governed by any specific legislation, other than general data protection legislation, and only by regulations drawn up by the police themselves."[33] There is great merit in allowing the police to collect biometrics[34] to track down wanted criminals.[35]

There ought to be a criminal offence with some teeth to deal with misuse by rogue employees including police officers. The information is too sensitive and could too easily be misused for cyberfraud, stalking including cyberstalking, and so on. Fines under the *Data Protection Act 2018* can be 4% of a corporation's annual turnover and thus do pressure big tech giants, banks, etc., to exercise due diligence to prevent data breaches and data misuse by employees. However, the police is a public body funded by the taxpayers and a lone employee is perhaps not too concerned about it being fined. What happens when a rogue employee misuses such data? The current law is such that a person could suffer harm from their data being misused, but with the corporation avoiding having to pay compensation, if it can show that the employee was acting outside his or

---

33 *Ibid.* at 693E.
34 Caution needs to be exercised in delegating too much discretion to AI police decision-making. See the issues raised in J. G. Cino, "Deploying the Secret Police: The Use of Algorithms in the Criminal Justice System," (2018) 34 *Georgia State University College of Law* 1073.
35 M. P. J. Ashby, "The Value of CCTV Surveillance Cameras as an Investigative Tool: An Empirical Analysis," (2017) 23(3) *European Journal on Criminal Policy and Research* 441.

her contractual duties as an employee and if it exercised due diligence by putting checks and balances in place to make it difficult for a lone employee to be able to so act.[36]

The Supreme Court of the United Kingdom has held that a corporation is not vicariously liable nor liable under the *Data Protection Act* (if due diligence is exercised) when a rogue employee acts alone in disclosing sensitive data. In *WM Morrison Supermarkets plc v. Various Claimants*,[37] a rogue employee of the supermarket giant Morrisons unlawfully made available online personal data of Morrisons employees including their name, address, gender, date of birth, phone numbers, national insurance number, bank sorting code, bank account number and salary. The rogue employee was seeking personal vengeance against Morrisons due to a grudge he formed following an internal disciplinary dispute a year earlier. Since the rogue employee's leak of this data was not done as part of his authorised employment, but contrary to it, there were no grounds for holding Morrisons vicariously liable.[38] Coupled with that, Morrisons demonstrated it had exercised due diligence as a data controller and thus was not liable under *Data Protection Act 1998* for the rogue employee's unauthorised conduct. The rogue employee, Skelton, was jailed for eight years after being convicted of fraud, securing unauthorised access to computer material and disclosing personal data, but none of these offences really target the core wrong. The core wrong was the privacy loss for thousands of people with their information being put online for cyberfraudsters to use forever after.

There are no custodial sentences for any of the offences found in the *Data Protection Act 2018*, including the offence of unlawful disclosure found in Section 170. Like the repealed *Data Protection Act 1998*, under *Data Protection Act 2018*, there are no powers of arrest and all offences are punishable only by a fine. The offences found in Sections 3 and 3AZ of the *Computer Misuse Act 1990* carry maximum sentences of 10 and 14 years, respectively. However, a person might not misuse a computer to violate the privacy of others. The owner of a bar or café could collect the biometrics of his or her customers without or with their consent and post them online or share them on some sort of private national database without misusing a computer or unlawfully accessing a computer. If there is no

---

36 In *WM Morrison Supermarkets plc. v. Various Claimants* [2020] UKSC 12 at Para. 32, Lord Reed said (with whom Lady Hale, Lord Kerr, Lord Hodge and Lord Lloyd-Jones were in *concorditas*) that:

> [a]n employer would not be vicariously liable for its employee's deliberate disclosure of its clients data unless the "disclosure of the data was so closely connected with acts" he was authorised to do that, for the purposes of the liability of his employer to third parties, his wrongful disclosure may fairly and properly be regarded as done by him while acting in the ordinary course of his employment.

> Since the leak was not caused by a lack of due diligence, WM Morrison Supermarkets plc. was not liable for any breach of the *Data Protection Act*.

37 *WM Morrison Supermarkets plc. v. Various Claimants* [2020] UKSC 12.
38 *Ibid.*

fraud and the person does not misuse a computer, the fine only penalty for the offence in the *Data Protection Act 2018* is hardly likely to provide a deterrent for data misuse. It hardly seems controversial that people trespassing into a private property with an intent of burglarising it might have their biometrics captured and passed on to law enforcement agencies, but ought private individuals be allowed to collect biometrics on people while they are going about their "lawful" activities in public places?[39] Anyone can put a face recognition app on their smart-phone and have it perfectly placed in their lapel pocket to capture the face of other pedestrians in a public street.

Imagine a lawyer is sitting in a café and is overhead discussing an important case she is working on. The lawyer is careful not to use actual names, but a busybody on the next table decides to covertly record the discussion and takes a photo of the lawyer to identify the lawyer and also to try to deanonymise the people discussed by the lawyer. The busybody uses the app, Clearview,[40] which allows a private individual to reverse search just about anyone with any profile online anywhere.[41] Clearview AI's massive database of images increases a person's chances

---

39 In a civil lawsuit in the United States, it was ruled that Facebook collecting facial biometrics without consent was unlawful. cf. *Patel v. Facebook, Inc.* (2019) 932 F.3d 1264.

40 In a class action for damages against Clearview AI, the plaintiffs are suing because their images and biometrics have been harvested and used without their consent. The trial pleading states:

> Specifically, Clearview has amassed a database of more than three billion photographs that it scraped from sources including Instagram, Twitter, YouTube, Facebook, Venmo and millions of other websites. Using this data, Clearview created a facial recognition tool that can identify virtually anyone by simply uploading a photograph. Users can take a picture of a stranger on the street, upload it to Clearview's tool and instantly see photos of that person on various social media platforms and websites, along with the person's name, address and other identifying information.

Mario CALDERON and Jennifer Rocio, individually and on behalf of all others similarly situated, *Plaintiffs, v. CLEARVIEW AI, INC. and CDW Government LLC* (2020) WL 746679 (S.D.N.Y.)

41 See: LINKEDIN CORPORATION, Petitioner, v. HIQ LABS, INC., Respondent., 2020 WL 1479902 (U.S.)

> Clearview, which has deployed bots to engage in the systematic scraping of social media websites to amass a database of more than three billion photos, without the consent of those websites or their users. Clearview has exploited that scraped data to support a powerful facial recognition technology that it has already licensed to more than 600 law enforcement agencies and offered to some private individuals and companies.

See On Petition for a Writ of Certiorari to the United States Court of Appeals for the Ninth Circuit, *LINKEDIN CORPORATION, v. HIQ LABS, INC.* (2020) WL 1479902 (U.S.) at 5. Cf. *Campbell v. Facebook, Inc.* (9th Cir. 2020) 951 F.3d 1106 at 1113, where the:

> Plaintiffs had focused their claims on three specific uses of the URL data that had been collected from private messages: (1) Facebook's counting URL shares as a "Like" of the relevant third-party web page; (2) Facebook's sharing data regarding URLs in messages with third parties, enabling those third parties to generate customized content and targeted

of success when performing a reverse image search. Suppose the busybody posts the video online or emails it to the lawyer's colleagues.

The barrister representing the former First Minister of Scotland (Alex Salmond), in a trial concerning nine women who made sexual assault and attempted rape allegations against Salmond, was covertly recorded discussing the case on a public train. The barrister was recorded without consent having a private conversation on the train where he says: "I don't know much about senior politicians but he was quite an objectionable bully to work with, in a way that I don't think Nicola [the current first minister Nicola Sturgeon] is. . . . I think he was a nasty person to work for . . . a nightmare to work for." Unfortunately, he also mentioned two of the women accusers by name even though sexual offence complainants have anonymity. He did not mention them publicly and thought he was having a private conversation around people who did not know him or the exact case he was discussing. Because of the recording, his "carelessness" has resulted in him having to refer himself to the Scottish Legal Complaints Commission. Mr. Salmond has since been cleared of all charges. However, if his own barrister's views (which may have been completely taken out of context) had been leaked to the press earlier, it could have a prejudicial effect on the trial.[42] In times gone by, this could have been dismissed as gossip. After all, it was a private conversation and those nearby had no right to be listening to it, let alone recording it. However, in the digital age, people can be held to account for every private thought and moment, if they exercise the liberty of having a private conversation on a train or in a café. This case was high profile, so it was easy for the covert recorder to identify the barrister and who he was talking about, but just about anyone can be identified with the use of Clearview.

Similarly, suppose X sees a woman on the beach either topless or fully nude[43] and films her and uses the Clearview app to track her down and send her video to her friends and colleagues. Worse still, he might use the app to trace her home or work address for the purpose of stalking her. Privacy is currently not protected by any criminal offence. Facial recognition smart-glasses or augmented reality glasses (Vuzix Blade Smart Glasses can be purchased by anyone, and these come with access to a massive database of images),[44] using apps such as Clearview, could allow any wearer to identify those they walk past in public places. Gargantuan databases of images, combined with information gleaned from social media profiles, public work profiles, and digital search and location histories, among

---

advertising on their own websites informed by this data; and (3) Facebook's use of the URL data to generate recommendations for other Facebook users.

42 "Alex Salmond's Lawyer Faces Inquiry After 'Sex Pest' Comment," (London: *BBC News*).

43 Cf. the sexual harassment discussed in *R. v. Lebenfish* (2014) ONCJ 130; *R. v. Taylor* (2015) ONCJ 449, where D took thousands of photographs of a young woman on a nude beach in Canada.

44 On the company's blog, it is stated: " 'iFalcon face recognition software . . . paired with the Vuzix Blade Smart Glasses provides up to eight hours of continuous operation and the portable database can store over one million unique faces,' – Paul Travers, CEO and President, Vuzix." www.vuzix.com/Blog/50.

other things, could allow individuals to effortlessly track where a person lives or works. The very best cybercriminals do a fairly good job at covering their digital tracks,[45] but everyday citizens too often publicly present information that assists cyberfraudsters and others to misuse their information. This sort of technology is not emerging in the distance future, but is a current reality.[46] It is now widely used by law enforcement agencies, as well as private corporations in Europe, China and the United States. In the United Kingdom, the current practice is to use cameras that are moved about in police vans, but it should not be long before the police are equipped with smart-glasses that have face recognition technology in them – or at least smart-phones with such apps on them. Add to the mix that this technology is also attached to drones. The European Union Agency for Fundamental Rights has reported that the public have less concern with face recognition technology being used in policing than when it is used in other contexts.[47] In its report, the Agency for Fundamental rights also gives a brief overview of where face recognition is being used in Europe.[48]

To the extent that any private individual can purchase this sort of technology to record others, discover their identity, find their work and home addresses, and publish private information about them without consent, data laws and constitutional privacy rights offer little protection. Even if a fair balance can be struck between the police using face/gait recognition body cameras in narrowly defined public places such as train stations, airports, shopping malls and some busy High

45 Jang-Jaccard *et al.* write:

> Why cyberattacks flourish? It is because cyberattacks are cheaper, convenient and less risky than physical attacks. Cyber criminals only require a few expenses beyond a computer and an Internet connection. They are unconstrained by geography and distance. They are difficult to identity and prosecute due to anonymous nature of the Internet.

Julian Jang-Jaccard *et al.*, "A Survey of Emerging Threats in Cybersecurity," (2014) 80(5) *Journal of Computer and System Sciences* 973. See also T. J. Holt, "Regulating Cybercrime through Law Enforcement and Industry Mechanisms," (2018) 679(1) *The Annals of the American Academy of Political & Social Science* 140.

46 See J. Vincent, *Facial Recognition Smart Glasses Could Make Public Surveillance Discreet and Ubiquitous*, (The Verge, 10 June 2019), where it is reported:

> The AR glasses have an 8-megapixel camera embedded in the frame which allows the wearer to scan faces in a crowd and compare with a database of 1 million images. Notifications about positive matches are sent to the glasses' see-through display, embedded in the lens.

47 See:

> The results of the survey show that, among the general population in the United Kingdom, only 9% feel completely uncomfortable when facial recognition is used for policing purposes, and 10% when used at airports. However, 24% do not feel comfortable with the use of facial recognition in public transport, 28% at schools, 37% in supermarkets, and 37% at the workplace.

Facial Recognition Technology: Fundamental Rights Considerations in the Context of Law Enforcement, (Venna: FRA, 2019) at 19.

48 *Ibid. et passim.*

Streets in the larger cities, it is troubling that private individuals and corporations are also being allowed to collect such biometrics without consent and without any imprisonable offence to deter misuse.[49]

Consent can only be given if the shopping mall does not make it a condition of entry that one allow his or her biometrics to be collected. Hence, if the condition of entry is that one must comply, then there is no real consent. If the public space is open to all and there is a way of opting in or opting out of having one's biometrics captured, then consent might be possible. Basing consent on people being forced to accept something or forgo some lawful liberty such as shopping in a shopping mall is not feasible. The trade-off might be for the police to operate such cameras in these quasi-private places (that a shopping mall is privately owned does not turn it into a private space – it is a public space where access is permitted for public consumption, even if the ulterior private aim of the provider is to make money).

Mass surveillance in public places (done openly and transparently by state enforcement agencies) is distinguishable from interception and targeted surveillance against a particular suspect which ought always require a warrant.[50] If the police need to use covert means in certain special cases, then access to such means ought to be subject to a court order. More generally, the police ought to be open and make it publicly known what technological surveillance and interception policing is being used and ought to have clear statements in the Police Code of Conduct[51] about the guiding rules and laws it will follow when using such surveillance and interception.[52]

Similarly, passing laws that allow law enforcement agents to attack encryption (i.e., install tools to decrypt or perform a lawful interception)[53] or bypass

---

49 Hill writes:

> Clearview AI, devised a ground-breaking facial recognition app. You take a picture of a person, upload it and get to see public photos of that person, along with links to where those photos appeared. The system – whose backbone is a database of more than three billion images that Clearview claims to have scraped from Facebook, YouTube, Venmo and millions of other websites – goes far beyond anything ever constructed by the United States government or Silicon Valley giant.

> K. Hill, "The Secretive Company That Might End Privacy as We Know It," (New York: *The New York Times*, 18 January 2020).

50 See the discussion in *Capenter v. United States* (2018) 138 S. Ct. 2206.
51 See for example the very comprehensive requirements set out for covert surveillance in *Covert Surveillance and Property Interference: Revised Code of Practice*, (London: Home Office, August 2018).
52 It has been pointed out that in the United States, there has been a growth in covert interception and surveillance with very little transparency. J. Manes, "Secrecy & Evasion in Police Surveillance Technology," (2019) 34 *Berkeley Technology Law Journal* 503.
53 Rozenshtein writes:

> Encryption can certainly make it harder for national-security and foreign-intelligence agencies to do their jobs, but . . . [w]ith enough effort, . . . [it is possible to] hack . . . into even the most sophisticated adversary's systems (or, as occurred in the San Bernardino case, purchase third-party tools that do the same).

encryption by allowing them to issue a notice requesting/ordering a suspect or third party to hand over an access key (i.e., smart-phone password) for the unencrypted data, ought to be balanced carefully with the right to privacy and freedom of expression.[54] There is increasing pressure on tech giants to build backdoors so that enforcement agencies can access encrypted data.[55] Arguably, enforcement agencies ought only be allowed to access encrypted data when there is other strong evidence demonstrating that someone has perpetrated a serious crime (arguably a crime carrying a minimum prison sentence of more than two years), and the encrypted data is likely to help prove as much.

The digital age has led to privacy being invaded through smart-speakers recording conversations for Amazon and Google, among others.[56] In the United Kingdom under Part III of the *Regulation of Investigatory Powers Act 2000* and Section 20 of the *Police and Criminal Evidence Act 1984*, a third party can be ordered to disclose access keys to make data accessible in an unencrypted format. Much of the data collected by smart-speakers is not encrypted, so law enforcement would have little difficulty obtaining it from a third party such as Amazon or Apple Inc. However, service provides such as Apple Inc. have encrypted communications such as FaceTime calls and iMessages from end to end, and thus are able to defend any request for a key to decrypt such information by asserting (truthfully) that it does not have the key that is required to decrypt the data in question. The key for decryption is normally with the suspect him or herself – that is, his or her face, fingerprint, password, and so forth.[57]

A. Z. Rozenshtein, "Wicked Crypto," (2019) 9 *UC Irvine Law Review* 1181 at 1188. See also *In re Order Requiring Apple, Inc. to Assist in the Execution of a Search Warrant Issued by this Court*, 149 F.Supp.3d 341 (E.D. N.Y. 2016); *State v. Stahl* (2016) 206 So. 3d 124 at 128. However, it is an overstatement to say it is always possible to break encryption. In many cases, it will not be possible or simply will be too expensive. This in a sense means that it will only be the most serious crimes where such an attempt might be tried and this offers some sort of balance between privacy and crime prevention.

54 "A third potential ground for a right to go dark is the law of evidentiary privileges. Evidentiary privileges protect the contents of certain communications against 'involuntary disclosure.' " See D. Gray, "A Right to Go Dark," (2019) 72 *SMU Law Review* 621 at 655 *et seq*.

55 A backdoor to encryption is a mechanism integrated into the particular device or technology that allows others to access encrypted data without requiring the key.

56 With respect to digital evidence, the Crown Prosecution Service notes:

Digital evidence and communications data can also be obtained directly from Communication Service Providers ("CSPs") as well as from computers and digital storage devices. Investigators have the power to serve orders on CSPs that oblige them to disclose communications data. Many CSPs are based in the US and may be obtained through Mutual Legal Assistance.

www.cps.gov.uk/legal-guidance/cybercrime-prosecution-guidance The United States has passed an Act titled *Clarifying Lawful Overseas Use of Data Act 2018*, which among other things, allows European Union members to acquire (expeditiously) data from US service providers without resorting to MLA procedure.

57 D. Casciani and G. Portal, "Phone Encryption: Police 'Mug' Suspect to Get Data," (London: *BBC News*, 2 December 2016), where the police knew they had no power to force a

Smart-speakers and iCloud backups do not come with the same sort of end-to-end encryption that calls and messages come with. Controversially, it was found that some providers of smart-speakers had set them so they were always listening and sending data including audio data back to Amazon, Google and Apple so their employees could analyse it.[58] This scandal led to these firms tightening up security and implementing stronger privacy protections, but no smart-speaker provider provides end-to-end encryption for all the information sought and communicated through a smart-speaker. People ought to be made aware of this fact and what encryption means.

Apple Inc. does not even provide end-to-end encryption for iCloud backups, so any information backed up can be handed to law enforcement. Presumably, law enforcement would need probable cause and a warrant to access such information. Apple Inc. does use encryption so that a customer's information is only accessed either because he or she has forgotten his or her own password or because law enforcement has required the backed up information. This might be the trade-off that is necessary to prevent governments forcing tech companies to stop end-to-end encryption for messages and calls. Apple Inc. also has refused to create a backdoor into its iOS operating system to allow enforcement agencies to unlock password-protected iPhones. There is only a weak justification for making the privacy of law-abiding citizens less secure to assist law enforcement, because criminals would soon avoid using products that have backdoors in them. It is likely they already avoid the use of smart-speakers and do not back up information concerning their criminality onto iCloud, where Apple Inc. does decrypt information when requested to do so by the authorities.

Obviously, if the information collected by a tech company is sought by a third party such as the police, then a warrant ought to be sought.[59] In England, Section 49 of the *Regulation of Investigatory Powers Act 2000* allows the police to give a person a notice ordering him or her to unlock his or her phone or computer. In the United States, it has been said that this does not violate a person's right not to self-incriminate himself or herself, since he or she is simply allowing the police to search for existing evidence. There is not real difference in searching a house for physical evidence and searching a phone for digital evidence.[60] In the

---

criminal mastermind's finger onto his iPhone to unlock it, so followed him and waited for him to use the phone and then snatched it from him while it was unlocked.

58 "Amazon, Apple and Google all employ staff who listen to customer voice recordings from their smart speakers and voice assistant apps." "Smart Speaker Recordings Reviewed by Humans," (London: *BBC News*, 11 April 2019).

59 See *Benedik v. Slovenia* (2018) (Application no. 62357/14), where the European Court of Human Rights held there had been a violation of Article 8 (right to respect for private and family life) since the police failed to obtain a court order before accessing subscriber information associated with a dynamic IP address. See also *R. (on the application of National Council for Civil Liberties (Liberty)) v. Secretary of State for the Home Department* [2020] 1 W.L.R. 243.

60 See *Commonwealth v. Jones* (2019) 481 Mass. 540 at 541, 547; cf. *In re Of* (2019) 354 F. Supp. 3d 1010, (N.D. Cal.).

United Kingdom, refusal to comply with a notice to unlock a smart-phone, etc., can result in a maximum sentence of two years imprisonment, or five years if the case being investigated concerns terrorism (national security) or child indecency. Since the maximum term of these offences can be much higher than five years, the penalty for non-compliance is not likely to encourage a guilty party to unlock evidence that might result in a life sentence for terrorism.

People have been both cleared and convicted based on information collected and stored on smart-devices.[61] However, people ought to be informed in advanced that their conversations are not only being recorded but are being kept an analysed by these tech giants. It should be made clear that there is no end-to-end encryption and that any data will be kept for whatever period of time the particular jurisdiction's data retention laws allow for. If a person is suspected of murder or some serious crime, there is nothing objectionable about the police seeking a warrant to obtain from a third party digital evidence collected by the suspect's smart-phone or smart-speakers. A murder conviction was obtained through such evidence in the United States.[62] However, we have also seen a rise in warrantless border searchers by immigration and customers officers in circumstances where there is no probable cause for searching through a person's private information.[63] The current law in the United Kingdom and United States is that when a person enters a customs zone in an airport, his or her human rights are null and void, especially the right to privacy. Anyone can be ordered to unlock their phone or computer without there needing to be any probable cause other than the immigration officer is bored.

A further issue is the collection and use of big data. Big data is a necessity and its benefits normally outweigh any privacy harm that might be caused by its collection and use, but it ought to be anonymised fully to preserve privacy.[64] It is necessary to have big data to properly determine how to treat and manage pandemics like the current COVID-19 pandemic. Concern has been raised about anonymised confidential health records being used, but as long as the anonymisation is done well, it is hard to see how any privacy loss would outweigh the benefits. For example, not removing a person's postcode from the information would be poor anonymisation in England, because English postcodes link to

---

61 See the cases mentioned in J. G. Browning and L. Angelo, "Alexa, Testify New Sources of Evidence from the Internet of Things," (2019) *82 Tex. B.J.* 506.

62 P. Ohm, "The Many Revolutions of Carpenter," (2019) 32 *Harvard Journal of Law & Technology* 357 at 416.

63 This is the norm in the United Kingdom, United States and China, among other countries. In *Rabbani v. D.P.P.* [2018] 2 Cr. App. R. 28, D was convicted for failing to give the password for his computer and the pin for his phone to officers when requested to do so. See also the American cases discussed in A. Das, "Chilling Social Media: Warrantless Border Searches of Social Media Accounts Infringe Upon the Freedom of Association and the Freedom to Be Anonymous Under the First Amendment," (2019) 84 *Brooklyn Law Review* 1287.

64 Big data and artificial intelligence (supercomputers) are being used in the fight against COVID-19. J. Hruska, "The Fastest Supercomputer on Earth Is Being Deployed Against Coronavirus," (*Extreme Tech*, 10 March 2020).

exact addresses – not to larger postal areas.[65] "Germany has proposed using big data and location tracking to isolate people with coronavirus once social distancing measures now in force have slowed its spread, media reported on Friday."[66] Similarly,

> Korea has used Big Data, such as GPS tracking data from phones and cars, credit card transactions, travel histories, CCTV footage, and artificial intelligence to identify high-priority cases and track the routes of infected individuals. Smartphone apps have been deployed for inbound international travellers who are undergoing the 14-day self-monitoring period and for suspected coronavirus cases who are in mandatory self-isolation. By facilitating self-monitoring and reporting data to the government, this prevented a ban on entry by international travellers.[67]

Of course, when emergency laws are enacted that compromise fundamental liberties, governments need to ensure that are such laws are repealed as soon as the emergency has passed. The need sunset clauses on them.

Big data is essential for improving healthcare and information can be sufficiently anonymised to make it useable without causing any real privacy loss. However, big data is also being used to discover people's predilections and thereafter bombard them with algorithmic chosen advertisements or news stories. Big data is being used to profile each consumer and thereafter aggressively target them. Big data analytics involves information being traced over time and used to build very detailed personal profiles. Smart-phone information such as location information (most use this to label photos automatically while travelling) and fitness and activity trackers found in smart-watches, along with stories people read on social media or the products they purchase on sites such as Amazon, allow large corporations to have a very detailed and personal profile of their customers. The *Data Protection Act 2018* (U.K.) (based on the *General Data Protection*

---

65 It has been reported by a credible newspaper, "Technology firms are processing large volumes of confidential UK patient information in a data-mining operation that is part of the government's response to the coronavirus outbreak." The Guardian story reports that patient postcodes are revealed in the data, which is worrying. See P. Lewis *et al.*, "UK Government Using Confidential Patient Data in Coronavirus Response," (London: *The Guardian*, 12 April 2020).

66 The German "Interior Ministry's strategy paper recommends following South Korea in aggressively testing for COVID-19 and using smartphone location data to help trace people who have come into contact with those infected with the flu-like disease." P. Carrel, "Germany Looks at Tracking Patients to Rein in Coronavirus-Reports," (New York: *The New York Times*, 27 March 2020).

67 D. Chung and H. S. Soh, "Korea's Response to COVID-19: Early Lessons in Tackling the Pandemic," (*World Bank Blog*, 23 March 2020) <https://blogs.worldbank.org/eastasia pacific/koreas-response-covid-19-early-lessons-tackling-pandemic>.

Regulation [GDPR]) does offer some protection. At least one state in the United States has tried to implement similar protections. Voss and Houser observe:[68]

> The motivation behind the [California Consumer Privacy Act] is similar to the GDPR and is to provide statutory protection and remedies for all California residents. It defines "personal information" as "any information that . . . relates to . . . a particular consumer or household." The term "personal information" is defined broadly and includes unique identifiers, geolocation data, and inferences from consumer behaviour. It gives consumers a right to know how their information is being used, the right to delete, and the right to stop businesses from selling their personal information.

The GDPR and the *Data Protection Act 2018* (U.K.) enact stringent privacy protections that require large entities to protect data or face a fine of up to 4% of their annual turnover. This means big banks, tech giants, employers, and so on, have to ensure that personal data is collected under strict conditions and is not leaked or exploited without consent. Data controllers, including tech companies, have to tell the user how they collect and use data.

Not all data types collected by entities result in the sort of harm that would justify a criminal law response. Much of its use, even when done without consent, does not cause any direct mental, physical or economic harm. It could lead to indirect economic harm when social engineering is used to convince unwitting consumers to make purchases they would not otherwise have made, but this sort of remote influence seems not to be sufficiently tangible to require the heavy hand of the criminal law. Class actions in the United States and the GDPR in Europe probably provide sufficient deterrence.

4. Censoring the Internet at large to prevent online harms

A recent White Paper, titled *Online Harms*,[69] has proposed to regulate cyberspace to prevent harmful content from remaining online. What is proposed can be conceptualised as: (1) regulating harmful expression such as offensive speech and extreme pornography; and (2) thwarting online facilitation of crimes perpetrated by others such as the sales of drugs and guns. The aim is not only to ensure websites containing information that may harm people by influencing their independent decisions to self-harm, but to have content removed that could cause offence or distress and thus affect the long-term psychological health of those exposed to it. Technology is required to filter information into two information streams so that adults can view information that is safe for adults and that children and

---

68 W. G. Voss and K. A. Houser, "Personal Data and the GDPR: Providing a Competitive Advantage for U.S. Companies," (2019) 56 *American Business Law Journal* 287 at 307–308.
69 H. M. Government, White Paper, *Online Harms*, (London: April 2019).

minors can view information that is safe for them. It would be absurd to limit the content of the Internet so that the only available information would be information that is safe for a 15-year-old.[70] Censorship has long been in place to protect minors from information that is not harmful to adults such as pornography and violence. Filters and lockouts can be applied to prevent minors accessing harmful material,[71] but this has to be done in a way that allows users of adult content to maintain anonymity.[72] Technology needs to be adapted to ensure fail-proof parental lockouts can be placed on devices used by children.[73]

The problem with trying to regulate the content of the Internet is: (1) information flows across jurisdictions; (2) the offensiveness of the diverse information that can be accessed across the globe is socially contingent – nude images can be seen on newsstands in public places in Berlin, but would cause outrage in Dubai; (3) there is a risk of removing useful and beneficial information as a consequence of intermediary Internet service providers applying AI filters to too narrow range of information to avoid penalties; and (4) the instantaneous nature of the Internet means that often a good deal of harm is done before the information can be removed. There is a strong element of paternalism behind the proposals to regulate the content of Internet as far as adults are concerned. The state wants to protect consenting adults from themselves and from them exposing themselves to information that might harm their psychic make-up or lead them into temptation. It is not only aimed at protecting them from content that is criminal per se (i.e., content promoting or inciting terrorism, extreme pornography, etc.), but other content that the state deems harmful to the health of consenting adults.

Content that is harmful to children such as pornography or horror film violence ought to be filtered so that they cannot access it. Content that harms others in the manufacturing process such as child pornography is already criminalised, and rightly so. The White Paper acknowledges that most criminal activity is not likely to be conducted on the open web, but rather is done through the Dark Web – but seems to use crime reduction as a justification for regulating the fountain of knowledge contained online. If a person is dealing in child pornography, illegal arms, illegal drugs, people trafficking, and so on, it is likely to be via the Dark Web.[74] There seems nothing too controversial about making terrorist information and child pornography unsearchable on the Internet, but Internet service

---

70 See the decision of the Supreme Court of the United States in *Reno v. American Civil Liberties Union* (1997) 521 U.S. 844. Cf. 15 U.S.C. §§ 6501–6506, *The Children's Online Privacy Protection Act of 1998* a U.S. federal law.

71 G. Mas, "#NoFilter: The Censorship of Artistic Nudity on Social Media," (2017) 54 *Washington University Journal of Law & Policy* 307; B. Chang, "From Internet Referral Units to International Agreements; Censorship of the Internet by the UK and EU," (2018) 49 *Colum. Hum. Rts. L. Rev.* 114.

72 In 2019, the Government of the United Kingdom was proposing an age verification system for adults to be able to access adult content such as pornography.

73 See Sections 18–19 of the *Digital Economy Act 2017*, not yet in force.

74 Cf. The U.S. statute, *Justice for Victims of Trafficking Act of 2015* with respect to advertising services that facilitate trafficking.

providers are already applying rigid filters to remove such content. And recent laws in China and Germany[75] mandate that such content ought to be removed. The European Union also intends to include a raft of new regulations (see the debate concerning the *Digital Services Act*)[76] that will include adopting mandatory and transparent notice-and-action rules which would require the provider to remove hate speech, child abuse images, and so forth. Provisions concerning fake news need to meet some sort of harm standard or risk an over-criminalising harmless speculating. There has been a spate of fake news concerning COVID-19 treatments, but we would not want to prosecute every ignorant person for passing on fake news such as that UV kills COVID-19. By placing a burden on the Internet service provider to remove fake news, rather than criminalising every person who posts fake news, we are able to avoid over-criminalising the conduct by targeting individuals who post the misinformation. To not overburden ISPs, it is hoped only seriously harmful fake news would be ordered for removal. Determining what this is will require a case by case assessment.

The White Paper aims to introduce a regulatory framework that will allow very substantial fines to be imposed on companies and for its senior management to be personally liable. Companies providing services where people can publish harmful material such as on Facebook, YouTube and Twitter will have a legal duty. The duties and obligations will be set out in a Code of Practice.[77] Often all that is being prevented is offence to others, not harm to others. It is doubtful offence to others is a sound justification for censoring the entire Internet, because it is best regulated through free debate.[78] Some of the content is hate speech, but it simply does not cause the sort of mental harm that would necessarily justify using criminal offences carrying prison sentences to educate people into being politically correct, decent, well-mannered and enlightened.[79] Administrative type

---

75 See Chapter 4 of this volume.

76 <https://forum-europe.com/news/2020/digital-services-act-conference>.

77 H. M. Government, White Paper, *Online Harms*, (London: April 2019) at Para. 21.

78 See further, E. T. Kasper and T. A. Kozma, "Absolute Freedom of Opinion and Sentiment on All Subjects: John Stuart Mill's Enduring (and Ever-Growing) Influence on the Supreme Court's First Amendment Free Speech Jurisprudence," (2020) 15 *U. Mass. L. Rev.* 2. M. Ammori, "The First Amendment Moves Beyond the Courts," (2014) 27 *Harv. L. Rev.* 2259 at 1173, notes:

> the terms of service for Google Search, Google's main search engine, are different from the terms of service for Google's YouTube. Links that connect to pornography or hate speech are not removed from Search, even if both would be re-moved from YouTube, as Search is designed to reflect the content of the entire web, including any site created by any person or organisation.

D. J. Baker and L. X. Zhao, "The Normativity of Using Prison to Control Hate Speech: The Hollowness of Waldron's Harm Theory," (2013) 16 *New Crim. L. Rev.* 621.

79 See:

> Speech that demeans on the basis of race, ethnicity, gender, religion, age, disability, or any other similar ground is hateful; but the proudest boast of our free speech jurisprudence is that we protect the freedom to express "the thought that we hate."

Matal v. Tam (2017) 137 S. Ct. 1744 at 1764.

offences carrying fines of up to £500 would be more than enough to deter most hate speech and other offensive forms of speech, but avoid imposing the sort of very severe restrictions on marginal speech that might simply be testing the boundaries.[80] Too often the courts are clogged up with cases where people have caused offence rather than any real mental harm, when criminal justice resources need to be reserved for more serious wrongs that cause tangible harm.[81] A repeat offender could be managed by suspending their social media accounts. Serious harassment, whether done via the Internet or other means, is already a serious criminal offence under Section 4 of the *Protection from Harassment Act 1997*. The media campaigns conducted in the tabloids that go on for weeks and weeks ought to be prosecuted under that the *Act of 1997*, but never are.

Recently in the *Daily Mail*, there was a story of a married manager sending flirtatious texts to a younger woman in his employ.[82] The only person caused mental harm by a national newspaper making a big story about a trivial private wrong was the wife of the man who was the subject of the story. The extensive trolling conducted by the tabloid press goes unchecked and laws concerning hate speech are applied randomly and inconsistently.[83] Famous people choose to live in the public eye and receive enormous rewards from fame, so by implication consent to some form of media harassment, but the everyday campaigns by tabloids in the United Kingdom against people who are not choosing to be in the public eye beggars belief. The tabloid press trolling is often far worse than any sort of trolling an individual might carry out against another private individual, but goes unchecked. It is justified as being in the public interest, when it simply

---

80 Feminists such as Germaine Greer, whose views on the distinctions between biologically born women and transgender women have resulted in her being no platformed, no doubt would pay a fine to continue to debate important issues where her opinions might offend some, but to use prison deter such debate would have too great a chilling effect on free speech.

81 See L. Purves, "Boiled Egg Case Shows What's Rotten in the Legal System," (London: *The Times*, 15 November 2019), where a trivial dispute between two ladies over the smell of the eggs one was eating on the public train ended up in a very expensive criminal trial in the Crown Court, resulting in the accused being cleared of the charge of racially aggravated public disorder, but being convicted and "fined only" for causing alarm or distress. These trivial disputes involving heated verbal arguments where any hint of offensive speech is clutched with alacrity to escalate the matter into a criminal matter are clogging the courts in the United Kingdom. The fine could have been issued on the spot as a fixed penalty for the offensive speech or better still a caution could have been given, without wasting police and court time.

82 H. Dawson and J. Middleton " 'Let's Kiss and see what Happens': Married New Boss of Premier League David Pemsel, 51, Called Former Female Colleague in her 20s 'Staggeringly Sexy' and Bombarded her with Inappropriate Messages," (London: *The Daily Mail*, 28 November 2019). Despite the headline, there were only half a dozen texts and the woman had sent kisses in her texts to him, and so on.

83 The celebrity, Harry Mountbatten-Windsor, is suing the press for negative reporting about him. "Prince Harry's Lawsuit Against Tabloids Could Backfire, Commentators Claim," (London: *The Guardian*, 5 October 2019).

is not. Perhaps some of it is staged and the victims accept payments to endure the humiliation, but it is hard to know if that is the case.[84]

There is a public interest in reporting serious crime or the wrongdoing of famous people, but the standards are applied fairly haphazardly. Prince Harry wore a Nazi uniform for self-amusement while Justin Trudeau blacked up for self-amusement, but neither were charged with a hate crime for the deep offence they caused.[85] Trudeau did it more than once, but was re-elected prime minister in Canada. The reach of the laws covering hate speech are so wide that there are no gaps whatsoever in English law. There is no need to have another layer of Internet law. Arguably, the hate speech laws in England cover a wide range of speech that would be better regulated through a penalty notice rather than through direct criminalisation. When this conduct is done online, the fine ought to reflect that, but again it seems there is no need for prison sentences or trials in such cases. Facebook, Google, Microsoft and Twitter have all agreed to an E.U. code of conduct obligating them to deal with valid notifications for removal of illegal hate speech from their servicers within 24 hours of notification. Content analysis algorithms might not catch all speech, but if a person is offended by speech and reports it to the ISP, then it should act. If no one complains and it is not noticed by the AI filter, it would be too much to punish the service provider for not noticing it.

Much of the material referred to in the White Paper refers to the removal of content that is already illegal to upload or market online.[86] For example, uploading child pornography is criminal conduct;[87] uploading information about terrorism is criminal conduct;[88] uploading extreme pornography is criminal conduct;

---

84 Presumably, those who allow themselves to be humiliated on reality TV programmes such as *U.K. Border Force* do so for payment.

85 N. Tweedie and M. Kallenbach, "Prince Harry faces outcry at Nazi outfit," (London: *The Telegraph*, 14 January 2005); "Justin Trudeau: New video of Canada's PM in blackface," (London: *BBC News*, 19 September 2019).

86 See for example, s. 63 of the *Criminal Justice and Immigration Act 2008* (possession of extreme pornography); s. 62 of the *Coroners and Justice Act 2009* (possession of child pornography); s. 69 of the *Serious Crime Act 2015* (possession of a paedophile manual); s. 57 of the *Terrorism Act 2000* (possessing articles for terrorism); s. 5 of the *Misuse of Drugs Act 1971*; the ss. 19 and 21 of the *Firearms Act 1968* and ss. ss.1, 1ZA of the *Prevention of Crime Act 1953*, (offensive weapons and firearms in public places); s. 139 of the *Criminal Justice Act 1988 (possession of blades)*; ss. 1–4 of the *Knives Act 1997 (marketing knives)*; Similarly, using the internet to sell an article that has not use other than to facilitate fraud, surely should be regulated by asking service providers to remove the advertisement. Cf. s. 6(1) of the *Fraud Act 2006*.

87 Not only is the act itself criminal, so is incitement and communication. Clearly, the Internet can be used to facilitate a range of sexual offences against children and such content needs to be deleted by providers to help reduce harm to children. See for example, ss. 14–15 and 15A and 47–51 of the *Sexual Act 2003*. Similarly, there is no question that child pornography (criminal conduct covered by ss. 1–3 of the *Protection of Children Act 1978*) ought to be removed from cyberspace by service providers to reduce harm to children.

88 S. 2(2)(e) of the *Terrorism Act 2006*. See too M. Lavi, "Do Platforms Kill?" (2020) 43 *Harv. J.L. & Pub. Pol'y* 477.

uploading intimate photographs and films of a former partner engaged in sexual activity is criminal conduct;[89] uploading hate speech or using the Internet to engage in hate speech is criminal conduct;[90] using electronic communications to assist or encourage crimes is criminal conduct; using the Internet to sell illegal goods[91] or services[92] is not necessarily always criminal conduct, but the sale of such goods or services is likely to result in criminal conduct.

The White Paper also makes specific reference to coercive behaviour which is criminal in itself,[93] but does not make it clear how this is an online issue. It makes reference to violent content, but violent content is not generally criminalised. Horror movies and horrific images and films can be viewed by consenting adults, even if such materials might have a tendency to make society more violent.[94] Advocating self-harm is not a crime[95] since it is not a crime to harm oneself.[96] Encouraging a person to commit suicide is already an offence under Section 2 of the *Suicide Act 1961.* The paper also makes specific reference to the modern slavery, but beyond applying complicity liability to the offences found in Sections 1–5 of the *Modern Slavery Act 2015,* it is not clear how this is cyberspace or online censorship issue.

It is not clear why the White Paper makes specific reference to female genital mutilation,[97] since encouraging or assisting it would already be covered by Sections 44–46 of the *Serious Crime Act 2007.* More might be done to crack down

---

89 Ss. 33–35 of the *Criminal Justice and Courts Act 2015.*
90 *Norwood v United Kingdom* (2005) 40 E.H.R.R. SE11; *DPP v. Collins* [2006] UKHL 40; [2007] 1 Cr.App.R. 5. See also s. 32 of the Crime and Disorder Act 1998 and the Protection from Harassment Act 1997; Sections 17–23 of the *Public Order Act 1986.* For a general discussion, see Baker, 2015.
91 It will be illegal to supply some goods such as drugs, equipment for terrorists, or fraud.
92 It would not be a criminal act to advertise your services as a professional assassin, but if a person were to be encouraged to use her services, the offences found in Sections 44–46 of the *Serious Crime Act 2007* would apply. The White Paper makes specific reference to using the Internet to market activities that facilitate organised immigration crime. This might involve promoting sham marriages or dodgy diplomas. Cf. R. (on the application of *London St Andrew's College) v Secretary of State for the Home Department* [2018] EWCA Civ 2496; *R. (on the application of Westech College) v Secretary of State for the Home Department* [2011] EWHC 1484. See the offences in ss. 24; 24A, 25, 25A, 25B & 27 of the *Immigration Act 1971;* and ss. 28–30 of the *Immigration and Asylum Act 1999.* Clearly, online advertising and social media facilities could be used to facilitate some of those crimes, but it is not clear that such conduct generally would come within the purview of a general internet censorship regime that is meant to protect consumers from harmful information on the Internet: such information might facilitate immigration fraud, but is not likely to harm any individual consuming the information. Cf. s. 3 of the *Export Control Act 2002; and* s. 3 of the *The Technical Assistance Control Regulations 2006* (technical assistance controls).
93 S. 76 of the *Serious Crime Act 2015.*
94 Empirical evidence is not conclusive on this and much more research is needed.
95 This is why a special provision was enacted to catch those who assist or encourage suicide after suicide itself was decriminalised. See s. 2 of the *Suicide Act 1961.* See also s. 2 of the *Female Genital Mutilation Act 2003.*
96 Cf. R v Wright; consent.
97 S. 1 of the *Female Genital Mutilation Act 2003.*

on minors having plastic surgery that is not necessary for medicinal or therapeutic purposes than focusing on the very rare crime of female genital mutilation.[98] Cosmetic surgery and the way it is advertised online should be reviewed as should the question of whether minors should be allowed to consent to such surgery when they do not need it to cure some medical problem, when it often has long-term harmful effects.

5. Overview of the chapters herein

In Chapter 2 of this volume, Lord Hodge examines financial technology (Fintech) and smart contracts. He argues that greater attention needs to paid to emerging technologies and their use in financial services. It is important that our laws and regulatory systems evolve to be apt for the Fintech age. Lord Hodge takes the view that British judges and the common law are in a good position to make an important contribution in this area. He cautions that there needs to be greater collaboration between judges, lawyers, computer experts, financiers, law reform bodies and legislators. "Data is power, and AI is power," and thus legislation and regulation has to be innovative and keep pace with emerging technology. Secure financial transactions also guard against potential cyberfraud in a global e-commerce economy spanning jurisdictions and legal systems. Therefore, Lord Hodge concludes that there needs to be "international agreement on legal and regulatory norms if Fintech is to achieve its potential in wealth creation and poverty reduction through cross-border transactions while maintaining market integrity and protecting the consumer."

In Chapter 3, Clough argues that intelligence-led policing and disruption has increasingly become a tactic in the fight against cybercrime. He argues that initially focused such methods were adopted against organised criminal networks, but that disruption as a policing method has expanded to incorporate many other serious transnational crimes, including cybercrimes. Clough argues that while it is a core feature of modern policing, little has been done to evaluate its effectiveness for tackling cybercrime. Its scope has not been clearly demarcated in relation to cybercrime prevention. Disruption often draws upon powers conferred for the purposes of enforcement, and therefore appropriate oversight is required. There is a danger of blurring of policing and security activities and a balance needs to be struck to protect fundamental rights such as sovereignty and privacy. This chapter discusses the nature of disruption and its application in the context of cybercrime, with a particular focus on legal frameworks. It begins with the nature of disruption and the role of intelligence in disruptive practices, before providing examples of how disruption may apply in the context of cybercrime. The role of legal frameworks is then considered, with a focus on the need for disruptive criminal offences, investigative powers and international cooperation. Although

---

98 D. J. Baker, *Glanville Williams: Textbook of Criminal Law*, (London: Sweet & Maxwell, 2015) at Chapter 26.

drawing primarily on examples from Australia and cognate common law jurisdictions, these issues are of potential relevance to all jurisdictions. The chapter aims to raise awareness of the role of disruption in combating cybercrime and the importance of legal frameworks if such techniques are to be both effective and subject to appropriate safeguards.

In Chapter 4, He and Jing explore some of the duties being placed on internet service providers in China. The note that China has introduced not only new pre-inchoate offences to deter individuals from misusing cybermeans to perpetrate crimes, but have introduced E.U.-style data retention laws and notification and removal duties (i.e., a duty for a ISP to remove fake news or other illegal content such as child abuse images upon being notified by the regulator). They argue that China needs to carefully evaluate the case for adopting some of the panicked approaches that have been adopted in places like Germany and Australia. They provide the example of Australia, where its entire population's digital data has to be kept by ISPs for a two-year period. While Apple Inc. provides end-to-end encryption for calls and messages, this is not the norm across the world and different tech companies in different jurisdictions take different approaches depending on the local law. They examine the effectiveness of data retention obligations and obligations on ISPs to monitor content and remove any illegal content from the Internet. They also examine the case for criminalising pre-inchoate wrongs that contribute to some end cyberharm.

In Chapter 5, Zhang and Wang examine the concept of virtual property for the purposes of applying Chinese property offences to the dishonest acquisition of it. The examine the debate about whether virtual property can be protected by the property offences found in Chinese law. Since Chinese property offences require the property to have some economic value, this is an important element for applying theft and fraud to a dishonest acquisition of virtual property. They point out that if such property is not property for the purposes of theft and fraud, then the only other way to deal with its wrongful acquisition is to treat it as a computer and network misuse offence, which is what often happens in China. They present a cogent analysis to draw out of the legal limitations of deeming all acts of illegal acquisition of virtual property as computer crimes. They argue that virtual property ought to be treated as property for the purposes of applying property offences when the core harm is the loss of property rather than the altering of computer data.

In Chapter 6, Liang and Baker examine a range of recent amendments to Chinese law and compared them with some of the inchoate, pre-inchoate and remote harm offences found in English law. Chinese law does not have the sort of wide inchoate conspiracy offence like that found in common law jurisdictions, but it will criminalise an agreement under Article 22 when a preparatory act has been done towards making the conspiracy succeed. They conceptualise some of the problems and justifications for applying pre-inchoate liability and omissions liability to cybercrime problems in Chinese law. They conclude is that Chinese law does not go nearly as far as English law with respect to inchoate, pre-inchoate and remote harm liability. Furthermore, the Chinese law of complicity is far more limited in that it requires the actual perpetrator and accessory to both be caught and convicted; otherwise, complicity is not made out. Likewise, in English law, it does not matter that it is not possible to determine which one was the accessory, and which one was the perpetrator, as long as it can be proved one had to be the perpetrator and the other the accessory.

They also introduce the new network offences found in Articles 286(1) and 287(1) of the *Criminal Code of China* and argue that the offences seem to strike at serious harm that needs deterring, but that there will be obstacles for imputation due to the corporate nature of ISPs. In English law, it has been notoriously difficult to impute fault to CEOs and senior managers of companies because they have been able to argue that they were too far removed from the breach to have sufficient knowledge to be responsible. They argue that the Chinese law effectively deals with this, because liability depends on a warning being served on particular officers within the corporation.

Finally, they argue that pre-inchoate and remote harm offences can be helpful as long as they result in fair labelling of the harm and wrong done, and as long as the sentence takes into account that the act was pre-inchoate or a remote harm. This is necessary not only because of the sheer number of victims that can be targeted through cybermeans, but also because of the very different roles that differ cybercriminals play. By having criminal offences to cover each step in the process, there is a higher chance of catching more people either at the pre-inchoate stage or remote harm stage, if not at the inchoate stage. It ought not matter that one party does preparatory acts (remote harms) for another without having any intention of assisting the other.

In Chapter 7, Professors Lao and Baker argue that the new provision on data protection found in Chinese law brings China much closer to the position taken with respect to data protection in the European Union. They demonstrate that China moved away from the minimalist approach that the United States takes with respect to data protection and has adopted a public law model of protection. They argue that data is best protected by public law including criminal law, because it allows all to have equal protection regardless of their ability to litigate data misuse as a private wrong such as the tort of misuse of information. Such litigation is expensive, and in China, like many common countries, would limit protection based on a person's ability to pay for lawyers to bring private actions. By having data protection covered by public laws, including criminal law, a person would have to do no more than phone the police or write to the regulator, should his or her data be misused. Also, they demonstrate that it is not helpful to simply assume that one can have a property interest in data.

In Chapter 8, Li, Zhao and Baker consider the problem of cyberfraud in China and carryout a comparative study with English law to provide China with some insights for reforming its law to catch a wider range of conduct concerning cyberfraud and related crimes. The aim to demonstrate that having remote harm offences that criminalise the act of selling or manufacturing articles for use in fraud is one way to plug the gap that is left when there is not any conspiracy or complicity between the seller/manufacturer and the end-user. They demonstrate that the law of complicity and conspiracy could be developed in China to cover a wide range of situations. Also, they point out that the preparation provision found in Article 22 of the *Criminal Code of China* could be supplemented with a new provision that criminalises criminal agreements per se. This could be limited to apply only to crimes that carry a three-year or longer prison sentence, to ensure that inchoate from of criminality is not stretched to cover agreements to perpetrate non-serious crime. They argue that law of complicity found in Articles 25 of the *Criminal Code of China* (the joint perpetration offence) would be enhanced in the field of cybercrime if it were supplemented with an inchoate from of complicity like that found in Sections 44–46 of the *Serious Crime Act 2007* (U.K.).

In Chapter 9, Creese addresses artificial intelligence and its use in cyberattacks and its use in preventing cyberattacks. Creese notes that artificial intelligence (AI) and associated technologies have been receiving increasing attention in recent years. The research investment both in academia and industry is significant, and this has resulted in methods being adopted widely as organisations seek to increase the value they can extract from data. Such value is created in a variety of ways, as it involves deploying a choice of a number of technologies, and associated analytical methods, that make up what is generally thought of as AI. But a simplified view of what these, in essence, can deliver is enhanced service and product due to an ability either: (1) to predict what the user will want, enjoy or need to use in the future; or (2) to learn and advise on an optimal decision, given data on current and past context, and past outcomes.

In Chapter 10, Hallevy examines the possibility of criminal liability and punishment for artificial intelligence. He argues that criminal liability can be imposed upon an entity include artificially intelligent beings and that the same may also be subject to punishment. He argues the sort of capacity for autonomous decision-making that gives rise to criminal liability can already be found in some artificially intelligent instruments. This capacity for autonomous decision-making is not in the very distance further, but is already raising serious questions for law, including criminal law. AI technology urgently needs regulating, and the question of criminal liability ought to be given equal treatment as is given to civil law issues. He makes a convincing case for demonstrating this is a present rather than a future problem and that artificially intelligent machines will be sufficiently autonomous in some case to relieve their human creators of any criminal responsibility for their choices, even if there may still be civil liability or product if the flawed decision could have been adequately guarded against by the manufacturer. Also, he presents a fairly convincing case for punishing artificially intelligent instruments as entities while outlining some of the difficulties that will raise.

In Chapter 11, Dsouza takes a more conservative approach than Hallevy and argues that there is no need to worry about criminal liability for artificially intelligent instruments, because mental capacity for establishing agency does not yet exist in machines. Thereafter, he applies the doctrines of criminal liability found in the general part to existing technology and assert the issue of criminal liability is moot. He writes, "the process of explaining why this is so gives us a chance to reflect once more on the resources that the criminal law has at its disposal, and reconsidering these in this new context brings out nuances that are sometimes overlooked."

2 Financial technology
Opportunities and challenges to law and regulation

The Right Hon. Lord Hodge

1. Introduction

In recent years, as concerns have grown about the use of our data by large commercial organisations, it has become increasingly clear that data is power. So is artificial intelligence. The theme of my chapter is both the opportunities which technology has created in the field of financial services and whether, and if so how, law and regulation can cope with the challenges which the use of data and AI by the financial community is posing.

There are four technological developments which have created the new opportunities and challenges. They are, first, the huge increase in the computational and data processing power of IT systems. Second, data have become available on an unprecedented scale. Third, the costs associated with the storage of data have fallen. And, fourth, increasingly sophisticated software services have come onto the market.

There are various definitions for artificial intelligence, or AI, which focus on its ability to perform tasks that otherwise would require human intelligence. Turner, in his recent book on regulating AI, *Robot Rules*, speaks of AI as "the ability of a non-natural entity to make choices by an evaluative process."[1] That is so, but AI is not confined to matching human intelligence in the performance of its tasks.[2] Machines can beat grand masters at chess and outperform expert players

---

1 J. Turner, *Robot Rules: Regulating Artificial Intelligence*, (London: Palgrave Macmillan, 2019) at 16; see also J. A. Schnader, "Mal-Who? Mal-What? Mal-Where? The Future Cyber-Threat of A Non-Fiction Neuromancer: Legally Un-Attributable, Cyberspace-Bound, Decentralized Autonomous Entities," (2019) 21 *N.C. J. L. & Tech.* 1.
2 Casey draws the following distinctions:

> First, "artificial intelligence" (AI), a term notoriously resistant to definition. It refers roughly to a suite of technologies that attempt to automate the complex behaviors we refer to as exhibiting "intelligence." Notionally, as the level of machine intelligence increases, intervention by humans decreases. Ultimately, AI systems aim to create discrete operating states in which machines can perform tasks by purely automated means. . . . Although automation exists on a spectrum, its immediate legal consequences are better understood as binary. Automating a complex task can produce a system with a discrete operating state involving neither a need (nor expectation) of appropriate human intervention – referred to

of "Go."[3] I would prefer to define AI as computer systems able to perform tasks which traditionally have required human intelligence or tasks whose completion is beyond human intelligence.

Within AI, there is machine learning, which involves the designing of a sequence of actions to solve a problem, known as algorithms, which optimise automatically through experience and with limited or no human intervention.[4] This ability poses significant challenges to our law, as I will seek to show.

There is also the process known as "big data analytics."[5] Computers can now find patterns in large amounts of data from many and diverse sources.[6] And our data is readily available. In 2016, 68% of adults in the 11 most economically advanced countries owned a smart-phone, giving access to the Internet and machine learning. It is a great empowerment. But it has its downside. As Turner stated: "Every time we use a search engine, that search engine is using us."[7] It raises major questions about our privacy and about manipulation of decision-making via the use of targeted advertising or other pernicious uses of social media, as recent concerns about the misuse of Google and Facebook have shown.

There are many benefits from the new innovations, and, in particular, the new processing capacity and storage infrastructure. The new capacity can be used beneficially in the diagnosis of diseases, the translation of foreign languages and the development of driverless vehicles. Law enforcement authorities increasingly use these techniques to both detect and deter crime early. It may also prove to be very useful when authorities decide on the likelihood that a person will re-offend. The United Nations Global Pulse has an interesting initiative using machine learning in combination with natural language processing to analyse material on the web, in social media, in newspapers and from other sources to assess the effectiveness

---

as "human-out-of-the-loop" or "closed-loop." Or, automating a complex task can produce a system that still envisages some degree of human intervention – referred to as "human-in-the loop" or "open-loop." Critically, a liability loop needn't encompass an entire operating domain to be considered "closed." Automatic emergency braking (AEB) systems, for instance, are closed-loop technologies that constantly scan for impending collisions, without ever actually taking over control of the larger driving task. Nor must a given loop be particularly "intelligent." In fact . . . automated loops don't actually need to involve software at all.

B. Casey, "Robot Ipsa Loquitur," (2019) 108 *Geo. L.J.* 225 at 245–246.

3 In 1997, IBM's Deep Blue defeated Gary Kasparov at chess, and in 2016, Google Deep-Mind's AlphaGo program beat the 18-time world champion Lee Sedol. M. A. Bruckner, "Regulating Fintech Lending," (2018) 37(6) *Banking & Fin. Services Pol'y Rep.* 1; M. R. Anderson, "Twenty Years on from Deep Blue vs Kasparov: How a Chess Match Started the Big Data Revolution," (London: *The Conversation*, 6 December 2017).

4 These definitions are taken from a paper by the Financial Stability Board, "Artificial Intelligence and Machine Learning in Financial Services" (1 November 2017).

5 See generally, C. K. Odinet, "The New Data of Student Debt," (2019) 92 *S. Cal. L. Rev.* 1617.

6 See also K. Johnson *et al.*, "Artificial Intelligence, Machine Learning, and Bias in Finance: Toward Responsible Innovation," (2019) 88 *Fordham L. Rev.* 499.

7 Turner, *op. cit. supra*, note 1 at 23.

of policies and to detect and anticipate emerging socio-economic or political problems.

There are also uses to which big data analytics and AI can be put which can cause more concern in Western perceptions, because they which pose serious challenges to our concepts of human rights.[8] Repressive regimes in the Middle East and elsewhere are purchasing technology to carry out surveillance activities on their citizens.

In Western society, governments have not sought to exercise such control, but there are very serious concerns about the potential for abuse of big data by commercial organisations, such as the misuse of data by tech giants including Facebook and Google.[9] There are also concerns about the use of data in relation to access to health insurance or to credit.[10]

Concerns about foreign intervention in our democratic processes have grown.[11] The grand jury's indictment in *United States v Internet Research Agency LLC* dated 16 February 2018,[12] which is a product of the enquiry by special counsel, Robert Mueller, is a sobering read, giving an account of the employment by agents of the Russian Federation of hundreds of individuals and the expenditure of millions of dollars on online operations, the creation of fictitious persons as opinion formers, and the carrying on of a misinformation operation on YouTube, Facebook, Instagram and Twitter to spread distrust of presidential candidates and the political system in the lead up to the 2016 U.S. presidential election.

The speed of technological development poses a real challenge to the law and to regulation. The business consultancy McKinsey has estimated that, compared with the Industrial Revolution, the changes being effected by AI are happening 10 times faster and at 300 times the scale, thus having roughly 3,000 times the impact.[13] The McKinsey Global Institute highlights the increasing pace of technological change and quotes an estimate from an industry insider that humankind will generate more data in the next five years than it has created in 5,000 years.[14] It is necessary to ask: how can the law respond to that challenge?

8 R. H. Sloan and R. Warner, "Algorithms and Human Freedom," (2019) 35 *Santa Clara High Tech. L.J.* 1; cf. M. M. Maas, "International Law Does Not Compute: Artificial Intelligence and the Development, Displacement or Destruction of the Global Legal Order," (2019) 20 *Melb. J. Int'l L.* 29 at 42.
9 See further, A. Alben, "Privacy, Freedom, and Technology-or How Did We Get into This Mess?", (2019) 42 *Seattle U. L. Rev.* 1043.
10 N. P. Terry, "Appification, Ai, and Healthcare's New Iron Triangle," (2018) 20 *J. Health Care L. & Pol'y* 117 at 164.
11 D. E. W. Johnson, "Russian Election Interference and Race-Baiting," (2019) 9 *Colum. J. Race & L.* 191.
12 See 2018 WL 3857077. See further A. Denton, "Fake News: The Legality of the Russian 2016 Facebook Influence Campaign," (2019) 37 *B.U. Int'l L.J.* 183.
13 Turner, *op. cit. supra*, note 1 at 35. See also D. Kim, "Intellectual Property in the Fourth Industrial Revolution Era," (2018) 53 *Les Nouvelles* 20.
14 R. Dobbs *et al.*, *No Ordinary Disruption: The Four Global Forces Breaking All Trends*, (New York: Public Affairs, 2015) at 33–41. See also Tom C.W. Lin, "Artificial Intelligence, Finance, and the Law," (2019) 88 *Fordham L. Rev.* 531.

2. Fintech

My topic in this chapter is not so much these wider concerns but the more focused question of the use of AI, big data and other financial technology by financial firms. Many of the concerns about the wider use of AI and big data are replicated in the world of financial technology (Fintech). I will examine some of the benefits or potential benefits of Fintech, before looking at blockchain technology, AI and machine learning, and data protection. Then I will seek to set out some ideas on the need to reform the law of contract to address smart contracts and contracts created between machines, the attribution of responsibility in delict (tort) for harm caused by semi-autonomous or autonomous machines, and the development of new concepts in property law. Finally, I will ask how this is to be done and make some observations concerning regulatory initiatives.

The power of AI and machine learning to analyse data should be able to contribute to a more efficient financial system in those economies which embrace Fintech. Lenders will have more information to assess the credit quality of borrowers and to make decisions on whether and how much to lend quickly. Insurers will better be able to assess risk and market their insurance contracts more efficiently. Customers of financial institutions increasingly rarely visit their bank branch but obtain money from ATMs and, if they have the patience to do so, solve problems by speaking to "chatbots" (which are computer programs which simulate conversations with human customers in natural language). Banks are thus able to provide their services with many fewer staff and branches.

Banks are using AI and machine learning to maximise profits from scarce capital, to improve their models for risk management and stress testing, and to carry out market impact analysis, by creating so-called "trading robots" which evaluate the impact of the business's own trading on the market in which it operates.[15] Asset managers and trading firms can use machine learning to devise trading and investment strategies and, in portfolio management, to predict price movements.

Advocates of Fintech assert that consumers and investors should benefit from lower fees and borrowing costs if the new technology reduces the cost of financial services. The technology also has the potential to make financial services available to consumers who are currently excluded from or have only limited access to such services, for example because of having no credit profile.[16] Access to reasonably priced credit can do much to alleviate poverty, both at home and internationally.

3. DLT

The development of algorithms has enabled the collaborative creation of digital distributed ledgers by which a database of assets is shared across a network of

---

15 Cf. G. Scopino, "Do Automated Trading Systems Dream of Manipulating the Price of Futures Contracts? Policing Markets for Improper Trading Practices by Algorithmic Robots," (2015) 67 *Fla. L. Rev.* 221.

16 Cf. D. C. Vladeck, "Consumer Protection in an Era of Big Data Analytics," (2016) 42 *Ohio N.U. L. Rev.* 493 at 496.

sites, geographies and institutions and in which all participants have their own identical copy of the ledger.

The European Securities Markets Authority[17] has described distributed ledger technology (DLT) systems as records of electronic transactions which are maintained by a shared or "distributed" network of participants (known as "nodes"), thereby forming a distributed validation system, that make extensive use of cryptography – that is, computer-based encryption techniques such as public keys and private keys and hash functions, which are used to store assets and validate transactions on distributed ledgers.

This technology originated in the blockchain which a person or persons under the pseudonym "Satoshi Nakamoto" developed in about 2008 to create the peer-to-peer cryptocurrency Bitcoin. In his paper on Bitcoin,[18] Nakamoto emphasised the attraction of a decentralised payment system by which electronic cash could be sent from one party to another without going through a financial institution or other trusted intermediary and which would make the payments irreversible or at least impractical to reverse, thus removing the need for a merchant to trust his customer to pay for his goods or services.

This concept has undoubtedly appealed to anti-establishment libertarians. Disenchantment with banking intermediaries and regulators after the banking crisis of over a decade ago has encouraged some to hanker after a dis-intermediated world. But Bitcoin has not been without its problems.[19] As a permissionless system, it is open to the public, and members of the public can effect and verify changes to the ledger. But the method of maintaining the validity of the record on the ledger is extravagant in its energy use. The "proof of work" validation method used by Bitcoin involves the use of large quantities of computing power, as people "mine" to obtain further Bitcoins. It has been estimated that Bitcoin already uses as much electricity per year as the annual consumption of the Republic of Ireland (which has a population of 4.8 million), and that by 2020, it will consume as much as Denmark, which has a population of 5.7 million.[20]

Bitcoin has also proved to be the object of speculative bubbles. It suffered crashes in value in 2011, 2013 and 2014, and particularly in 2017 when the coin rose from $1,000 to over $19,000 before falling back sharply. When I gave

---

17 Financial Markets Law Committee, "Fintech: Issues of Legal Complexity," (June 2008) at 61; European Securities Markets Authority, "The Distributed Ledger Technology Applied to Securities Markets," (7 February 2017) at 4.

18 S. Nakamoto, "Bitcoin: A Peer-to-Peer Electronic Cash System," (2008).

19 See C. R. Goforth, "How Blockchain Could Increase the Need for and Availability of Contractual Ordering for Companies and Their Investors," (2019) 94 *N.D. L. Rev.* 1; W. Magnuson, "Financial Regulation in the Bitcoin Era," (2018) 23 *Stan. J.L. Bus. & Fin.* 159; M. Ryznar, "The Future of Bitcoin Futures," (2019) 56 *Hous. L. Rev.* 539.

20 The records of Bitcoin transactions are thought to be almost impossible to falsify because the collective computer power required to validate transactions is so great: World Bank Group, "Distributed Ledger Technology (DLT) and Blockchain," (2017), at 6; C. L. Reyes, "Cryptolaw for Distributed Ledger Technologies: A Jurisprudential Framework," (2018) 58 *Jurimetrics J.* 283.

a lecture on Fintech in Shanghai in October last year, the price of a Bitcoin was about $6,400. In March of this year, the price was about $3,800. This price would be disappointing to someone who bought in when a Bitcoin fetched in the tens of thousands of dollars. But in a fit of exuberance after the recent announcement of a Facebook cryptocurrency, to which I will return, the price of a Bitcoin had risen to $11,661.60 as of the time of writing. It is, in short, a speculator's toy.

Other concerns about the cryptocurrency have included the pseudonymous nature of the participants in its transactions. It appears to be attractive to criminals who wish to launder money, and concerns have been expressed about its use in tax evasion, drug trafficking and the funding of terrorism.[21] Europol estimates that £3–4 billion is laundered using cryptoassets each year in Europe. While that is a small proportion of money laundering in Europe, a recent report by the Financial Action Task Force to the G20 states that suspicious transaction reporting linked to cryptoassets is rising.[22] Digital currencies have also been used by the controllers of ransomware, the malicious software used to prevent users from accessing their computer system unless a ransom is paid.[23] While there may not have been breaches of the DLT ledger supporting the cryptocurrency, there have been major problems with the software at Bitcoin exchanges at which the digital currency is exchanged for fiat currency. Thus, a Tokyo-based Bitcoin exchange, Mt Gox, which had handled 70% of the world's Bitcoin trades, had to be shut down in 2014 after thefts of over $450 million worth of Bitcoin were discovered, and in August 2016, $72 million worth of Bitcoin was stolen in a hack of the Bitfinex exchange. In the first 10 months of 2018, $927 million was stolen from coin exchanges by hacking, including $500 million from a hack on the Coincheck exchange.[24] More recently, it has been reported that the sudden death of the 30-year-old founder of QuadrigaCX, Gerald Cotten, has left up to $190 million of cryptocurrency beyond the reach of their owners as they were stored offline in "cold wallets" on his encrypted laptop and nobody knows how to get access to them.

The extent of fraud and serious misrepresentation in initial coin offerings (ICOs) has done much to discredit this means of unregulated funding. At a recent seminar in the Royal Society, it was stated that there are currently 2,231 live cryptocurrencies. The use of smart contracts (which I will discuss) has been described as "uniquely dangerous" because of the capacity for mistakes or deliberate flaws in the programme which cause investors to lose their money. There is plenty of scope for criminal activity.[25]

21 E. Engle, "Is Bitcoin Rat Poison? Cryptocurrency, Crime, and Counterfeiting (Ccc)," (2016) 16 *J. High Tech. L.* 340.
22 Financial Conduct Authority, "Guidance on Cryptoassets," Consultation Report CP19/13, para. 2.31.
23 L. J. Trautman and P. C. Ormerod, "Wannacry, Ransomware, and the Emerging Threat to Corporations," (2019) 86 *Tenn. L. Rev.* 503.
24 Financial Conduct Authority, *op. cit. supra*, note 22 at para. 2.28.
25 A. Verstein, "Crypto Assets and Insider Trading Law's Domain," (2019) 105 *Iowa L. Rev.* 1.

In the United Kingdom, the Financial Conduct Authority has spoken of market volatility and the lack of transparency and oversight heightening the risk of market manipulation and insider dealing on exchanges and trading platforms and there are proposals to extend the regulatory reach of the Financial Conduct Authority (FCA) to bring in further types of cryptoassets and to apply anti-money laundering regulations to them.

I doubt whether the future lies with permissionless cryptocurrencies with decentralised validation. But I expect that there remains a bright future for distributed ledger technology and probably also for digital currencies which are developed (and possibly underwritten) by mainstream financial institutions and central banks. Several central banks are exploring the introduction of DLT-based digital currencies issued by a central bank and backed by fiat currency,[26] and large international banks are examining the introduction of digital currencies backed by reserves of fiat currency.[27] In February 2019, J. P. Morgan announced that it had created and successfully tested a digital coin representing a fiat currency using a blockchain-based technology.[28] J.P. Morgan sees the digital coin as a means of achieving instantaneous transfers of value, reducing their clients' counterparty and settlement risk and decreasing requirements to hold capital. They are currently seeking regulatory approval. More recently still, Facebook in June 2019 announced a proposal for a new virtual currency, Libra, as the basis of a payment service operating on a version of blockchain, which has the support of several substantial companies and payment networks, including Visa and Mastercard. It would use its WhatsApp messaging service to transfer funds. It would be backed by reserves of fiat currency. It would not be a permissionless system but would entail a private network of about 100 trusted companies which would post the transactions instead of relying on independent validation. It has been described as a "full frontal assault on finance."[29] And it raises very serious questions about the ability of central banks to control their financial systems and operate normal monetary policy and the ability of countries or groups of countries to impose effective sanctions on other countries.[30]

Distributed ledger technology offers many benefits. You can trace the ownership of assets on blockchain. If a trusted institution controls the ability to alter the blockchain, DLT can provide an accurate record of prior transactions without incurring great expense. DLT has the potential to reduce the costs of banking transactions and international trade by eliminating the need for the transmission and handling of paper documents and simplifying cross-border payments. The

26 World Bank Group, *op. cit. supra*, note 20 at 34.
27 M. Dell'Erba, "Stablecoins in Cryptoeconomics: From Initial Coin Offerings to Central Bank Digital Currencies," (2020) 22 *N.Y.U. J. Legis. & Pub. Pol'y* 1.
28 J. P. Morgan Chase & Co website, announcement published on 14 February 2019. www.jpmorgan.com/global/news/digital-coin-payments
29 *Financial Times*, 24 June 2019.
30 Sebastian Omlora, "The CISG and Libra: A Monetary Revolution for International Commercial Transactions?" (2020) 3 *Stan. J. Blockchain L. & Pol'y* 83.

FCA reports that there have been cases in the regulatory sandbox, which I will discuss shortly, which have demonstrated on a small scale that exchange tokens have made payment services, such as international money remittance, cheaper and faster.[31] There is the potential to speed up and reduce the costs of transaction by reducing or even eliminating intermediaries in financial transactions. The World Bank quotes an estimate that the financial sector alone could achieve savings in the range of $15–20 billion per year.[32]

An important part of the savings may result from the use of "smart contracts," which are contracts whose terms are recorded in a computer language and which are automatically executed by a computing system. At its simplest, the smart contract involves an instruction to the computer that if X happens, then the computer is to act to make Y the result. In other words, the smart contract is performed automatically, without human intervention. This removes or reduces the risk of default and avoids the cost of enforcement of contractual obligations. If you agree to transact by computer using smart contracts, you get automatic performance. It is like putting money into a vending machine to buy a bottle of water. The computer's "if-then" logic operates: money in, bottle out.

The reduced dependence on intermediaries, such as central counterparties (CCPs), and the reduced risk of default which blockchain technology can offer, are seen as a means of improving financial market infrastructure. In a recent paper,[33] Professor Avgouleas and Professor Kiayias argue that the use of DLT systems in securities and derivatives trading, clearing and settlement has the potential to transform the structure of the financial services industry. The dependence on and concentration of power in the hands of a few CCPs in derivatives trading is seen as giving rise to systemic risk and also creating moral hazard because a CCP may be too big to fail. In securities transactions, the costs of the use of investment intermediaries which hold securities as depositaries and the risks associated with the re-hypothecation of securities which have been received as collateral in one transaction, as collateral in a second transaction are seen as problems. The authors suggest that DLT systems can reduce that dependence on intermediaries, give the ultimate investor more control over the securities which it owns, and increase transparency and traceability. The new technology can reduce costs and, the authors suggest, create greater transparency and liquidity for long-term finance by creating markets for previously illiquid investments.

There is considerable international interest in the potential of DLT technology. Securities exchanges in Canada and Australia have declared their intention to move to blockchain-operated trading and clearing, and the South Korean capital markets regulator advocates collaboration in developing an integrated blockchain system for stock transactions. The Bank of England has been studying how a

---

31 Financial Conduct Authority, *op. cit. supra*, note 22 at para. 3.54.

32 World Bank Group, *op. cit. supra*, note 20 at 16.

33 E. Avgouleas and A. Kiayias, "The Promise of Blockchain Technology for Global Securities and Derivatives Markets: The New Financial Ecosystem and the 'Holy Grail' of Systemic Risk Containment," (2019) 20 *European Business Organization Law Review* 81.

real-time gross settlement service could be adapted to support settlement in systems using DLT technology. A consortium of Hong Kong- and Singapore-based banks have started using DLT technology for processing trade finance documentation, following a successful trial which suggested that there were savings in time and cost from the use of the technology.

AI and the ability to process rapidly so much more data than was possible in the past should assist institutions to make better evidence-based decisions. Sophisticated investors and commercial organisations may be able to benefit greatly from what technology can offer, including in the area of peer-to-peer lending. But there are also important risks that ought not to be underestimated. The availability of big data and the ability of computers to process and analyse the data in ways which were previously not possible give rise to unprecedented ethical and regulatory questions. Since at least 2008, the ethical standards and responsibility of financial institutions have been the subject of adverse public debate. More recently, similar questions are being asked of the principal providers of technology such as Facebook and Google. In short, can financiers and big tech be trusted with the power which the information revolution gives them? Most people say no.

Concerns have been expressed about the potential for data to be used in unacceptable ways. Big data threatens privacy. The increased capacity to combine and process data from various sources has made it easier to identify individuals who are data subjects. Reidentification technology may undermine the current views of what is personal data.[34] Algorithms could be used to restrict certain people's access to finance or insurance on unlawfully discriminatory grounds; they can be used as means of social control. The misuse or loss of data stored "in the cloud" will be a concern if financial services are provided in this way;[35] cybersecurity is a challenge, for, while financial institutions constantly build their defences, cyber-criminals develop ever more sophisticated means of attack.[36]

There may be a need to protect retail consumers from risky products by limiting access to certain platforms only to sophisticated investors. This may be the case with platform lending, as currently platform providers do not owe any form of a fiduciary duty to lenders in crowd funding should things go wrong, and things did go wrong in many ways in China where these platforms first claimed a substantial market share, forcing a government response.[37] But there may also be problems for financial institutions. Fifty-five per cent of trades in United States equity markets and 40% of such trades on European markets are automated with

---

34 C. Chang, "Bank on We the People: Why and How Public Engagement Is Relevant to Biobanking," (2019) 25 *Mich. Tech. L. Rev.* 239 at 249.

35 A. S. Y. Cheung and R. H. Weber (eds.), *Privacy and Legal Issues in Cloud Computing*, (London: Edward Elgar Publishing Ltd., 2016).

36 J. Mitts and E. Talley, "Informed Trading and Cybersecurity Breaches," (2019) 9 *Harv. Bus. L. Rev.* 1.

37 Jay P. Kesan and Carol M. Hayes, "Bugs in the Market: Creating A Legitimate, Transparent, and Vendor-Focused Market for Software Vulnerabilities," (2016) 58 *Ariz. L. Rev.* 753 at 771; cf. O. Lobel, "The Law of the Platform," 101 *Minn. L. Rev.* 87 at 144 *et seq.*

all key decisions made by algorithmic programmes.[38] The Financial Stability Board (FSB) has warned of the danger of "herding" in financial markets. This is the process by which traders adopt similar machine-learning strategies and so amplify financial shocks. The FSB has also warned about the danger that insiders and cybercriminals may be able to manipulate market prices by identifying predictable patterns in the behaviour of automated trading strategies.[39]

Another concern which has been identified is the risk that financial markets may become too dependent on a limited number of technology suppliers so that the insolvency of, or other disruption to, the business of a big supplier could disrupt the market.[40]

The development of Fintech also poses a challenge to the legal systems of the United Kingdom. We have long taken pride in having legal systems which promote commercial activity and which can be adapted to cope with changing circumstances. Lord Goff, in an extrajudicial writing, spoke of judges being there to give effect to the transactions of business people and not frustrate them; we, he said, "are there to oil the wheels of commerce, not to put a spanner in the works, or even grit in the oil."[41] Oiling the wheels of commerce when businesses are developing novel means of transacting though the use of AI, and machine learning poses a serious challenge to lawyers, judges and legislators.

Much of the literature on the challenges posed by AI and machine learning has focused on robotics, including the development of weapons and driverless cars. Perhaps the principal concern is the attribution of responsibility for the acts and omissions of robots.[42] In March 2019, the Lord Chief Justice of England and Wales announced the establishment of an advisory body to offer guidance to the senior judiciary on AI and its impact, including its effect on the law. I welcome that initiative.

4. Contract law

Because of the importance of contract law in financial transactions, I will begin with that. Both English law and Scots law should not have much difficulty with questions about parties' intention to enter into contracts and the interpretation of the contracts, because of the objective approach which we adopt. So long as the operation of the computer program can be explained to judges who, like me, may be deficient in our knowledge of computer science, it should be relatively

---

38 Turner, *op. cit. supra*, note 1 at 26.

39 Report, *Financial Stability Implications from FinTech*, (London: FSB, 2017) at 37–39 et passim it is noted: (1) "Financial stability implications from FinTech: supervisory and regulatory issues that merit authorities' attention" (27 June 2017); and (2) "Artificial intelligence and machine learning in financial services."

40 *Ibid.* at 33.

41 Sir Robert Goff, "Commercial Contracts and the Commercial Court," (1984) *LMCLQ* 382 at 391.

42 S. Gless *et al.*, "If Robots Cause Harm, Who Is to Blame? Self-Driving Cars and Criminal Liability," (2016) 19 *New Crim. L. Rev.* 412.

straightforward to conclude that people who agree to use a programme with smart contracts in their transactions have objectively agreed to the consequences of the operation of the "if-then" logic of the programme. In the context of financial transactions, the English law requirement for consideration should not be a serious difficulty and the flexible law of estoppel can, if needed, ride to the rescue.

The self-executing smart contract cannot be unscrambled in the same way as a traditional contract, because it is not possible to annul it and halt its performance in the course of execution. The smart contract's strength in eliminating default by causing X to bring about Y prevents the courts from stopping the performance of the contract. Rescission is not an option for the contracting party.[43] This means that the remedies for, say, fraud or misrepresentation inducing the contract are to order the re-transfer of property which has passed under the contract. This could be achieved by a declarator or declaration that the contract was induced by fraud or other misrepresentation and an order for re-transfer, by developing the law of unjust enrichment to reverse the effect of a contract which has not been rescinded.

Much greater problems in the law of contract may arise if computers are developed to use machine learning to optimise the transactions which they enter into. If businesses were to use computers with machine learning capability to deal with other computers with similar ability, they could autonomously generate transactions which would not fit easily into our contract law. Could one party to the contract turn to the other and say, like Aeneas to Dido, "*non haec in federa veni*," or "that wasn't the deal"? Or should the law say that those who willingly use computers with machine learning to effect their transactions are to be taken as intending to be contractually bound by the deals which those autonomous machines make? If a financial institution could walk away from a machine-created transaction, that might create chaos in the commercial world. If there is to be a contract drafted or adapted by machines, there will have to be significant development to our law of contract which will require careful and imaginative consideration.[44]

It may sound rather fanciful that commercial organisations would allow computers autonomously to devise and enter into contracts with each other. But it may not be beyond the realm of possibility, since there are commercial advantages in allowing computers to optimise trading deals. And there is always the risk of unintended consequences. It seems to me that there is great merit in the concept of the regulatory sandbox, which I will discuss, as a means of testing innovative Fintech in a relatively safe environment.

---

43 Unscrambling an executed contract on blockchain is difficult to achieve, requiring one to go back in the chain to a point before the contract, creating a fork and re-creating the chain without the impugned transaction. See also H. Hughes, "Blockchain and the Future of Secured Transactions Law," (2020) 3 *Stan. J. Blockchain L. & Pol'y* 21.

44 Cf. S. Agnikhotram and A. Kouroutakis, "Doctrinal Challenges for the Legality of Smart Contracts: Lex Cryptographia or A New, 'Smart' Way to Contract?" (2019) 19 *J. High Tech. L.* 300 at 307.

It is sufficient at this stage to state that if Fintech is developed to use machine learning to optimise contractual transactions, there is a need for our commercial law to develop new concepts to address that phenomenon. Questions about the intention to enter into legal relations, to whom that intention is to be attributed – and how the terms of a computer-generated contract are to be recorded to achieve legal validity and be interpreted – will require innovative thinking.

5. Tort/delict

The law of tort or delict will need to be revised to attribute liability for harm caused by machines exercising AI. Taking the most common form of delict, the law of negligence, how does one develop concepts akin to the neighbourhood principle in *Donoghue v Stevenson*[45] and the carefully crafted rules by which judges have developed the common law to place boundaries on the involuntary obligations which the law imposes? Sadly, it is not just a matter of the reasonable bot on the San Francisco tramcar replacing the reasonable man on the Clapham omnibus – these are just legal abstractions.

Ulpian's three classical legal precepts – "to live honourably, to injure no one and to give everyone his due" – can provide a basis for the regulation and self-regulation of human activity. In the law of negligence, reasonable foresight and proximity – the neighbourhood principle – have fixed the boundaries of involuntary obligation in many contexts. But how do you impose liability and give compensation for the failure of a machine to comply with Ulpian's precepts – to injure no one and to give everyone his due? And when one addresses economic torts, namely the intentional infliction of harm by unlawful means, inducing breach of contract or conspiracy, which require a mental element of an intention to cause harm, or the delict of fraud, in which the knowledge or belief of the representor is relevant,[46] how do you impose liability for the harm caused by the autonomous acts of computers?

Where financial institutions choose to use AI in transactions with each other, the participants in such transactions can regulate their relationship, including responsibility for the outcomes of AI, by contract. But when harm is caused to persons who are not parties to the contractual relationship, we enter the field of involuntary obligation; that is, tort (delict) or liability imposed by statute, or unjustified enrichment.

Questions of the attribution of liability are arising in relation to driverless cars.[47] There the principal concern is to have remedies for personal injury and damage to property caused by the vehicle. Part 1 of the *Automated and Electric Vehicles Act 2018* imposes liability for third-party personal injury or property

---

45 [1932] A.C. 562.

46 J. Thomson, *Delictual Liability*, (London: Bloomsbury, 5th edn., 2014) at Chapter 2.

47 A. B. Lemann, "Autonomous Vehicles, Technological Progress, and the Scope Problem in Products Liability," (2019) 12 *J. Tort L.* 157; M. A. Lemley and B. Casey, "Remedies for Robots," (2019) 86 *U. Chi. L. Rev.* 1311 at 1352 *et seq.*

damage caused by an automated vehicle driving itself on a road or other public place on the insurer of the vehicle or, if it is uninsured, on the owner.

Similar but more difficult questions will arise in relation to attribution of liability and causation in the context of transactions performed by Fintech. Is liability for harm caused by the decisions of the machine to be imposed on the producer of the machine on a product liability model? Or should the owner or organisation which operates the machine be answerable for such harm? More fundamentally, in a market system in which it is entirely legal to impose economic harm on a competitor if one trades within the boundaries of the law, how do you define what is an economic wrong resulting from the autonomous acts of machines? Having identified what is an economic wrong in such circumstances, should the law impose strict liability for the harm caused by the acts of machines, or should liability be imposed on the natural or non-natural person producing, owning or operating the machine only if a natural person could reasonably have foreseen the risk of harm? These are fundamentally important questions of legal policy, and the common law does not provide any ready-made answers.

To my mind, a no-fault compensation scheme funded by a levy or taxation, such as is available in New Zealand to compensate personal injury, is a non-starter in Fintech because of the potential scale of economic loss compared with the compensation paid under such a scheme for personal injuries.

There seems to me to be scope for a regime of compulsory third-party insurance which like that of the driverless vehicle could be on a no-fault basis, but there is a problem as to the amount of insurance coverage which could sensibly be required. In the United Kingdom, compulsory third-party motor insurance in respect of property damage has been fixed at the comparatively modest level of £1.2 million.[48] The potential scale of liability for economic loss from financial transactions is on a quite different level from liability for personal injury or physical damage to property. What would be a prudent and economically manageable level of compulsory insurance for Fintech, and how many insurers will be prepared to offer such cover in the absence of product standardisation and a legal certification process?

6. Property law

There is also a need to adapt the law of property to cope with the assets which are the product of Fintech. The Financial Conduct Authority does not view exchange tokens such as Bitcoins, Ether and Litecoin as money. While used as a means of exchange within digital communities, their volatility, which I have mentioned, militates against their use as a unit of account or a store of value. Fewer than 600 merchants in the United Kingdom accept exchange tokens as a payment tool.[49] The Financial Markets Law Committee (FMLC) has suggested that digital

---

48 *Road Traffic Act 1988*, Section 145(4).
49 Financial Conduct Authority, *op. cit. supra*, note 22 at paras. 3.31–3.34.

currencies which are pegged to fiat currencies could be regarded as "e-money" and be negotiable. The FMLC suggests that the traditional categories of English law could be extended to recognise virtual choses in possession as a new form of property.[50] In Scotland, where our property law has a strong civilian framework we would need to recognise a new form of intangible moveable property.

A re-examination of the suitability of the tools of property law and trust law for our modern financial system would be a good idea in any event. There has been a debate for several years now on modernising, or at least clarifying, the law to accommodate intermediated securities. Intermediation at its simplest is the chain from the issuer of a security through the registered holder (such as a central securities depositary in the CREST securities depository system), via one or more intermediaries to the ultimate account holders. The question of the rights of the various parties in the chain and, in particular, the protection of the interest of the ultimate account holder has engaged the FMLC, the Law Commission, the U.K. government and, in relation to private international law, international bodies for several years.[51] DLT is seen by some as a possible solution to some of the problems created by intermediation. A careful examination of this possibility, together with an examination of appropriate legal rules for digital currencies and DLT transactions, would be a major undertaking, but if successful, would serve to provide a legal infrastructure to facilitate Fintech.

Another matter which needs to be addressed is whether the AI involved in Fintech should give rise to intellectual property which the law should recognise. If machines act autonomously to create new contracts, should there be copyright, and who should own it? Similar questions arise in relation to patents if such machines invent things which have industrial application.[52] In relation to copyright, U.K. law treats as the author of a computer-generated work the person by whom the arrangements necessary for the creation of the work are undertaken.[53] This approach appears to have considerable potential to create disputes, particularly if a machine is involved in the arrangements.

7. Separate legal personality

One option for addressing the various questions arising out of the use of AI in Fintech is to explore whether to give a computer separate legal personality.[54]

---

50 Financial Markets Law Committee, "Fintech: Issues of Legal Complexity," (June 2018) at 30, 38.

51 L. Gulliver and J. Payne (eds.), *Intermediation and Beyond*, (London: Hart Publishing, 2018), especially the chapters by V. Dixon (Chapter 3); R. Goode, (Chapter 5) and Richard Salter (Chapter 7).

52 Cf. W. M. Schuster, "Artificial Intelligence and Patent Ownership," (2018) 75 *Wash. & Lee L. Rev.* 1945.

53 Sections 9(3) and 178 of the *Copyright, Designs and Patents Act 1998*.

54 Cf. L. B. Solum, "Legal Personhood for Artificial Intelligences," (1992) 70 *N.C. L. Rev.* 1231; G. Hallevy, "The Criminal Liability of Artificial Intelligence Entities-from Science Fiction to Legal Social Control," (2010) 4 *Akron Intell. Prop. J.* 171; H. T. Greely,

While at first blush, that may sound far-fetched, there is no reason in principle why the law cannot create such personality. English law has for a long time allowed an office occupied by a natural person to be a corporation sole, the separate legal personality of a "one-person" company has been recognised since 1897[55] and, more recently, in *Bumper Development Corporation*,[56] it has recognised the separate legal personality in Indian law of a ruined temple which was little more than a pile of stones.

It would be possible for the machine as a separate legal person to own intellectual property and in turn to be owned by a financial institution. That institution's licence, or the general regulatory law, could impose on the firm responsibility for any malfunction, if, for example, it had been involved in the design of the algorithm. The law could confer separate legal personality on the machine by registration and require it or its owner to have compulsory insurance to cover its liability to third parties in delict (tort) or restitution. And as a registered person, the machine could own the intellectual property which it created.

(a) How the law should be adapted

It will be clear from what I have said up until now that it is not practicable to develop the common law through case law to create a suitable legal regime for Fintech.[57] The judiciary does not have the institutional competence to do so; it will play an important role in adapting the law, but more is needed. The changes in the law which are required are not interstitial law, the making of which is the long-recognised task of judges; they will require inter-disciplinary policy-making and consultation which a court cannot perform when resolving individual disputes and developing case law.

The Lord Chief Justice's initiative in setting up an advisory body is very welcome as a means of alerting the judiciary and the court system to the opportunities and challenges of AI. But a larger-scale collaboration involving the executive branch of government, focusing on AI and Fintech and aiming to produce facilitating legislation is probably needed if the United Kingdom is to facilitate the development of Fintech without harming the integrity of the markets or financial consumers. As the Law Society of England and Wales has stated (in a related

---

"Neuroscience, Artificial Intelligence, Crispr-and Dogs and Cats," (2018) 51 *U.C. Davis L. Rev.* 2303 at 2324.

55 *Salomon v. A Salomon and Co Ltd* [1897] A.C. 22.

56 *Bumper Development Corporation v Commissioner of Police of the Metropolis* [1991] 1 W.L.R. 1362.

57 Sir Geoffrey Vos, the Chancellor of the High Court, in two very interesting lectures has expressed more optimism that judges can facilitate the development of Fintech: Joint Northern Chancery Bar Association and University of Liverpool Lecture, "Cryptoassets as property: how can English law boost the confidence of would-be parties to smart legal contracts? (2 May 2019), "LawTech, Smart contracts and Artificial Intelligence," Bunderministerium Der Justiz Und Für Verbraucherschutz, Berlin (14 May 2019).

context): "The statutory approach ensures that there is a framework in place that everyone can understand."[58]

(b) International conventions and model laws

Financial transactions cross borders. If Fintech is to achieve its potential and contribute to the economic welfare of this country and other countries, legal reform and regulatory change cannot be confined to the domestic market, but must aspire to promote cross-border financial transactions and to facilitate international trade.

The current conflicting approaches to the treatment of cryptoassets by key jurisdictions such as the United States, the European Union and the United Kingdom support the case for international cooperation in the creation of Fintech law.

One option would be to develop a model law along the lines of model laws which the U.N. Commission on International Trade Law (UNCITRAL) has developed and states have adopted. Another is the preparation of an international convention. At the very least, there needs to be international cooperation to establish agreed rules of private international law to establish the governing law in relation to contracts executed and property held in a distributed ledger which operates across borders. I wonder if UNIDROIT, the International Institute for the Unification of Private Law, might have a role to play. It seems to me that the involvement of an intergovernmental body might reduce the suspicion by developing countries that large developed economies were dictating the rules. An alternative would be to build up a multilateral consensus between the leading trading nations.

(c) Regulation and regulatory sandboxes

There is an increasing awareness outside the field of financial services of the risks that AI and big data analysis pose to privacy and human rights.[59] Fintech can be designed to promote social control and achieve social exclusion. It will all be in the algorithms.

The preparation of statements of ethical standards has a role to play. But there is no public appetite for exclusive self-regulation in the financial services and tech industries. There needs to be official regulation to protect investors and consumers, to promote market integrity and to preserve financial stability. The FCA is busy addressing whether to ban the sale of certain cryptoassets to retail consumers. The European Banking Authority and the European Securities and Markets

---

58 The Law Society's written evidence to the House of Commons Science and Technology Committee Report on *Robotics and artificial intelligence* (12 October 2016), quoted by Turner, *op. cit. supra*, note 1 at 223.

59 See for example P. Margulies, "Surveillance by Algorithm: The NSA, Computerized Intelligence Collection, and Human Rights," (2016) 68 *Fla. L. Rev.* 1045.

Authority have been active in providing advice on the appropriate regulatory framework for cryptoassets.

The *Fifth E.U. Money Laundering Directive* came into force in 2020 and has been implemented in the United Kingdom, despite the fact that the U.K. has left the European Union. The aim is not to regulate cryptocurrencies themselves, but to regulate the providers of cryptocurrency exchanges by requiring them to register and by empowering the National Crime Agency's Financial Intelligence Unit to obtain from those exchanges the addresses and identities of owners of virtual currency. The Financial Action Task Force (FATF), an intergovernmental body, has undertaken a work programme in relation to virtual assets and on 21 June 2019 adopted an Interpretative Note and has given further guidance on its standards for the regulation and monitoring of the providers of virtual asset services.[60]

At the same time, a regulatory regime must not stifle innovation. The FATF seeks to promote responsible financial innovation by providing a platform for sharing developments and initiatives.

The FCA's invention in 2015 of the "regulatory sandbox" is to my mind a very important innovation. A regulatory sandbox is a framework set up by a financial services regulator to allow small-scale live testing of innovations by private firms (operating under a special exemption or limited temporary exception) under the supervision of the regulator.[61]

The sandbox allows the private firm to test products and services on a small scale with appropriate financial backing to indemnify consumers against loss and enables the regulator to assist in identifying safeguards to protect consumers which should be built into such products and services. This collaboration should enable them to be taken to market speedily.

Another possible use of a regulatory sandbox would be to analyse transactions to test the efficacy of proposed legal rules which could form a statutory framework of applicable rules on contract law, delict or tort, and property.

The regulatory sandbox has proved to be popular internationally, and in August 2018, the FCA and 11 other regulators announced the creation of the "Global Financial Innovation Network." This is intended to create a so-called global sandbox which would enable firms to trial new products in several countries at the same time, and allow regulators to exchange ideas on policy.

---

60 *Interpretative Note to Recommendation 15 on New Technologies (INR. 15) and Guidance for a Risk-Based Approach to Virtual Assets and Virtual Asset Service Providers.* http://fatf-gafi.org/publications/faftrecommendations/documents/public-statement-virtual-assets.html.

61 This definition is derived from Ivo Jenik and Kate Lauer, "Regulatory Sandboxes and Financial Inclusion," Working Paper (Washington, DC: CGAP, October 2017). See also C. Tsang, "From Industry Sandbox to Supervisory Control Box: Rethinking the Role of Regulators in the Era of Fintech," (2019) *U. Ill. J.L. Tech. & Pol'y* 355; Dirk A. Zetzsche *et al.*, "Regulating A Revolution: From Regulatory Sandboxes to Smart Regulation," (2017) 23 *Fordham J. Corp. & Fin. L.* 31.

The international harmonisation of regulatory standards would serve to discourage financial institutions from seeking out jurisdictions with the least effective regulation as a base for their Fintech business. Discouraging such regulatory arbitrage ought over time to enhance market integrity and consumer protection.

8. Conclusion

Financial services play a very important role in the economy of the United Kingdom and other countries. An important precondition of establishing and maintaining the United Kingdom as a centre of excellence in the development and operation of Fintech is the development of our laws and regulatory systems to facilitate the use of such technology. This is a big undertaking. British judges and the common law are well placed to make an important contribution. But we need more; we need a collaboration between financiers, computer specialists, judges, lawyers, law reform bodies and legislators.[62]

Data is power, and AI is power. We will need legislation. There also needs to be innovative regulation. Further, we must work for international agreement on legal and regulatory norms if Fintech is to achieve its potential in wealth creation and poverty reduction through cross-border transactions while maintaining market integrity and protecting the consumer. Conversations between the common law and China, such as in the conference that gave birth to this volume, make a valuable contribution to that goal.

---

62 The Fintech Delivery Panel and LawTech Delivery Panel, which have been established with the encouragement of the U.K. government, should be well placed to consult and advise on the law reform needed to facilitate the safe development of Fintech. The U.K. Jurisdiction Taskforce of the LawTech Delivery Panel has recently conducted a consultation on areas of legal uncertainty regarding cryptoassets, DLT and smart contracts which may provide useful insights into the principal areas of concern.

3 Between prevention and enforcement

The role of "disruption" in confronting cybercrime

Jonathan Clough

1. Introduction

Evolving from the move towards intelligence-led policing in the 1990s, disruption has increasingly become a key performance indicator for many law enforcement agencies (LEAs) around the world. Initially focused on organised criminal networks, disruption as a policing method has expanded to incorporate a broad range of serious transnational crimes, including cybercrimes. Although increasingly a feature of modern policing, it remains unclear in its scope and in the measurement of its effectiveness, particularly in relation to cybercrime, where it has received relatively little attention. Because disruption often draws upon powers conferred for the purposes of enforcement, concerns may be raised about appropriate oversight, the blurring of policing and security activities, and the need to balance competing interests and rights such as sovereignty and privacy.

This chapter discusses the nature of disruption and its application in the context of cybercrime, with a particular focus on legal frameworks. It begins with the nature of disruption and the role of intelligence in disruptive practices, before providing examples of how disruption may apply in the context of cybercrime. The role of legal frameworks is then considered, with a focus on the need for disruptive criminal offences, investigative powers and international cooperation. Although drawing primarily on examples from Australia and cognate common law jurisdictions, these issues are of potential relevance to all jurisdictions. It is hoped that this chapter will raise awareness of the role of disruption in combating cybercrime and the importance of legal frameworks if such techniques are to be both effective and subject to appropriate safeguards.

2. The nature of disruption

Since the early 1990s, policing agencies have increasingly moved away from a reactive prosecution-directed mode of crime control towards a form of policing known as intelligence-led policing.[1] Because of its more proactive nature,

---

1 M. Innes and J. W. E. Sheptycki, "From Detection to Disruption," (2004) 14(1) *International Criminal Justice Review* 1 at 2.

intelligence-led policing lends itself not only to crime prevention and reduction, but to the use of other techniques to disrupt criminal activity without necessarily proceeding to prosecution.[2]

It has been suggested that disruption is, in part, a product of widespread disenchantment with the traditional enforcement model.[3] In contrast to the use of intelligence for the purposes of prevention, the enforcement model requires admissible evidence, is costlier, and holds less certainty of outcome.[4] While achieving a prosecution is "rarely discounted,"[5] intelligence-led policing may produce a change in policing attitudes away from prosecution and towards objectives that "are increasingly more pragmatic, aiming to disrupt and disorganize criminal networks and markets."[6]

The reference to criminal networks and markets highlights that disruptive policing has most commonly been employed in relation to organised criminal groups, albeit of varying levels of sophistication.[7] The challenges to a prosecution-directed model presented by organised criminal groups are exacerbated by globalisation,[8] and disruption has assumed greater significance as an approach to policing that seeks to address the inability of local policing to address transnational and organised crime.[9]

Although part of the lexicon of intelligence-led policing, disruption remains "ambiguous and still not clearly defined by most agencies."[10] While the precise meaning will vary according to context, in broad terms, disruption may be seen as sitting on a spectrum of approaches to policing.[11] At one end of the spectrum, crime prevention is proactive and may be defined as "any activity by an individual or group, public or private, which attempts to eliminate crime either before it occurs or before any additional activity results."[12] At the other end of the spectrum, an enforcement-directed model is reactive and prosecution focused. Disruption may serve either or both of these purposes.[13] For example, the disabling

---

2   J. H. Ratcliffe, *Intelligence-Led Policing*, (Oxford: Routledge, 2nd edn., 2016) at 5.

3   *Ibid.* at 132.

4   P. Gill, "Organised Crime," in R. Dover, M. S. Goodman and C. Hillebrand (eds.), *Routledge Companion to Intelligence Studies*, (Oxford: Routledge, 2013) at 317.

5   Ratcliffe, *op cit. supra*, note 2 at 6.

6   Innes and Sheptycki, *op. cit. supra*, note 1 at 3.

7   S. Kirby and N. Snow, "Praxis and the Disruption of Organized Crime Groups," (2016) 19(2) *Trends in Organized Crime* 111.

8   Z. Shiraz and R. J. Aldrich, "Globalisation and Borders," in Dover *et al.*, *op. cit. supra*, note 4 at 267.

9   Ratcliffe, *op. cit. supra*, note 2.

10 *Ibid.* at 11. For an extensive list of disruptive techniques, see College of Policing, "Disrupting Serious and Organised Criminals: Menu of Tactics," (College of Policing Research, 2016) <https://whatworks.college.police.uk/Research/Documents/Menu_of_tactics.pdf> accessed 18 February 2020.

11 Kirby and Snow, *op. cit. supra*, note 7 at 112; Ratcliffe, *op cit. supra*, note 2 at 122.

12 Ratcliffe, *op. cit. supra*, note 2 at 133 citing S. P. Lab, *Crime Prevention: Approaches, Practices and Evaluations,* (Cincinnati, OH: Anderson Publishing, 1988).

13 *Ibid.* at 133 citing S. Chainey and J. H. Ratcliffe, *GIS and Crime Mapping*, (Chichester: John Wiley & Sons, 2005) at 17.

of a botnet may result in prosecution, but is primarily aimed at preventing further offending.[14] Prosecution of offenders in an online forum may have the incidental effect of disrupting further criminal activity.

Such disruption-directed policing is relatively new, at least in terms of being formally identified as such.[15] Described in 2004 as an "emergent, and as yet little remarked upon" phenomenon,[16] it is now identified as a key strategy for many agencies, both nationally and internationally. For example, the National Crime Agency in the United Kingdom states as one of its four strategic priorities the "relentless disruption of serious and organised crime which affects the U.K. and its interests."[17] The Australian Criminal Intelligence Commission states that one of its roles is to "provide critical intelligence contributions to partners that drives the disruption, disabling and dismantling of serious and organised criminal enterprises."[18]

Although the precise role of disruption is both fluid and contextual, it does not supplant prosecution as the goal of policing, but rather supplements and supports it.[19] However, in the context of serious and organised crime, it is clearly a response to circumstances where prosecution is impractical, if not impossible. For example, one of the Operational Priorities of the National Crime Agency is to "operate proactively at the high end of high risk, undertaking significant investigations resulting in offenders being brought to justice through prosecution or, *if that is not possible*, disrupted using other means."[20] It is in this context that its importance apropos cybercrime becomes apparent. Given the limits to the effectiveness of criminalisation to address transnational crimes in general, and cybercrimes in particular, the focus of policing moves increasingly towards prevention of crime.[21]

3. The role of intelligence

As previously noted, disruption as a policing strategy arose out of intelligence-led policing.[22] A distinction is commonly drawn between information and intelligence,[23] the latter requiring "the systematic and purposeful acquisition,

---

14 *Ibid.* at 11, see the discussion of the "Avalanche" botnet.
15 Innes and Sheptycki, *op. cit. supra*, note 1 at 2.
16 *Ibid.*
17 National Crime Agency, "Annual Plan 2018–19," ' (NCA Annual Plan, 2018) at 8 <www. nationalcrimeagency.gov.uk/who-we-are/publications/168-nca-annual-plan-2018-19/ file> accessed 24 January 2020.
18 Australian Criminal Intelligence Commission, "Strategic Plan 2018–23," (2018) <www. acic.gov.au/files/australian-criminal-intelligence-commission-strategic-plan-2018-23-17 957-kb> accessed 24 January 2020.
19 Innes and Sheptycki, *op. cit. supra*, note 1 at 3.
20 National Crime Agency, *op. cit. supra*, note 17 at 9 (emphasis added).
21 S. W. Brenner, "Toward a Criminal Law for Cyberspace: A New Model of Law Enforcement," (2004) 30 *Rutgers Computer & Technology Law Journal* 1.
22 See generally, Innes and Sheptycki, *op. cit. supra*, note 1 at 5–11. Also see Jerry Ratcliffe, *Strategic Thinking in Criminal Intelligence*, (Sydney: Federation Press, 2nd edn., 2009).
23 Innes and Sheptycki, *op. cit. supra*, note 1 at 6.

sorting, retrieval, analysis interpretation and protection of information."[24] While some police intelligence will be gathered through covert means, other intelligence may be based on information that is already in existence or, indeed, is publicly available.[25] Although the digital environment undoubtedly presents considerable challenges to law enforcement, it also presents many opportunities for intelligence gathering.

First, modern technology facilitates the collection of information that may then be analysed for the purpose of providing intelligence. Second, it facilitates the production of intelligence, with modern systems, particularly those incorporating machine learning, increasingly able to look for meaningful patterns and connections between vast amounts of data, which can then facilitate human analysis. Third, digital technology has accelerated the formal and informal sharing of intelligence between agencies, nationally and internationally.[26]

Another important feature of the modern intelligence environment is the blurring of law enforcement and national security. In recent years, the use of intelligence has moved beyond foreign and military intelligence to include crime and domestic law enforcement, particularly where criminal activity is seen as a threat to national security.[27] Security agencies and LEAs may therefore face similar challenges, as well as opportunities for collaboration, despite the ostensibly clear difference in their objectives.[28]

For example, LEAs may look to security agencies[29] or foreign governments[30] for technical assistance. Equally, intelligence gathered for the purposes of law enforcement may also be of interest to security agencies. Increasingly, the distinction between the domestic and the external becomes blurred, with potentially serious consequences. The ability of LEAs to access data outside the jurisdiction would once have been the preserve of intelligence agencies, and collaboration with the technology sector may give rise to geopolitical concerns, given potential state involvement.

4. The role of disruption in cybercrime

As previously noted, disruption as a policing approach has primarily been employed in the context of serious and organised crime. Its use in the context of cybercrime has been relatively little discussed. Although some cybercrimes may overlap with serious and organised crime, it is a distinct phenomenon presenting

---

24 R. Whitaker, *The End of Privacy: How Total Surveillance is Becoming a Reality*, (New York: New Press, 1999) at 5.
25 Ratcliffe, *op. cit. supra*, note 2 at 6.
26 *Ibid.* at 4. Also see S. Chermak *et al.*, "Law Enforcement's Information Sharing Infrastructure: A National Assessment," (2013) 16(2) *Police Quarterly* 211.
27 Gill, *op. cit. supra*, note 4 at 313.
28 Shiraz and Aldrich, *op. cit. supra*, note 8 at 270–271. Also see D. Clemente, "Cybersecurity," in Dover *et al.*, *op. cit. supra*, note 4 at 256.
29 *Dotcom v. Attorney-General* [2017] NZHC 1621.
30 *R. v. Porter* [2006] Cr. App. R. 25.

its own unique challenges. In broad terms, cybercrime is used to describe the use of technology in the commission of criminal offences, and is generally understood to describe three different forms of technology-related crimes.[31]

The first category is so-called cyberdependent crimes "that can only be committed using a computer, computer networks, or other form of ICT."[32] These include offences such as hacking, malware and distributed denial of service (DDoS) attacks.[33] This is the context in which disruption is most commonly used in relation to cybercrime, and particularly lends itself to the use of technical means to disrupt future offending.

The second category is cyberenabled crimes; that is, "traditional crimes that are increased in their scale or reach by the use of computers, computer networks or other ICT."[34] The range of offending is extremely broad, and commonly involves a combination of online and offline conduct. The focus here is on disruption of the particular offence type. For example, sexual offences will require different disruptive techniques to fraud offences, and techniques used in one context may need to be adapted to another.

The third category, "computer-supported crimes,"[35] encompasses any crime in which the use of technology is incidental but may afford evidence of the offence. Of particular relevance in this context is the use of technology to support criminal enterprises, and to support criminal networks. In addition to disrupting specific offences, disruptive techniques may be utilised against organisational and financial structures.

The need for alternatives to prosecution in the context of cybercrime has been known for some time.[36] The same motivations that drive disruptive practices in relation to organised crime apply equally to cybercrime, and which strategies are adopted will often depend on whether offenders can be identified or not. If there are known offenders, then enforcement may seem the logical approach.[37] However, even if suspected actors can be identified, they may be beyond the reach of enforcement. For example, they may be in a jurisdiction where they are safe from prosecution and/or where extradition is unlikely or impossible, or obtaining evidence via conventional means may be impractically slow. In some cases, they may be state actors or supported by state actors; hence, enforcement is unlikely to work as a practical measure.[38] In such circumstances, disruption may

---

31 P. N. Grabosky, *Cybercrime*, (Oxford: O.U.P., 2016) at 2.
32 M. McGuire and S. Dowling, *Cyber Crime: A Review of the Evidence*, (London: Home Office, 2013) Research Report 75 at 5.
33 J. Clough, *Principles of Cybercrime*, (Melbourne: Cambridge University Press, 2nd edn., 2015) at 11.
34 McGuire and Dowling, *op. cit. supra*, note 32.
35 *Ibid.* at 6.
36 G. Allan, "Responding to Cybercrime: A Delicate Blend of the Orthodox and the Alternative," (2005) 1 *New Zealand Law Review* 149.
37 Gill, *op. cit. supra*, note 4 at 316–317.
38 M. Kilger, "The Evolving Nature of Nation State Malicious Online Actor Relationships," in T. J. Holt (ed.), *Cybercrime Through an Interdisciplinary Lens*, (Oxford: Routledge, 2016).

be seen as a valid means of pursuing offenders that, in all likelihood, would never be prosecuted.

As previously noted, disruption describes a range of strategies. For example, the FBI defines disruption in the context of cyberoperations as:

> interrupting or inhibiting a threat actor from engaging in criminal or national security related activity. Disruptions are the result of direct actions and may include, but are not limited to arrest, seizure of assets, or impairing the operational capabilities of key threat actors.[39]

For the Australian Federal Police, it may take the form of dismantling and disrupting transnational serious and organised crime syndicates.[40]

It is suggested that disruptive practices in the context of cybercrime may usefully be discussed under three headings. The first is the use of criminal or other regulatory mechanisms to disrupt and inhibit further offending. The second is the use of technical means to disrupt the ability of offenders to continue their criminal activity. The third is the use of intelligence gathering to support disruptive practices. While not exhaustive, these categories illustrate the breadth of disruptive strategies that may be adopted, and the importance of legal frameworks to support them.

(a) Enforcement

One of the most common forms of disruption is actually a form of enforcement; that is, the offender is not prosecuted for the primary offence(s) of which he or she is suspected, but is prosecuted for a lesser offence that is more easily proved and may achieve a similar objective, at least in the short term. Such an approach disrupts the activities of the target person, making it difficult to continue their operations while under sanction. It may also make other potential offenders wary and more restricted in their activities. For example, the potential presence of undercover officers within online forums has the potential to disrupt criminal activity due to the fear of participants that their activities may be monitored.[41]

Such an approach may be opportunistic; that is, once LEAs become aware that the suspect is engaged in some form of criminality, any available offence may be utilised.[42] Of particular interest are those offences which are, at least in part,

---

39 Office of the Inspector-General, U.S. Department of Justice, "Audit of the Federal Bureau of Investigation Annual Financial Statements Fiscal Year 2018," (2018) 8 <https://oig.justice. gov/reports/2018/a1907.pdf> accessed 25 January 2020.

40 Australian Federal Police, "International Engagement: 2020 and Beyond," (2017) 10 <www. afp.gov.au/sites/default/files/PDF/AFPInternationalEngagement2020Strategy.pdf?v=1> accessed 25 January 2020.

41 T. J. Holt and A. M. Bossler, *Cybercrime in Progress: Theory and Prevention of Technology-Enabled Offenses*, (Oxford: Routledge, 2015) at 144–145.

42 The classic example being Al Capone, the notorious American gangster who was ultimately sentenced to imprisonment for tax evasion rather than for his more extensive criminal activities; *Capone v. United States* (1932) 56 F.2d 927.

enacted to assist disruption of more serious activities. These may take broadly two forms.

The first is when prosecution for the principal offence is likely to be difficult, if not impossible. Offences are drafted which therefore target conduct further upstream to try to prevent or disrupt the commission of the ultimate offence.[43] For example, so-called identity theft provisions are concerned with the misuse of identity information, such as biographical details, credit card numbers, usernames and passwords, and even biometric information.[44] While existing fraud offences may be employed to prosecute the fraudulent use of identity information, identity theft offences are typically based around a broadly defined concept of "identity information," and then criminalise conduct such as possession, trafficking and manufacturing of that information.[45]

Such offences may be described as disruptive as they aim to strike at the market for such information, theoretically reducing demand but also hampering efforts to use such information in further offending. It is a response that may lead to broad-based possession offences in a variety of contexts such as malicious code,[46] credit card skimmers,[47] child abuse material,[48] digital blueprints[49] and "things" connected with terrorist acts.[50]

The second example is when there is too great a risk of waiting until the offender has attempted to commit the completed offence. Offences are therefore drafted that allow intervention at an early stage. A good example is so-called grooming offences. The term grooming is commonly used to describe a "process by which a person prepares a child, significant adults and the environment for the abuse of [a] child."[51] Legislatures in some jurisdictions have responded by enacting a broad range of inchoate offences which are intended to allow for intervention at an early stage. For example, the relevant Australian federal offences not only criminalise conduct such as procuring a child to engage in sexual activity,[52] but also communications that are made with the intention of making it easier to procure the child to engage in sexual activity.[53] It is even an offence to engage

---

43 Ratcliffe, *op. cit. supra*, note 2 at 47.
44 Australasian Centre for Policing Research and the Australian Transaction Reports and Analysis Centre, Standardisation of Definitions of Identity Crime Terms: A Step Towards Consistency' (2006) *Report Series No.* 145.3, 9–10.
45 See, for example, *Criminal Code Act 1995* (Cth.) pt. 9.5. See generally J. Clough, "Towards a Common Identity? The Harmonisation of Identity Theft Laws," (2015) 22(4) *Journal of Financial Crime* 492.
46 Section 478.3 of the *Criminal Code Act 1995* (Cth.).
47 Section 372.3 of the *Criminal Code Act 1995* (Cth.).
48 Section 474 and 22A of the *Criminal Code Act 1995* (Cth.).
49 Section 51F(1) of the *Firearms Act 1996* (N.S.W.).
50 Section s 101.4 of the *Criminal Code Act 1995* (Cth.).
51 S. Craven *et al.*, "Sexual Grooming of Children: Review of Literature and Theoretical Considerations," (2006) 12(3) *Journal of Sexual Aggression* 287 at 297.
52 Section 474.26 of the *Criminal Code Act 1995* (Cth.).
53 Section 474.27 of the *Criminal Code Act 1995* (Cth.).

in conduct such as misrepresenting the person's age as part of a plan to engage in sexual activity with a child.[54]

Such actions are not limited to criminal offences, but may extend to legal mechanisms that are utilised as an alternative to, or in conjunction with, prosecutions. These may be civil or administrative, public or private. For example, in the United States, the primary computer crime legislation, the *Computer Fraud and Abuse Act*,[55] contains provisions that allow for civil actions.[56] While the resources required ordinarily place civil actions beyond the reach of most individuals, the size of many technical companies, together with their technical expertise, means that civil actions are a real possibility, either alone or in collaboration with government agencies. For example, in 2013, Microsoft's Digital Crimes Unit partnered with LEAs including EC3[57] and the FBI, as well as other industry partners, to disrupt the "Zero Access" botnet.[58] The action involved civil suits filed by Microsoft which gave judicial authorisation for blocking incoming and outgoing communications between computers in the United States and 18 IP addresses associated with the fraudulent schemes.[59]

In terms of public enforcement, the primary examples are provisions that are aimed at the profit motive. Digital technology is increasingly used by transnational organised criminal networks to support their operations,[60] and the Dark Web contains a variety of illicit materials, with one study observing "a dominance of commerce within Tor, largely around narcotics and illegal financial services."[61] Therefore, steps to attack the profit motive are significant, both in support of other prosecutions and as a form of disruption.

Many jurisdictions have legislation that is suitable for this purpose. These include anti-money laundering and counter–terrorism-financing legislation, confiscation of proceeds of crime and taxation legislation. For example, when Ross Ulbricht was sentenced to life in prison for his activities on the Dark Net site Silk Road, the charges against him included money laundering.[62] Prosecution may also be used against intermediaries, for example prosecuting payment processors

---

54 Section 474.25C of the *Criminal Code Act 1995* (Cth.).
55 18 USC § 1030.
56 18 USC § 1030(g).
57 European Cybercrime Centre.
58 R. Boscovich, "Microsoft, the FBI, Europol and Industry Partners Disrupt the Notorious Zero Access Botnet that Hijacks Search Results," (*Microsoft EU Policy Blog*, 5 December 2013) <https://news.microsoft.com/2013/12/05/microsoft-the-fbi-europol-and-industry-part ners-disrupt-the-notorious-zeroaccess-bot net/> accessed 27 January 2020.
59 *Ibid.*
60 Shiraz and Aldrich, *op. cit. supra*, note 8 at 267 citing M. Naím, *Illicit: How Smugglers, Traffickers and Copycats Are Hijacking the Global Economy*, (New York: Doubleday, 2005).
61 J. Dalins *et al.*, "Criminal Motivation on the Dark Web: A Categorisation Model for Law Enforcement," (2018) 24 *Digital Investigation* 62 at 71.
62 U.S. Attorney's Office, "Ross Ulbricht, aka Dread Pirate Roberts, Sentenced in Manhattan Federal Court to Life in Prison," (New York: *Federal Bureau of Investigation News*, 29 May 2015) <www.fbi.gov/contact-us/field-offices/newyork/news/press-releases/ross-ulbricht-aka-dread-pirate-roberts-sentenced-in-manhattan-federal-court-to-life-in-prison> accessed 27 January 2020.

under money laundering laws in order to disrupt payment systems used by criminal actors.[63] More recently, the Joint Chiefs of Global Tax Enforcement are engaged in cooperative efforts to address transnational crimes including cyber-crimes and cryptocurrencies.[64] At a broader level, given that nation states may themselves be responsible for cyberattacks, disruptive responses at the political level may include trade sanctions and related remedies.[65]

(b) Technical means

There are numerous examples of technology-based disruptive techniques, some of which will not require legislative oversight. For example, financial institutions putting measures in place to ensure two-factor authentication, warning of the presence of suspicious websites, and the like, may all disrupt offending and form part of a good business model to protect consumers. A particularly novel example was the use of chatbots to waste scammers' time by using AI to automatically respond to spam emails.[66]

Other forms of technical disruption may require legislative support. For example, the use of take-down regimes in relation to child exploitation material can be a very effective way of limiting the presence of such material within the jurisdiction. The Internet Watch Foundation in the United Kingdom estimates that in 2018, only 0.04% of known child sexual abuse URLs were hosted in the United Kingdom, down from 18% in 1996.[67] Australia recently adopted a civil enforcement regime to support take-down notices in relation to image-based abuse.[68]

Such systems are, however, limited by the territorial reach of the country concerned. Without international cooperation, sites will still be accessible from countries that do not have similar mechanisms in place. For example, the IWF estimates that in 2018, 79% of child sexual abuse URLs were hosted in Europe (including Russia and Turkey).[69] Although not perfect, international coordination limits the number of jurisdictions from which such material will be accessible, at least via conventional URLs.[70] More recently, large technology companies

63 Holt and Bossler, *op. cit. supra*, note 41 at 152.
64 United States Government IRS, "Joint Chiefs of Global Tax Enforcement: Tackling Tax Crime Together," (IRS, *IRS Joint Chiefs of Global Tax Enforcement,* 23 January 2020) <www.irs.gov/compliance/joint-chiefs-of-global-tax-enforcement> accessed 27 January 2020.
65 The George Washington University Centre for Cyber and Homeland Security, *Into the Gray Zone: Active Defense by the Private Sector against Cyber Threats,* (2016) Centre for Cyber and Homeland Security Project Reports, at 9.
66 J. Vincent, "Send Scam Emails to This Chatbot and It'll Waste Their Time for You," *The Verge,* (online, 10 November 2017).
67 The Internet Watch Foundation, Annual Report 2019 <www.iwf.org.uk/report/2018-annual-report> accessed 27 January 2020.
68 *Enhancing Online Safety (Non-consensual Sharing of Intimate Images) Act 2018* (Cth.).
69 Internet Watch Foundation, *op. cit. supra*, note 67 at 21.
70 See generally, Weixiao Wei, "Online Child Sexual Abuse Content: The Development of a Comprehensive, Transferable International Internet Notice and Takedown," (2011) *Internet Watch Foundation* <www.iwf.org.uk/sites/default/files/inline-files/IWF%20Research%20

have agreed to improve their processes in relation to online live streaming of terrorist acts, including greater sharing of information and the use of artificial intelligence and other digital tools.[71]

More challenging are those circumstances where LEAs engage in active measures, often in collaboration with the private sector, to disrupt unlawful conduct or to gain intelligence in order to disrupt/prosecute. For example, in 2016, the Avalanche botnet was dismantled using the largest example of a technique known as sinkholing.[72] The Avalanche network was used as a platform for malware and money mule recruiting, and during the operation, over 800,000 domains were either seized, sinkholed or blocked.[73] The operation involved collaboration between Europol, Eurojust, EC3, the U.S. Department of Justice, FBI and prosecutors and investigators from over 30 countries, as well as industry partners.[74] The primary goal of the exercise appears to have been disruptive, as although victims were identified in 180 countries, and 221 servers put offline, the operation resulted in only five arrests.[75]

Such activities should be distinguished from so-called "hacking back," which is typically used to describe illegal offensive cybermeasures;[76] for example, when private entities engage in active measures to deter unlawful conduct which is against their interests, including compromising peer-to-peer networks and even DDoS attacks.[77] Much of this conduct is of questionable legality, and would typically be an offence under the cybercrime laws of many jurisdictions.[78]

It should also be distinguished from conduct carried out by security agencies, when the more accurate term is "active cyber defence." For example, the

---

Report_%20Development%20of%20an%20international%20internet%20notice%20and%20 takedown%20syste_1.pdf> accessed 27 January 2020.

71 J. Duke, "Tech Giants Pledge Unprecedented Cction to Tackle Terrorist Content," (Sydney: *The Sydney Morning Herald*, 26 May 2019).

72 Sinkholing "is an action whereby traffic between infected computers and a criminal infra-structure is redirected to servers controlled by law enforcement authorities and/or an IT security company"; Europol, "Avalanche" Network Dismantled in International Cyber Operation," *Europol Press Releases*, (online, 1 December 2016) <www.europol.europa.eu/ newsroom/news/%E2%80%98avalanche%E2%80%99-network-dismantled-in-international-cyber-operation> accessed 27 January 2020 (' "Avalanche' Network dismantled").

73 *Ibid.*

74 *Ibid.*

75 *Ibid.* Similarly, it is unclear whether any prosecutions arose out of the Zero Access take-down, despite extensive cooperation between LEAs, see page 9.

76 The George Washington University Centre for Cyber and Homeland Security, *op. cit. supra*, note 65 at 8–9.

77 T. J. Holt, "Regulating Cybercrime through Law Enforcement and Industry Mechanisms," (2018) *The ANNALS of the American Academy of Political and Social Science* 140 at 146–147. Private entities may also play a disruptive role by releasing threat information to the public, making it more difficult for offenders to operate, and easier for users to avoid risk, *Ibid.* at 148.

78 C. Cook, "Cross-Border Data Access and Active Cyber Defence: Assessing Legislative Options for a New International Cybersecurity Rulebook," (2018) 29 *Stanford Law & Policy Review* 205.

Australian Signals Directorate (ASD) is a secret intelligence agency which operates to "inform, protect, and disrupt,"[79] and provides:

> high-impact, full-spectrum offensive cyber-operations to support a range of Australian Government priorities including supporting military operations, *law enforcement and criminal intelligence* activity against cyber criminals, and responding to serious cyber incidents against Australian networks.[80]

(c) Intelligence gathering

While the digital environment presents many challenges to LEAs, it also presents extraordinary opportunities for increased surveillance and intelligence gathering. Such powers are often justified as necessary to address threats to national security,[81] however, and the blurring of law enforcement and security matters means that they are often conferred on both.[82] To the extent that disruption is a form of intelligence-led policing, it is the beneficiary of this increased access to data and intelligence.

A good example is Australia's data retention scheme, which came into effect on 13 October 2015.[83] In broad terms, this scheme requires telecommunication service providers to retain data about their subscribers' online activity for a period of two years. The information to be kept includes subscriber identity information; billing information; the nature of the services(s); source, destination, date, time and duration of communications; type of communication or service; and location of equipment.[84] Although the legislation specifically precludes the disclosure of the contents of a communication,[85] the range of data that is accessible is potentially highly incriminating. Further, the distinction between content and data is notoriously blurred and constantly changing.[86]

Another example is so-called Network Investigative Techniques (NIT), the most well known being the FBI's operation against the child exploitation network known as PlayPen.[87] At one time estimated to have approximately 150,000 users,[88] PlayPen was a hidden service accessed using the Tor network, the effect

---

79 Australian Signals Directorate, "About ASD," (2020) <https://asd.gov.au/about/index.htm> accessed 27 January 2020.
80 *Ibid.*
81 Gill, *op. cit. supra*, note 4 at 319.
82 Shiraz and Aldrich, *op. cit. supra*, note 8 at 264.
83 *Telecommunications (Interception and Access) Amendment (Data Retention) Act 2015* (Cth.), inserting Ch 5, Pt 5–1A *Telecommunications (Interception and Access) Act 1979.*
84 Section 187AA of the *Telecommunications (Interception and Access) Act 1979.*
85 Section 172 of the *Telecommunications (Interception and Access) Act 1979.* It also precludes information relating to IP addresses and the like; Section 187A(4)(b).
86 N. Suzor *et al.*, "The Passage of Australia's Data Retention Regime: National Security, Human Rights, and Media Scrutiny," (2017) 6(1) *Internet Policy Review* 1 at 8–9.
87 For a detailed discussion, see *U.S. v. Levin* (2017) 874 F. 3d 316 at 319–321.
88 *U.S. v. Levin* (2017) 874 F. 3d 316 at 319.

of which was to conceal the IP addresses of those accessing the site.[89] Pursuant to warrants, the FBI seized control of the server hosting PlayPen, and operated an NIT on the site. This is software similar to a Trojan which infects computers accessing the site and causes those computers to send identifying information back to the host.[90] The information that could be accessed using the NIT included IP addresses, date and time of access, operating system and username.[91]

5. Legislative frameworks and oversight

The preceding discussion has provided some examples of how disruption may apply in the cyberenvironment. Disruption is not without its critics, and a number of concerns may be raised, including that disruption will skew policing away from enforcement, that it is difficult to measure its effectiveness,[92] that only lower-level offenders will be targeted[93] or that it may simply displace offending or have unintended consequences.[94]

A particular concern is that disruption may avoid the scrutiny associated with the criminal justice system.[95] The issuing of warrants, presentation of evidence at trial, scrutiny of evidence by defence counsel and judicial oversight are all potential checks on misconduct associated with disruptive techniques.[96] Because disruption does not necessarily result in prosecution, these oversight mechanisms may not be present to the same degree.[97] Scrutiny can be made more complex by the fact that agencies are often reluctant to reveal the technology underpinning their surveillance.[98] Requests for such information have led to cases being dropped rather than disclosing the investigative technique or exploit relied upon,[99] a phenomenon known as greymailing.[100]

---

89 *Ibid.*
90 M. Weidman, "Jurisdiction, the Internet, and the Good Faith Exception: Controversy over the Government's Use of Network Investigative Techniques," (2018) 122 *Dickinson Law Review* 967 at 973–974.
91 *U.S. v. Levin* (2017) 874 F. 3d 316 at 320.
92 C. Harfield, "SOCA: A Paradigm Shift in British Policing," (2006) 46(4) *British Journal of Criminology* 743 at 752.
93 Gill, *op. cit. supra*, note 4 at 317.
94 J. Ratcliffe and J. Sheptycki, "Setting the Strategic Agenda," in Ratcliffe, *op. cit. supra*, note 22 at 264; F. Jansen and J. van Lenthe, "Adaptation Strategies of Cybercriminals to Interventions from Public and Private Sectors," in Holt, *op. cit. supra*, note 38.
95 Ratcliffe, *op. cit. supra*, note 2 at 132; Gill, *op. cit. supra*, note 4 at 317; Ratcliffe and Sheptycki, *op. cit. supra*, note 94.
96 Gill, *op. cit. supra*, note 4.
97 Ratcliffe, *op. cit. supra*, note 2 at 133.
98 R. K. Garcha, "Nits a No-Go: Disclosing Exploits and Technological Vulnerabilities in Criminal Cases Notes," (2018) 93 *New York University Law Review* 822. Infamously, Apple refused to assist investigators to gain access to data on the iPhone of the San Bernardino gunman; see A. E. Waldman, "Designing Without Privacy," (2018) 55 *Hous. L. Rev.* 659 at 713.
99 L. H. Newman, "The Feds Would Rather Drop a Child Porn Case Than Give Up a Tor Exploit," *Wired*, (Online, 7 March 2017).
100 C. W. Chen, "The Graymail Problem Anew in a World Going Dark: Balancing the Interests of the Government and Defendants in Prosecutions Using Network Investigative

The focus of this chapter is on the importance of legal frameworks. From a legal perspective, the greatest challenge is reconciling the many competing interests of states, agencies and citizens.[101] It is vital that appropriate safeguards are put in place to ensure that other rights and interests are properly considered, and that oversight and accountability mechanisms are put in place. There is otherwise the very real danger that police operations will outpace the ability of legislatures to regulate them, leaving the situation whereby questionable conduct is carried out without clear lawful authority. The ramifications of such conduct go beyond the domestic to the potential for international controversy.[102]

The next section considers three contexts in which legislative action may be required in order to provide both the necessary legal powers and appropriate oversight. These are: the need for criminal offences that support disruptive techniques, investigative powers that may be utilised for disruptive purposes and provisions that support transnational cooperation.

6. Criminal offences

As previously noted, an important aspect of disruptive policing techniques is the enactment of disruptive offences. As validly enacted laws, such offences are at least subject to legislative oversight, providing the opportunity for competing considerations to be weighed. However, in order to be effective, these offences must necessarily be broad and often inchoate. In Australia, for example, the identity theft provisions have been criticised as being unnecessary and overbroad, and as reflecting gross over-criminalisation.[103] Particularly when these offences are addressing a global problem, it is important that legislatures are careful not to unduly broaden domestic laws in order to disrupt conduct occurring outside the jurisdiction, especially when other jurisdictions refuse to prosecute the principal offenders.

In addition, although often aimed at transnational crimes, the nature of these offences may be such that they do not support effective international cooperation. A country's criminal laws are a clear statement of its values, and these may differ considerably between jurisdictions. This is likely to be compounded in the case of lower-level disruptive offences, the justifications for which may not easily be agreed upon between countries.[104]

Techniques (NITs) Note," (2017) 19(1) *Columbia Science and Technology Law Review* 185.
101 N. A. Pollard and J. P. Sullivan, "Counterterrorism and Intelligence," Dover *et al.*, *op. cit. supra*, note 4 at 250.
102 Shiraz and Aldrich, *op. cit. supra*, note 8 at 272; Gill, *op. cit. supra*, note 4 at 319.
103 A. Steel, "True Identity of Australian Identity Theft Offences: A Measured Response or an Unjustified Status Offence," (2010) 33 *University of New South Wales Law Journal* 503; I. Leader-Elliott, "Framing Preparatory Inchoate Offences in the Criminal Code: The identity Crime Debacle," (2011) 35 *Criminal Law Journal* 80.
104 Allan, *op. cit. supra*, note 36 at 155; Also see M. D. Goodman and S. W. Brenner, "The Emerging Consensus on Criminal Conduct in Cyberspace," (2002) 10(2) *International Journal of Law and Information Technology* 139.

Even when cooperative agreements are in place, investigation may be hampered by a lack of specific offences and/or differences in terminology.[105] In particular, so-called dual criminality is a common requirement of mutual assistance and extradition. This requires that the offence must be an offence under the laws of both jurisdictions, usually subject to a minimum level of penalty. Therefore, if conduct is criminalised in one jurisdiction but not another, then dual criminality will not be satisfied.

For this reason, other jurisdictions may be encouraged to enact suitable offences, the rationale being that it is "more effective to fight crime at the source."[106] According to the international engagement strategy of the Australian Federal Police, "[p]ushing crime back to its point of origin for disruption has a positive effect on crime locally, nationally and internationally."[107] Such an approach does, however, require those countries to have offences suitable for early intervention or the capacity to prosecute the principal offence.

7. Investigation powers

As previously discussed, modern technology has given LEAs access to extraordinary powers of surveillance. This, in turn, has the potential to intrude on fundamental rights and has been accompanied by increasing calls for rights protection, in particular rights to privacy and protection against unreasonable search and seizure.[108] It is incumbent on individual states to justify these intrusions, consistent with their obligations under domestic and international law.

Given the transnational nature of cybercrimes, of particular relevance are the terms of the Council of Europe *Convention on Cybercrime*.[109] Although there is a range of regional and transnational agreements relating to cybercrime,[110] in the absence of truly international agreement,[111] it remains the most complete and influential.[112] At the time of writing, 63 states have ratified, representing one-third of member states of the United Nations, and a diversity of regions and legal systems.[113]

---

105 Clough, *op. cit. supra*, note 45 at 501.
106 Australian Federal Police, *op. cit. supra*, note 40 at 15.
107 *Ibid.*
108 Shiraz and Aldrich, *op. cit. supra*, note 8 at 268.
109 Council of Europe, *Convention on Cybercrime* (ETS No 185, 2001).
110 United Nations Office on Drugs and Crime, "Comprehensive Study on Cybercrime," (2013) 67 <www.unodc.org/documents/organized-crime/UNODC_CCPCJ_EG.4_2013/CYBER CRIME_STUDY_210213.pdf> accessed 27 January 2020.
111 Most recently, the United Nations has supported a Russian resolution "to establish an open-ended ad hoc intergovernmental committee of experts, representative of all regions, to elaborate a comprehensive international convention on countering the use of information and communications technologies for criminal purposes"; UN General Assembly, Seventy Fourth Session, A/74/401, 25 November 2019, F. Hassan, "Countering the Use of Information and Communications Technologies for Criminal Purposes," at 6.
112 United Nations Office on Drugs and Crime, *op. cit. supra*, note 110 at 75.
113 Council of Europe Treaty Office, "Chart of Signatures and Ratifications of Treaty 185," (*Council of Europe website*, 18 February 2020) <www.coe.int/en/web/conventions/full-list/-/conventions/treaty/185/signatures?p_auth=H6EpSzMQ> accessed 18 February 2020.

The *Cybercrime Convention* adopts a conventional prosecutorial model. For example, the Preamble states that it provides for the criminalisation of certain conduct and "the adoption of powers sufficient for effectively combating such criminal offences, by facilitating their *detection, investigation and prosecution* at both the domestic and international levels and by providing arrangements for fast and reliable international co-operation."[114] Similarly, Article 14(1) states that "[e]ach Party shall adopt such legislative and other measures as may be necessary to establish the powers and procedures provided for in this section for the purpose of *specific criminal investigations* or proceedings."[115] Nonetheless, as the examples previously discussed illustrate, intelligence gained for criminal investigations may in fact be used for a range of disruptive purposes.

Of particular relevance to this discussion is Section 2 of the Convention's Chapter I, which is concerned with procedural law. Under the *Cybercrime Convention*, these procedural powers must be subject to "conditions and safeguards provided for under its domestic law" that "shall, as appropriate in view of the nature of the procedure or power concerned, inter alia, include judicial or other independent supervision, grounds justifying application, and limitation of the scope and the duration of such power or procedure."[116] In addition,

> [t]o the extent that it is consistent with the public interest, in particular the sound administration of justice, each Party shall consider the impact of the powers and procedures in this section upon the rights, responsibilities and legitimate interests of third parties.[117]

The *Cybercrime Convention* therefore provides a framework around which such powers may be exercised.[118] Parties are required to draw upon their own standards under international and domestic law[119] to:

> ensure that the establishment, implementation and application of the powers and procedures provided for in this Section are subject to conditions and safeguards provided for under its domestic law, which shall provide for the adequate protection of human rights and liberties.[120]

These include rights arising under the *International Covenant on Civil and Political Rights*, as well as "other applicable international human rights instruments."[121] Parties must also incorporate the principle of proportionality.[122]

---

114 Preamble of the *Convention on Cybercrime* (ETS No 185, 2001) (emphasis added).
115 Art. 14(1) of the *Convention on Cybercrime* (ETS No 185, 2001) (emphasis added).
116 Art. 15(2) of the *Convention on Cybercrime* (ETS No 185, 2001) (emphasis added).
117 Art. 15(3) of the *Convention on Cybercrime* (ETS No 185, 2001).
118 J. Clough, "A World of Difference: The Budapest Convention on Cybercrime and the Challenges of Harmonisation," (2014) 40 *Monash University Law Review* 698.
119 Council of Europe, Explanatory Report to the Convention on Cybercrime (ETS No 185, 2001) [145] <https://rm.coe.int/16800cce5b> accessed 18 February 2020.
120 Art. 15(1) of the *Convention on Cybercrime* (ETS No 185, 2001).
121 *Ibid.*
122 *Ibid.*

It is left to individual parties to determine the extent to which rights will be protected, with no specific minimum standards of due process.[123] This is very much a pragmatic response, allowing countries to pursue common goals while respecting legitimate national differences.[124] It does, however, mean that rights protections may vary considerably, which becomes of particular significance when intelligence may be shared between countries with differing levels of protection for human rights.

The Australian data retention regime provides an interesting illustration, albeit one which falls outside the terms of the *Cybercrime Convention*.[125] In terms of oversight, information may be disclosed to enforcement agencies without warrant.[126] Authorisation may be granted by authorised officers of the enforcement agency, the officer having to be satisfied that the disclosure is reasonably necessary for the enforcement of the criminal law, location of missing persons, enforcement of a law imposing a pecuniary penalty or protection of the public revenue.[127]

Although justified as necessary to fight terrorism and serious crime, there is a real risk that the data may be accessed "by a wide range of bodies for a wide range of other purposes, without the judicial oversight that a warrant would require."[128] Prior to the 2015 amendments, the data could be accessed by a broad range of agencies including Australia Post, the RSPCA, and local councils.[129] This was reduced to a much more limited number of law enforcement and intelligence agencies,[130] but it has since been reported that many more agencies are seeking to access the data via other legislation.[131] Although subject to review by two Parliamentary committees prior to being enacted,[132] the concerns raised by the

---

123 M. F. Miquelon-Weismann, "The Convention on Cybercrime: A Harmonized Implementation of International Penal Law: What Prospects for Procedural Due Process?" (2005) 23 *Journal of Computer and Information Law* 329 at 341.

124 Clough, *op. cit. supra*, note 116 at 710.

125 The *Cybercrime Convention* only requires a system of data preservation, not data retention; Art. 16 of the *Convention on Cybercrime* (ETS No 185, 2001). See Chapter III of the *Telecommunications (Interception and Access) Act 1979.*

126 A warrant is only required where the disclosure relates to a journalist; Part 4.1, Div 4C of the *Telecommunications (Interception and Access) Act 1979.*

127 Sections 178–180 of the *Telecommunications (Interception and Access) Act 1979.*

128 Suzor *et al.*, *op. cit. supra*, note 86 at 5. For another example of a provision imposing safeguards in relation to retention and disclosure of material obtained under warrant, see Section 129 of the *Investigatory Powers Act 2016* (U.K.).

129 Attorney-General's Department, "Telecommunications (Interception and Access) Act 1979 Annual Report 2015–16," (2016) 41 <www.homeaffairs.gov.au/nat-security/files/telecommunications-interception-access-act-1979-annual-report-15-16.pdf> accessed 18 February 2020.

130 Section 110 of the *Telecommunications (Interception and Access) Act 1979.*

131 G. Churches and M. Zalnieriute, "Unlawful Metadata Access Is Easy When We're Flogging a Dead Law," (2019) *The Conversation* <http://theconversation.com/unlawful-metadata-access-is-easy-when-were-flogging-a-dead-law-127621> accessed 18 February 2020. The Minister may also declare an agency to be an enforcement authority; Section 176A(3) of the *Telecommunications (Interception and Access) Act 1979.*

132 Parliamentary Joint Committee on Human Rights, "Examination of legislation in accordance with the Human Rights (Parliamentary Scrutiny) Act 2011: Bills introduced 20–30

Human Rights Committee were largely rejected.[133] For example, the Committee's recommendation that access be subject to warrant was dismissed by the Attorney General as "impractical."[134] The operation of the scheme is currently undergoing further review.[135]

In contrast to many cognate jurisdictions, Australia has no constitutionally protected rights that would allow courts to strike down legislation. In the United States, revelations of bulk surveillance of telecommunications data has raised serious legal and constitutional issues.[136] Similar data retention regimes were struck down by the European Court of Justice,[137] which held that E.U. law precludes access of national authorities to retained data,

> where the objective pursued by that access . . . is not restricted solely to fighting serious crime, where access is not subject to prior review by a court or an independent administrative authority, and where there is no requirement that the data concerned should be retained within the European Union.[138]

It has been argued that the Australian scheme suffers many of the same deficiencies.[139]

The use of NITs by the FBI was also subject to considerable oversight, albeit largely supportive of the practice. First, the use of NITs was authorised under

---

October 2014, Legislative Instruments received 20 September–10 October 2014," (2014) <www.aph.gov.au/Parliamentary_Business/Committees/Joint/Human_Rights/Scru tiny_reports/2014/Fifteenth_Report_of_the_44th_Parliament> accessed 18 February 2020; Parliamentary Joint Committee on Intelligence and Security, "Advisory report on the Telecommunications (Interception and Access) Amendment (Data Retention) Bill 2014," (2015) <www.aph.gov.au/Parliamentary_Business/Committees/Joint/Intelligence_and_ Security/Data_Retention/Report> accessed 18 February 2020.

133 Suzor *et al., op. cit. supra*, note 86 at 6.
134 Parliamentary Joint Committee on Human Rights, *op. cit. supra*, note 130 at 41.
135 The Parliamentary Joint Committee on Intelligence and Security has commenced a review of the mandatory data retention regime prescribed by Part 5–1A of the *Telecommunications (Interception and Access) Act 1979*. See Parliament of Australia, "Review of the Mandatory Data Retention Regime," (2019) *Parliamentary Joint Committee on Intelligence and Security Review* <www.aph.gov.au/Parliamentary_Business/Committees/Joint/Intel ligence_and_Security/Dataretentionregime> accessed 18 February 2020.
136 L. K. Donohue, "Bulk Metadata Collection: Statutory and Constitutional Considerations," (2014) 37(3) *Harvard Journal of Law & Public Policy* 757; P. Margulies, "Surveillance by Algorithm: The Nsa, Computerized Intelligence Collection, and Human Rights," (2016) 68 *Fla. L. Rev.* 1045.
137 Cases C-293/12 and C-594/12 *Digital Rights Ireland Ltd v Minister for Communications, Marine and Natural Resources* [2014] 3 CMLR 44; *Tele2 Sverige AB v. Post-och telestyrelsen (C-203/15) Secretary of State for the Home Department v. Watson (C-698/15)* [2017] Q.B. 771. For a recent decision concerned with oversight of surveillance powers in the United Kingdom, see *R. (on the application of Privacy International) v. Investigatory Powers Tribunal* [2019] 2 W.L.R. 1219.
138 *Tele2 Sverige AB v. Post- och telestyrelsen (C-203/15) Secretary of State for the Home Department v. Watson (C-698/15)* [2017] Q.B. 771 at para. 134.
139 Suzor *et al., op. cit. supra*, note 86.

warrant. Second, there were numerous legal challenges to the use of the technique.[140] Finally, there was legislative oversight in the form of amendments to the rules of criminal procedure, such that a warrant may be issued for property outside the district, but within the jurisdiction of the United States.[141] However, such oversight was largely due to the fact that prosecutions were pursued. The seizure of the PlayPen server arose out of a tip from a foreign law enforcement agency. Authorities could have immediately shut down the server, but chose to assume control of it in order to continue their investigation.[142] Had they shut the site down, or not proceeded to prosecution, there would likely have been no public scrutiny of the sharing of intelligence. Equally, amendments to the rules of criminal procedure were concerned with extraterritorial application within the United States; the provision is silent in relation to the targeting of foreign computers.

8. International cooperation

Although cybercrime is a relatively new phenomenon, it draws on trends that have been developing in other forms of policing, particularly counter-terrorism and organised crime.[143] In particular, the trend towards global metropolitan policing involves cooperation between policing agencies at the national, transnational and international levels, but also includes cooperation with intelligence agencies, non-governmental organisations and the private sector.[144] These changes are an inevitable product of globalisation and the increasingly borderless nature of information sharing; this presents a clear challenge to Westphalian notions of borders and sovereignty.[145]

Emblematic of both the opportunities and pitfalls that this modern environment presents is the use of intelligence sharing; that is, where states share their intelligence with another state.[146] For example, the Australian Federal Police expressly state that "[w]e share information and criminal intelligence with our partners to improve crime detection and disruption efforts."[147] To say that effective enforcement, including disruptive practices, will depend on intelligence sharing is at once obvious and simplistic. On the one hand, the ability to share intelligence seems like a logical response to the challenges of transnational crime, and may seem appealing to both governments and the public.[148] On the other hand, there are conflicting needs of enforcement versus sovereignty and rights protections which are not easily overcome.[149]

---

140 See generally Garch, *op. cit. supra*, note 98 and Weidman, *op. cit. supra*, note 90. For some recent examples, see *United States v. Grisanti* (2019) 943 F.3d 1044; *Anzalone v. United States* (2019) 205 L.Ed.2d 176; and *United States v. Caswell* (2019) 788 Fed.Appx. 650.
141 Rule 41(5) of the *Federal Rules of Criminal Procedure*.
142 *U.S. v. Matish* (2016) 193 F. Supp. 3d 585.
143 Pollard and Sullivan, *op. cit. supra*, note 101 at 249.
144 *Ibid.*
145 Shiraz and Aldrich, *op. cit. supra*, note 8 at 264.
146 J. I. Walsh, "Intelligence Sharing," in Dover *et al.*, *op. cit. supra*, note 4 at 290.
147 Australian Federal Police, *op. cit. supra*, note 40 at 15.
148 Shiraz and Aldrich, *op. cit. supra*, note 8 at 269–270.
149 *Ibid.*

The challenges of sharing intelligence, even between local agencies, are well known, and often lead to the development of task forces or centres to coordinate such intelligence sharing and cooperation.[150] Even in a country with a relatively small population, such as Australia, there can be a complex web of agencies and entities, state and federal, government and private, all of which are potentially involved in the sharing of intelligence.[151]

The problem is, of course, magnified when applied to the transnational environment. In addition to differences in language and legal structures,[152] there is the sheer volume of data that may be shared uncritically.[153] For many developing (and even some developed) countries, there is also the question of capacity. New areas of activity are likely to emerge in developing countries that do not necessarily have the infrastructure nor technical skills to address them.[154]

To the extent that disruption relies upon effective intelligence sharing, it will benefit from the progress that has been made in intelligence sharing as an aspect of transnational law enforcement.[155] However, in addition to the operational challenges of intelligence sharing, there remain considerable obstacles at the state level, described as "the bargaining problem and the enforcement problem."[156]

The bargaining problem describes the challenges associated with determining with whom the state will share intelligence, what types of intelligence will be shared and on what terms.[157] Globalisation has presented both new targets and new partners.[158] It may be seen as necessary, in pursuing broader goals of crime prevention, to engage with countries that take different views on certain rights, such as privacy or freedom of expression, or where recognised human rights may not be observed or are in fact abused.[159] Further confusion may arise when "economic partners may simultaneously be geopolitical adversaries."[160]

The problems are even more acute where the intelligence is not necessarily shared for enforcement. Oversight of foreign intelligence sharing presents additional challenges,[161] and the role of private entities further complicates matters.[162]

---

150 Gill, *op. cit. supra*, note 4 at 318.
151 Just at the federal level, key agencies include the Australian Security Intelligence Organisation (ASIO), Australian Signals Directorate (ASD), Australian Criminal Intelligence Organisation (ACIC), Australian Federal Police, Australian Tax Office (ATO), Australian Transaction Reports and Analysis Centre (AUSTRAC), Australian Securities and Investments Commission (ASIC), Australian Competition and Consumer Commission (ACCC), the Australian Communications and Media Authority (ACMA), and the Australian Centre to Counter Child Exploitation (ACCCE).
152 Gill, *op. cit. supra*, note 4.
153 Shiraz and Aldrich, *op. cit. supra*, note 8 at 269–270.
154 Clough, *op. cit. supra*, note 116.
155 Gill, *op. cit. supra*, note 4 at 318.
156 Walsh, *op. cit. supra*, note 144 at 291.
157 *Ibid*.
158 Shiraz and Aldrich, *op. cit. supra*, note 8 at 266.
159 J. I. Walsh, *The International Politics of Intelligence Sharing*, (New York: Columbia University Press, 2009) at 140; Shiraz and Aldrich, *op. cit. supra*, note 8 at 269–270.
160 The George Washington University Centre for Cyber and Homeland Security, *op. cit. supra*, note 65 at 6.
161 C. Hillebrand, "Intelligence Oversight and Accountability," in Dover *et al.*, *op. cit. supra*, note 4 at 307–308.
162 *Ibid*. at 310–311.

For example, is it permissible for LEAs to approach private entities in another jurisdiction and seek access to data? Even where intelligence is shared, there is then the "enforcement problem"; that is, how to enforce any agreement on intelligence sharing if it is breached, whether deliberately or inadvertently.[163] Two observations may be made in relation to these challenges.

First, mutual trust is obviously crucial in facilitating intelligence sharing, and may be used effectively with examples such as the Five Eyes Network, or within regional organisations such as the European Union whereby there are more formal mechanisms available to monitor and "enforce" agreements that are in place. However, the nature of cyberinvestigations is such that they will necessarily involve states with whom the other state may have a limited or even difficult relationship. Such obstacles can, however, be overcome, when there is seen to be mutual interest. Investigations involving child exploitation, for example, often involve a broad range of countries that may not otherwise operate cooperatively.[164] This is not to underestimate the effort and diplomacy involved in ensuring such sharing is possible, but rather that mutual interest can go some way to encouraging mutual trust.

Second, the problems are magnified in the context of disruption because the basis for sharing is less clear than for enforcement where more transparent mechanisms and principles are often in place. Reciprocity, for example, will usually be expected but may be difficult to provide if there are concerns about the purpose to which such intelligence will be used. We see examples of this, in a more formal context, with mutual assistance and extradition which may be refused, inter alia, on the basis that the offence is a political one. As previously noted, lack of dual criminality is likely to be more common in relation to disruptive offences, potentially leading to a refusal to cooperate.

The frameworks that are put in place will vary according to the level of trust between parties. It has been suggested that the sharing of intelligence may be more anarchic between close and trusted allies, than where there is a greater risk of defection.[165] This may lead to more fluidity amongst trusted allies, which exacerbates the lack of oversight. When there is an imbalance, and perceived or actual risk of defection, then the imbalance may need to be addressed by mechanisms which seek to minimise the risk of defection.[166]

International cooperation may occur informally in accordance with relevant domestic laws and agreements.[167] It may also be facilitated by agencies such as Interpol and Europol, intelligence collaborations such as Five Eyes and 24/7 networks such as the G8 network of contact points. Chapter III of the *Cybercrime Convention*, which is concerned with international cooperation, requires parties

---

163 Walsh, *op. cit. supra*, note 144 at 291–292.
164 T. Krone, "International Police Operations against Online Child Pornography," (2005) 296 *Trends & Issues in Crime & Criminal Justice* 1.
165 Walsh, *op. cit. surpa*, note 144 at 133.
166 *Ibid.* at 134.
167 Clough, *op. cit. supra*, note 116.

to "co-operate with each other, in accordance with the provisions of this chapter, and through the application of relevant international instruments on international co-operation in criminal matters, arrangements agreed on the basis of uniform or reciprocal legislation, and domestic laws, to the widest extent possible."[168]

An example of a legislative framework governing intelligence sharing with foreign agencies is found in the Australian data retention scheme discussed previously. In addition to disclosure to domestic agencies, an Authorised Officer of the Australian Federal Police may authorise the disclosure of specified information or documents to foreign LEAs[169] for "(a) the enforcement of the criminal law of a foreign country; or (b) an investigation or prosecution of a crime within the jurisdiction of the ICC; or (c) an investigation or prosecution of a War Crimes Tribunal offence."[170] Although limited to authorisation by the Australian Federal Police, whether disclosure is made merely requires that the officer is satisfied that the disclosure "is appropriate in all the circumstances" and that it is "reasonably necessary" for the relevant purpose.[171] Foreign law enforcement agency is defined to mean a foreign police force "however described," and "any other authority or person responsible for the enforcement of the laws of the foreign country."[172]

Whether the disclosure is made to a local or foreign enforcement agency, the Authorised Officer is required to be "satisfied on reasonable grounds that any interference with the privacy of any person or persons that may result from the disclosure or use is justifiable and proportionate."[173] In making this determination, the officer must consider the gravity of the matter for which the information is sought, e.g., the seriousness of the offence, the likely relevance and usefulness of the information/documents, and the reason why the disclosure is sought.[174] Where disclosure is made to foreign law enforcement, disclosure must be made on condition that the information will be used only for the requested purpose, that it will be destroyed when no longer required for that purpose, and in the case of disclosure of prospective information, any other condition imposed by the Attorney General.[175]

---

168 Art. 23 of the *Convention on Cybercrime* (ETS No 185, 2001).

169 Chapter 4, Pt 4.1, Div 4A of the *Telecommunications (Interception and Access) Act 1979*.

170 Section 180A(3) of the *Telecommunications (Interception and Access) Act 1979* (existing information/documents). The *Telecommunications (Interception and Access) Act 1979* also allows for prospective disclosure of documents in relation to foreign law enforcement (s 180B), as well as secondary disclosure of information authorised for disclosure to an enforcement agency (s 180C). Information disclosed to a foreign agency may also be authorised for disclosure to the Australian Security Intelligence Organisation.

171 Section 180A(4) of the *Telecommunications (Interception and Access) Act 1979*.

172 Section 5 of the *Telecommunications (Interception and Access) Act 1979*. It also includes agencies responsible for investigations/prosecutions at the ICC or a War Crimes Tribunal.

173 Section 180F of the *Telecommunications (Interception and Access) Act 1979*.

174 Section 180F. Under the *Telecommunications Act 1997*, Technical Assistance and Technical Capability Notices may also extend to assisting the enforcement of the criminal laws of a foreign country in relation to serious offences; Sections 317L(2)(c) and 317T(3)(b).

175 Section 180E of the *Telecommunications (Interception and Access) Act 1979*. For another example of a prevision placing restrictions on disclosure to overseas authorities see Section 130 of the *Investigatory Powers Act 2016* (U.K.).

In addition to privacy rights, access to transnational information may infringe on the sovereignty rights of other nations, with modern communications all but obliterating traditional jurisdictional boundaries. Probably the most well-known example involved the question of whether a provider in the United States could be compelled by a *Stored Communication Act*[176] warrant to disclose data stored in another jurisdiction. Conflicting authority was set to be resolved by the Supreme Court,[177] but the decision was vacated due to the enactment of the *Clarifying Lawful Overseas Use of Data (CLOUD) Act*.[178] This Act is intended to address the challenges faced by LEAs in accessing overseas data under the SCA, and requires data holders to provide data on equipment that they operate, subject to lawful process, wherever it is stored.[179]

The Act also provides for a challenge mechanism where the provider reasonably believes that the customer or subscriber is not a U.S. citizen and does not reside in the United States, and "that the required disclosure would create a material risk that the provider would violate the laws of a qualifying foreign government."[180] A "qualifying foreign government" is, inter alia, a foreign government that has entered into an executive agreement with the United States.[181] The Act also preserves a common law comity claim for those countries that are not qualifying foreign governments, and allows a U.S. court to determine whether the competing foreign interests should override the warrant requirement.[182] For example, the European Union's *General Data Protection Directive* restricts the circumstances in which data may be transferred out of the European Union, and may come into conflict with U.S.-issued warrants.[183]

The *CLOUD Act* also provides an expedited mechanism for certain foreign governments to access data stored in the United States. Ordinarily, the SCA prohibits U.S. providers from disclosing data to foreign governments, even where the investigation relates to foreign nationals and laws.[184] The *CLOUD Act* seeks to avoid the notoriously cumbersome mutual legal assistance treaty (MLAT) process[185] by allowing certain governments to enter into bilateral agreements with the United States conferring reciprocal data access rights.[186] In order to qualify, the Attorney General must certify that the domestic laws of the foreign government "affords robust substantive and procedural protections for privacy and civil

---

176 121 USC §§ 2701–2712 (SCA).
177 *United States v. Microsoft Corp* (2018) 584 U.S. 1.
178 H.R. 1625, 115th Cong. div. V (2018).
179 18 USC § 2713.
180 18 USC § 2703(h)(2).
181 18 USC § 2703(h)(1).
182 J. Daskal, "Microsoft Ireland, the CLOUD Act, and International Lawmaking 2.0 Essay," (2018) 71 *Stanford Law Review Online* 9 at 11–12.
183 *Ibid*. at 12.
184 *Ibid*.
185 Clough, *op. cit. supra*, note 116 at 706.
186 18 USC § 2523.

liberties in light of the data collection and activities of the foreign government that will be subject to the agreement."[187] To date, only the United Kingdom has entered into such an agreement,[188] although negotiations are underway with Australia.[189] It has also been suggested that it may be possible for regional agreements to be made, for example, with the European Union.[190]

Some aspects of the U.S.-U.K. agreement are particularly notable for this discussion. Although the agreement is limited to serious crime, it extends to the "prevention, detection, investigation, *or* prosecution of Serious Crime."[191] In terms of further disclosure, the issuing party (that is, the country receiving the data), agrees not to transfer data received pursuant to the agreement, "to a third country or international organization" without first obtaining the consent of the party providing the data.[192]

Some commentators have argued that such transborder access of data may violate the sovereignty of other nations.[193] Others are more sanguine, arguing that such virtual intrusions do not violate sovereignty, and that actual experience of transnational investigations suggests "a norm of cooperation not confrontation."[194] While it is true that there are examples of extensive cooperation between nation states, particularly in the context of child exploitation investigations, the potential for transborder access to data cannot be dismissed as inevitably being acceptable to other countries.[195] It is not difficult to imagine other forms of investigation where countries may not be willing to respond uncritically to unauthorised intrusions into their computer networks, whether it be controversial prosecutions such as terrorism, countries where there is heightened tension, or offences for which countries may have different values.

---

187 18 USC § 2523(b)(1).
188 U.K. Government and U.S. Government, "Agreement between the Government of the United States of America and the Government of the United Kingdom of Great Britain and Northern Ireland on Access to Electronic Data for the Purpose of Countering Serious Crime," (3 October 2019) <www.gov.uk/government/publications/ukusa-agreement-on-access-to-electronic-data-for-the-purpose-of-countering-serious-crime-cs-usa-no62019> accessed 18 February 2020.
189 U. S. Department of Justice, "Joint Statement Announcing United States and Australian Negotiation of a CLOUD Act Agreement by U.S. Attorney General William Barr and Minister for Home Affairs Peter Dutton," (7 October 2019) <www.justice.gov/opa/pr/joint-statement-announcing-united-states-and-australian-negotiation-cloud-act-agreement-us> accessed 18 February 2020.
190 Daskal, *op. cit. supra*, note 179 at 15.
191 Art 2 (emphasis added).
192 Art 8(2).
193 A. Ghappour, "Searching Places Unknown: Law Enforcement Jurisdiction on the Dark Web," (2017) 69(4) *Stanford Law Review* 1075.
194 O. S. Kerr and S. D. Murphy, "Government Hacking to Light the Dark Web: What Risks to International Relations and International Law?" (2017) 70 *Stanford Law Review* 58 at 65.
195 See generally *United States v. Gorshkov* (WD Wash, No CR00–550C, 23 May 2001); *United States v. Ivanov* (2001) 175 F. Supp. 2d. 367.

In the Microsoft Ireland case,[196] for example, the proposed access under warrant was objected to by the Irish government as in breach of Irish law,[197] the Irish government even going so far as to take the unusual step of filing an amicus curiae brief.[198] There is also the potential for collateral damage, with allegations that Microsoft sinkholed the server of a legitimate security researcher, and also caused damage to benign domain names in its botnet operations.[199] Although these issues were known at the time the *Cybercrime Convention* was drafted, agreement could not be reached other than in limited circumstances.[200] It is only relatively recently that the Council of Europe has developed draft recommendations on an additional protocol dealing specifically with transborder access to data.[201]

9. Conclusion

The inherently transnational nature of cybercrimes presents considerable challenges to the traditional enforcement model of policing. It is not surprising that LEAs will increasingly look to disruptive measures in an effort to prevent or impede crimes that might otherwise never be prosecuted. These are not new problems, nor are they unique to disruptive activities. However, the nature of disruption brings into stark relief the need for oversight and the protection of fundamental rights.

Perhaps the most significant impact of this environment will be a move away from international agreements towards bilateral or multilateral instruments between like-minded countries and/or regions. This may further arrest progress towards a global cybercrime instrument, and encourage the regional. "Economic globalisation is well advanced, but the engines of global governance that were supposed to help to police it have not arisen naturally and, in so far as they exist, they have proved to be notably weak."[202]

On the one hand, it may be argued that to be effective, they require international frameworks to support cooperation.[203] These are complex issues which crucially regulate the extent to which LEAs may infringe the privacy rights of

---

196 *Microsoft Corporation v. U.S.* (2015) 829 F. 3d 197.
197 T. Brier, "Defining the Limits of Governmental Access to Personal Data Stored in the Cloud: An Analysis and Critique of Microsoft Ireland," (2017) 7 *Journal of Information Policy* 327 at 351–352 ("Defining the Limits of Governmental Access to Personal Data Stored in the Cloud").
198 *Ibid.* at 351.
199 R. Adhikari, "Microsoft's ZeroAccess Botnet Takedown No 'Mission Accomplished,'" (*Tech News World*, 9 December 2013) <www.technewsworld.com/story/79586.html> accessed 27 January 2020.
200 Clough, *op. cit. supra*, note 116 at 719.
201 Council of Europe, "(Draft) Elements of an Additional Protocol to the Budapest Convention on Cybercrime Regarding Transborder Access to Data," (T – CY 14, 2013).
202 Shiraz and Aldrich, *op. cit. supra*, note 8 at 267.
203 Europol, *op. cit. supra*, note 72 quoting J. King, the then European Commissioner for the Security Union.

individuals and potentially the sovereignty of nation states. Resolving these issues can only be done at the international level. It is not for local governments to provide assurances that conduct does not infringe the law of another country. This may, in turn necessitate greater international, or at least regional agreements to address these issues on a broader basis.[204]

On the other hand, the reality is that global cooperation is likely to be difficult to achieve. "Despite the public commitment of policy-makers to achieve wider intelligence cooperation, the vast majority of intelligence cooperation remains clumsily bilateral."[205] We see here a tension between the importance of harmonisation and international agreement in the prosecution of cybercrimes, and the need for more closely targeted bilateral or regional agreements to address specific concerns or that reflect different legal cultures. Although more limited in scope, it is possible that these bilateral agreements may nonetheless raise the human rights standards of countries wishing to enter into them.[206]

Although the focus of this chapter is on cybercrime, technology has merely accelerated features of transnational crime which were already evidence, and which are an inevitable product of globalisation.[207] LEAs and other agencies "grapple with a range of contradictory demands – more active operations, increased global cooperation, and a wider set of security threats – all set against the expectations of ethical behaviour and good governance from civil society."[208] These are extremely complex matters involving multiple agencies and the public and private sectors across multiple jurisdictions. The pace of technological change, and the constantly evolving human rights landscape, only add to the complexity.[209]

The purpose of this chapter has been to highlight the additional dangers and complexities that may arise when these powers are used for disruptive purposes, beyond the reach of conventional oversight mechanisms. Legal frameworks are vital in providing the constraints within which agencies implement disruptive practices and develop supervision and monitoring structures.[210] Disruption will only become more prevalent in policing the cyberenvironment, and policy makers must ensure that any offences created or powers conferred are both properly targeted and appropriately monitored.

204 Daskal, *op. cit. supra*, note 179 at 13.
205 Shiraz and Aldrich, *op. cit. supra*, note 8 at 269.
206 Daskal, *op. cit. supra*, note 179 at 15.
207 Shiraz and Aldrich, *op. cit. supra*, note 8 at 264.
208 *Ibid.* at 271.
209 Pollard and Sullivan, *op. cit. supra*, note 101 at 250.
210 Ratcliffe, *op. cit. supra*, note 2 at 133.

4 Preventive cybercrime and cybercrime by omission in China

He Ronggong and Jing Lijia

1. Introduction

In the face of rapidly growing cybercrime risks, the Chinese government recently enacted some omissions liability offences for Internet service providers (hereinafter ISPs). Additionally, it introduced some new pre-inchoate offences for individual offenders. The shift in policy is aimed at regulating online harms and ensuring that cybermeans such as fake webpages are not used to facilitate criminal offending. We shall attempt to demonstrate that criminalisation in this area is influenced by considerations of putative national security concerns rather than by a purely rational penal policy. The global trend has been towards excessive criminalisation when it comes to terrorism, but then the strict approach adopted in terrorism offences start to be implemented more broadly to apply in cases where there is not potential threat to human lives.

We will argue that China needs to carefully evaluate the case for adopting some of the panicked approaches that have been adopted in places like Germany and Australia. As we will see later, Australia has justified a data retention law that allows it to look back at its entire population's digital messages for a two-year period on the grounds that it will help prevent terrorist attacks, even though terrorism is an almost non-existent problem in that country.

The pre-inchoate offences we focus on are those that have been enacted to tackle the use of cybermeans for perpetrating crime. We shall examine the cyberspace principles enshrined in the *Cyber Security Law* in China to try to ascertain whether they are apt for solving the particular cybercrime problems that they are designed to stem. The new forms of cybercrimes in China are omissions offences for ISPs based on the fact that ISPs might not invest properly in security and retain data that may be needed for solving crimes. Coupled with that, they might not invest in the latest artificial intelligence filters to remove illegal content from the Internet such as child sex abuse images, literature promoting terrorism, and so forth. The Internet provider will be given a warning to remove the harmful expression from its platform and if it fails to do so its senior managers and compliance department employees may face a three-year prison sentence pursuant to Article 286(1) of the *Criminal Code of China*. Liability is not strict, nor is it based on objective negligence. Rather, the ISP's senior managers and compliance department employees will be given a warning, and if they fail to comply with the warning, their deliberate failure to do will result in criminal liability.

The other theme explored in this chapter is the legitimacy of criminalising pre-inchoate wrongdoing. There is nothing new about criminalising pre-inchoate conduct. Chinese law has long had pre-inchoate and possession offences. Article 128 of the *Criminal Code of China* provides: "Whoever, in violation of the regulations governing control of guns, illegally possesses or conceals any guns or ammunition shall be sentenced to fixed-term imprisonment of not more than three year[s]." Meanwhile, Article 130 provides: "Whoever illegally enters a public place or gets on a public transportation vehicle with any gun, ammunition, controlled cutting tool or explosive, inflammable, radioactive, poisonous or corrosive materials and thereby endangers public security. . . ."

Article 128 criminalises harmless conduct on preventive grounds. A gun and/or ammunition locked up and securely stored by a sane and rational person poses not risk of harm; it is only a remote harm in that someone somewhere out of the general population will misuse a gun, if they are readily available to the general population.[1] From 1999–2013, the very liberal gun ownership laws in the United States resulted in close to 500,000 Americans being killed by guns.[2] Criminalisation of gun ownership need not be based on demonstrating a particular owner harmed another by misusing his or her gun or that a particular owner poses such a risk of harm, but on the statistic that widespread gun ownership endangers all those residents in the United States.[3]

Statistically, widespread gun ownership increases the chance one will be misused by someone somewhere, resulting in very serious consequences. Similarly, if people were allowed onto the Metro with explosives, this would make travel on the Metro considerably more dangerous, even if the traveller had no intention of using the explosives, but was merely transporting them to sell them to a terrorist. The *telos* of explosives or carrying two or more guns on the Metro is such that there is no social utility in allowing private citizens to possess them and deal with them in that way. These sorts of offences are pre-inchoate in that they precede an attempt to shoot another or to causes and explosion to harm others.

It is the risk of danger that makes such conduct worthy of punishment and deterrence, but it is hard to know when to draw the line in the endangerment cases. Mere preparation seems to be one step back from attempts, but endangerment not involving preparation such as when a person sells guns without a care about how they are used, seems to be one step back from preparation. What also

---

1 M. D. Dubber, "Policing Possession: The War on Crime and the End of Criminal Law," (2001) 91 *J. Crim. L. & Criminology* 829 at 897; C. Slobogin, "A Jurisprudence of Dangerousness," (2003) 98 *Nw. U. L. Rev.* 1; G. Yaffe, "In Defence of Criminal Possession," (2016) 10 *Crim. L. & Phil.* 441.
2 S. Resnick *et al.*, "Firearm Deaths in America: Can We Learn From 462,000 Lives Lost?" (2017) 266(3) *Ann Surg.* 432.
3 D. J. Baker, "Collective Criminalization and the Constitutional Right to Endanger Others," (2009) 28(2) *Crim. Just. Ethics* 168.

needs to be put on the scales when determining the case for criminalising such conduct is the gravity of any harm that might be caused. If the endangering conduct is that the accused possessed a large bomb, that would justify criminalisation even though he does not possess the bomb to use himself and even though he has not attempted to use it.

However, if the endangering conduct is posting online a legitimate chemistry textbook from which the accused might learn how to make a bomb, we really need to question the need for extending the law back to something as innocuous as a textbook, because it is not an inherently dangerous item. Nor does it contain messages of incitement; it simply gives basic technical information that might be used to make a bomb, but is more likely to be used by thousands and thousands of students to pass their chemistry examinations. We will consider these nuances when considering the new offence in Section 287(1) of the *Criminal Code of China*. We will argue that when the item is not inherently dangerous and when the information or online post does not incite others to perpetrate a crime or specifically provide instructions on how to perpetrate a crime, the criminal law ought not be invoked.

2. Pre-inchoate criminalisation and early harm prevention

(a) Background of the latest amendments to PRC criminal law

According to the 43rd Statistical Report on Internet Development published by China Internet Network Information Centre (CNNIC) in 2019, the People's Republic of China (PRC) has 829 million netizens, with an Internet penetration rate of 59.6% at the end of December 2018.[4] Everything from travel bookings to banking is now done on mobile apps. Internet usage is highly diversified and affects nearly every person's life either directly or indirectly. That a person has no mobile phone, computer or Internet does not mean that the shops that serve her or the hospital that treats her do not use such technology.

The increasing number of online users in China means that cyberspace and the technology for participating in that space is shaping and creating new social norms. The social norms will vary depending on the social context, but people feel able to say things on Weibo or Twitter that they might not say to another to their face. New norms have arisen in relation to privacy and expression, since every social media account holder and smart-phone owner can publish information including private information. New norms have also arisen with respect to the best way to perpetrate property crimes such as fraud.

Technology will be used in different ways, depending on the social context and the profile of the user: a student environment might have a higher concentration

---

4 See the 43rd Statistical Report on Internet Development published by CNNIC, <www.cnnic.net.cn/hlwfzyj/hlwxzbg/hlwtjbg/201902/t20190228_70645.htm> accessed 28 February 2019.

of its population using social media and gaming apps, while a business environment might have a higher concentration of its users using email, travel apps, accounting apps, news apps, and so on. People socialise as much – if not more – online than they do in person, and so forth.[5]

Not only has technology led to social changes, but so too has data harvesting by large corporations. Large tech corporations have been able to take advantage of their technology provisions to consumers such as social media platforms (e.g., WeChat and Facebook), online shopping platforms such as Amazon and Alibaba, and search engines such as Google and Baidu, to amass vast quantities of personal data which can then be used to manipulate consumers into buying certain products and services or into reading certain suggested news articles, and so forth.[6] Of course, even with this level of manipulation occurring, there is a wealth of information online that is more diverse than in the days when a couple of media outlets controlled the entire public narrative on all subjects.

Smart-speakers[7] and smart-doorbells, along with programmes such as Geofeedia, have been used to put unsuspecting consumers under constant surveillance to gain even more information about them.[8] Hence, sophisticated analytics powered by artificial intelligence is used to survey customer data and profile customers to influence their future preferences.[9] The ability of these corporations to influence social preferences and beliefs is a form of "social engineering."[10] Big data can be used to also give an individual a credit score that might not necessarily be accurate.[11] Hence, it is not only individuals misusing the Internet and related technology, but also large corporations.

5 T. C. Antonucci *et al.*, "Social Relations and Technology: Continuity, Context, and Change," (2017) 1(3) *Innov. Aging* 1.

6 J. Shkabatur, "The Global Commons of Data," (2019) 22 *Stan. Tech. L. Rev.* 354.

7 R. Davidian, "Alexa and Third Parties' Reasonable Expectation of Privacy," (2018) 54 *Am. Crim. L. Rev.* 58.

8 M. Hu, "Cybersurveillance Intrusions and an Evolving Katz Privacy Test," (2018) 55 *Am. Crim. L. Rev.* 127 at 134.

9 S. Valentine, "Impoverished Algorithms: Misguided Governments, Flawed Technologies, and Social Control," (2019) 46 *Fordham Urb. L.J.* 364.

10 O. Tene and J. Polonetsky, "Taming the Golem: Challenges of Ethical Algorithmic Decision-Making," (2017) 19 *N.C. J. L. & Tech.* 125 at 126 commenting on Amazon's approaches to social engineering. Cf. "Social engineering in the context of cybercrime is really about the use of psychological manipulation to trick a person into doing something that isn't going to be in their best interests." M. Bassingthwaighte, "Cybercrime and Social Engineering," (2018) 61 *Advocate* 42.

11 Allen writes:

> Today, the consequences of the era of redlining have stained the "big data" that determines conditions for housing financing. For example, scholars have recently made persuasive arguments that there have been racist practices in the credit reporting industry, which produces metrics that evaluate a person's ever-important credit score.

J. A. Allen, "The Colour of Algorithms: An Analysis and Proposed Research Agenda for Deterring Algorithmic Redlining," (2019) 46 *Fordham Urb. L.J.* 219 at 236.

(b) The harm justification for criminalising pre-inchoate cyberharm

The main principle put forward to prevent harmless conduct being criminalised is the harm principle. Mill's harm principle proposes that,

> the only purpose for which power can be rightfully exercised over any member of a civilized community, against his will, is to prevent harm to others. To make any one answerable for doing evil to others is the rule; to make him answerable for not preventing evil is, comparatively speaking, the exception.[12]

The harm principle has not been enshrined into any constitution either in the East or West, apart from in France.[13] To respect the right not to be unfairly punished and criminalised is something lawmakers aspire to, but normally fail to achieve. Enshrined in the *Constitution of the People's Republic of China* (hereinafter referred to as the *Constitution*) are a number of important protections that largely mirror those found in Europe and the United States.[14] China takes the idea that the criminal law should be invoked as a last resort seriously,[15] but like Western states, has let criminalisation expand unnecessarily. While criminalisation in China is minimal compared to that in the United States,[16] it needs to take care not to end up with the same sort of over-criminalisation crisis as the United States.

Endangerment is a valid justification for criminalisation. There is no reason to wait for harm-doing to be consummated before punishing it,[17] but pre-inchoate

---

12 J. S. Mill, *On Liberty and Other Essays*, (Oxford: O.U.P., 1991) at 14.
13 D. J. Baker, *Glanville Williams Textbook of Criminal Law*, (London: Sweet & Maxwell, 2015) at 82.
14 Baker notes that constitutional rights can put a check on over-criminalisation, but largely have been interpreted to mean little in the United States, thereby causing an over-criminalisation crisis. *Ibid*.
15 N. Jareborg, "Criminalization As Last Resort (Ultima Ratio)," (2005) 2 *Ohio St. J. Crim. L.* 521.
16 Mushlin writes:

> According to a comprehensive census of the world's prison population conducted by Kings College International Centre for Prison Studies, the United States had the highest prison population in the world and also had the highest rate of imprisonment – 698 per 100,000 – of any country in the world. In terms of numbers, even though the United States has only 5% of the world's population, it houses 25% of the world's prisoners. According to the International Centre for prison studies: There are more than 2.2 million prisoners in the United States of America, more than 1.65 million in China (plus an unknown number in pre-trial detention or "administrative detention"), 640,000 in the Russian Federation, 607,000 in Brazil, 418,000 in India, 311,000 in Thailand, 255,000 in Mexico and 225,000 in Iran.

> M. B. Mushlin, *Rights of Prisoners*, (Westlaw online, 5th edn., updated 2019) at § 1:1.

17 A. Ashworth, "Taking the Consequences," in S. Shute *et al* (ed.), *Action and Value in Criminal Law*, (Oxford: Clarendon Press, 1993).

conduct needs to be punished far less severely than consummated harm. For example, a terrorist attack might involve a person: (1) buying a chemistry book; (2) reading the chemistry book; (3) understanding the content of the chemistry book well enough to construct a bomb; (4) buying the materials for making the bomb; (5) making the bomb; (6) attaching a detonator to the bomb; (7) attaching a remote sensor to the bomb to be able to set it off from a smart-phone while a kilometre away from the bomb; (8) taking it to the planned bomb site such as a busy carriage on the Metro; (9) leaving the bomb in an old suitcase on the Metro; (10) getting off the Metro and travelling a kilometre away from it; and (11) pressing the trigger code through a smart-phone to detonate the bomb. No one is actually harmed until step 11 is successfully completed.

Suppose the bomber presses the code on his smart-phone but it does not set the bomb off, because the he did not know what he was doing and all he has constructed is a harmless big blob of chemicals that cannot explode and thus is harmless. Here we have a complete attempt. The bomb-maker did all he could to succeed, and genuinely believed that he had triggered a bomb that would have killed everyone within the Metro carriage had the facts been as he believed. The evil state of mind of the bomb-maker is no less simply because he failed in his attempt at making and exploding the bomb. He pushed the button and thought it would explode and kill many, and that is what he was intending to do. It is only due to chance that he failed to construct a workable bomb and thus did not kill anyone.

The point here is that the harm is zero. No one was hurt. However, the terrorist tried to kill many people on the Metro and had genuinely tried to build a bomb and is clearly a dangerous person. The attempt deserved punishment, and that is beyond debate.[18] But how far back should the law go as far as covering his preparatory acts? Should it go right back to the purchase of the chemistry book? If it is to go back that far, how ought that be punished given its remoteness from

---

18 See:

> But the fact that endangering a participant is not an aggravating circumstance for arson does not erase the difference in culpability between endangerment and death. It is true that in a system of morality in which only intentions and behaviours, but not consequences, count, there is no moral distinction between dangerous conduct that causes harm and otherwise identical dangerous conduct that does not. The only difference is luck, not usually considered a moral attribute. But 'moral luck,' as philosophers refer to distinctions in culpability that are based on consequences rather than intentions, is, rightly or wrongly, a pervasive characteristic of moral thought in our society, at least the moral thought that informs the criminal law. Two people drive at the same unlawful speed under identical road conditions. One hits a child; one hits no one. The first is guilty of involuntary manslaughter; the second of a violation of the highway code. The only difference between their conduct is the consequence. The difference, though fortuitous, counts for the severity of the punishment deemed appropriate for the defendants' behaviour.

United States v. Martinez (1994) 16 F.3d 202 at 205–206. See also B. Williams, *Moral Luck*, (Cambridge: Cambridge University Press, 1981).

the end harm and given that the terrorist might change his mind along the way and withdraw from his evil plan?

The way to regulate pre-inchoate criminalisation is to impose a strict proportionality test, as is currently the case under Article 13 of the *Criminal Code of China*, which provides "if the circumstances are obviously minor and the harm done is not serious, the act shall not be considered a crime." Article 22 of the *Criminal Code of China* criminalises preparation and Article 25 criminalises joint crimes, so if A, B and C agree to perpetrate a burglary, and prepare for such a burglary, they all could be liable. Suppose B and C purchase the tools to break into a jewellery shop late at night, and C drives them there an acts as a lookout. When they arrive, they change their minds and decide it is too risky and drive home. On their way home, they are pulled over by the police for a routine breath test to make sure C has not been drinking alcohol while driving. While the police are doing this, they notice the car has burglary tools in the back seat. The police also find messages on their phone in a group-chat among A, B, and C outlining what their plans were.

Suppose C decides not to drive A and B, and tells them before they buy any tools that she no longer wants any part of the planned burglary and that they should remain honest citizens and avoid perpetrating the planned burglary. Here, Article 13 could be applied to C since she has only agreed in principle to the crime and no overt act of preparation was commenced before she unequivocally withdrew. Similarly, Article 13 might apply if all there were overhead sitting in Costa discussing their plan, but with none of them doing any overt act of preparation towards the plan. A bare agreement to perpetrate a crime is not sufficient to incur criminal liability in China. However, the new offence we are about to examine would make them all liable, should they set up a WeChat group for the purpose of communicating about the potential burglary, as opposed to merely meeting in the Costa café to discuss it.

Let us look at the new law as laid down in Article 287(1) of the *Criminal Code of China*. Article 287(1) makes it an offence to make use of information networks to conduct any of the following actions:

(1) Establishing websites or chat groups that are used to commit fraud, spread criminal methods, create or sell prohibited or controlled items, or promote other illegal or criminal activities.
(2) Publishing information on the production or sale of drugs, guns, pornography, and other prohibited or controlled items, or other illegal or criminal information.
(3) Publishing information in order to conduct illegal or criminal activities such as fraud.
    A unit that commits the crime in the preceding paragraph should be fined. The persons who are directly in charge and others who are directly responsible for the offence should be punished, if the circumstances are serious, for a term of imprisonment not exceeding 3 years.

A person who commits any two of the acts listed in the preceding paragraph, which also constitutes another crime, should be convicted and punished in accordance with the heavier punishment provisions.

Article 287(2):

A person commits an offence if he provides Internet access, server hosting, network storage, communication transmission and other technical support, or assists in advertisement, promotion, payment and settlement transactions, knowing that others use such information networks to commit crimes.

A unit that commits the crime in the preceding paragraph should be fined. The person who are directly in charge and others who are directly responsible for the offence should be punished, if the circumstances, for a term of imprisonment up to 3 years.

Like in the West, much of this expansion of the criminal law is justified not by the need for the law to operate long before any harm is done.[19] The gravity of the harm that would result, were a terrorist to succeed, might justify early intervention, but it is not clear that this law is simply being applied to serious harms.[20] Professor Glanville Williams said more than 40 years ago, that "double inchoate" liability (i.e., an attempt to conspire or an attempt to attempt) means "the

---

19 Lacey writes:

> The extraordinary events of September 2001 are, of course, an important part of the genesis of this new legislative concern with the criminalization of terrorism. The anti-terror reaction has created a wave of criminalization – particularly of what we might call preliminary or pre-inchoate activities – that significantly expands the boundaries of criminal law.

N. Lacey, "Populism and the Rule of Law," (2019) 15 *Ann. Rev. L. & Soc. Sci.* 79 at 91; D. J. Baker, "Treason Versus Outraging Public Decency: Over-Criminalisation and Terrorism Panics," (2019) 84(1) *J.C.L.* 19 at 31, Baker writes (emphasis added):

> There are many terrorism offences of preparation that reach such remote wrongs one wonders if some of the *life sentences are appropriate*. The operation of the law is pushed back in the realm of what (from the point of view of the ultimate criminal intent and ultimate harmful action) is not much more than an overt manifestation of a "thought crime." Criminalising attempts with proportionate punishment for the harm attempted is normatively justifiable, but one has to question life sentences with minimum terms of 20–40 years for *preparation* that falls well short of an actual attempt.

20 Hallevy writes:

> It might be argued that the extremely high severity of terrorist crimes justifies such a concept of inchoate offenses, but as a new general concept it creates an unjustified slippery slope. . . . Originally, in the Middle Ages, inchoate offenses were applied only to severe crimes.

G. Hallevy, "Incapacitating Terrorism Through Legal Fight-the Need to Redefine Inchoate Offenses Under the Liberal Concept of Criminal Law," (2012) 3 *Ala. C.R. & C.L.L. Rev.* 87 at 116–117.

operation of the law is pushed still further back in the realm of what (from the point of view of the ultimate criminal intent) is mere preparation."[21] The new offence of setting up a chat group can be applied to any crime. It could be applied to a couple of teenagers who set up a chat group to plan to steal a pair of shoes for the school dance. It is not clear the proportionality requirement found in Article 13 would apply given that the very purpose of this offence is to criminalise the means created by social media groups for communicating about crime.

The problem with the new pre-inchoate offences outlined in Article 287(1) is that they are not subject to a proportionality constraint and are not limited to serious preparatory or endangering acts such as those involved when a person prepares for terrorism or where a person prepares for grand fraud by setting up a major Internet scheme that is likely to deceive thousands of victims. Terrorism has to be an exception due the threat to human life involved, but ought we be extending the criminal law to cover a WeChat group set up by teenagers to steal shoes and so forth? How do we draw the line between legitimate pre-inchoate criminalisation that rightly operates at an early stage to prevent very serious harm to others, and pre-inchoate criminalisation that targets the network means that might be set up to facilitate minor property offences?

There are many difficulties with the collection of evidence, the identification of facts and the application of law. Preparatory acts of cybercrime may not only threaten significant legal interests, but are harder to detect since the harm-doing might not even be attempted. The necessity of early intervention of criminal law is normally justified as a harm prevention measure. If it is highly probable that the harm will occur (as is the case with millions of incidents of cyberfraud), it does not matter that the harm is not great in each individual case. It is the harm caused in aggregate, plus the fact that theft is normally a crime even when the value is not great, that provides the case for criminalisation. While terrorism is a very rare crime and the general probability of it being perpetrated is low compared to property crimes and other crimes of violence,[22] if a person is preparing for terrorism, its probability increases by the fact a particular person is preparing for it, and since its potential harm is so great, there is compelling case for early intervention.

Although China's criminal law permits the punishment of preparatory offences, attributing responsibility for preparatory offences is difficult in theory and practice. In order to fully protect the legal interests, maintain the network order and prevent future harms, legislators believe that it is necessary to make special provisions in the form of substantive preparatory offences for certain online harms. The idea is that these offences would be narrowly tailored to tackle the specific problem.

Criminal law mainly aims at to attribute liability for past wrongdoing so that a person can be appropriately punished.[23] There has been a move toward preventive

21 G. Williams, *Textbook of Criminal Law*, (London: Stevens & Sons, 1978) at 389.
22 C. J. Finlay, "Just War, Cyber War, and the Concept of Violence," (2018) 31 *Philosophy & Technology* 357; M. Montgomery, "Proliferation of Cyberwarfare Under International Law: Virtual Attacks with Concrete Consequences," (2019) 28 S. *Cal. Interdisc. L.J.* 499.
23 A. von Hirsch, *Past Or Future Crimes: Deservedness and Dangerousness in the Sentencing of Criminals*, (Manchester: Manchester University Press, 1986).

criminalisation to deter harm before it is attempted or done.[24] In the last few years, the position of Chinese lawmakers has been changing, and there has also been greater use of omissions liability in the area of cybercrime prevention. It is hoped that moving forward proportionality and fair labelling constraints will be put in place to ensure that Article 287(1) is not applied so widely as to result in unfair crime labelling and disproportionate punishment.

The *Criminal Code of China* Article 13 seems too vague to mirror Article 49(3) of the *Charter of Fundamental Rights of the European Union*, which provides: "The severity of penalties must not be disproportionate to the criminal offence." A more fine-tuned provision can be found in Section 143(3) of the *Criminal Justice Act 2003* (U.K.), which provides: "In considering the seriousness of any offence, the court must consider the offender's culpability in committing the offence and *any harm* which the offence *caused*, was *intended to cause* or *might foreseeably have caused*" (emphasis added).

Article 29 of Amendment IX of the *Criminal Code*, amending Article 287, adds the crime of illegal use of an information network. In addition, this provision directly criminalises certain preparatory acts such as creating a fake webpage, establishing a criminal group via a social network group-chat, publishing illegal information online such as terrorism content or child pornography, and so forth.

According to Article 287(1)(b) of the criminal law, if a person commits the crime of illegal use of an information network, and at the same time it constitutes other crimes such as disseminating child pornography or terrorist content, and the circumstances are serious, his or her act constitutes both the crime of illegal use of information network and the dissemination of obscene articles (for profit). These would be treated as two crimes for the purposes of conviction and punishment. If the crime of illegal use of the information network is committed and the prepared cybercrime is put into practice, such as the creation of a fake hotel website to seek money from people trying to book hotel rooms (i.e., where such people pay money believing it is a genuine webpage and a room will be provided for the money), these will be punished as independent crimes. The person's criminal record will also list each crime that he or she has been found guilty of having perpetrated.[25] We think there needs to be a proportionally constraint applied, and it ought to take into account that assisting another to be prepared for crime is fairly remote conduct that ought to be punished less severely, because of its remoteness from the actual harm that might be caused.

---

24 See A. Ashworth and L. Zedner, "Prevention and Criminalization: Justifications and Limits," (2012) 15 *New Crim. L. Rev.* 542 at 450; A. Ashworth, "Preventive Orders and the Rule of Law," in D. J. Baker and J. Horder (eds.), *The Sanctity of Life and the Criminal Law*, (Cambridge: Cambridge University Press, 2013) at 45 *et seq*; M. S. Moore, "A Tale of Two Theories," (2009) 28(1) *Criminal Justice Ethics* 27 at 31.

25 J. C. Ginsburg and L. A. Budiardjo, "Liability for Providing Hyperlinks to Copyright-Infringing Content: International and Comparative Law Perspectives," (2018) 41 *Colum. J.L. & Arts* 153 at 179.

3. Omissions liability for internet service providers

In Chinese criminal law theory and judicial practice, the following requirements should be met in order to define a crime of omission: (1) the actor has a specified duty to do a certain act; (2) it is possible for the actor to perform the specified duty; and (3) the actor fails to do the specified act, which results in criminal liability. As for the first requirement, "a specified duty to commit a certain act" is the source of citizens' positive duties.[26] Normally, in theory and legal precedents, a duty could rise under the following circumstances: (1) the duty is expressly stipulated in statute; (2) the duty is required by the actor's position or business; (3) the duty results from the actor's prior conduct; or (4) the duty is based on a contractual duty.[27]

Article 286(1):

> A person commits an offence if, being an Internet Service Provider, it fails to fulfil the information network security management obligation as stipulated in the laws and administrative regulations, and refuses to take corrective measures when ordered to do so by the relevant regulator. A term of imprisonment not exceeding 3 years is the maximum punishment for an individual.

The offence elements under Article 286(1) are:

(1) The ISP allowed (by failing to prevent upon being warned) mass dissemination of illegal information.
(2) The ISP allowed or caused the leakage of users' information, which leads to serious consequences.
(3) The ISP allowed or caused the loss of criminal evidence in serious circumstances.
(4) Other serious circumstances.

> A unit that commits the crime mentioned in the preceding paragraph should be fined. The persons who are directly in charge and others who are directly responsible for the offence should be punished in accordance with the provisions in the preceding paragraph.
>
> A person who commits any two of the acts listed in the preceding paragraph, which also constitutes another crime, should be convicted and punished in accordance with the heavier punishment provisions.

Similarly, due to threats of terrorism in Chinese, anti-terrorism criminal legislation has also adopted a duty approach. For example, Article 311 of *Chinese*

---

26 "It is only proper to speak of something as an omission if it constitutes a failure to carry out a duty." A. Ashworth, *Positive Obligations in Criminal Law*, (Oxford: Hart Publishing, 2013) at 31–32.
27 See Chen Xingliang, "The Generation of Omission," (2012) 4 *Peking University Law Journal* 666 at 667.

Criminal Code was amended to create an offence of refusing to provide evidence of crimes of espionage, terrorism or extremism. It does have a fault requirement (mental element), however. Pursuant to Article 311, whoever knowing that another person has committed the crime of espionage, terrorism or extremism, but refuses to provide relevant information or evidence when asked by the authorities, should be subjected to imprisonment for a term not exceeding three years. England has had similar laws from some years. Alternatively, the person might be put under surveillance and supervision, if the circumstances are serious.[28] This amendment shows that citizens' positive duties have been extended in the field of combating terrorism and extremist crimes.[29]

The duty placed on ISPs under Article 286(1) is not only omissions liability, but also borders on requiring people to police their fellow citizens. This type of offence comes within the concept of what Baker calls an "allowing" or "permitting" offence.[30] Article 286(1) creates "the crime of failing to perform the information network security management obligation."[31] The *Cyber Security Law* was passed on 7 November 2016 and came into effect on 1 June 2017. Although the *Cyber Security Law* is promulgated later than the Ninth Amendment of Chinese criminal law in terms of the time, the new provisions in the Ninth Amendment of Chinese criminal law have had a strong influence on the development of the *Cyber Security Law* and its draft.

There are three guiding principles of the *Cyber Security Law*: (1) the principle of cyberspace sovereignty; (2) the principle of attaching equal importance to the development of cybersecurity and development of informatisation; and (3) the principle of joint governance, which indicates that cyberstakeholders such as government agencies, enterprises, social organisations, technical communities and citizens should all participate in the governance of cyberspace. For example, Article 9 of the *Cyber Security Law* stipulates that:

> network operators carrying out business and service activities must follow laws and administrative regulations, respect social morality, abide by commercial ethics, be honest and credible, perform obligations to protect cyber

---

28 In England, terrorists are kept under surveillance after they leave prison if they are considered to pose a continuing threat. It was recently held that a police pilot project using automated facial recognition surveillance was not contrary to the right of privacy found in Art. 8 of the ECHR, see *R. (Bridges) v. Chief Constable of South Wales Police* [2020] 1 W.L.R. 672 See also V. Mitsilegas, "European Criminal Law and the Dangerous Citizen," (2018) 35(6) *Maastricht Journal of European and Comparative Law* 733.

29 See He Ronggong, "Thoughts on 'Preventive' Anti-terrorism Criminal Legislation," (2016) 3 *China Legal Science* 150.

30 Baker, *op. cit. supra*, note 13 at 273, noting in England the offence for not reporting crimes perpetrated by others was abolished because it put too great a burden on people to betray family and friends to the police. It also caused untrained citizens to pry into matters where trained police would suspect no crime.

31 See Jing Lijia, *Preventive Turn and Limits of Criminal Governance on Info- and Cybercrime*, (Beijing: Social Science Academic Science, 2019) at 56.

security, accept supervision from the government and public, and bear social responsibility.

Article 47 of the *Cyber Security Law* stipulates that:

> network operators shall strengthen management of information published by users and, upon discovering information that the law or administrative regulations prohibits the publication or transmission of, they shall immediately stop transmission of that information, employ handling measures such as deleting the information, prevent the information from spreading, save relevant records, and report it to the relevant competent departments.

These provisions clearly show that the Ninth Amendment of Chinese criminal law adopts the principle of joint governance of cyberspace as required in the *Cyber Security Law*. The criminalisation of assisting information network criminal activity, especially the criminalisation of failing to perform the information network security management obligation, is a bold attempt to regulate online harms with the help of the private entities who run and profit from providing network services.

(a) Effective governance of cybercrime and the addition of citizens' positive duties

The practicality of enforcing cybercrime is complex, because of the cybermeans used to perpetrate them.[32] Let's take fraud as an example; an actor might commit fraud anywhere in the world through the Internet, as long as the actor has access to it. That is to say, both wrongdoers and victims are extremely scattered and mobile because of the wide reach of the Internet and the mobility provided by modern devices. Under these circumstances, targeting only the perpetrator who might be based in some foreign country would not be very effective at deterring this sort of crime.[33]

A criminal might set up a webpage in the Philippines that sells child sex abuse images and videos. This might be set up in a way that makes it difficult to trace the perpetrator and also difficult to enforce the law across national jurisdictions. One way to minimise the potential harm to the children who are abused to make these ghastly materials is to make ISPs in China find such material and remove it or make it unsearchable. Of course, this will not prevent this material appearing on the Dark Web, but the level of skill required to operate on the Dark Web would at least mean this sort of content would not readily accessible to the general public on mainstream platforms.

32 *Ibid.* at 23–24.
33 See Liang Genlin, "Internalization of Traditional Crimes: Obstacle of Imputation, Response of Criminal Law and Restriction of Doctrine," (2017) 2 *Law Science Magazine* 4.

As far as fraudulent advertisements are concerned, fake bank and hotel websites are vastly more lucrative to the fraudsters, if they appear on the open Internet rather than on the Dark Web. After all, members of the general public do not go onto the Dark Web and anyone operating there is likely to see through fake webpages and so forth. Hence, the most lucrative place for fraudsters to place their fake advertisements and fake webpages is on the open Internet for all to see and find readily. Therefore, placing some duties on ISPs could have a real impact on reducing online harms, even though it would not mean getting the perpetrator who might be operating in some remote jurisdiction. The perpetrator would have his or her criminal activities disrupted, even though he or she might never face justice.

The most convenient way to prevent such materials appearing online is to require ISPs to have positive duties to remove such content upon being informed of its existence and upon being requested to remove it. Accordingly, ISPs become the "focus of Internet control"[34] in this sense. Therefore, in the field of China's cyberlaw, the addition of positive duties is based on harm prevention and disruption rather than criminalising the perpetrator who has made the illicit materials or promoted the illicit materials in cyberspace, since that perpetrator could be in another jurisdiction where law and order is lax.[35] If the perpetrator is found, he or she will be liable for a range of offences including some cybercrimes.

The aim of criminalising the conduct referred to in Article 286(1) is to make ISPs responsible to prevent harm that is done by independent others, on the simple basis that they are in a position of "control" and can take the most effective steps to prevent some of the harm at the remote stage.[36] Under the "control theory" Baker expounds,[37] A has a duty not to give A's car keys to B to "allow" B to drive, if A knows that B is inebriated from drinking a bottle of Kweichow Moutai. Here, if A does the "positive act" of providing the keys, a factfinder might infer intentional assistance. Similarly, if B is sober and B is driving A's car and B starts to drive dangerously, A would have a duty as the controller (owner) of the car to control its use so that it is only used lawfully. A has to take reasonable steps to try to stop B using A's car in an unlawful way. If A omits to do so, in England and Wales and most other common law jurisdictions, A would be equally liable for the criminal act of dangerous driving on the basis that A through omission intentionally encourages B to continue to drive in such a way.[38]

---

34 See L. Lessig, *Code v2*, translated by L. Xu and W. Shen (Beijing: Tsinghua University Press, Rev. edn., 2018) at 75.

35 See He Ronggong, "The Popularization of Prevention-oriented Criminal Law and Its Limits," (2017) 4 *Chinese Journal of Law* 147–148.

36 Cf. Baker, *op. cit. supra*, note 13 at 260, 657 *et passim*, states that certain people have a duty under the "control theory" to prevent others from misusing their premises or equipment such as a motorcar to criminally harm others and if they fail they will be complicit and thus equally liable. See also I. Leader-Elliott, "Framing Preparatory Inchoate Offences in the Criminal Code," (2011) 35 *Crim. L.J.* 80 at 82.

37 *Ibid.*

38 *Ibid.*

The new law in China is different, as it targets remote assistance. The ISP has no direct connection with the wrongdoers, but simply allows illegal content and advertisements and so forth to appear on its platform. It can be expensive to find and delete such material, and ISPs also make profits from such content.[39] Chinese law grounds criminal liability on the ISP's refusal "to take corrective measures which are ordered by the regulator."[40] If the ISP fails to prevent others from "continuing" to cause mass dissemination of illegal information online, it will be liable for failing to prevent the "continuing illegal act" from continuing upon being warned to stop it from continuing.

If it fails to prevent "information from leaking," it will be liable, if the data breach has serious consequences. Article 286(1) also has a data retention provision which deals with situations where data is not properly secured upon being informed that it is required "as evidence of criminal activity." It is not clear how long the ISP has to secure a person's search history, emails, WeChat messages, and so on. The law is vague, and it is not clear whether the law adopts a "reasonableness standard" as far as any due diligence defence might be concerned. For instance, it is not clear whether an ISP could argue it took all reasonable steps to remove any illegal content, etc., and had a robust compliance department and applied the best available artificial intelligence filters to find and remove such content, but unfortunately missed some illegal content and thus inadvertently continued to host it on its server. It appears that criminal liability is based on refusing to comply with an order to remove such content after being warned by a regulator, so perhaps sloppy and reckless censoring by the ISP will not result in punishment unless it has already been warned.

Compare this to Australia, where Schedule 1 of the *Telecommunications (Interception and Access) Amendment (Data Retention) Act 2015* mandates that ISPs and telecommunications providers retain information about their users' online activity for two years. Under this law, ISPs must keep identifying information about their customers, including billing information.[41] The data has to be retained for two years and must be encrypted and stored securely. The Act allows some authorised law enforcement agencies to access the stored information without a warrant, apart from the specific case of data relating to journalists. The draconian law in Australia was justified on the grounds that it was necessary for national security, even though terrorism is an almost non-existent problem in Australia.

---

39 P. Olson, "New Tactics Punch Holes in Big Tech's Ad-Fraud Defences," (New York: *The Wall Street Journal*, 7 January 2020). The European Commission has drafted a Code of Practice on Disinformation, to among other things, "improve the scrutiny of advertisement placements to reduce revenues of the purveyors of disinformation." Cf. The Notes on Amendment to the Criminal Law of the People's Republic of China (ix).

40 Article 286(1) of the *Criminal Code of China*.

41 The new Section 187AA of the *Telecommunications (Interception and Access) Act*) outlines the information the ISP must retain, and it includes "voice, SMS, email, chat, forum, and social media."

In Europe, where there is an occasional terrorist attack, data retention laws are very limited due to the right to privacy enshrined in Article 8 of the *European Convention on Human Rights* among other Charters. In *Tele2 Sverige AB v. Post-och telestyrelsen (C-203/15)*,[42] the Court of Justice of the European Union held that the data retention law contravened the right to privacy, because it was not targeted only at very serious crime, but indiscriminately covered all citizens whether they had a criminal profile or not. Thus, it was held to be incompatible with the *Charter of Fundamental Rights of the European Union* and *Directive 2002/58/EC of the European Parliament and of the Council of 12 July 2002*. It was held that not only did it disproportionately impinge the freedom of expression right of citizens, but citizens would fear the constant surveillance and long retention times. It was held that the:

> General data retention obligations were in fact a serious interference with the right to privacy, enshrined in article 7 of the *Charter of Fundamental Rights of the European Union*, and the right to the protection of personal data guaranteed by article 8 of the *Charter*.[43]

The *Cyber Security Law* also emphasises that ISPs shall fulfil the obligation of cybersecurity protection and bear social responsibilities to realise the joint governance of cyberspace. Article 47 of *Cyber Security Law* provides that:

> network operators shall strengthen the management of information published by users and, upon discovering information that the law or administrative regulations prohibits the publication or transmission of, they shall immediately stop transmission of that information, employ handling measures such as deleting the information, prevent the information from spreading, save relevant records, and report to the relevant competent departments.

In this context, the *Decision of the Standing Committee of the National People's Congress on Safeguarding Internet Security* put most of the burden of information network security management on ISPs.[44] Furthermore, criminalisation of illegal use of the information network in Article 287(1) of the Ninth Amendment of the *Criminal Code of China* adopts a legislative approach that is prevention-oriented, because this simplifies the standards and procedures of proof, and provides potential perpetrators at each level of the crime. Somewhere along the cybercrime chain of law enforcement prosecutors hope to convict one of the role players, whether for a preparatory act, an inchoate act or for a consummated crime.

---

42 *Tele2 Sverige AB v. Post-och telestyrelsen (C-203/15)* [2017] 2 W.L.R. 1289.
43 *Ibid.* at 1314.
44 See Zhou Guangquan, "The Thinking and Approaches of Criminal Law Legislation in a Transitional Period," (2016) 3 *Social Sciences in China* 130.

4. The constitutional dilemma: the deviation from marketplace norms

Providing Internet services is a private commercial transaction, and as long as the server does not deliberately host illegal content, it seems it ought not have to take on the financial burden of acting as state censor. Moreover, ISPs only engage in commercial activities; they are not national functional departments. In this case, they cannot be considered, in accordance with Chinese criminal law, as being accountable for examining the authenticity and legality of the transmitted information and preventing network participants from committing crimes. These obligations need to be fulfilled by the relevant national functional departments.

As a basic law in China to regulate cyberspace, Article 8 of the *Cyber Security Law* indicates that:

> the competent telecommunication department of the State Council, public security departments and other relevant authorities shall be responsible for protecting, supervising and administering cyber-security within the scope of their respective responsibilities in accordance with the provisions of this Law and other relevant laws and administrative regulations. The national cyber-space administration authority is responsible for the overall planning and coordination of cyber security work and relevant supervision and administration work.

If the crime of failing to perform the information network security management obligation stipulated in Chinese criminal law is regarded as conferring positive duties of maintaining information network security on ISPs, it puts ISPs in the position of state censors and gives them a quasi-policing role, which does not conform to the relevant provisions of the *Cyber Security Law*. Furthermore, it would lead to a situation where ISPs bear the duty of cyberspace administration, but lack the corresponding power to take actions against wrongdoers who misuse their services. From this point of view, the legitimacy of this crime is questionable.[45]

However, we see similar duties placed on ISPs in Europe and the United States – especially in relation to hosting pirate movie sites, and so forth. However, under the *Digital Millennium Copyright Act of 1998*, 17 U.S.C. 512(c), a safe harbour is created for online intermediaries such as video platforms like YouTube. Online intermediaries can, under certain circumstances, avoid being held liable for any user-generated content that infringes copyright and is posted on the platform. Article 14 of the European Commission *E-commerce Directive* is similar to the text of *Digital Millennium Copyright Act of 1998*, 17 U.S.C. 512(c). According to this Article 14, an ISP is not criminally liable unless it had

---

45 Lijia, *op. cit. supra*, note 31 at 165.

actual knowledge of the infringement or was aware of facts or circumstances from which infringement was blatantly apparent.

Many Western states have excessive wide data retention laws, and China seems merely to be borrowing these ideas from the West. Perhaps the focus going forward is to ensure that any criminalisation is proportionated to the remote contribution made to the end harm by the ISP. Furthermore, attention should be put on making sure only inherently harmful content is regulated. Content such as adult pornography is better dealt with by implementing parental lockout systems. A new filter that Twitter uses deletes naked pictures from messages and Facebook has a filter to remove nude images, but if these images are being sent privately between two consenting adult lovers, is it really the business of a private corporation to decide what they can send to each other privately?[46] However, there would be nothing wrong with putting an app on a phone belonging to a minor (aged younger than 18) to prevent him or her from taking a nude selfie – since this would prevent such a person from exploitation and from making decisions in youth that might be regretted later in life.[47] The same could apply to violent games and movies, which harm children. Nunziato has noted:

> The European Union, as well as several European countries, have generally implemented speech regulations to hold platforms liable for failing to police their sites, and have recently imposed sweeping regulations on such platforms. And, in their efforts to comply with such regulations, online platforms like Facebook and Twitter may end up implementing these European regulations in ways that affect what U.S. audiences can access online – since it is often difficult for platforms to implement national regulations in a geographically targeted manner with no spill-over beyond the regulating nation's borders. The European Union and European countries have recently undertaken sweeping efforts to remedy perceived imperfections in the marketplace, including by requiring online platforms to rapidly remove a wide swath of harmful content. Among European nations, Germany has led the way by enacting drastic legislation requiring social media sites like Facebook and Twitter to remove false news, defamatory hate speech, and other unlawful content within twenty-four hours of receiving notice of the same, upon pain of multi-million-euro fines. . . . In addition to government regulation by the European Union and by European governments, the online platforms themselves are undertaking self-regulatory measures with respect to content accessible by U.S. audiences.[48]

46 "New Twitter Filter Deletes Naked Pictures from Messages," (London: *BBC News*, 15 February 2020).

47 R. Morrison, " 'Child Friendly' Tone e20 Smartphone that Blocks Users from Taking Naked Selfies, doesn't Save 'Inappropriate' Images and Lets Parents Check up on their Kids is Launched in Japan," (London: *The Daily Mail*, 19 February 2020).

48 D. C. Nunziato, "The Marketplace of Ideas Online," (2019) 94 *Notre Dame L. Rev.* 1519 at 1521–1522.

Nunziato continues:

> Opponents of the [German] legislation also contend that Facebook's "delete when in doubt" practice has a chilling effect on speech both online and offline, and that in the [German *Network Enforcement Act*] era, "people are more careful what to think, what to write" and "[l]ots of people are afraid of losing of their accounts." Critics also complain about the process through which such censorship occurs. They lament the fact that NetzDG has created a regime in which "companies can play judges" and through which the legislation "outsource[s] censorship to private companies and infringe[s] on civil liberties." As one public official complained, under NetzDG, "too many competences that require legal expertise are delegated to tech companies."[49]

(a) The principle of personal responsibility

The general principle of bearing responsibility solely for one's own wrongdoing requires that citizens ought only to be held criminally responsible for their own actions. When an ISP is held responsible, it is its managers and compliance department employees who will be imprisoned for up to three years for wrongdoing by independent others who they do not know, who they have not conspired with, who they have not intentionally encouraged or assisted. Any assistance is continued after the event, and fault only occurs after the relevant senior managers in the ISP or compliance experts become aware that they are facilitating the "continuing act" of publishing illegal content by failing to remove such content.

We have explained that if a warning is given and the senior managers or compliance experts working for the ISP intentionally refuse to comply, this can be reconciled with the basic principle of complicity by omission.[50] However, the sort of "control theory"[51] or "allowing" theory of complicity adopted in some common law countries is almost impossible to reconcile with the narrow from of joint perpetration crime found in Article 25 of the *Criminal Code of China*. Hence, the law is being extended beyond what Article 25 allows for.[52]

Comparatively, we can see that the German law supports such an approach, but the law in the United States is far more restrictive.[53] In *Zeran v. AOL*,[54] the

---

49 *Ibid.* at 1535.
50 D. J. Baker, *Reinterpreting Criminal Complicity and Inchoate Participation Offences*, (Oxford: Routledge, 2016) at 33–41, 63, 107, 216–217.
51 *Ibid.*
52 Wang Huawei, "A Comparative Study on the Liability of Internet Service Providers Based on the Criminal Law," (2016) 4 *Global Law Review* 46.
53 They can be summarized as: The transmission, searching or retaining of information must be initiated by the subscriber, i.e., the service provider must be the passive receiver and transmit information at the user's request without interfering with information communications; the service provider must have the negative knowledge of the content of the infringing material; the provider must immediately remove, block or deny access to the infringing material, once receiving the relevant notification complying with statutory requirements; and the provider must adopt and implement a policy of terminating the account of repeat infringers or authorizing their access and inform the subscriber of the policy. *Digital Millennium Copyright Act*, Subsections 512(a)–(d), (i).
54 *Zeran v. America Online, Inc.* (1997) 129 F. 3d 327.

notorious Section 230 of the *Communications Decency Act* was interpreted to provide platform and ISPs with complete immunity for the acts of others publishing illegal content on their servers.[55] Similarly, in the case of copyright violations, the law requires the "copyright owner to take responsibility for searching for infringing material and notifying the service provider."[56] ISPs could be exempted from such liability as long as they do not actively and culpably participate in transmitting illegal information.[57]

Germany's *Network Enforcement Act* (*Netzwerkdurchsetzungsgesetz*) came into force on 1 October 2017. This law, among other things, aims to combat online "hate speech, agitation and fake news." Pursuant to this Act, the German government has imposed duties on social media giants such as Facebook and Twitter to ensure that they remove unsafe and abusive content from their platforms. Thus, platform providers should check complaints immediately, delete patently illegal content within 24 hours and delete any illegal content within seven days after checking and block access to it. A fine up to €50 million could be applied to any platform that inactively or poorly employs handling measures. In this regard, the law is similar to the safe harbour principles that apply to copyright infringements, because providers are only liable upon being informed of the illegal content. The safe harbour immunity only applies if the service provider does not have any *knowledge* of the fact that the copyright infringing material is published on its server. If an ISP such as YouTube becomes aware of an infringement as a consequence of a notification from the right holder, it has to take down the material.[58]

Omissions liability for ISPs in China is also based on a "notification and removal" process. In order hold an ISP criminally liable rather than liable for the lighter administrative liability that exists in China, there must be a proven failure to act by the ISP upon being notified by the regulator. To hold ISPs liable for any breach without warning would be too great an extension of criminal liability, because these organisations have millions of content creators uploading information every minute, no compliance department could hire enough people to censor every bit of information uploaded and even the best artificial intelligence filters are not going to be perfect. It is also better to risk some harmful content accidentally appearing on the web than having panicked ISPs over-censor the content of the web. Much of the offensive expression censored in Germany is not censored at all in the United States, because the United States only criminalises speech that might lead to physical harm and only when such speech creates a real and imminent risk of inducing violence.[59]

55 *Viacom Int'l, Inc. v. YouTube, Inc.*, (2012) 676 F.3d 19.
56 R. A. Gorman and J. C. Ginsburg, *Cases and Materials*, (New York: Foundation Press, 7th edn., 2006) at 887.
57 A. Savin, *EU Internet Law*, (Edward Elgar Publishing, 2013) at 50.
58 B. Holznagel, *Das Compliance System des Entwurfs des Netzdurchsetzungsgesetzes* – Eine kritische Bestandsaufnahme aus internationale Sicht, Zeitschrift für Urheber – und Medizinrecht 2017, S. 615.
59 See:

> The constitutional guarantees of free speech and free press do not permit a State to forbid or proscribe advocacy of the use of force or of law violation except where such advocacy is

5. The normativity of private censorship and pre-inchoate criminalisation

Criminal law is a necessary harm prevention mechanism, but it is subject to a number of justice constraints, including the retributive constraint the punishment fit the crime.[60] There needs to be strong normative grounds for invoking the criminal law and generally it should be used as a last resort. Chinese criminal law's coercive power is subject to some constitutional constraints, but like the legal systems in Europe, this is fairly minimal when it comes to controlling what is made a substantive crime. The harm principle has no constitutional power in most jurisdictions,[61] even if it did some of the omissions liability and pre-inchoate liability would be normatively justified under it.

Requiring ISPs to remove material that is harmful to children or that risks inciting acts of terrorism clearly meet the requirements of the harm principle and there are no constitutional considerations of any weight on the other side of the scales, because there is no freedom of expression interests in expressing this content online or elsewhere. However, criminalising the mere creation of an online chat group is hard to reconcile with the normative claim that we ought to criminalise conduct that harms others. Even trivial and remote harm might cross the threshold set by Article 13 of the *Criminal Code of China*, if the harm has no social utility whatsoever and the *telos* of the product causing the harm is purely criminal, as would be the case with a fake hotel webpage that sells rooms that do not exist. Nonetheless, something with a dual lawful and unlawful purpose such as an online chat group seems too far removed from any real harm in the real world to warrant the criminal law being invoked so early.[62]

In order to strike a proper balance between network security and civil liberties, a restrictive interpretation of the "information network security management obligation" and of the pre-inchoate offences is a necessity. The pre-inchoate offences could be made safer if they were to apply to only very serious harms that risk human life such as potential terrorism or to items that can only be used for a criminal purpose such as ATM card skimmers or have the potential to target victims en masse (i.e., fake webpages or false online advertisements).

The are some legislative constraints: Article 286(1) "the crime of failing to perform the information network security management obligation" of Chinese criminal law lists three grounds for criminalisation: (1) "allowing *mass* dissemination of illegal information to continue to remain online"; (2) "causing or allowing

---

directed to inciting or producing imminent lawless action and is likely to incite or produce such action.

Brandenburg v. Ohio (1969) 395 U.S. 444 at 447.

60 Baker, *op. cit. supra*, note 13 at 39; 42–44.

61 D. J. Baker, "Constitutionalizing the Harm Principle," (2008) 27 *Crim. Just. Ethics* 3 at 4–6.

62 R. Peeters, "The Price of Prevention: the Preventive Turn Consequence for Role of State," (2015) 17(2) *Punishment & Society* 167 at 168.

user information to leak with serious consequences"; or (3) "causing or allowing the loss of criminal evidence with serious circumstances."[63] (Emphasis added.)

Suppose pornography starring consenting adults and viewed only by consenting adults, through a system that an age verification filter prevents children from accessing, were to appear online in China. Such content would not harm the adults who voluntarily access it. However, it is illegal content (even if objectively harmless), and if it were online in China, it would reach the masses, but the circumstances are not objectively serious because only consenting adults are able to access the material (assuming proper age verification technology is implemented) and the material is likely to be less harmful than viewing violent films. That something is a crime in the *Criminal Code* (Articles 263 and 264) might be all it takes to deem it is a serious circumstance for it to be published online, regardless of whether only consenting adults can access it and regardless of whether it causes any objective harm.[64] Hence, the "serious circumstances" constraint is no constraint at all, as it is not a normative constraint but simply a constraint that rests on legal positivism, meaning the seriousness of the circumstances might be based simply on the illegality of the content and the fact it is put online for millions of consenting adults to access, rather than on whether it has the potential to cause objective harm to any of them.

6. Conclusion

The new provisions in China seem to try to borrow ideas and concepts from other jurisdictions without giving much thought to how well those laws are working in those places.[65] However, it is a commendable first step to try to combat the harm caused by cyberfraud and other online crimes. The main crime that takes place online is fraud, but these sweeping laws will require everyone's data to be retrained for a period of time not given in the legislation. The level of evidence that might be obtained in the case of preparation crimes from a digital trail is

---

63 Lijia, *op. cit. supra*, note 31 at 26.

64 Huigens writes:

> Legal positivism, for example, has as its centrepiece the separation thesis: the idea that law and morality are two different normative systems, so that to insist, as natural law theorists once did, that an immoral law is no law at all is just confused. (Among other things, it overlooks the distinction between descriptive and normative claims.) The separation thesis itself is descriptive. But many legal positivists also make normative arguments from the separation thesis. They place value on the formality and perspectivity of legal rules in contrast to ordinary morals, and advance a distinctive rule of law agenda according to which legal norms ought to be different from and independent of moral norms to a very great degree. The theory of punishment tends to work in the opposite direction, in that normative claims tend to drive the descriptive account.

> K. Huigens, "On Aristotelian Criminal Law: A Reply to Duff," (2004) 18 *Notre Dame J.L. Ethics & Pub. Pol'y* 465 at 469–470.

65 See Jing Lijia, "The Application of Legal Dogmatic of the Criminal Law in Information Network Security Management Obligation," (2017) 5 *Oriental Law* 84.

likely to be compelling. In the past, many preparatory acts perhaps went unnoticed due to a lack of evidence, so digital evidence does have the potential to help law enforcement bring cases and for the prosecution to prove cases. We think the approach taken in Europe is a better model than that taken in Australia – since Europe requires all data to be destroyed after six months, while Australia required it to be kept for two years. The European model strikes a fairer balance between usefulness of making such evidence available and the right to privacy and expression of the bulk of the population who will never be involved in crime.[66]

Perpetration of crimes through the Internet and online platforms has a ubiquitous aspect to it, because perpetrators can perpetrate across jurisdictional borders and do so anonymously.[67] We have argued that there is both a normative and legal case for criminalising certain preparatory acts and facilitation acts that do not come within the purview of complicity, such as selling fake websites without engaging in a joint crime of fraud, but simply to make money from one's information technology skills. We have cautioned that these crimes ought to be subject to stringent proportionality and fair labelling constraints similar to the constraint found in Article 13 of the *Criminal Code of China*. As for the omissions liability placed on ISPs to remove terrorist content, we have no objection to such a law, as it only results in a conviction after a warning is given and the ISP refuses to comply. However, we are concerned about private enterprises carrying out this sort of regulatory role. They will often lack the expertise to draw a careful line between permissible content and impermissible content and might over-censor for the fear of incurring liability. However, the warning system might guard against that to some extent.

---

66 T. Cai *et al.*, "Characteristics of Cybercrimes: Evidence from Chinese Judgment Documents," (2018) 19(6) *Police Practice & Research* 582.
67 J. Clough, *Principles of Cybercrime*, (Melbourne: Cambridge University Press, 2015).

5 Criminal law protection of virtual property in China

Zhang Mingkai and Wang Wenjing

1. Introduction

In Chinese criminal jurisprudence, various views exist on the act of illegally acquiring virtual property belonging to another. At the core of the debate is whether virtual property can be protected by property offences such as theft. The question is: should the act of acquiring virtual property belonging to another, that has real economic value,[1] be defined as property for the purposes of treating any wrongful and dishonest acquisition as theft or fraud?[2] Or should such wrongful acquisitions be deterred through applying computer and network misuse offences?[3] There are legal limitations to deeming all acts of illegal acquisition of virtual property as computer crimes. We will argue that virtual property can

---

1 Odinet writes:

> It is worth noting that the Second Life economy is not insignificant. In 2014 alone, users 'cashed out over $60 million . . . by selling their Linden Dollars for good old USD." With about 600,000 active users, and assuming that about 20% of them are engaged in the buying and selling of goods and services on Second Life (and exchanging Linden dollars for U.S. currency), that equates to a "very very rough guess" of a $500 average payout. According to Linden Lab's Chief Executive Officer in a 2015 interview, "[t]here's a woman in New Zealand who makes hundreds of thousands of dollars making hands and feet for avatars and feeds her family by doing that." . . . The buying and selling of goods is not, however, the only way in which a Second Life user can monetize her virtual world experience. Users can also rent or acquire their own real estate. The "land" itself merely represents space on the Second Life servers that individuals can come to acquire rights in for a limited duration. But, practically speaking, within the virtual world this server space manifests itself as actual acreage. To acquire rights in land in Second Life, a user can 'rent' the land from Linden Labs or from some other renter of land for a weekly or monthly price.

C. K. Odinet, "Bitproperty and Commercial Credit," (2017) 94 *Wash. U.L. Rev.* 649 at 667–668.

2 Cf. *Bragg v. Linden Research, Inc.* (2007) 487 F.Supp.2d 593. Some jurisdictions have held virtual property can be property for the purposes of the law of theft. See T. van der Linden, "Stealing Masks and Amulets: What's Law Got to Do with It?" (2013) 46 *U.B.C. L. Rev.* 665; W. Rumbles, "Theft in the Digital: Can You Steal Virtual Property," (2013) 17 *Canterbury L. Rev.* 354.

3 Cf. Rain Xie, "Why China Had to 'Ban' Cryptocurrency but the U.S. Did Not: A Comparative Analysis of Regulations on Crypto-Markets Between the U.S. and China," (2019) 18 *Wash. U. Global Stud. L. Rev.* 457; S. Chen, "Path Transformation in the Construction of Virtual Property Rules: From the Perspective of Research Paradigms," (2019) 6 *Renmin Chinese L. Rev.* 102.

be the object of property crime and that theft is a more apt offence to apply when the core harm is the loss of property rather than the altering of computer data.[4] Furthermore, the value of the property can be used to determine the level of criminality involved: for the act of illegally acquiring any users' virtual property, the sentence should reflect the value of the virtual property that dishonestly appropriated.

2. Conceptualising virtual property

(a) General concept of a virtual asset

There are two schools of thought on virtual property in China. Some theorists define it narrowly, while others adopt a broader conceptualisation. We will call the broader conceptualisation "virtual existence theory" and the narrow conceptualisation "online game theory." The virtual existence theory stresses that the existence of virtual property is confined to a network environment. A typical view is that virtual property is "a competitive, perpetual and interlinked information resource which exists in digital form in a virtual world and can be governed by man and appreciated by its user,"[5] or "a specific service or something intangible that is valuable and able to meet a certain need in cyberspace."[6] The virtual existence theory draws a line between virtual property and digital property. Virtual property depends on cyberspace, while digital property is different because it is an extension of physical property in an electronic space that is not dependent on cyberspace. Nonetheless, this theory includes several different views, but further study is needed to decide which elements should be chosen to define virtual property.

Meanwhile, the "online game theory" confines the scope of virtual property to online games. A typical point of view is that virtual property is electronic data modules designed and offered by a game operator in an online game that can be owned and used by a game player, including weapons, game currencies, land and buildings, and articles of everyday use.[7] The emergence of the online game theory is attributed to the reality that nearly all virtual property cases are related to online games in China, which is what triggered the present debate over crimes involving online game-centred virtual property. Compared with the virtual existence theory, the online game theory has a more specific and more operable scope. The existence of online virtual property should not be confined

---

4 See generally, M. M. Chew, "Virtual Property in China: The Emergence of Gamer Rights Awareness and the Reaction of Game Corporations," (2011) 13(5) *New Media & Society* 722.

5 M. Xiaying and X. Ke, "The Theory and Legislation of Virtual Property Inheritance," (2013) 6 *The Jurist* 82; cf. B. M. Owens-Filice, " 'Where's the Money Lebowski?' – Charging Credit and Debit Card Larcenies Under Article 121," (2014) *Ucmj, Army Law* at 3.

6 Zhao Wensheng and Liang Genlin, "How to Apply the Law to the Theft of Traffic Packets and Other Virtual Property," (2014) 4 *People's Procuratorial Semimonthly* 42.

7 H. Guoyun, "On the Improper Nature of Criminal Protection of Network Virtual Property – Let The Virtual Property Stay in the Virtual World Forever," (2008) 3 *Journal of People's Public Security University of China (Social Science Edition)* 33.

to online games. Predictably, with the advance of network technology, more and more virtual property will exist outside of online games (e.g., Bitcoin),[8] which should be treated equally in law.

3. Categorising virtual property

As for virtual property, the present mainstream viewpoint in Chinese academic circles is that virtual property refers to property whose property value exists in cyberspace in the form of electromagnetic data. This view does not directly adopt the virtual existence or the online game conceptualisation of virtual property, but lists three marked characteristics essential to virtual property in comparison with traditional property: (1) virtual property uses electromagnetic data as its carrier; (2) property value as content; and (3) the Internet as the space.[9] On this basis, virtual property is divided into three types.[10]

---

8 In China's judicial practice, Bitcoin has been identified as virtual property and an object of protection for property infringement. For example, in the *Pei Siyuan* case, the Higher People's court of Guangdong province pointed out that:

> The currency is a kind of network virtual goods. Although the transaction of Bitcoin in China is illegal, there are objective transaction facts on the Internet and real currencies, which can be converted into real material benefits, and it should be recognized as property in terms of legal attributes.

China Judgment Online, <http://wenshu.court.gov.cn/content/content?DocID=2a9f27 d9-32f6-47dd-9131-a9c9014c8c1d&KeyWord=%E8%AF%88%E9%AA%97%7C%E6%AF% 94%E7%89%B9%E5%B8%81> accessed 12 Mach 2019. Cf. G. I. Zekos, "Economics and Legal Understanding of Virtual Currencies," (2019) *Banking & Fin. Services Pol'y Rep* 1; R. M. Lastra and J. G. Allen, "Virtual Currencies in the Eurosystem: Challenges Ahead," (2019) 52 *Int'l Law.* 177.

9 This aligns somewhat with views held by Anglo-American theorists. Fairfield writes:

> Another commonly occurring example of virtual property is a chat room devoted to discussing stocks. There is a focusing effect that draws people to the chat room – the more people that are involved in the conversation, the more valuable the discussion becomes. You cannot take over the chat room from its creator, so it is rivalrous. But people can join the conversation because of the interconnectivity and persistent traits of the space, just as they might go to a restaurant where stockbrokers are known to meet. There is a reason we call it a chat "room," entirely divorced from the pseudo psychological sense of being in a space: the space may be electronic, but it has encoded into it some of the characteristics of a real room. Virtual property also plays an important part in financial institutions – a bank account may be one of the earliest forms of virtual property. Bank accounts exist as loci within an interconnected network. The owner of an account has an exclusionary right over a nexus of electronic credits and debits located at that nexus. The bank account is persistent – even though the account balance is merely an entry, that entry remains in the bank if undisturbed. The bank account is interconnected – other people can send money to the account, and the owner of the account can authorize money to flow to other account holders.

J. A. T. Fairfield, "Virtual Property," (2005) 85 *B.U. L. Rev.* 1047 at 1057.

10 Jiang Bo, *Research on Judicial Protection of Virtual Property*, (Beijing: Peking University Press, 2015) at 31.

(a) The problem with virtual property in China

Account virtual property refers to all account and password types that involve user information, including game accounts, email accounts and QQ numbers. Arguably, digital and virtual property overlap in many places, and it is unhelpful to completely compartmentalise them.[11]

Besides common online game accounts and email accounts, QQ accounts are conceptualised as virtual property in China. The software QQ is an instant message application developed by Tencent in 1999. It provides users with several functions, including written and voice communication, sending files, audio and video communication, email service, network hard disk and online games. The user applies to Tencent for a free QQ number after accepting the conditions of Tencent's agreement. The user sets his or her own password and obtains the right to use the software with his or her QQ number. According to Tencent's agreement, the right to use the QQ number belongs only to the initial applicant, and that registrant is not allowed to transfer or sell it. It also cannot be inherited by another user. If the user violates the agreement or discontinues use of their QQ number for an extended time period, Tencent has the unconditional right to take it back.[12]

Before 2011, QQ became China's major tool for sending instant messages, especially for young users.[13] QQ was seen as the best for communicating on the Internet because of its speed, stability and convenience, among other characteristics.

---

11 Compare the conceptualization of digital property in the Anglo-American common law system.

> The definition of "digital property" includes both "digital accounts" (defined as "an electronic system for creating, generating, sending, receiving, storing, displaying, or processing information to which the account holder has access") and "digital assets" (defined as "information created, generated, sent, communicated, received, or stored by electronic means on a digital device or system that delivers digital information,' including a contract right).

> S. S. Varnado, "Your Digital Footprint Left Behind at Death: An Illustration of Technology Leaving the Law Behind," (2014) 74 *La. L. Rev.* 719 at n. 319. See also *Taxation of certain digital property in North Carolina* 2019 WL 5447078 (RIA) where it is said: "Certain digital property includes the following items: an audio work; an audiovisual work; a book, magazine, a newspaper, a newsletter, a report, or another publication; and a photograph or a greeting card." Similarly the *St. & Loc. Taxes Weekly* Art. 9, outlining the law for tax purposes in Alabama, states: "Digital property" includes any of the following that is transferred electronically:

>> digital audio works (such as ringtones, recorded songs, music, books or other sound recordings), digital books, finished artwork, digital photographs, periodicals, newspapers, magazines, video greeting cards; audio greeting cards, video games, electronic games or any digital code related to this property.

12 Clearly, this raises issues of contract and tort law, as well. D. B. Koburger, "Legal Implications of Public Spaces in Virtual Reality," (2019) 12 *Landslide* 10 at 12.

13 Around 2008, QQ had 500 million registered users, with a market share of 76.7%. At the time, QQ was the undisputed leader in instant messaging in China, and it remains one of the most important online communication tools for Chinese netizens today.

Short QQ numbers or those with special meanings gradually became scarce resources, like desirable phone numbers, leading to the emergence of many organisations and individuals illegally selling QQ numbers on the Internet, and to the creation of software used to steal QQ numbers. Just like losing many contacts because of losing a cell phone, losing a QQ number is an unquantifiable loss for the user. Against this backdrop, whether a QQ number can be seen as a property for protection remains markedly controversial theoretically, legislatively and in juridical practice.

In December 2005, the Nanshan District Court in Shenzhen accepted China's first case of suspected stolen QQ numbers.[14] The defendant, Zeng, entered Tencent in May 2004 and was responsible for system monitoring at his company's security centre. In March 2005, he acquainted himself with another defendant, Yang, when he purchased a QQ number on *Taobao.com*. Together they conspired and stole others' QQ numbers and sold them for profit. From March to July, Yang sent randomly selected QQ numbers to Zeng via the Internet. Zeng then used an ex-colleague's account to access the back-end system for password protection information (i.e., IDs and email accounts) for those QQ numbers and sent that information to Yang. Yang cracked the password protection questions for those QQ numbers, changed the passwords and sold them. In all, the two defendants sold approximately 130 QQ numbers and illicitly earned 61,650 yuan.

The court held that the prosecution had proved its case but held that theft was not the appropriate offence. The court decided this to treat it as a network communication service violation, because a QQ number as a code was covered by that area of the law, while QQ numbers per se were not subject to property protection in criminal law. A number essentially is only information, but it is also a tool for controlling one's communications.[15] A QQ number was held to be a code for communication.[16] The two defendants falsified the passwords of more than 130 QQ numbers, making the original users of these members unable to contact their contacts; this violated their freedom of correspondence.[17] In the

---

14 *Criminal Judgment No. 56* of Nanshan District People's Court of Shenzhen City, Guangdong Province (2006).

15 The English law of theft does not recognise information as property. See D. J. Baker, *Glanville Williams Textbook of Criminal Law*, (London: Sweet & Maxwell, 2015) at 1243–1245, 1319–1332. Baker points out that in the United States, law of theft recognises information (especially valuable trade secrets) as property for the purposes of the law of theft. Baker also shows how if a person copies another's door key, to gain entry to their property at some later date, that this sort of copying of information is theft because it makes the original key valueless.

16 For a compendious and convenient overview (in English) of China's network and communications offences, see Xingan Li, "Regulation of Cyber Space: An Analysis of Chinese Law on Cyber Crime," (2015) 9(2) *International Journal of Cyber Criminology* 185.

17 Article 252 of the *Criminal Code of China* provides: "Those infringing upon the citizens right of communication freedom by hiding, destroying, or illegally opening others' letters, if the case is serious, are to be sentenced to one year or less in prison or put under criminal detention." S. Daocui, "Criminal Protection of Network Property Interests: Judicial Trend and Theory Coordination," (2016) 6 *Political Science and Law* 44.

end, the court defined the crime as a violation of freedom of correspondence and judged the defendants conduct as a network offence. This case is considered China's first virtual asset case, but it ended up denying that virtual assets possess property attributes.

This shows how difficult it is to define infringement on account virtual property involving user information as a property violation from the outset. In later judicial precedents, such cases are typically treated as crimes of invading the victim's freedom of communication rights. Later, in 2011, the Supreme People's Court issued Article 11 of *Explanations on Laws Applicable to Criminal Cases of Hazarding Computer Information System Security*. As a result, the Supreme People's Procuratorate now treats it as identity authentication information, so the act of acquiring any other user's account password and then selling it for profit using computer techniques is deemed an illegal acquisition of a computer information data.[18] Therefore, account virtual property is not the object of property tort in Chinese criminal law, and this opinion is already universally accepted in theory and in practice.

(b) Virtual property articles

Virtual property articles (or chattels)[19] typically include online game gears, characters, ornaments of avatars, props used in live video streaming, and so forth. This type of virtual property is essentially a computer character string, but it is manifested as articles with gaming or recreational functions in a network environment. Different from account virtual property, there is no consensus about whether virtual property articles are subject to property crime.[20]

Initially, many advocated for this type of virtual property infringement to be defined as property crime; however, this caused the dispute to focus on the determination of a specific amount (in China, to establish theft, a certain amount is required)[21]. Without a generally accepted value calculation method

---

18 Cf. the *Computer Misuse Act 1990* (U.K.).

19 Moses writes:

> While "land" is created by the program's developers, virtual chattels are generally created by the characters themselves using software tools provided by the developers. Both virtual chattels and virtual land are bought with "Linden dollars" which can be purchased, through an online currency exchange, with real currency (for example, via credit card).

> L. Bennett Moses, "The Applicability of Property Law in New Contexts: From Cells to Cyberspace," (2008) 30 *Sydney L. Rev.* 639.

20 The secondary value argument rests on the traditional monetary value of virtual chattels in the secondary market: "Because the money in virtual worlds is convertible to real world money, virtual work is having an impact on real world economies." M. A. Cherry, "Cyber Commodification," (2013) 72 *Md. L. Rev.* 381, 407–408. However, can hours spent playing a game equate to property? See F. G. Lastowka and D. Hunter, "The Laws of the Virtual Worlds," (2004) 92 *Cal. L. Rev.* 1.

21 Almost all the property crimes in China's criminal law are crimes committed in amount, and the conviction and sentencing are based on the property value. The minimum amount for theft is 1,000–3,000 yuan.

for virtual property, the definition of a crime against property does not exist.[22] For example, in 2003, a player (Li) of the online game *Red Moon* discovered that all of his gears in the game had been stolen. He filed a lawsuit against the operator, Arctic Ice Company. The court decided that the fact that the defendant had violated the victim's virtual property rights, but held the remedy was simply to order the defendant to restore the lost game gears to the plaintiff. This seems to have been based on the fact that the court was unable to determine the economic value of the virtual chattels in the real world. In another example, in 2004, defendant Yan used his role as a staff member to steal personal data from three game players who attended a ceremonial gaming event held by NetEase. Yan counterfeited the victims' IDs and captured their NetEase permit numbers; he then got NetEase to send him new security codes on the pretext that the victims' codes were lost. Thereafter, Yan logged into those games with the new security codes to steal the victims' game gears, which he sold, illegally earning CNY 3,750 yuan. NetEase estimated that the stolen gears were worth 69,070 game coins, which is the equivalent of 4,605 yuan. The court ruled that virtual gears were personal property, so the defendant's act constituted larceny, but the court's instruction did not include information about how to calculate the specific value of the game gears. The punishment handed down was a flat fine of 5,000 yuan.

In recent years, verdicts about virtual chattels have changed in juridical practice. For instance, in 2014, a court decided that the act of setting traps to obtain game gears to sell them on behalf of the defendant Kong was theft.[23] But, in 2016, another court decided that the act of acquiring game gears in game accounts in a similar way constituted illegal acquisition of computer information system data.[24] As we will see, the viewpoint that virtual property has data attributes is developing into a more common occurrence, causing virtual property disputes increasingly to be considered computer crimes.

The illegal acquisition of virtual property using computer techniques has also been held to be a computer crime, because the methods used to obtain the property involves computer and network violations. For example, in Hu's case,[25] the defendant Hu bought a type of Trojan virus; he then befriended chosen game players on the Internet and sent those files with the Trojan virus while chatting with them and thereafter controlled their transactions by controlling their access to their game roles. Hu transferred two game gears from the victims worth 9,259 yuan. The court believed that the defendant illegally invaded and controlled others' computer information systems by implanting the Trojan virus and that the

22 W. Zuofu, *Practical Research on Specific Provisions of Criminal Law*, (Beijing: China Fangzheng Press, 2012) at 1078.
23 *Criminal Judgment No. 120* of Donggang District People's Court of Rizhao City, Shandong Province (2014).
24 *Criminal Judgment No. 143* of Guangdong 1323 Initial Punishment of Huidong County People's Court (2016).
25 *Criminal Judgment No. 299* of Guangdong 0891 Punishment of the People's Court of Zhanjiang Economic and Technological Development Zone (2017).

act of acquiring stored, processed, or transmitted data from these systems constituted a crime.

Yet, it is worth noting that illegal acquisition of game gears without using any computer technique can also be defined as computer crime. For example, in Wang's case,[26] the defendant Wang bought more than 60,000 sets of online game accounts and passwords (all of which had been illicitly acquired by others) and resold them via the Internet, earning 69,093 yuan. In the first instance, the court sentenced him according to the crime of illegal acquisition of computer information system data, and in the second instance, the court supported this verdict.

(c) Virtual currency as property

Virtual currency here refers to virtual currency used on a network platform, including game currency, QQ coin, Bitcoin, and so forth.[27] Compared with

26 *Criminal Order No. 364* of Beijing First Intermediate People's Court (2017).
27 See:

> Virtual currency is a digital representation of value that can be digitally traded and functions as (1) a medium of exchange; and/or (2) a unit of account; and/or (3) a store of value, but does not have legal tender status (i.e., when tendered to a creditor is a valid and legal offer of payment) in any jurisdiction. . . . Defendant acted as 'payment instrument seller' and engaged in business of money transmitter by exchanging virtual currency for cash and marketing business of selling other's virtual currency, and thus defendant was required to register under statutory chapter governing money service businesses, although virtual currency did not have legal tender status and did not fall under definition of payment instrument under statutory chapter governing money service businesses; virtual currency was redeemable for currency, and virtual currency was used by several restaurants, doctors, and as payment for expert testimony.

> *State v. Espinoza* (Fla. Dist. Ct. App. 2019) 264 So. 3d 1055 at 1058. A New York Statutory regulation:

> defines virtual currency broadly, and includes all digital units of exchange that: (1) have a centralized repository or administrator; (2) are decentralized and have no centralized repository or administrator; or (3) may be created or obtained by computing or manufacturing effort. Virtual currency shall not be construed to include any of the following: (i) digital units that: (a) are used solely within online gaming platforms; (b) have no market or application outside of those gaming platforms; (c) cannot be converted into, or redeemed for, Fiat Currency3 or Virtual Currency; and (ii) may or may not be redeemable for real-world goods, services, discounts, or purchases; digital units that can be redeemed for goods, services, discounts, or purchases as part of a customer affinity or rewards program with the issuer and/or other designated merchants or can be redeemed for digital units in another customer affinity or rewards program; or (iii) digital units used as part of Prepaid Cards. (Regulations of the Superintendent of Financial Services: Virtual Currency [23 NYCRR] § 200.1 [p]). Virtual currency business activity includes the following conduct involving New York or a resident of New York: (1) receiving Virtual Currency for Transmission or Transmitting Virtual Currency, except where the transaction is undertaken for non-financial purposes and does not involve the transfer of more than a nominal amount

virtual chattels, virtual currency as an object of property crime seems more acceptable, because it has some monetary relation with real currency in the marketplace. For example, QQ coin is a type of virtual currency issued by Tencent and used to pay for QQ number services,[28] membership services, QQ game props and other QQ services. Normally, QQ can only be acquired by direct purchase (1QQ coin = 1 yuan). Therefore, for users who rely on QQ services, there is no difference between a loss of 1 QQ coin and a loss of 1 yuan.

Earlier cases of illegally obtained virtual currency were usually defined as property crime regardless of whether any computer technique was used. For example, in 2007, a court decided that the act of Xu and his accomplices stealing QQ coins by making fake calls, transferring QQ numbers and selling them for money constituted theft.[29] In the case of Lu and Li, Lu used an Internet software called *ADSL Password Terminator* to steal accounts, passwords and corresponding user information from many broadband users of the Jiangsu Branch of China Telecom Corporation Limited. Lu converted the points in each account into QQ coins to steal the victims' virtual property and sold them at the price of 1QQ coin for 0.85 yuan. Additionally, Lu gave partial information to Li to buy QQ coins for use and for sale. The defendant Lu stole 107,400 QQ coins in total, worth CNY 103,104 yuan. In this case, the court held Lu stole a huge amount of private and public property, constituting illegal possession and therefore theft.

However, at present, there is also a changing trend toward treating these sorts of dishonest property acquisitions as computer crimes. Zhou's case reflects this shift in attitude. The defendant Zhou exercised remote control over the computers of others by embedding the computer virus PCShare into their computers; he then stole their game coins in online games and sold them for approximately 70,000 yuan via the Internet. The court of the first instance sentenced Zhou to 11 years' imprisonment and fined him 10,000 yuan for the crime of larceny. Zhou lodged an appeal that resulted in the court of the second instance overturning the first-instance judgement by changing the accusation to illegal acquisition of computer system data on the grounds that the game coins as a virtual asset could not be assessed accurately. It was held that existing evidence made it impossible to give the asset a monetary value and thus it would not be punished as theft.[30]

---

of virtual currency; (2) storing, holding, or maintaining custody or control of Virtual Currency on behalf of others; (3) buying and selling Virtual Currency as a customer business; (4) performing Exchange Services as a customer business; or (5) controlling, administering, or issuing a Virtual Currency.

Chino v. New York Department of Financial Services (2017) 94 N.Y.S.3d 537.

28 QQ number service mainly includes: member level password protection, mobile phone retrieve password, mobile phone lock, member mailbox and other services.

29 *Criminal Judgment No. 73* of Zhejiang Higher People's Court (2007).

30 *Criminal Judgment No. 0097* of Bengbu Intermediate People's court, Anhui Province (2010).

(d) Questions raised

The term *virtual property* itself is similar to a protected object in property crime, and virtual property has real property value. Therefore, initially, the illegal acquisition of virtual property was usually treated as property crime in Chinese juridical practice. The main reason for the existing contradictions and repeated changes in the determination of the nature of the previously mentioned cases is that China's current legislation neither makes clear the nature of virtual property nor directly stipulates the method of deciding on the act of stealing virtual property. In Chinese criminal law, the property needs to reach a certain value to come within the purview of the criminal law of theft, but when the amount remains, it is impossible to determine whether the value crosses the threshold required for property offences. On the other hand, based on the proposal that virtual property has data attributes, the protection of data attributes over virtual property as a legal interest has begun to draw serious attention. As a result, illegal acquisition of virtual property is defined as computer crime, but the acts that used to be limited to those using computer techniques have begun to develop based on the expanded definition. Judicial practice has already rendered verdicts on cases of stolen virtual property based on accusations of sabotaging computer information, illicitly acquiring computer system data, and so forth.

This chapter argues that virtual property can constitute property for the purposes of bringing it within the protection of property offences. Treating virtual property as property in penal law does not go against the principle of legality, because some wrongs will be better labelled property crimes rather than computer network crimes, because the weight of the wrong will be the dishonest acquisition of the property, not the computer and network means used to acquire that property. The harm will be the loss of property, not the way that loss was caused. Sentencing also needs to reflect the wrongfulness and harmfulness of the defendant's conduct. Mislabelling the wrong gives the sentencing judge less guidance about what is an appropriate sentence.[31]

4. Virtual property as property

When an actor illegally obtains another's virtual property by stealing it, it can be confirmed that this conduct belongs in the category of theft and fraud because the actor's purpose is to deliberately and dishonestly possess another's virtual property. It would be incongruous to argue that virtual property is property of sufficient value to warrant criminal law protection, but not treat the wrong of a dishonest acquisition as a property offence. We take the view that in Chinese law, property must have three characteristics: the possibility of management or control, transfer possibility and value. Without these three characteristics, there is no

---

31 D. J. Baker, *The Right Not to be Criminalized: Demarcating Criminal Law's Authority*, (Oxford: Routledge, 2011).

property for the purposes of invoking a property offence rather than a network or computer misuse offence.

First, there is a possibility of management or control. Sir James Fitzjames Stephen writes:

> A thing is the property of a man when the man is enabled by law to deal with the thing at his pleasure in every way in which the law permits him to deal with it, and to exclude all other persons from dealing with it in any way whatever except by his consent.[32]

Relative to the victim, we cannot say that the victim possesses a certain property if it is impossible for the victim to manage and control that property. Baker writes: "When another assumes the right to control (even intangible property such as digital images) property that belongs to another he deprives the owner of her right to control and exclusively use that property."[33] Crimes such as theft manifest that others' possession or control of property is either transferred to or possessed by another without consent or lawful justification. Only property that an owner has the exclusive right to control and manage can be property for the purposes of establishing a property offence.

As we all know, the possibility of managing virtual property is mainly realised through having exclusive control of the account. As a user, one exclusively controls virtual property by purchasing and saving it to a registered and secure account. This is the same as controlling one's bank funds through exclusive password access (usually face recognition nowadays) to one's banking app. In other words, the account is a warehouse for storing virtual property and is also a mark of the user having exclusive control over the virtual property. It is not only having such control that counts, but also having the legal right to exclusive control.[34]

Second, there is transfer possibility.[35] An actor infringes on another's property rights if he or she interferes with the owner's ability to transfer that property.

---

32 J. F. Fitzjames Stephen, *A History of the Criminal Law of England*, (London: Macmillan, 1883) Vol. III, at 122.

33 Baker, *op. cit. supra*, note 15 at 1245.

34 Gray writes:

> Assignment (whether voluntary or involuntary) constitutes the ultimate release or abnegation of control over the access of strangers to the benefits of an excludable resource. In the absence of such assignment, "property" in an excludable resource can be vindicated against third parties precisely because the resource is excludable.

K. Gray, "Property in Thin Air," (1991) 50 *Cambridge L.J.* 252 at 302.

35 Anderson writes:

> Snare formulaically suggests that property exists when three primary rules are satisfied, namely (1) A has the right to use P, (2) others may use P if, and only if, A consents, and (3) A may permanently transfer the rights under 1 and 2 to other specific persons by consent. To these three primary rules, three supplementary rules can be added, namely (4) punishment rules detailing what may happen to B if she wrongfully interferes with A's use of P,

There is no doubt that virtual property can be transferred and that a person can interfere with that right if he or she takes control of virtual property belonging to another without consent or lawful justification.[36] The Ministry of Culture in June 2010 issued a guidance note titled "Interim Measures for Administration of Online Games," which indicates that:

> virtual currency of online games refers to virtual exchange tools issued by online game organisations, represented in specific digital unit, purchased directly or indirectly by online game users with legal tender in a certain proportion, which exists outside a game program and is saved into the server in the form of electromagnetic records.[37]

It is because virtual property has transfer possibility that it can be an object of infringement.

Third, there is economic value.[38] Relative to the protection of legal interests, an object is not worthy of being protected if it has no value.[39] The problem is how we understand value. There are three main theories of value in Chinese penal theory. In the first, property value includes objective and subjective value.[40] Here, the goods can be an object of property crime as long as they have objective or subjective value. Objective value means that the property has objective economic value. For example, automobiles, food, money and other items have objective value. Subjective value means the property has emotional value to the owner

---

(5) damage rules requiring B to pay compensation if she damages P without A's consent, and (6) liability rules specifying that if A's use of P results in damage to others then she will be held responsible.

G. Anderson, "Towards an Essentialist Legal Definition of Property," (2019) 68 *DePaul L. Rev.* 481 at 489 quoting F. Snare, "The Concept of Property," (1972) 9 *Am. Phil. Q.* 200.

36 Baker argues that the police can lawfully take control of contraband without the consent of its owner, because it would have a lawful justification for taking control of such property. "However, this does not mean that illegal drugs are not property: *R. v. Smith* [2011] 1 Cr. App. R. 30." Baker, *op. cit. supra*, note 15 at 1333.

37 However, Gray, like Sir James Fitzjames Stephen, points out: "It is that the criterion of 'excludability' gets us much closer to the core of 'property' than does the conventional legal emphasis on the *assignability* or enforceability of benefits." Gray, *op. cit. supra*, note 34 at 294; 301 (emphasis added).

38 Similarly, in English Law,

> One may steal, for example, a commercially worthless piece of paper, because there are many pieces of paper that people want to keep, even though they have no market value. If a thing were derisively worthless, like a used matchstick, the prosecution could not establish dishonesty.

Baker, *op. cit. supra,* note 15 at 1233.

39 "The criminal law involves censure, punishment and stigma. Therefore, it should be used as a last resort." Baker, *op, cit. supra*, note 31 at 153. The criminal law cannot be used to resolve petty disputes, but should be invoked to deter conduct that threatens to harm the interests of others in a substantial sense.

40 K. Yoshio, *Specific Provisions of Criminal Law*, (Tokyo: Seirin Shoin, 1963) at 264.

and possessor, which does not need to be evaluated by money. For example, love letters and photos have subjective value.[41] In the third viewpoint, property value includes exchange value (monetary value) and use value. The goods can also have use value without exchange value. For example, love letters are considered goods with use value.[42]

Doubt exists in the first viewpoint. Goods with subjective value can be the object of property crime only when they have objective economic value, if they can be evaluated in monetary terms. In essence, this view denies that goods with subjective value can be an object of property crime, even if taking them could cause sufficient harm to warrant a criminal law response.[43] Therefore, it is difficult for people to accept that worthless property that has great subjective value is left unprotected by property offences. In some cases, the harm caused by the theft of subjectively valuable property might be a privacy loss and be best dealt with through a privacy law, but in many cases, no other law will apply. In many cases, the harm might be limited to losing something that only has semimetal value and the loss of which will not cause a collateral harm such as a violation of privacy.

Goods with use value include reading and viewing value, as well as the value of meeting the owner and possessor's spiritual needs. Here, use value is not meant in the economic sense, but only signifies objective action or spiritual/emotional meaning for the owner and possessor. Ordinary citizens purchase the property not to exchange it, but for their personal use. For example, a patient's medical history over the long term is not likely to have economic value, but it has important use value for the patient. It is arguable that property with use value ought to be protected by property offences[44] when it can be demonstrated that its loss could cause collateral harm beyond trivial mental annoyance and that harm is sufficiently serious to warrant using the criminal law to deter it. The court system and criminal justice system would be completely clogged if every trivial dispute over otherwise valueless property were brought to trial. This ought not exclude trying to guard against rare remote harms that are out of the ordinary.[45]

It is also certain that virtual property has both objective value and use value. For example, people can use game currency to purchase game products or play

41 D. Shigemitsu, *Outline of Criminal Law*, (Tokyo: Sōbunsha, 1972) at 551; Ohtsika Hitoshi, *Introduction to Criminal Law* (Tokyo: Yuhikaku Supplement, 2005) Vol. 3, at 173.

42 N. Atsushi, *The Division of Criminal Law*, (Tokyo: Seibondou, 2009) at 231.

43 Take the case given in Baker, *op. cit. supra*, note 15 at 1333, where the builder copied nude photographs of a woman he found in her bedroom while employed to do building repairs in her house. Suppose he had posted the private nude photographs online and caused the woman great mental distress. In Chinese law, he might be liable for some other kind of offence, but he would not be liable for the theft of the photographs.

44 See *Criminal Code of the People's Republic of China*, Article 269.

45 In one dispute over virtual property, the aggrieved party took the law into his own hands and murdered the person who stole his property. J. Rogers, "A Passive Approach to Regulation of Virtual Worlds," (2008) 76 *Geo. Wash. L. Rev.* 405 at 409–410. This was not a remote harm of the crimianlisable kind (D. J. Baker, "The Moral Limits of Criminalizing Remote Harms," [2007] 10 *New Crim. L. Rev.* 370 [2007]), but an extraordinary an unforeseeable crime that was independent of any property crime.

games. People can also use game equipment to play games. It has been reported that in some cases, a divorcing couple put greater emphasis on keeping game equipment instead of their real estate in the divorce settlement. The paid transfer of virtual property has become a universal phenomenon. Therefore, virtual property has objective value (exchange value) in the secondary market.[46]

That virtual property is recognised, as property in Chinese penal law does not mean *any* virtual property qualifies. There are many types of virtual property, including account numbers, goods and currency. The property tests mentioned previously concerning control/exclusivity, assignability and value seemed to be recognised as giving rise to property under theft- and fraud-type offences. Otherwise, even virtual property that is universally acknowledged as property is excluded from the protection of these offences. For example, although ordinary QQ numbers and email accounts have the possibility of management and transfer possibility, they do not have value because they are only a means of communication. Therefore, they are not recognised as property in Chinese criminal law. Hence, it is contended that that any virtual property not coming within the purview of the previously mentioned property tests are not protected by property offences in Chinese criminal law.

5. The principle of legality

When crimes involving virtual property came into Chinese view for the first time, a huge controversy was triggered about whether virtual property is property for the purposes of invoking the criminal law. Most scholars argued it could not be, because it would violate the principle of legality. The example given by Baker[47] of a builder copying a woman's subjectively valuable nude photographs might not come within Articles 363–364 of *Criminal Code of the People's Republic of China* (the "Crime of Producing, Selling, or Disseminating Obscene Materials"), since the photographs were not posted online, but rather were kept for the builder's personal use. The American court treated the privacy violation caused by the builder copying the nude photographs he found in her house while doing building work as theft, but it was really a privacy violation and the theft label does not really reflect the wrongfulness and harmfulness of his conduct. Merely copying a person's photographs would not come within the computer network offences, because they are not being taken from or downloaded to a computer if they are simply copied onto a digital camera.[48] Article 286 of the *Criminal Code* provides:

> Whoever violates states regulations and deletes, alters, adds, and interferes in computer information systems, causing abnormal operations of the systems and grave consequences, is to be sentenced to not more than five years of fixed-term imprisonment or criminal detention; when the consequences are

46 Cherry, *op. cit. supra*, note 20.
47 Baker, *op. cit. supra*, note 15 at 1333.
48 *Ibid.*

particularly serious, the sentence is to be not less than five years of fixed-term imprisonment.

Whoever violates state regulations and deletes, alters, or adds the data or application programs installed in or processed and transmitted by the computer systems, and causes grave consequences, is to be punished according to the preceding paragraph.

Whoever deliberately creates and propagates computer virus and other programs, which sabotage the normal operation of the computer system and cause grave consequences, is to be punished according to the first paragraph.

It also would be nonsense to try to say that copying such photos interfered with the victim's freedom of communication, so such conduct would go unpunished in China. The only case of virtual property theft to be reported in the United Kingdom was prosecuted as a computer misuse offence, when it would have been better labelled as theft given the amount of money stolen.[49] Japan, Korea, Germany and Italy also take the position that theft only covers property that has some economic value beyond sentimental value. If virtual property cannot be determined to be objectively valuable, it simply cannot meet the requirements laid down by the principle of legality.[50] In other words, although virtual property would come within a wider normative theory of property such as "the utilitarian theory of Bentham, the labour theory of Locke, and the personhood theory of Radin,"[51] it does not currently meet the legally recognised definition of property required by the *Criminal Code of China*.

Chinese scholars are heavily influenced by legal theories from civil law jurisdictions rather than those from common law jurisdictions, but this is due to the tendency to look for simple comparisons rather than deeper conceptual meanings. This sort of comparative methodology is sometimes very unhelpful. First, the stipulations in Chinese criminal law are different from those in Germany, Japan and other countries. Therefore, we cannot indiscriminately imitate their stipulations and practices. These jurisdictions have their own complex private law rules and social factors that determine the compass of what they define as property. For

49 See:

> In court Ashley Mitchell admitted penetrating the systems of online gaming firm Zynga to steal the chips. He laundered the haul via a series of Facebook accounts in a bid to escape being caught. The billions of virtual poker chips had a face value of $12m (£7.4m) but Mr Mitchell realised only £53,000 from sales before he was apprehended.

"Hacker Faces Jail Over Poker Chip Theft," (London: *BBC News*, 3 February 2011). This case would meet the virtual property test for the purposes of theft outlined in this chapter, not only because the virtual chips had a real monetary value, but because the virtual property is controllable and transferable.

50 C. Yunliang and Z. Xin, "The Choice of Protection Path of Virtual Property in Criminal Law," (2009) 2 *Law Review* 146.

51 M. S. Boone, "Virtual Property and Personhood," (2008) 24 *Santa Clara Computer & High Tech. L.J.* 715 at 721.

a concept like property, it is necessary to look at the wider area of the private law of property. Virtual property as a concept has been recognised in Holland and New Zealand,[52] and has been conceptualised and widely debated in the common law literature. The literature we have quoted from the common law jurisdictions is more instructive on how virtual property might be conceptualised to bring it within the concept of property that the *Criminal Code of China* requires.

It is important to look at the substance, since legal definitions are relative to the given jurisdiction. Prior to 2011,[53] there was a fierce controversy in Japan about whether saving obscene images and image data to a computer hard drive as information should be considered obscene goods.[54] However, what is regarded as obscene is in the eye of the beholder, and thus is socially contingent.[55] In China, any nudity apart from that for medical purposes is considered obscene and would be caught without the sort of debate that took place in Japan.[56] Similarly, the conduct of an adult female having sexual intercourse with a boy is identified as child molestation (compulsory indecency) without controversy in Japan[57] and England, but many people think that it violates the principle of legality to apply Chinese law to this wrong.[58] Most would agree it is a great wrong that requires punishment, but it does not fit within the strict legal definition in the *Criminal Code of China*.

A strictly literal interpretation means one legal definition is unlikely to include another definition when two legal provisions are stipulated. In English criminal law, there are wide and narrow offences, so if the prosecution cannot bring

---

52 See note 2 *supra*.
53 Before 2011, according to Article175 of the Japanese criminal law, the object of obscenity is *obscene documents, pictures or other obscenities*. In 2011, the obscenity of "recording media related to electromagnetic records" was added.
54 Yamaguchi Atsushi, *The Division of Criminal Law*, (Tokyo: Hashige, 2010) *at* 508.
55 Baker writes:

> It is not a crime to feed homeless people in China or Britain, but it is in some parts of the U.S.. . . . The harmfulness of many acts is dependent on convention and socialization. If x were to paint a bright yellow stripe across the Mona Lisa her conduct, but unless we consider the underlying social norms it is not possible to comprehend the wrongness, badness or harmfulness of intentionally painting a bright yellow stripe on an old painting. Some might argue that the additional stripe is art in itself and thus adds to the aesthetics of the original painting, if they have not been socialized into perceiving it as a cultural artefact. Painting a stripe on it would not diminish anyone's essential or primitive-type survival resources in the way that destroying a remote tribe's only source of water and food would. There is something much more universal about the latter harm, because suffering severe dehydration and starvation would impact all humans in the same way. The objective wrongness of conventional harms and umbrages can only be ascertained by considering contextual, circumstantial, social and empirical factors.

Baker, *op. cit. supra*, note 31 at 12; 20.

56 This also shows that in China's criminal law, *things* and *articles* are not limited to physical objects.
57 N. Noliyuki, "The Division of Criminal Law," (2012) *Koubundou* 89.
58 G. Mingxuan and M. Kechang, *The Criminal Law*, (Beijing: China Legal Publishing House, 1999) at 833.

conduct within one offence, it will try for another.[59] Chinese prosecutors do the same. This sometimes means a wrong is not given the crime label that is most apt for describing the wrong involved, or it is not punished at all. When the principle of legality is applied, the conduct has to fit within the definition of a pre-existing crime. It is entirely possible the wrong to include the content brings it within the definition of more than one crime.

Alas, Chinese thinking on the subject has been led astray by the influence of foreign law that is often outdated and in need of reform itself.[60] For example, a recent review in Japan recommended:

> The Act on Prevention of Transfer of Criminal Proceeds is amended to add Virtual Currency Exchange Service Providers to 'Specified Business Operators' who assume obligations thereunder, thereby imposing on them the following obligations, etc., prescribed by the same Act: 1. Obligation to identify customers; 2. Obligation to prepare and maintain verification records; 3. Obligation to prepare and maintain transaction records; 4. Obligation to report suspicious transactions to the relevant authority; and 5. Measures to appropriately conduct verification at the time of transaction.[61]

When people say there is a difference between property interests and property per se, the term *property* is obviously used in the narrow sense of the word. For example, a mobile phone is a property and the associated creditor's rights are interests in the property. However, when people use a broad property concept, the term *property* includes both the narrow definition of property and interests of property. On the other hand, the existing difference between interests of property and the narrow definition of the term *property* is not a reason to deny that interests of property can be the object of theft. Section 263 of the *German Criminal Code* provides:

> (1) Whosoever with the intent of obtaining for himself or a third person an unlawful material benefit damages the property of another by causing or maintaining an error by pretending false facts or by distorting or suppressing true facts shall be liable to imprisonment not exceeding five years or a fine.

---

59 Baker, *op. cit. supra*, note 15 at Chapter 1.
60 *Penal Code of Japan (Act No.45 of 1907)* Article 235, provides: "(Theft) A person who steals the property of another commits the crime of theft and shall be punished by imprisonment with work for not more than 10 years or a fine of not more than 500,000 yen." Meanwhile, Article 246–2 of the *Penal Code of Japan* provides:

> (Computer Fraud) In addition to the provisions of Article 246, a person who obtains or causes another to obtain a profit by creating a false electromagnetic record relating to acquisition, loss or alteration of property rights by in putting false data or giving unauthorized commands to a computer utilized for the business of another, or by putting a false electromagnetic record relating to acquisition, loss or alteration of property rights into use for the administration of the matters of another shall be punished by imprisonment with work for not more than 10 years.

61 T. Nakazaki and K. Kawai, "Development of Legal Framework for Virtual Currencies in Japan – Bill Submitted to the Diet," (2016) *FSTGN* 1.

This provision does not define property, but simply states that those who damage property with the particular purpose of obtaining unlawful material benefit shall be liable. Simple theft is covered in Section 248a of the German code which provides: "1) Whoever takes movable property belonging to another away from another with the intention of unlawfully appropriating it for themselves or a third party incurs a penalty of imprisonment for a term not exceeding five years or a fine." This, unlike English and American[62] common law, does not protect intangible property.[63] The *German Criminal Code* Section 202a provides:

> (1) Whoever, without being authorized to do so, obtains access, by circumventing the access protection, for themselves or another, to data which were not intended for them and were specially protected against unauthorized access incurs a penalty of imprisonment for a term not exceeding three years or a fine.

This offence also seems totally inapt for dealing with the theft of intangible property.

The Dutch Supreme Court in its judgement (No. S 10/00101 J Criminal Chamber), applied Section 310 of the *Dutch Penal Code*[64] to virtual property and held it could be subject to theft, even though that section does not expressly provide protection for intangible or virtual property. Nonetheless, the Dutch decision does lend support to the claim that China ought to recognise controllable and valuable virtual property as property for the purpose of the law of theft. At Paragraph 3.3.2. of the judgement, the Justices of the Supreme Court of the Netherlands said: "[T]he legislature has, through various penal provisions such as those in art. 310 Penal Code, provided for punishment for those who intentionally evade the effective control of any property which belongs to another with the intention of unlawfully appropriating it." The case hinged on the fact that

---

62 "And intangible property, such as '[c]onfidential business information has long been recognized as property.' " *United States v. Yihao Pu* (N.D. Ill. 2014) 15 F. Supp. 3d 846 at 850.
63 Baker *op. cit. supra*, note 15 at 1243 writes:

> Section 4(1) of the *Theft Act 1968* (U.K.) mentions "things in action and other intangible property" as the subject of theft. "Things in action" (also archaically called "choses in action") are rights that can be enforced only by bringing an action and not by taking possession; they are "property rights" to the extent that they can be bought and sold. The most obvious thing in action is the creditor's right to payment of a debt. Shares, patents, copyrights, and trade marks have also been called things in action, but Parliament has taken away that name from patents (which, however, remain intangible property, otherwise called incorporeal property.)

64 Section 310 simply provides:

> Any person who takes any property belonging in whole or in part to another person with the intention of unlawfully appropriating it, shall be guilty of theft and shall be liable to a term of imprisonment not exceeding four year s or a fine of the fourth category.

> The Supreme Court of the Netherlands drew on the old electricity theft cases to imply that the law covered intangible property such as virtual property.

the virtual items had an objective value and was under the exclusive control of a player.

In English and American law, the law of property determines what is property, which is a branch of private law. The criminal law then expressly acknowledges the types of property that are subject to theft. The private law of property recognises a range of intangible property rights as property per se such as a chose in action.[65] Some forms of intangible property are expressly excluded from the law of theft because they copyright or patent laws protect these rights.[66] The problem with the special provisions in the *Criminal Code of China* is that the interpreter cannot discover whether property includes property rights based only on the concept of *property* in Article 264 of the Code.[67] A conclusive interpretation of a concept must be based on specific reasons. Among these, if the interpreter's conclusion can be verified by other articles of law, it can be considered valid. For instance, Article 224 of Chinese criminal law stipulates that one form of crime of contractual fraud is going into hiding after receiving the other party's goods, payment for goods, cash paid in advance or property for guaranty.

Goods, payment for goods and cash paid in advance are all property, yet property for guaranty not only limits the definition to property in the narrow sense, but includes property rights such as creditor's rights. Obviously, the object of a crime of contractual fraud can involve property rights.[68] In other words, the property in Chapter 5 of the special provisions of criminal law includes property rights. For additional explanation, *Amendment (IX)* to the criminal law of the People's Republic of China further affirms that property rights belong to property. For instance, Paragraph 1 in the newly added Article 307–1 in *Amendment (IX)* to the criminal law expressly provides for a crime of false action. Paragraph 3 then stipulates that someone who commits any other crime while committing the crime of illegally occupying another person's property or evading his or her lawful

---

65 See:

> A "chose in action" is pertinently defined as "[a] proprietary right in personam, such as a debt owed by another person. . . ." . . . "Larceny of chose in action" occurs when 'any person shall feloniously steal, take and carry away, or take by robbery, any bank note, check or other order for the payment of money issued by or drawn on any bank . . . being the property of any other person. . . ."

> *State v. Grier* (2012) 224 N.C. App. 150, 153–154. See also L. Chambers, "Misappropriation of Cryptocurrency: Propelling English Private Law into the Digital Age?" (2016) 5 *Journal of International Banking and Financial Law* 263.

66 Baker, *op. cit. supra*, note 15 at 1243–1245. Baker argues that the English courts have erred in not recognizing that valuable trade secrets and confidential information fall within the definition of property provided for in Section 4 of the *Theft Act 1968*.

67 Without referring to the expression of other laws, it is considered that the property stipulated in Article 264 of the criminal law is property in a narrow sense and does not include property interests, which is just a previous understanding (or the opinion formed based on the provisions of other countries' criminal laws), rather than a natural conclusion.

68 Zhang Mingkai, "Property Interest is the Object of Crime of Fraud," (2005) 3 *Science of Law* 74.

debts as mentioned in Paragraph 1 shall be convicted and punished according to the provisions of the crime with the heavier penalty.

The draft of the Ninth Amendment of the *Criminal Code of China* once stipulated that:

> Whoever commits false action, occupying any other person's property or evading his or her lawful debts will be punished according to Article 226 of *Criminal Law* with the heavier penalty; (i.e., convicted of the crime of fraud and punished with the heavier penalty).

During the discussion of the draft, someone pointed out that this situation often constitutes the crime of fraud but that it may also constitute other crimes. If state functionaries take advantage of their position and collude with others to occupy public property by false action, it may constitute the crime of corruption. It is not reasonable to convict a defendant for these crimes as fraud. Therefore, the second instance of the draft revised the relevant stipulations to form this provision.[69] The property in occupying another's property apparently includes property in the narrow sense, as well as property rights. Evading his or her lawful debts obviously belongs to property rights. This stipulation demonstrates that the property stipulated in Chapter 5 of the special provisions of criminal law not only recognises property in the narrow sense, but includes intangible property such as proprietary right *in personam* (i.e., rights that can be enforced only by bringing a legal action and not by taking possession). Furthermore, the crime of theft may be made out when an actor maliciously collaborates with the judge to conduct a false action, resulting in victims delivering property rights to the actor.[70] People holding the negative opinion may consider that the stipulation in Paragraph 3 in Article 307–1 of the criminal law is a legal fiction. However, if the negative opinion is adopted, the following situation forms: the conduct of occupying another person's property rights by false action constitutes crimes such as fraud and corruption, while the conduct of occupying other's property rights by methods other than false action will not constitute crimes such as fraud or corruption. Therefore, the same actions of occupying another's property rights will result in the difference in whether a crime was committed or not due to the different methods, which is clearly incongruous.

Furthermore, whether a certain interpretation is prohibited by the principles of legality should be concluded by considering various factors, including the purpose of the articles in the criminal law, the necessity for punishment of actions, the possibilities of national prediction, the coordination of articles in criminal law and the distance between the interpretation of the conclusion and the core meaning

---

69 Z. Tiewei, *Interpretation of the Ninth Amendment to the Criminal Law of the People's Republic of China*, (Beijing: China Legal Publishing House, 2015) at 243.

70 The private law rules on choses in action means that such cases are normally treated as fraud rather theft in English law. See the discussion in Baker, *op. cit. supra*, note 15 at 1249–1251. See also *R. v. Darroux* (2019) Q.B. 33.

of certain words. In most cases, it is not a question of how words are applied, but rather how to assess the articles' purpose and the nature of the conduct, along with how to balance the legal rights protection mechanism and the human rights protection mechanism.[71] Whether one adopts a wide or narrow interpretation of an Article in the *Criminal Code of China* will not only depend on normative factors, but on the purpose beyond the relevant Article. If the offence were aiming to protect property and property rights within a general range such as intangible property, it would not be helpful to overanalyse every form of intangible property to determine whether it is covered by an offence.

An interpretation that completely deviates from the purposes of the articles of law would lack validity, but whether something is property ought to be judged by uniform tests such as control and value. In China, if property is considered to not include property rights, then an action whereby an actor kidnaps someone and demands a remittance or transfer to his bank account should not be applied to the article of kidnapping others in order to claim properties (since deposits do not belong to properties in the narrow sense). This interpretation of the law would not only be difficult for the public to accept, but it also would be incongruous given the clear purpose of the law.

The first paragraph of Article 225–2 in Japanese criminal law stipulates that:

> A person who kidnaps another by force or enticement, for the purpose of causing the kidnapped person's relatives or any other person who would be concerned about the kidnapped person's safety to deliver any property, taking advantage of such concern, shall be punished by imprisonment for life or for a definite term of not less than 3 years.

Property and property rights are clearly distinguished in Japanese criminal law, yet Professor Nishida Noriyuki still held the point that this article should also be applied when an actor kidnaps someone and then requires the kidnapped person's relative or any other concerned person to make remittance or transfer to the actor's bank account.[72] In China, if property rights are not considered to be property, the state functionary's extortion and acceptance of property rights does not constitute a bribery crime. This simply cannot be the case in China.

In summary, the viewpoint that virtual property cannot be treated as property in accordance with the provisions found in the *Criminal Code of China*, because it violates the principles of legality is without merit. Treating virtual property as property for the purposes of Chinese criminal law can easily be reconciled with the principle of legality. The criminal law of China does not expressly preclude intangible property or property rights more generally from its purview. Rather, the criminal law provisions discussed in this chapter strongly imply that such property was intended to be covered by the *Code*. In fact, such property is better

---

71 Zhang Mingkai, *The Criminal Law*, (Beijing: Law Press, 2016) at 59.
72 N. Noriyuki, *The Division of Criminal Law*, (Tokyo, Hiroshi Wentang, 2012) at 81.

protected by property offences when it is property that has been lost, rather than by narrow offences such as the freedom of communication offences. While some foreign jurisdictions might take a different view, the common law jurisdictions, and the position taken by the Supreme Court of the Netherlands, strongly supports the thesis we have presented in this chapter.

6. China's current practice concerning virtual property

As we have seen, Chinese criminal law has no similar provision to Section 4 of the *Theft Act 1968 (U.K.)* which outlines what property is protected by all the property offences in English law. While what constitutes property is a question for private (property) law, not criminal law, the British government was careful to include a provision in its *Theft Act 1968* to expressly state which forms of property were protected by property offences such as theft. Virtual property is not expressly defined in Chinese criminal legislation or in Chinese property legislation. Furthermore, the *Criminal Code of China* does not have a provision expressly stating what forms of property are covered by its property offences, rather it is implied that any property meeting the tests of control/management, transferability and value will be protected by the property offences found in the Code.

The majority of Chinese criminal lawyers take the view that virtual property has both property and data attributes, but there is still a great debate about when it should be treated as property rather than mere data. With the rapid development of network technology in recent years, the number of cases of illegal acquisition of virtual property belonging to another has increased. Academics have started to debate what kind of attributes virtual property needs for tort law to apply. The current situation continues to be that there are different criminal theories of what constitutes virtual property and different judicial judgements about when to treat its theft as theft rather than as a network crime. Some scholars insist that virtual property is a kind of property that comes within purview of property offences, but quasi-government organisations suggest it has the attributes of data and should be protected by computer misuse types of offences.[73] As we saw at the start of this chapter, the courts have sometimes treated the act of stealing virtual property as theft but at other times as a computer crime (that is, a crime of illegally acquiring data from a computer information system or the crime of destroying a computer system).

It is noteworthy that, although it is still difficult to determine the act of controlling another user's account and transferring game equipment and coins using false identity authentication information as a theft, the judgements made over the last two years show a tendency to determine such acts as crimes of illegal acquisition of computer information system data. The data attribute is starting to

---

73 Long Weiqiu, "Research on Data Property Right Construction and its System," (2017) 4 *Political and Legal Forum* 63.

become dominant in judicial practice. This approach works if the information has only a subjective value, but it does not properly label the conduct when theft of virtual goods worth thousands or millions are simply punished as data offences.

The change comes from quasi-government organisations which support the data attributes of virtual property. For example, in 2012, the policy research institute of the Supreme People's Court pointed out that virtual property was comprised of electromagnetic records and electronic data, not property, in its approval of a case of virtual property theft. In 2013, the Supreme People's Court and the Supreme People's Procuratorate issued the *Explanation on Several Issues about the Applicable Law for Dealing with Criminal Cases of Stealing* and stated it was not appropriate to treat the act of stealing virtual property as a theft since a series of practical problems would occur. Specifically, valuing the property would be impossible due to a lack of generally recognised values for virtual goods. It was held that if it was necessary to investigate the criminal responsibility of a given person for such wrongdoing, such an act could be treated as a cybercrime, such as the crime of illegal acquisition of computer information system data.[74]

Although "approval" and "interpretation" are not judicial explanations in a strict sense, they do represent the standpoints of quasi-government organisations and play a guiding role in judicial practice. Various judicial authorities no longer determine the act of stealing virtual property as a theft when convicting and punishing, but as a crime of illegal acquisition of computer information system data. Supportive scholars point out that infringement of virtual property consists of modifying a computer information data, but the same can be said of hacking into a bank account and removing its digital balance. The only difference is that the latter example does not raise a valuation issue.[75]

However, there are limitations if all acts of stealing virtual property are treated as cybercrimes. First, illegal acquisition of computer information system data will not always be the right label and will not reflect the wrong that is being deterred, and thus will not give the right warning to citizens about what not to do. Computer and network misuse will also be relevant at times, and in England, a defendant could be charged with both crimes if he or she hacked a computer to steal large sums of money.[76] It is obviously is crime mislabelling[77] simply to treat theft of virtual property that could be worth millions as a data breach. Crime labels should reflect the conduct that is being criminalised so that people have fair warning about the nature of the wrong being proscribed. For example, Zhang spent

---

74 Yu Haisong, "Network Crime Trend and Criminal Countermeasures Adjustment," (2018) *Qiaoqiao Lawyer* 12 at 14.
75 Chen and Zhou, *op. cit. supra*, note 51.
76 See for example, *R. v. Brown* [2014] EWCA Crim 695 where the defendant was charged with possession of articles for use in fraud, contrary to Section 6(1) of the *Fraud Act 2006* and of securing unauthorised access to computer material with intent, contrary to Section 2(1)(e) of *the Computer Misuse Act 1990*.
77 B. Mitchell, "Multiple Wrongdoing and Offence Structure: A Plea for Consistency and Fair Labelling," (2001) 64(3) *Modern L.R.* 393; C. M. V. Clarkson, "Theft and Fair Labelling," (1993) 56(4) *Modern L.R.* 554.

RMB 50,000 purchasing QQ coins and other virtual properties that were later stolen by Li. If Li's act were determined as simply a crime of illegal acquisition of computer information system data, Zhang's conduct would not be properly labelled as major theft. The harm and wrong is not only illegally accessing and manipulating computer data, but also a substantial dishonest acquisition of property belonging to another.

Furthermore, when an actor uses other methods to illegally acquire another's virtual property such as game coins, it is hard to fit the wrong within the definition of our current computer crimes. Example 1: A and others threatened a victim with violence in a game arcade, forced him to tell them his web account and password and then pocketed his QQ coins worth tens of thousands of yuan by setting a new password.[78] In this case, no computer information system was illegally invaded, let alone sabotaged, and such an act is not a key component of the crime of illegal acquisition of computer information system data. Example 2: B inveigled another person to transfer his QQ coins worth tens of thousands of yuan to B's account. This act is also impossible to determine as a computer crime. Example 3: C, a network operator employee, took advantage of his position to legally access a computer information system, from which he stole and then sold virtual properties. Such an act cannot be determined as a computer crime, either. Apparently, the point of view that all problems can be solved if all acts of stealing virtual property are determined to be crimes of illegal acquisition of computer information system data is undesirable as it is established without a comprehensive understanding of all possible circumstances, thus leaving obvious punishment loopholes.

Additionally, the principle of appropriate punishment for a crime will fail if all acts of stealing virtual property are treated as computer crimes. For example, A1 prepared RMB 500,000 in cash to buy QQ coins but had them all stolen by Party A before placing the order. B bought QQ coins worth RMB 500,000 immediately after RMB 500,000 cash was prepared but had not yet used them after the purchase. Party B immediately hacked the computer information system and stole all of B's QQ coins. In accordance with the previously mentioned viewpoint, Party A should be convicted of theft and sentenced to a fixed-term imprisonment of more than 10 years or life and Party B should be convicted of the crime of illegal acquisition of computer information system data and sentenced to a fixed-term imprisonment of less than three years or detention. Some may think that it is appropriate to sentence Party B based on the extremely severe circumstances of such a crime. However, Party B's act of illegal acquisition of computer information system data itself cannot be judged as an extremely severe case. If it were considered an extremely severe case, the amount of property infringed upon by the actor must be taken into consideration. In turn, this indicates that attention shall be paid to the protection of the victim's properties. In addition, even if the

---

78 Huo Shiming and Zhang Guoqiang, "Virtual Property Encounter Real Robbery Sentencing Confusion," (*Jurisprudence Daily*, 2009).

suitable statutory sentence for extremely severe cases is applied, it is still difficult to fit the punishment with the crime.

To sum up, the point of view and practice of determining the act of illegal acquisition of others' virtual properties as a computer crime have obvious limitations, because punishment loopholes may be formed, resulting in punishment that may not be suitable for the crime.

7. The value of virtual property

Although it is feasible to hold that virtual property is property for the purposes of applying the property offences found in Chinese criminal law, we need to be able to convincingly value virtual property if it is to be protected by such offences. The constraint against criminalising the theft of property that only has a sentimental value is a worthy constraint, because it prevents over-criminalisation. It means the criminal justice system is not clogged up with petty property disputes that do not warrant such a serious response as criminalisation. When property is stolen that can cause collateral harm such as a person's nude photographs, any gap in the law should be plugged by having a privacy offence that properly labels the wrong involved.

How can we set a standard for objectively valuating virtual property? We not only need to make sure it has sufficient value to make the law of theft relevant, but also need to know the value so that a proportionate sentence can be handed down. Chinese law, like English law, allows for a heavier sentence when the sum stolen is greater.

There are two academic theories about how to determine the value of virtual property: first, the value of virtual property shall be determined based on what the player spent generating it; second, the value of virtual property shall be determined based on the value of the virtual property itself; i.e., its market transaction price.[79] This allows for a straightforward conviction and sentence that is proportionate to the actual economic value of the property. However, if a broader analysis is taken, there is the risk of misidentifying services and labour per se as property.[80]

The only issue with this straightforward current market value analysis of the property is that any sentence would have to be proportionate with the value of the virtual property at the time the defendant stole it. If the defendant thought she was stealing virtual property worth 400 yuan but due to capital gains the real value is 40,000 yuan, then the defendant's sentence should only be for what she

---

79 Tao Xinping and Liu Zhiren, "On the Legal Protection of Network Virtual Property," (2017) 4 *Political Science and Law* 99; Cherry, *op. cit. supra*, note 20.
80 Baker, *op. cit. supra*, note 15 at 1477 *et seq.*, points out that labour is not property, even when supplied on contract as a legitimate service. It is for this reason that in England, Section 11 of the *Fraud Act 2006* is narrowly tailored to criminalize those who dishonestly obtain a service intending not to pay.

or he was intending to steal – 400 yuan of virtual property. Therefore, sentences should apply respectively to the value of the virtual property stolen.

The first category of virtual property is what is purchased by a user from an Internet service provider or a third party with a relatively stable price and a value that is unlikely to change due to the user's conduct, such as QQ coin, game currency, etc. The virtual property falling into this category has two characteristics: first, such virtual property is sold by the service provider at a definite price and it has a relatively stable price that will not change easily; second, such virtual coins do not belong to the service provider, but are acquired by the user (typically an ordinary consumer) by means of purchase rather than through the user's own work or game events. Based on these two closely related characteristics, the value of such virtual property stolen or defrauded by an actor should be calculated in accordance with the official price published by the service provider.

Taking QQ coins as an example: after purchasing a certain number of QQ coins with real money, a user can obtain online services equivalent to that sum, which has no difference from the user's entitlement to real property. If an actor illegally acquires virtual coins, the victim's loss is completely consistent with the official price published by the service provider. In other words, there should be no difference in the calculation method for this category of virtual property and general merchandise. In addition, general merchandise may depreciate, thus requiring professionals' evaluation. But virtual property like QQ coins will not depreciate. Therefore, the value of this virtual property category can be directly calculated in accordance with its official price.[81] However, in such cases, it is not feasible to calculate the level of the crime based on the amount of stolen goods disposed of by the actor because that amount would normally be lower than the official price, thus not matching the victim's loss. If the crime level were calculated based on the amount of stolen goods disposed of by the actor, the victim's legal interests would not be protected. In this regard, the sentence should reflect the value of what was stolen based on the defendant's knowledge of its value when he or she stole it.

The second category of virtual property is what a user purchases from an Internet service provider or a third party that is upgraded post-processing, such as game gears, characters, etc. This category of virtual property also has two characteristics: first, such virtual property has a definite but relatively lower price when the service provider sells it, and the user needs to upgrade it by investing a large amount of time and energy, thus giving it more value. Second, such virtual property belongs to the user, not to the service provider. How to determine the value of this type of virtual property is an important problem for trial judges, because the sentence has to reflect the value of the actual property loss while also punishing the defendant in proportion with the value he or she thought the property had.

---

81 There are actually two official prices for Internet service providers: the price at which they sell to users and the price they limit on their official trading platforms. This chapter argues that calculating the price at which Internet service providers are sold to users is convenient and uniform and does not result in a disadvantage to the defendant.

Complexity arises when the punishment and level of crime is based on the Internet service provider's original selling price. When a victim pays for virtual equipment or raw materials and then invests heavily in it (including costs for online gaming, expenses for surfing the Internet, time, technology, etc.) after the acquisition, the purchase price no longer reflects the level of crime because the user's investment is not part of the calculation. A comparison might be where an expert restorer of antique violins buys an old violin for 500 yuan then spends six months restoring it. The restored violin is now worth 10,000 yuan. If the thief intends to steal a 10,000-yuan violin, then there is no problem holding the thief liable for stealing a more valuable violin. It is not a matter of trying to argue that the thief stole the labour used to restore the violin, nor is it a matter of trying to argue that the thief stole the restoration "service," but simply a matter of arguing the thief knowingly stole a restored violin that had a value of 10,000 yuan.

Some people believe that the value of virtual property in online games can only be determined in accordance with the average market price at the time when the dispute occurs under current circumstances, specifically by performing statistical analysis on the price data from the market.[82] This chapter agrees with this viewpoint. At present, the player trading market for virtual property in China has become large scale. Players trade virtual properties online mainly through electronic transactions with the help of QQ, WeChat, other instant chat software, email or offline after communicating with each other online. Some websites have even established specialised service platforms for players to exchange and purchase virtual game properties, such as the virtual property trading platform Taobao. In fact, a whole set of virtual property conversion and trading mechanisms has been established among online player groups. In the virtual property trading market for players, most virtual properties have relatively stable market price.[83] Therefore, it is feasible to determine the value of virtual property based on the average market price. The same could be said of non-virtual property – value is determined by market norms.

The third category is virtual property of Internet service providers. For example, Tian and three others took advantage of the bugs in an online game in Shenzhen, broke through two servers' firewalls using specialised software, implanted more than 20 accounts with swiping cards and stole 130 billion game coins from the platform provider. After discussion, multiple experts decided that the price of this virtual property could be determined based on the points purchased by the player or on transactions made by the player with other players. The conclusion of the price evaluation was based on the crime date as the base date for price evaluation and on the market price of 100 million coins equal to RMB 350, so the 130 billion game coins stolen amounted to RMB 455,000.[84] However, the

---

82 Xinping and Zhiren, *op. cit. supra*, note 79.
83 Zhang Yuan, "A Discussion on the Determination of Virtual Property Value of Online Games," (2006) 11 *People's Judicature* 75.
84 The estimated value of 130 billion game coins of stolen virtual property is 450,000 yuan (in Chenduendu signature), *Qianjiang Evening News* 2009.05.21.

public might not accept that it is fair to sentence Tian to a fixed-term imprisonment of more than 10 years or even life, because the output of virtual property is viewed as different from the output of traditional property. The public simply do not generally believe that the platform service provider lost RMB 455,000.

Traditional output is linear. For example, how many grains a farmer can produce depends on how much land he has. Even if he uses more fertiliser and improves his planting technology, the growth of output per unit will still have a peak value. In general, it can only approach a certain higher land output per unit. If the farmer does not sleep or rest, he still cannot make much more money because his income is restricted to the relationship between output and input. In general, the output of any *res corporales* is confined to the total quantity of raw materials. Even if losses are reduced based on improvement of production technology, the output per unit of raw materials can only approach a certain high value.

However, virtual property is characterised by one-time output and unlimited sale. The production and development of software itself is a one-time investment, but its value can be generated through replication. How many people want to buy the virtual property, and how much value can the virtual property create? For example, the output and input of the virtual properties owned by Tencent have a non-linear or even no relationship to labour and other investment inputs. In the Tencent QQ zone, it may take several days for a couple of designers and programmers to design a virtual hat. Once that is done, the virtual hat will be sold at the price of 1 yuan per unit. If 1 million hats are sold, 1 million yuan of income is generated. Since the virtual hat is sold through electronic billing, there is no need to make a new hat when one sells. Therefore, there is nearly zero difference in cost no matter whether Tencent sells 100 million hats or 10,000 hats. This is perhaps why illegally downloading movies and books has never been categorised as a serious crime. It is barely enforced because an artist can live like a king 50 years after writing a single song, if the song is a hit. Most of the wealth protected by intellectual property rights has no relationship with the effort or labour used on producing it. A 2,000-page academic textbook will require far greater skill and effort to research and write than writing a 100-word song, but the income is likely to be little to nothing for the textbook while the song might earn its author millions every year for life. As a result, the relationship between income and cost of producing virtual property is very weak, but the profitability can be disproportionately high.

The loss of a user's virtual property is the same as the loss of property in real life. But the loss of an Internet service provider's virtual property is obviously different from the loss of property in real life. For example, 100 million QQ coins stolen from Tencent and 100 million yuan in cash stolen from Tencent are obviously two different things. If 100 million QQ coins are stolen, Tencent can still meet a user's requirements as long as he purchases QQ coins, no matter how many. Under the same conditions, Internet service providers' property loss cannot be compared with users' property loss. The same can be said of movies and ebooks.

8. Conclusion

We argue argued that virtual property should be taken seriously as a form of property that can be protected by property offences. We have tried to show how it is a form of property that has real value. While there are evaluation complexities, in many cases, a reasonable market value can be placed on virtual goods for the purposes of categorising the seriousness of the theft and for determining a proportionate sentence. We have also tried to show that the creator of virtual property, like the creator of copyright or patented material, will have an initial investment cost that will vary depending on what the intellectual property or virtual property is and on the expertise required to create it; repeated theft of digital copies of digital property, such as an e-book or movie, can cause great losses to a big corporation because it will sell fewer copies. A corporation might spend millions developing a new medicine, but an artist might spend little producing a song. Similarly, a corporation might not spend a great deal creating virtual property, but if others can steal it and sell it cheaply, then this will affect sales. It does not matter that sales simply rest on replicating the same property and selling it over and over, because if a person is not paying for it, there is less income.

It is the impact on sales that will be the real measure as far as a corporation is concerned, because it will have fewer people to sell its replicated virtual property to. Pirate movie sites do cost corporations millions each year in sales and royalties. The question for virtual property will be determining whether the sale of stolen property can affect the overall income for the corporation producing the virtual property. If it is cheaper to buy stolen virtual property, then why pay the corporation full value for the property? Hence, we think further research is required to evaluate the loss to a corporation when a secondary market of stolen virtual property is in place. However, the when it comes to private individual X stealing private individual Y's virtual property, we can see no barrier to evaluating it and treating it as property within the definition of the existing property offences found in the *Chinese Criminal Code*. However, we would recommend that *Chinese Criminal Code* adopt an enactment similar to Section 4 of the *Theft Act 1968*, which clearly outlines what property is protected by all the property offences in the *Criminal Code*, to prevent lawyers relying on misplaced "principle of legality" arguments to exclude certain thefts from being treated as thefts as opposed to being treated as data and network communications crimes.

6 Criminalising cybercrime facilitation by omission and its remote harm form in China

Liang Genlin and Dennis J. Baker

1. Introduction

Since the 1990s, the information society and the Internet have permeated almost every aspect of human activity, and this is now being compounded by artificial intelligence.[1] Information technology and the information society has passed the Web 1.0 era and has entered the Web 2.0 era and is moving towards the Web 3.0 era and beyond.[2] The basic feature of the Web 1.0 era was that human participation was mainly passive as far as online content was involved. The essence of the Web 2.0 era is that it involves greater human interaction and active participation. Comprehensive interconnection between humans and computers, netizens and netizens, netizens and networks, especially the "point-to-point" interaction with peer-to-peer (P2P) technology has become the basic feature of the network world.[3] Netizens are no longer passive audiences of information products, but are also participants in the creation, dissemination and sharing of information and related products. We are now in the mobile technology age.[4] Mobility has

---

1 G. Wagner, "Robot, Inc.: Personhood for Autonomous Systems?" (2019) 88 *Fordham L. Rev.* 591; U. Pagallo *et al.*,"The Middle-out Approach: Assessing Models of Legal Governance in Data Protection, Artificial Intelligence, and the Web of Data," (2019) 7(1) *T. & P.L.* 1; K. Raustiala and C. J. Sprigman, "The Second Digital Disruption: Streaming and the Dawn of Data-Driven Creativity," (2019) 94 *N.Y.U. L. Rev.* 1555.

2 Niesel writes:

> The evolution of the web has been marked with increased user interactivity and, even more concerning, a move towards background processes that create interactivity and user-provider relationships with relatively little action on the part of the user. The evolution of the internet from the earliest days of Web 1.0, to the burgeoning of Web 3.0, and eventually Web 4.0, shows how blurred the lines of interactivity have and will become.

Z. Niesel, "Personal Jurisdiction: A New Age of Internet Contacts," (2019) 94 *Ind. L.J.* 103 at 127.

3 C. Soghoian, "Caught in the Cloud: Privacy, Encryption, and Government Back Doors in the Web 2.0 Era," (2010) 8 *J. Telecomm. & High Tech. L.* 359. See further M. Graham and W. H. Dutton, *Society and the Internet: How Networks of Information and Communication are Changing Our Lives,* (Oxford: O.U.P., 2019).

4 M. Saliternik, "Big Data and the Right to Political Participation," (2019) 21 *U. Pa. J. Const. L.* 713 at 723.

allowed the masses to collect and publish information while walking about without exercising the levels of reflection that a trained and experienced newspaper or other editor might exercise before posting information.

In a nutshell, the first generation of the web stated in 1989 after its creation by Sir Tim Berners Lee and lasted until around 2005. It was by and large "view-only" with little to no interaction or input from users. It is true that it was interactive and participatory, but most of the information posted required the disseminator to have control over a formal website. Web 2.0 was far more interactive because platforms such as social media networks, wikis and blogs allowed users to create and share their own content. Web 3.0 will be a web of data that will be able to interpret, comprehend and combine information to provide users with a focused and tailored interactive experience.[5] It is likely to be much more decentralised, and thus might affect the monopoly currently held by the tech giants.[6] Web 3.0 will give users much greater control, and this will be achieved primarily through cloud applications and smart-phones.[7] "The Semantic web is more likely to be open source, widely distributed, available anywhere and using natural language."[8] The third-generation Internet services will be a combination of semantic web and artificial intelligence,[9] and will raise a host of new legal issues as it emerges.

With such rapid technological changes taking place every couple of years, it is challenging for lawmakers to keep abreast of the many ways that criminals might use this technology to perpetrate crimes. It is not only the increasing misuse of

---

5 G. René *et al.*, *The Spatial Web: How Web 3.0 Will Connect Humans, Machines and AI to Transform the World*, (New York: 2019).

6 Widener writes:

> Thus, the "read-write-execute" Web, where users can create and execute their own tools and software to manipulate and extract information, rather than relying upon other people's software and websites. The term, like the phrase "the semantic Web," focuses on the concept of enhancing the "intelligence" of the underlying Internet architecture – the idea that information will be organized and identified in ways that makes searches more effective because the platform "understands" and makes connections between pieces of data. In full flower, Web 3.0 will be "applications that are pieced together" – with the characteristics that the apps are relatively small, the data is in the cloud, the apps can run on any device (PC or mobile), these applications are very fast and very customizable to any machine, and are distributed virally.

> M. N. Widener, "Populist Placemaking: Grounds for Open Government-Citizen Spatial Regulating Discourse," (2018) 121 *W. Va. L. Rev.* 461 at 530.

7 M. Zanker *et al.*, "Measuring the Impact of Online Personalisation: Past, Present and Future," (2019) 131 *International Journal of Human-Computer Studies* 160; M. S. Gal and D. L. Rubinfeld, "Data Standardization," (2019) 94 *N.Y.U. L. Rev.* 737.

8 P. Ohm and J. Frankle, "Desirable Inefficiency," (2018) 70 *Fla. L. Rev.* 777; J. J. A. Shaw, "Lefebvre and Law: Social Justice, New Technologies and the Spatial Imaginary," in M. E. Leary-Owhin and J. P. McCarthy (eds.), *The Routledge Handbook of Henri Lefebvre, the City and Urban Society*, (Oxford: Routledge, 2020) at 187–206.

9 P. K. Yu, "Data Producer's Right and the Protection of Machine-Generated Data," (2019) 93 *Tul. L. Rev.* 859.

technology as a means for perpetrating crime that is of concern to lawmakers, but also the ways in which critical technology infrastructure might be hijacked for ransom or otherwise criminally damaged. The regulation, management and control of the risks facilitated by the Internet have become more urgent, important and complex. It is a global challenge to cope with the development of information technology and to make and improve the relevant technical rules and legal rules to keep a balance between technology innovation and human dignity.

With major advances in network technology, many traditional crimes have become cyberised, and cybermeans tend to be the dominant means used to perpetrate some offences such as fraud. The crime trends and structures are changing in China. For example, illegal online gambling, cyberfraud, the dissemination of fake news, the infringement of copyright and the theft or sale of personal information are all on the increase.

The attack against and destruction of computer systems has been an evolving problem since the Web 1.0 era. It therefore has become a challenge of our times to respond effectively to the cyberisation of traditional crimes as well as the normalisation of cybercrimes.[10] In this chapter, we will try to look at some of the key reforms introduced in China as far as liability for Internet service providers (hereinafter ISPs) are concerned. In this chapter, we aim to shed some light on some of the problems that have arisen in China and discuss some of the legal solutions that have recently been put forward. There are two main streams of offences we examine. We examine the new obligations imposed on ISPs under Article 286(1) of the *Criminal Code of China* in relation to having a duty to keep information secure and to remove illegal content from their platforms upon being warned. This provision also requires ISPs to retain data that might be evidence for proving criminal matters. We also examine the new preparatory offences that have been created in Article 287(1) of the *Criminal Code of China* to evaluate the harm justification for letting the criminal law cover mere preparatory acts.[11]

2. Cybercrime: extending the reach of the current law

The doctrines that exculpate and inculpate, and the general principles of punishment that have long been applied in criminal law, are apt for dealing with most cybercrime.[12] There is a difference between a cybercrime and the use of cyber*means* to perpetrate a crime that can also be perpetrated though non-cyber*means*.[13] For example, phishing is one way of facilitating fraud, but the same

---

10 See Yu Zhigang, "The Evolution of Network Thinking and the Thought of Sanctioning Cyber Crimes," (2016) 4 *Peking University Law Journal* 1047 at 1049. See also J. Grimmelmann, "Consenting to Computer Use," (2016) 84 *Geo. Wash. L. Rev.* 1500.

11 J. Feinberg, *Harm to Others*, (New York: O.U.P., 1984).

12 See generally, H. L. A. Hart, *Punishment & Responsibility*, (Oxford: Clarendon, 1968); C. Payne and L. Finlay, "Addressing Obstacles to Cyber-Attribution: A Model Based on State Response to Cyber-Attack," (2017) 49 *Geo. Wash. Int'l L. Rev.* 535.

13 Baker points out:

> Most crimes that are referred to as cybercrimes are not in fact attacks on cyber technological cyber devices, data, programs and services per se, such as computers, databases, servers

information that can be obtained from phishing can be obtained through a burglar photographing a person's credit card, driving licence, passport, and so on. A burglar could break into a house and copy as much information as a cyberfraudster might obtain from phishing. Nevertheless, cyberisation of traditional crimes has, to a substantial extent, changed the nature and extent of such crimes, because it not only allows a fraudster to target millions at once, but also allows such a criminal to operate with a higher level of remoteness from the crime and with a better layer of anonymity.

The most common problem has been cyberfraud whereby criminals have been using the four-in-one network technology (Internet, mobile phone, television and telephone) to steal and sell citizens' personal information. This is done by using an arbitrary display number software and voice-over-Internet protocol (VOIP)[14] telephone technology to set up fake websites including fake online banking websites. These sites carefully impersonate the telecommunication sector, banks, the police and the justice department. The process also involves criminals making threatening phone calls and sending false information through emails.[15] The cybermethods used allow them to target people indirectly and remotely, so that they need not have direct contact.

Phishing has been a common cybermethod for perpetrating fraud for some years, but criminal gangs are employing more sophisticated schemes to circumvent the increasing awareness of potential victims. A large number of vulnerable and disadvantaged retirees have been the main targets for these fraudsters. According to the *China Telecommunication Fraud Analysis Report 2016*, based

---

and so on. Rather the bulk of cyber offences are simply traditional crimes such as fraud, theft, incitement of hatred, incitement of crimes of violence, obscenity offences, blackmail and extortion, copyright theft, fake news (slander and libel), and terrorism, which are perpetrated with the help of cyber technology.

D. J. Baker, "The Concept of Cybercrime: Applying the General Part to Limit Offending via Cyber Means," (2019) 5 *People's Procuratorial Semimonthly* 35.

14 See:

VoIP technology is simply another mechanism for delivering voice communication. VoIP transmits the voice data over internet protocol (IP) instead of through traditional telephone lines on the PSTN. The voice data is converted into digital bits which are placed in packets and sent over the same pathways as internet data. VoIP can be provided over the public Internet or a private IP network. The packets of information run through various computers, routers, and switches before they are reconstituted at their destination. VoIP-to-VoIP communications are those that originate and terminate at IP addresses existing in cyberspace without regard to the person's geographic location. . . . In contrast, interconnected VoIP involves communication of VoIP to or from a traditional PSTN landline connection. Interconnected VoIP is defined as a service that provides real-time, two-way voice communication over a broadband connection from the user's location using special equipment that permits the user to receive calls from or terminate calls on the PSTN.

In *re Investigation into Regulation of Voice Over Internet Protocol Servs.* (2013) 193 Vt. 439 at 441–442.

15 "The purpose of hackers' phishing is to trick unsuspecting users into clicking on links that take them to fake websites or install malware on their device." J. Cullen, "Future Crimes," (2017) 33 *Syracuse J. Sci. & Tech. L.* 35 at 38.

on research conducted by the Internet Security Centre, a mere 360 mobile phone guards intercepted 445 million fraudulent telephone calls in a single month, with an average of 14.35 million calls per day. Statistically, it has been estimated that there are at least 100,000 criminals operating from both inside and outside China. These criminals are connected with the network mainly through fixed phone-lines or mobile phones. The main crime they perpetrate is cyberfraud.[16]

If China had an inchoate form of fraud like that found in England under Section 2 of the *Fraud Act 2006* (U.K.), even an attempt to dishonestly defraud another through cybermeans would be an offence. However, in China, there must be actual deception and an actual loss of money or property before the offences of fraud can be proved.[17] A form of inchoate liability would allow many more people to be prosecuted, but the numbers might be so high that they could block the criminal justice system completely. The question as far as the criminal law is concerned is not only about how to criminalise this sort of conduct, but how to enforce such offences. There could be preparation offences (that is, pre-inchoate offences)[18] such as those that do not punish an actual attempt or actual assistance or encouragement, but punish preparation.[19] Professor Lacey has noted:

> Moreover, a significant number of these new offences draw the boundaries of responsibility-attribution at an earlier stage, inviting a characterization of them as not merely inchoate, but pre-inchoate offences. The offence of engaging in any conduct in preparation for giving effect to an intention to commit acts of terrorist or assist another to do so under section 5 of the *Terrorism Act 2006* would be a good example. Note that this tendency to push back the boundaries of responsibility-attribution in time is far from being restricted to areas such as counter-terrorism or drug regulation. As Lindsay Farmer has shown, developments in offences against the person and sexual offences – the extension of the conception of psychological assault,

---

16 Source: 360 Internet Security Centre: "China Telecommunication Fraud Situation Analysis Report 2016," <http://zt.360.cn/1101061855.php?Dtid=1101061451&did=490024605>.

17 See for example, Articles 175; 192–200; 264 and 265 of the *Criminal Code of the People's Republic of China*.

18 Steward notes:

> "preparation offences" as types of conduct that may be "necessary precursors of the commission of an attempt but do not constitute an attack in the sense required for a criminal attempt." Preparation offences are not "dangerous in themselves," and are connected to the harm that they ultimately may cause "only through the subsequent intervening choices of the actor . . . choices that have not yet been made.

> H. Stewart, "The Normative Structure of Criminal Law: Moral or Political?" (2015) 9 *Crim. L. & Phil.* 719 at 723.

19 A. Ashworth, "Preventive Orders and The Rule of Law," in D. J. Baker and J. Horder (eds.), *The Sanctity of Life and the Criminal Law*, (Cambridge: Cambridge University Press, 2013) at 45 *et seq.*

the creation of a sex offender register – as well as in property offences – notably in the example of money-laundering – also move in this pre-inchoate direction.[20]

Besides preparatory (pre-inchoate) offences, there are also "remote harm" crimes such as those found in Sections 6 and 7 of the *Fraud Act 2006* (U.K.), which prevent people from possessing, making and supplying articles that might assist others or themselves to perpetrate fraud. These are not preparation or complicity offences, but offences that aim to prevent people facilitating preparation, but there would be an overlap when the manufacturer of the articles for use in fraud manufactures them for fraud that he or she personally plans to perpetrate or manufactures them for someone he or she intends to assist to perpetrate a crime. When there is no overlap, acts such as manufacturing articles for use in fraud are simply criminalised as remote harms (providing there is a remote harm justification for criminalisation),[21] and thus, we shall label such offences "remote harm" offences. The problem for attribution of criminal liability for China is not dissimilar to that in common law jurisdictions. The problem of deterrence and disruption is also the same. While the use of indirect remote harm liability and direct pre-inchoate (preparatory) liability can lead to unfair over-criminalisation,[22] it can

20 N. Lacey, *In Search of Criminal Responsibility: Ideas, Interests, and Institutions*, (Oxford: O.U.P., 2016) at 48.

21 A. von Hirsch, "Extending the Harm Principle: 'Remote' Harms and Fair Imputation," in A. P. Simester and A. T. H. Smith (eds.), *Harm and Culpability*, (Oxford: Clarendon Press, 1996); D. J. Baker, "The Moral Limits of Criminalizing Remote Harms," (2007) 10 *New Crim. L. Rev.* 370 at 375. For an example of a remote harm crime, see Section 3A of the *Computer Misuse Act 1990* (U.K.), which criminalises "making, supplying or obtaining articles for use" in a computer crime. Section 3A provides:

> (1) A person is guilty of an offence if he makes, adapts, supplies or offers to supply any article intending it to be used to commit, or to assist in the commission of, an offence under section 1, 3 or 3ZA. (2) A person is guilty of an offence if he supplies or offers to supply any article believing that it is likely to be used to commit, or to assist in the commission of, an offence under section 1, 3 or 3ZA. (3) A person is guilty of an offence if he obtains any [article – (a) intending to use it to commit, or to assist in the commission of, an offence under section 1, 3 or 3ZA, or (b) with a view to its being supplied for use to commit, or to assist in the commission of, an offence under section 1, 3 or 3ZA. (4) In this section 'article' includes any program or data held in electronic form.

22 By way of analogy, Ashworth and Zedner argue that "Such offenses are specific to terrorism, and so do not come within the general part of the criminal law. They are ad hoc extensions based on a preventive rationale in the hope that they will provide extra security." A. Ashworth and L. Zedner, "Prevention and Criminalization: Justifications and Limits," (2012) 15 *New Crim. L. Rev.* 542 at 545. Cancio gives the example of association crimes such as gang membership and concludes: "Therefore, offences of unlawful association constitute instances of pre-inchoate crimes. In spite of this, the punishment imposed for such offenses is very harsh, considering the fact that the criminalized conduct does not even come close to causing harm to others." M. C. Cancio, "The Wrongfulness of Crimes of Unlawful Association," (2008) 11 *New Crim. L. Rev.* 563 at 564.

be reconciled with the fundamental principles of justice if it is applied narrowly to comply with the principles of fair labelling and proportionate punishment.

There are a number of ways of tackling this sort of criminality: (1) direct liability for the consummated crime; (2) complicity liability for involvement in the underlying offences; (3) inchoate liability for attempting such offences; (4) direct (pre-inchoate) preparatory liability; and (5) indirect remote harm liability such as offences that criminalise possession and manufacture of equipment or websites that might be used to perpetrate crimes. In addition to that, unexplained wealth orders[23] might be placed on those who have significant unexplained wealth. A further barrier could be placed by properly regulating cryptocurrencies to remove the anonymity of account holders. Cryptocurrencies allow cyberfraudsters to hide and transfer the proceeds of crime without detection.[24]

3. Liability for indirect remote harm and direct pre-inchoate harm

There are many papers discussing the use of complicity to try to reach the members of cyberfraud syndicates, so we intend to avoid that topic in this chapter. We want to focus on how extending the law back further in time might help to reduce cybercrime while at the same time not compromise the fundamental principles of criminal justice. In addition, we want to focus on criminal liability for those ISPs that provide enabling technology and fail to withdraw their enabling technology after being warned that their technology is facilitating cybercrime. A fairly important rule for lawmakers when considering whether to criminalise conduct is whether that conduct warrants criminalisation for good reason. The core reason given in most societies is harm to others. A mere thought crime is harmless, so it ought not be criminalised. However, once a person starts doing more than thinking about perpetrating a crime, the law could be invoked even though the criminal's acts are mere preparation or are remote from the primary crime. If a terrorist has a storeroom full of bombs, there is no need to wait until he attempts to explode them on a train before invoking the protection of

---

23 Bell writes:

> The U.K.'s Unexplained Wealth Order, passed in 2018, is a great example. The law requires individuals to reveal the sources of their wealth used to purchase an asset worth more than 50,000 pounds (about $65,000). If they can't, the government has a right to seize the property.

A. Bell, "Taking a Stand Against Ginancial Crime: Building a Culture of Compliance," (2019) 34(20) *Westlaw Journal Corporate Officers and Directors Liability* 1. Similarly, "The Australian Federal Police may seek a preliminary unexplained wealth order. The Court may make such an order if there is evidence the wealth may have been acquired from unlawful means." A. D. Gray, "Forfeiture Provisions and the Criminal/civil Divide," (2012) 15 *New Crim. L. Rev.* 32.

24 J. O. McGinnis and K. Roche, "Bitcoin: Order Without Law in the Digital Age," (2019) 94 *Ind. L.J.* 1497 at 1529.

the criminal law. However, a pre-inchoate act of terrorism should be labelled and punished less than an attempted act of terrorism, and *a fortiori*, less than a consummated act of terrorism.[25] The gravity of the harm posed by this sort of preparation would justify allowing the criminal law to operate at the pre-inchoate stage. There is no social utility in a private person having a storeroom full of explosives, and the risk of harm such a (direct) preparatory act poses is so serious that it warrants criminalisation.

Similarly, if a person is in possession of illegal weapons which she intends to sell to a terrorist group, this remote harm ought to be criminalised. There is no social utility in private individuals dealing in arms and weapons of mass destruction, and thus possession per se is a remote harm. It is remote as the possessor does not intend to harm anyone, but merely intends to sell the weapons to make money. If the seller has no intention of assisting any particular terrorist, it would be difficult to show that she intended to assist terrorism, which is what would be required to establish complicity liability. Hence, remote harm liability would allow the law to plug any gap left by the law of complicity and by direct preparatory offences. It is enough to show that dealing in such items is dangerous, not only because it puts the purchaser of the weapons in a more dangerous position, but also because it will remotely assist such a person to harm others.

When we reach the law back to cover acts of preparation that might not be harmful in themselves, we need to make sure that these sorts of acts are remotely harmful in that they pose a real risk of making a causative and normative contribution to some end harm. Lawmakers need to be able to explain why the remote harm is wrong and worthy of criminalisation. A person can still be charged with the primary offence, but a layer of remote harm liability can disrupt wrongful conduct early in the harm chain. Whether (direct) preparatory liability ought to have a role to play when there is no threat to human life is a complex normative matter, because many people who are intent on perpetrating a crime do change their minds. We need to leave room for people to change their minds, and thus the law of attempts is more than enough to protect society in most cases.[26]

Generally, pre-inchoate conduct is criminalised in China, but it is rarely punished in practice.[27] Article 22 of the *Criminal Code of the China* provides: "Preparation for a crime refers to the preparation of the instruments or the creation of the conditions for a crime."[28] The harm principle rationale for criminalising

---

25 D. J. Baker, "Treason Versus Outraging Public Decency: Over-Criminalisation and Terrorism Panics," (2019) 84(1) *J.C.L.* 19; J. Feinberg, "Criminal Attempts: Equal Punishment for Failed Attempts," in J. Feinberg (ed.), *Problems at the Roots of Law*, (New York: Oxford University Press, 2003) at 100; L. Crocker, "Justice in Criminal Liability: Decriminalizing Harmless Attempts," (1992) 53 *Ohio St. L.J.* 1057.

26 Cf. D. N. Husak, "Why Punish Attempts at All? Yaffe on 'The Transfer Principle,' " (2012) 6 *Crim. L. & Phil.* 399.

27 See Yan Erpeng, "Comment on the Phenomenon of Network Alienation of Crime and the Way to Deal With it in Criminal Law," (2015) 3 *Research on Rule of Law* 51–52.

28 There is no preparation provision in the general part of criminal law in the common law world. See G. Williams, *Criminal Law: The General Part*, (London: Stevens & Sons, 1953);

conduct covers not only harm caused, but also harms that are risked.[29] Endangerment is the rationale for criminalising certain acts of possession and supply, and is also the justification for criminalising preparatory conduct. Hence, if X without lawful justification (i.e., acting in self-defence or as a police officer preventing a crime) fires a gun at Y with an intention of killing Y but misses, X has endangered Y's life even if X has not killed Y. Suppose Y's back is turned and Y has headphones on and is listening to loud music so does not even know she has been shot at. Y disappears into the crowd before the police can tell her about the attempt on her life. Here, Y has not even suffered the mental shock of knowing someone tried to killer her. X is liable for attempted murder, even though Y suffered no harm whatsoever. Preparation takes this back a step further and would criminalise X's mere purchase and possession of a firearm. Some offences will target acts that a designed to help others prepare such as manufacturing and selling items that might be used for use in fraud or terrorism, but others are more general and might cover an item that can have both lawful and unlawful uses such as a can of petrol, which could be used to fuel a motorbike or to fuel a Molotov cocktail to perpetrate an act of terrorism. In this case, there needs to be strong evidence to demonstrate that while the petrol was an innocuous substance per se, the defendant had an unlawful purpose and was planning to use it in a petrol bomb.[30] In other cases, the item will be such that it can be deemed to have had no lawful purpose, such as where a private individual possesses automated teller machine (ATM) card skimmers[31] or military grade weapons.[32]

H. Wechsler *et al.*, "The Treatment of Inchoate Crimes in the Model Penal Code of the American Law Institute: Attempt, Solicitation, and Conspiracy," (1961) 61 *Colum. L. Rev.* 571.

29 C. Finkelstein, "Is Risk a Harm?" (2003) 151 *U. Pa. L. Rev.* 963; R. A. Duff, "Criminalizing Endangerment," (2005) 65 *La. L. Rev.* 941 at 950.

30 Cf. B. Middleton, "Preparing for Terrorism," (2011) 75(3) *J. Crim. L.* 177; J. Hodgson *et al.*, "How to Make a Terrorist Out of Nothing," (2009) 72(6) *M.L.R.* 984. Cf. the recent decision of the Supreme Court of the United Kingdom: *R. v. Copeland* [2020] UKSC 8 at para. 29, where the Supreme Court of the United Kingdom had to consider whether personal experimentation for private educational purpose, absent some recognised lawful purpose, could be treated as a "lawful object" for the purposes of the Section 4(1) of the *Explosive Substances Act 1883*. Lord Sales said:

> If the accused knew that his proposed use of the explosive substance in his possession would injure others or cause damage to their property or was reckless regarding the risk of this, the ostensibly lawful object identified by him would be tainted by the unlawfulness inherent in his pursuit of that object.

31 For example,

> A Lebanese loop is a device which can be surreptitiously inserted into a cash machine and which then traps the card of the next user. The fraudsters will, by one means or another, observe the PIN number being put in by the user, and as soon as he or she leaves the machine they retrieve the loop, which brings with it the card, which they can then use with the PIN to make fraudulent withdrawals.

R. v Munteanu [2013] 1 Cr. App. R. (S.) 107.

32 See for example, M. Krantz, "Walking Firearms to Gunrunners: Atf's Flawed Operation in A Flawed System," (2013) 103 *J. Crim. L. & Criminology* 585 at 590. Cf. *R. v. Copeland* (2020) U.K.S.C. 8.

Because some of these preparatory acts do not pose a real danger to others, it is difficult to know when to invoke the criminal law. There is nothing controversial about making it a crime to possess bombs or ATM card readers, if these acts of possession are fairly labelled[33] and published proportionately.[34] Nonetheless, it would not be possible to make it a crime to possess cans of petrol. There are limitations as many items are not axiomatically an item for preparing for a particular type of crime.

However, under Article 287(1) of the *Criminal Code of China*, it is an offence to make use of information networks to (a) establish websites or chat groups for use in crime, or to disseminate information on how to perpetrate crimes; (b) publish information about the sale of pornography, drugs, guns, and so on; or (c) publish information to facilitate criminal activities such as fraud. These offences targets pre-inchoate conduct. Setting up a WeChat or WhatsApp group could be a legitimate and lawful act such as when a group of students set up one to communicate with each other and with their professor. Also, such a group might be set up by a mastermind to reach fellow criminal gang members. It is a bit like the can of petrol; it could have a lawful or unlawful use. The law is pre-inchoate here, even on common law standards where it is a crime merely to agree to do a crime in the future, because the criminal gang members need not use the group-chat to agree to do a crime.[35] They will be liable simply because they set up the group-chat to communicate, if there is strong evidence it was set up to communicate about a criminal plan or to effect a crime.

It is one thing to find a person with an ATM card reader in his or her possession because it axiomatically is an instrument for use in fraud, but it is something entirely different to prove that a communication group (Facebook or WeChat group) was established for the purposes of perpetrating a crime. A person might set up a WeChat group and reach out to a group of people she suspects might be interested in participating in crime with her, but she has no way of knowing for sure if any of them will, but technically has done an act that putatively is

---

33 Husak writes:

> Andrew Ashworth points out, it is important "that widely felt distinctions between kinds of offences and degrees of wrongdoing are respected and signalled by the law, and that offences should be divided and labelled so as to represent fairly the nature and magnitude of the law-breaking.

D. N. Husak, "The Costs to Criminal Theory of Supposing That Intentions Are Irrelevant to Permissibility," (2009) 3 *Crim. L. & Phil.* 51 at 64.

34 A. von Hirsch, *Censure and Sanction*, (Oxford: Clarendon Press, 1993).

35 Unlike the common law, Chinese law does not have an inchoate crime of conspiracy. In common law jurisdictions, if two or more persons agree to perpetrate a crime, they will be liable for the crime of conspiracy, even if they do not attempt to carry out their plan. A and B might agree to steal the Crown Jewels, and after reading about the security at the Tower of London, might decide it is a hopeless plan and completely abandon it before doing a single act of preparation. If their agreement itself can be proved, they would be liable for conspiring to perpetrate a burglary, even though they never got past reading about the impossibility of penetrating the security at the Tower. See D. J. Baker, *Glanville Williams Textbook of Criminal Law*, (London: Sweet & Maxwell, 2015) at Chapter 19.

preparatory for the crime she intends to do with the group members. It will be difficult to apply the law to this example in practice, unless there are some overt acts such as an exchange of messages to indicate that the group is a criminal group.

Add inchoate liability to the preparatory act and we see acts being criminalised that are very remote from any real criminal harm such as a loss of property from a future fraud. For example, a person might set up a fake webpage for the purposes of making fraudulent representations to deceive people into making payments for a service that does not exist, but this preparatory act might not actually deceive anyone before it is exposed as a fake website. In Europe, many people have been deceived into paying money for flights or hotels on fake websites.[36] This is actual fraud, however. Setting up the webpage itself would be caught by the inchoate offence of fraud found in Section 2 of the *Fraud Act 2006* (U.K.), which does not require the false representation to actually cause any loss and does not require anyone to actually be deceived.[37] The false representation itself is treated as an act of fraud. A fake website claiming it is a real hotel webpage and that a room will be provided for money paid contains several false representations and is rightly treated as fraud, regardless of whether anyone is fooled into booking a room on it. Whether the law needs to cut in at an earlier stage in every case is questionable.[38]

Let us assume that X has set up a fake hotel website, but before X is able to launch it online, the police search X for some other matter and find the planned webpage on X's computer. Article 287(1)(c) of the *Criminal Code of China* would *not* catch this preparatory act, because it requires the fake website to go live online before its creator can be liable, but Section 6 of the *Fraud Act 2006* (U.K.) would catch this act of preparation. Section 6(1) provides: "(1) A person

---

36 It has been reported that,

> [Fifty-three per cent] of online holiday scams related to the sale of airline tickets: for example, booking a flight on a fake site and receiving an imitation ticket, or paying for a ticket that never arrives. . . . Scams relating to accommodation bookings were the second most common area. . . . This includes professional and convincing websites offering luxury villas for rent, often at a discounted rate. Some of these villas won't even exist, but some will be real properties being offered by scammers without the owner's knowledge, with Spain and France most commonly targeted. They often require you to pay a deposit, which travellers will never see again.

> A. Wilson, "Online Holiday Booking Scams and How to Avoid Them," (London: *The Guardian*, 14 June 2019).

37 Baker, *op. cit. supra*, note 35 at Chapter 37.

38 Husak writes:

> There is virtually no controversy that the state is justified in creating and enforcing at least some nonconsummate offences. The immediate question is whether and to what extent the progress described above in defending a general theory about the moral limits of the criminal law provides much insight into the issue of whether and under what conditions the enactment of nonconsummate offenses is a legitimate exercise of state authority.

> D. N. Husak, "The Nature and Justifiability of Nonconsummate Offences," (1995) 37 *Ariz. L. Rev.* 151 at 159.

is guilty of an offence if he has in his possession or under his control any article for use in the course of or in connection with any fraud." Endangerment to economic interests is the justification for Section 6 of the *Fraud Act 2006* (U.K.), but the harm risk is further back in time than harm risked by an attempt. The gravity of the endangerment can also depend on the type of end harm that might result. For example, carrying a large bomb on the Metro is more dangerous than carrying two unloaded handguns. Similarly, the risk to property interests is less when a person sells a jimmy bar to a putative burglar than it is when she sets up a fake webpage for a fraudster that allows the fraudster to target millions of potential victims.

Criminalising the act of publishing information to facilitate another's crime would overcome the barrier posed by trying to apply complicity liability to such a problem.[39] In England, there is a very wide form offence of inchoate "assistance or encouragement" found in Sections 44–46 of the *Serious Crime Act 2007* (U.K.), which criminalises not only actual assistance and encouragement/ incitement, but attempts to assist and incite. Suppose X posts a gun and letter offering £100,000 to Y, if Y kills V, but the police find the gun and letter in the mail and confiscate it before Y has a chance to learn about the offer or use the gun. X would be liable for attempting to assist and encourage Y to kill V. There is no need to show the assistance or encouragement actually had any impact, and there is no need for any crime to be perpetrated by Y. In the realm of *trying* to assist or encourage the general public to perpetrate a crime, there are a couple of older English precedents that are instructive, even though they predate the Internet. In *R. v. Marlow*,[40] it was said:

> the appellant was the author and publisher of the book and he had advertised it for sale in 1994 and sold about 500 copies. . . . The prosecution contended that the book amounted to an incitement of those who bought it to cultivate cannabis, which is an offence under section 4(2) of the *Misuse of Drugs Act 1971*. . . . It was argued that the book was too remote from the actions of those reading it to constitute incitement. The prosecution, on the other hand, argued that the appellant's intention in writing and publishing the book could be inferred from the book itself.

The common law offence of incitement was an inchoate offence that applied when a person encouraged/incited another to commit a crime regardless of whether the other person attempted or did in fact perpetrate that crime. The

---

39 Kadish writes:

> By its nature, the doctrine of complicity, like causation, requires a result. It is not a doctrine of inchoate liability. If the primary party does not act in violation of the law, there is no unlawfulness for which to hold the secondary actor accountable.

S. H. Kadish, "Complicity, Cause and Blame: A Study in the Interpretation of Doctrine," (1985) 73 *Cal. L. Rev.* 323 at 355–356.

40 [1998] 1 Cr. App. R. (S.) 273.

judges in this case were wrong to treat it as a case of incitement, because the author seems to have only been intending to assist. The author let the readers make up their own minds about growing cannabis. The common law offence incitement was abrogated in England and was replaced with an inchoate form of complicity as laid down in the *Serious Crime Act 2007* (U.K.). The main amendment to the law by the *Serious Crime Act 2007* was that it extended inchoate liability to attempted assistance, whereas the common law offence of incitement only applied to attempted encouragement.

If a person posts online illegal information about how to grow drugs, this would be caught by Section 45 of the *Serious Crime Act 2007* (U.K.), but that offence does contain a high threshold for establishing the fault element and thus a person would only be liable if he or she "believed" posting such information online "would" assist or encourage another to perpetrate the crime that such advice or encouragement is capable of assisting or encouraging. The encouragement may be directed to persons generally, as it was in *Invicta Plastics Ltd. v. Clare*,[41] and it may encourage a general course of crime. Hence, in English law, there is no need to show that the person who posted the criminal knowhow online intended to assist or encourage a particular offender, but it must be shown that he or she believed it would assist or encourage someone. In addition, the information must be capable of assisting another or inciting another to commit the target crime. The English law offers some support and guidance for the new provision found in Article 287(1) of the *Criminal Code of China* with respecting posting information online about how to perpetrate crimes.

Preparatory acts for perpetrating a property offence through cybermeans (i.e., setting up a fake website on a computer without having yet had a chance to make the webpage live online so that it is publicly searchable) is conceptually no different than preparatory acts to perpetrate a property crime through non-cybermeans (i.e., a burglar buys tools to break into a house, but has not yet attempted to break into the house). The main difference, however, is that cybermeans can be used to target millions of potential victims en masse, and this might add some weight on the utilitarian scales for bringing the criminal law in at an early stage and thus criminalising the preparation rather than waiting for the preparation to move to the attempt stage.[42]

---

41 [1976] R.T.R. 251.
42 See Liang Genlin, "The Dilemma and Breakthrough of General Principle of Punishing Preparatory Crime," (2011) 2 *China Legal Science* 150 at 156–162. See Network Security Law of the People's Republic of China (Standing Committee of the National People's Congress, Order No. 53 of the President of the People's Republic of China, 7 November 2016, eff. 1 June 2017); Information Security Specification – Personal Information Security Specification (GB/T 35273–2017) (Office of the Central Leading Group for Cyberspace Affairs, General Administration of Quality Supervision, Inspection and Quarantine; National Security Standardization Technical Committee, 29 December 2017, eff. 1 May 2018).

4. Internet service provider offences

A number of new laws have been enacted in China to ensure that Internet service providers minimise the criminal harm others cause by using their services. There is also a new law to ensure that ISPs retain data for the purposes of giving prosecutors relevant evidence to obtain convictions against those who use the service to perpetrate crimes. An email service provider such as Yahoo or QQ would be liable for failing to retain emails from a criminal suspect, upon being asked to do so. The suspect might have deleted the emails, but if the service provider has kept a record for a set statutory period and is requested to hand it over, then it should comply. The new offences found in Article 286(1) of the *Criminal Code of China* include a general duty to fulfil a management role to ensure network security. Internet service providers also have to make sure illegal content and fake news is removed from the Internet or platform in a timely manner after they are made aware of the content by the regulator.

(a) Criminalisation and the duty of the ISP to act

Cyberlibertarians emphasise the necessity to deter states from over-regulating the content of the Internet.[43] However, it is obvious that cyberspace cannot go unregulated any more than the real world can go unregulated, because many aspects of people's real lives are done online. The posting of material inciting terrorism, and the sale of child sex abuse images and videos, cannot be ignored simply because this is done online. There has to be "some" censorship, and there also has to be parental lockout systems[44] so that consenting adults can access a diverse range of harmless content, even if some of that content might offend others.[45] Some people are offended by harmless content, and the remedy for those people is not to search for such content.[46] When the content is objectively harmful in a universal sense (i.e., content that would be deemed wrongful by most people in most cultures),[47] it is only right to make it unsearchable and order ISPs to remove it in a timely manner.

It is necessary to have carefully constructed categories of what online content is impermissible. Otherwise, the regulator might get confused about what is and

---

43 P. Timmers, "Challenged by 'Digital Sovereignty,' " (2019) 23 *J. Internet L.* 1.

44 A. Phippen, "App Based 'Solutions' to Keeping Children Safe Online," (2017) 28(8) *Ent. L.R.* 264.

45 T. C. Arthur, "The Problems with Pornography Regulation: Lessons from History," (2019) 68 *Emory L.J.* 867.

46 J. Feinberg, *Offence To Others*, (New York: O.U.P., 1985).

47 If people across cultures inter-subjectively evaluate expression as harmful or wrongfully offensive (as is the case with extremist views supporting terrorism, and as is the case with child sex abuse images), then that provides a sound case for criminalizing it. On the normativity of evaluating conduct wrongful through an inter-subjective evaluation, see C. Korsgaard, *The Sources of Normativity*, (Cambridge: C.U.P., 1996).

what is not allowed, and this could lead to all sorts of legal disputes. For example, it is incongruous to prevent "consenting adults" from seeing other nude adults in a mainstream movie, while at the same time allowing extremely violent games and movies to be accessed by young people including children. No adult has ever been objectively harmed from seeing another nude adult in a movie, but many children and young people have been harmed from playing violent games and watching violent movies. The empirical evidence shows that exposure to this sort of violence makes young people violent in real life.[48] Videos inciting terrorism and child sex abuse images have no place online because they are objectively harmful. Similarly, advertisements for guns or drugs have no place online because the sale of such items leads to objective harm. However, if the law tries to cover a really wide range of content including content that is not actually harmful, but is only *contra bonos mores*, the law will be hard to apply in practice and hard to enforce. The U.K. government's recent proposal to regulate the content of the Internet has received robust criticism, because it is trying to regulate too wide a range of content. Phippen and Bond write:

> We have, over the past seven years, seen a policy direction that aims first, to prevent children and young people from accessing pornography, and failing (and we expect this to continue even with the enactment of age verification from the *Digital Economy Act*). The Online Harms White Paper takes this unsuccessful model and extends it to an all-encompassing duty of care on companies to ensure online harms become a thing of the past or risk the wrath of the regulator. Without defining what that duty of care looks like, the thresholds for liability, or even how a harm might be defined.[49]

Some of the content that is harmful to children but not harmful to adults needs to be subject to parental lockout filters to prevent children from accessing it. We would not want a society where everyone merely accessed information that

---

48 Gibson writes:

> The California legislature passed the Act because the state felt that violent video games appealed to the morbid interests of kids and research showed that playing violent games has a harmful impact on the children who play those games. The legislature specifically targeted violent video games because of their "unique capacity to cause children to experience automatic aggressiveness, increased aggressive thoughts and behaviour, antisocial behaviour, desensitization to violence, and reduced activity in the frontal lobes of the brain."

> A. L. Gibson, "Brown v. Entertainment Merchants Association: Violent Video Game Legislation Loses the Game Against the First Amendment: Independent Regulation of the Game Industry Scores A Point Instead," (2013) 32 *Miss. C. L.* Rev. 171 at 173.

49 "The [U.K.] government will establish a new statutory duty of care to make companies take more responsibility for the safety of their users and tackle harm caused by content or activity on their services." A. Phippen and E. Bond, "The Online Harms Spearmint Paper – Just More Doing More?" (2019) 30(6) *Ent. L.R.* 169 at 173; D. E. Bambauer, "Orwell's Armchair," (2012) 79 *U. Chi. L. Rev.* 863.

was only safe for a 15-year-old to access. As for pornography starring consenting adults and viewed by consenting adults, it is *malum prohibitum* rather than *malum in se*, so there is no normative justification for making it illegal,[50] but because the *Criminal Code of China* makes it illegal, there is a legal positivism justification for criminalising its dissemination online.[51] Regulating ISPs to ensure that harmful content is not appearing online should be designed to prevent genuinely harmful content such as child sex abuse images and material inciting terrorism from appearing online.[52] Such information is universally deplored and has no place online, but regulators will have difficulty in other areas because some content is not harmful to adults, but would be harmful for children to access. The United Kingdom has thought about having an age verification check for adults accessing certain websites, but is still discussing what technology to use and how to reconcile age verifications with anonymity and privacy.[53]

(b) Allowing others to cause harm through failures to prevent

Article 286(1)(a) of the *Criminal Code of China* seems to target intentional assistance by omission.[54] What the new offence in Article 186(1)(a) aims to do is to stop specific types of harms from being facilitated by Internet service providers. The type of liability found in Article 286(1)(a) is a form of omissions liability, best conceptualised as liability for "allowing."[55] There is a duty not to

---

50 Feinberg, *op. cit. supra*, note 46. Feinberg makes a distinction between wrongful offensive expression such as hate speech and expression that is only conventionally offensive, such as public nudity.

51 Legal positivism normally does not provide a sound normative justification for criminalisation, because it simply states something is illegal because the law says it is. Thus, if the law said it is a crime to wear green shirts, legal positivism would mandate that we comply with such a law. See H. L. A. Hart, "Positivism and the Separation of Law and Morals," (1958) 71 *Harv. L. Rev.* 593 at 627.

52 D. J. Baker, *The Right Not to be Criminalized*, (Oxford: Routledge, 2011) at Chapter 6.

53 A. Phippen and E. Bond, "Fare Thee Well Age Verification, You Will Not be Missed," (2020) 31(2) *Ent. L.R.* 41, where the authors discuss "the announcement that *the Digital Economy Act 2017* Pt 3, which aimed to introduce age verification checks for access to websites containing pornographic material, will not be brought into force."

54 On assistance by omission see D. J. Baker, *Reinterpreting Criminal Complicity and Inchoate Participation Offences*, (Oxford: Routledge, 2016) at 33–43, 267.

55 This is analogous to being held criminally liable for "allowing" and "permitting" as discussed in Baker. Baker writes:

> The various offences of "permitting" something to be done can be committed not only by giving words of authorization but by failing to prevent conduct when one is in control of the situation, and here again the person who must not permit is specified. The failure to control doctrine is controversial and its application is often difficult to reconcile with the fundamental principles of fair labelling and proportionate punishment. . . . The control doctrine has mainly been invoked along with the law of complicity to make people liable for failing to control others from using their property to perpetrate a criminal offence when it was possible for the owner to take reasonable steps to try to deter the perpetrator.

Baker, *op. cit. supra*, note 35 at 260.

allow your platform or Internet service to be used by others to perpetrate criminality. The relevant regulator gives the ISP a warning, and if it fails to comply with the warming, it is then liable for continuing to allow the illegal content to remain online. Article 286(1)(a) is a good fit with the concept of "allowing," since the provider allows content that is illegal to remain on its platform after being warned. It was reported recently in England that:

> Up to 90 per cent of adverts on Google for investment ISAs and bonds could be scams, the search giant has been warned [by the Financial Conduct Authority] – as it emerged that questionable sites have been taken down only to reappear again within hours.[56]

If a search engine or social media platform or other ISP allows fraudulent advertisements to appear on their webpages, they facilitate the conduct of the fraudsters, even if that is not their intention. Therefore, there is nothing objectionable about imposing a duty on them to take reasonable steps to check that the advertisements they host are not false representations designed to defraud members of the public. If an ISP misses some of the fraudulent advertisements, it will not be liable under Article 286(1)(a), unless it refuses to remove them after being informed of the remaining fraudulent advertisements by the regulator.

The problem is, even with a warning, it may be impossible to find all the fake news, child sex abuse images and videos inciting terrorism, and so forth. Presumably, the regulator will only impose liability under Article 286(1)(a) when it has given a specific warning as to a particular webpage or social media post, and so forth. If the warning is too vague, then it would be unfair to penalise the ISP if it has exercised due diligence (taken all reasonable steps) in trying to remove all content it thinks is covered by the warning. It might use artificial intelligence[57] to filter out the worse of the scam advertisements or other illegal content, but even this might not identify all the illegal material that needs removing. A due diligence defence[58] would mean the ISP would not be liable for missing some illegal content, if it has used the best technology (artificial intelligence filters), has invested in a proper compliance department to monitor content, and so forth.

Article 286(1) contains no due diligence defence, but merely holds that the offence only applies to Internet service providers and its responsible representatives

---

56 B. Chapman, "90% of Google Adverts for ISAs and Bonds May be Scams, Search Giant Told," (London: *The Independent*, 20 February 2020).

57 *Mutatis Mutandis*: in an American copyright violation case, it was said:

> UMG also argues that Veoh's removal of unauthorized content identified in RIAA notices demonstrates knowledge, even if Veoh complied with § 512(c)'s notice and take-down procedures. According to UMG, Veoh should have taken the initiative to use *search and indexing tools to locate and remove from its website any other content* by the artists identified in the notices.

UMG Recordings, Inc. v. Shelter Capital Partners LLC (2013) 718 F.3d 1006 at 1023–1024.

58 Baker, *op. cit. supra*, note 35 at 330 discussing due diligence defences based on taking reasonable steps to prevent others using your equipment to cause criminal harm.

(senior managers or those directly responsible for compliance) if they fail to remove the illegal material after being told to do so. Only those who intentionally refuse to do as requested will be liable, and they face a prison sentence of up to three years. It is not clear if in every case the ISP will be given very specific details of what to remove, or if it will be simply given a general warning to remove content of a certain kind such as extremist videos inciting terrorism, and so on. Given the long prison sentence, it is presumed that the warning will be fairly specific. This provision is more about criminalising facilitation than it is about criminalising preparation. It targets real harms and the way that ISPs facilitates (assists) others to perpetrate such harms. The law of complicity is not relevant, because there is no intentional assistance in advance, but simply intentional assistance after the prior inadvertent assistance is brought to the ISP's attention. However, a deliberate failure to remove content after being warned is intentional assistance by omission and clearly comes within the purview of complicity when the ISP intentionally decides to continue to assist knowing it is assisting by not removing that assistance.

(c) Responsibility for allowing others to leak data

Article 286(1)(b) also seems to meet the harm threshold for justifying criminalisation, because leaking confidential information or failing to prevent confidential information from being hacked and leaked, due to poor security, is harmful. If an ISP is given a warning that its security is weak, then it has a duty to ensure it is using the best possible security features to guard against hackers. It would be difficult to set an artificial intelligence filter to identify private and confidential information, but criminal liability only takes place if the ISP fails to remove the content after being warned or fails to have proper security features in place to protect that data. Many major data breaches have resulted from hacking where there has been poor security. It has been held in the United Kingdom that a corporation will not be vicariously liable when an employee deliberately and wrongfully leaks information to seek revenge against his or her employer. Nor will a corporation be liable under the *Data Protection Act 2018* (U.K.), if it has exercised due diligence to prevent information being leaked.[59] The majority of data breaches have occurred in circumstances when the ISP had impeccable security in place.

---

59 In *WM Morrison Supermarkets plc. v. Various Claimants* [2020] UKSC 12 at para. 32, Lord Reed wrote (with whom Lady Hale, Lord Kerr, Lord Hodge and Lord Lloyd-Jones were in *concorditas*) that an employer would not be vicariously liable for its employee's deliberate disclosure of its clients' data unless the:

> disclosure of the data was so closely connected with acts he was authorised to do that, for the purposes of the liability of his employer to third parties, his wrongful disclosure may fairly and properly be regarded as done by him while acting in the ordinary course of his employment.

At para. 48, Lord Reed wrote:

> The remaining issue in the appeal is whether the Data Protection Act excludes vicarious liability for breaches of its own provisions, committed by an employee as a data controller,

Big data breaches have caused a range of harms beyond the mental harm caused by having the private information made public. In some cases, people have been left open to blackmail and identity fraud. Take the Ashley Madison scandal. In the United States in 2015, a gang identifying as "The Impact Team" hacked and stole the user data of Ashley Madison, a commercial dating website dedicated to enabling extramarital affairs. The hackers copied personal information about the website's user base and threatened to publish users' real names and other personally identifying information online, if Ashley Madison did not meet certain demands. In August 2015, the gang leaked more than 25 gigabytes of company data, including search history and credit card transaction records, real names and home addresses.

Let us assume that the leaked data is not placed in the Deep Web or Dark Web, but simply posted on Weibo or WeChat. Under Article 286(1)(b), Weibo or WeChat would be given a warning to implement proper security measures or otherwise be held criminally liable for continuing to facilitate potential data leaks after being warned. Clearly, data breaches can facilitate cyberfraud, blackmail and identity theft, and cause a host of other harms, so it appears that Article 286(1)(b) does aim to prevent harm to others. It is preventive in that the law cuts in whether anyone is harmed or not, but its general aim is to prevent harm before it transpires, or at least to limit it in these cumulative situations when the cyber-means used could result in many victims.

(d) Allowing the loss of criminal evidence

Article 286(1)(c) targets the removal of criminal evidence. "Removal of extremist speech may make it difficult for law enforcement to do its work. Terrorism investigations often rely on clues left in social media activity. Thus, it may be difficult to investigate potential terrorism if online evidence is immediately removed."[60] Article 286(1)(c) contains a provision dealing with records and files stored by Internet service providers. It means email and other subscriber data stored by ISPs that could be evidence for criminal matters should not be destroyed and must be handed to the authorities upon request. The kind of authorisation required by law enforcement to access stored information is not our concern here, as our focus is on criminal liability for failing to keep such information secure upon being warned to do so. The European Court of Human Rights has held that

---

or for misuse of private information and breach of confidence. Having concluded that the necessary conditions for the imposition of vicarious liability do not exist in this case, it is not strictly necessary for the court to go on to consider those issues.

At para. 54, Lord Reed wrote:

That conclusion is not affected by the fact that the statutory liability of a data controller under the DPA, including his liability for the conduct of his employee, is based on a lack of reasonable care, whereas vicarious liability is not based on fault.

60 D. K. Citron, "Extremist Speech, Compelled Conformity, and Censorship Creep," (2018) 93 *Notre Dame L. Rev.* 1035 at 1061.

ISPs have disclosure obligations,[61] but it is hard to imagine an ISP destroying or deleting criminal evidence – at least intentionally.[62]

In the United Kingdom, ISPs are only obliged to retain communications data, if they have received a respective "retention notice." These notices are issued by the Secretary of State, if it necessary for dealing with serious crime. If the crime is not serious, then the ISP or other individual has no duty to retain the data.[63] The European Data Retention Directive requires European ISPs to retain telecom and Internet traffic data from customer's communications for at least six months and up to two years. In an ongoing review of the law, the European Council said:

> Data retention constitutes an essential tool for law enforcement, judicial and other competent authorities to effectively investigate serious crime, including terrorism. The use of data retention and similar investigative measures should be guided by the protection of fundamental rights and freedoms and the principles of purpose limitation, necessity and proportionality.[64]

This is more to do with enforcement and helping the police and other agencies put people in prison who have perpetrated crimes than it is about preventing past harm. It is not a question of preventive criminalisation, but an enforcement measure.

---

61 *Benedik v. Slovenia* (2018) 62357/14. Compare Sch.7 para.18(1)(c) of the *Terrorism Act 2000* (U.K.), which provides:

> (1) A person commits an offence if he – (a) wilfully fails to comply with a duty imposed under or by virtue of this Schedule, (b) wilfully contravenes a prohibition imposed under or by virtue of this Schedule, or (c) wilfully obstructs, or seeks to frustrate, a search or examination under or by virtue of this Schedule.

Under this law, the traveller in *Rabbani v. D.P.P.* [2018] 2 Cr. App. R. 28, was convicted for failing to give the password for his computer and the pin for his phone to officers when requested to do so. Cf. *Capenter v. United States* (2018) 138 S. Ct. 2206, where the Supreme Court of the United States held that such information could only be obtained with a warrant, even if held by a third party such as an ISP.

62 Brayne *et al.* write:

> In August 2017, YouTube's algorithmic content moderation system, in aiming to remove extremist propaganda from its site, inadvertently deleted thousands of videos documenting human rights atrocities in Syria–potentially jeopardizing war crimes prosecutions that might rely on those videos as evidence.

S. Brayne *et al.*, "Visual Data and the Law," (2018) 43 *Law & Soc. Inquiry* 1149 at 1159–1160. Similarly, legislation in the United States designed to get ISPs to remove material that violates copyright law has shown that while AI is helpful for identifying what material to remove, it is far from perfect. S. K. Mehra and M. Trimble, "Secondary Liability, Isp Immunity, and Incumbent Entrenchment," (2014) 62 *Am. J. Comp. L.* 685 at 690.

63 Section 87 of the *Investigatory Powers Act 2016*.

64 *Draft Conclusion of the Council of the European Union on Improving Retention of Data for the Purpose of Fighting Crime Effectively*, (Brussels: 2019) at 5.

(e) The crime of fabricating and disseminating false information

In order to deal with the chaos that can be caused by fake news in the information age, Article 5 of the *Interpretation on Several Questions of Applicable Law in Criminal Cases of Using Information Network to Implement Defamation was promulgated by Supreme People's Court & Supreme People's Procuratorate* on 2 September 2013. This provision provides:

> Whoever fabricates and disseminates false information on the information network, or knowingly disseminates such information on the information network, or organizes or directs others to disseminate such information on the information network, thus causing disturbances or serious public disorder, shall be convicted and punished for the crime of provoking trouble in accordance pursuant to Article 293(1) d. of the Criminal Law.

In order to fill the lacuna in the law for cases when people use the Internet or social media to spread fake news, this provision criminalises the manufacture and dissemination of fake news online. This provision aims to prevent the power of social media and its reach to millions of people from being misused to cause riots in public places and serious public disorder as provided for in Article 293(1) (d) of the *Criminal Code*.

However, Article 5 requires the context be examined to determine whether the fake news was capable of causing serious public disorder. Contextual factors include whether it is targeted at crowds in places such as wharfs, airports or shopping malls. Hence, what is the general nature of the public place and its purpose, and how might disorder in such a place have a serious impact? It is also necessary to determine how crowded the place might be, and so forth. In England, it would also be relevant to look if there was already a riot occurring. If a person went on social media and sent messages of support to rioters already in action, English law would hold such a person liable for rioting through the law of incitement.[65] A great deal of harm was caused by fake news about the coronavirus,[66] and this is a major problem in an age when anyone can publish anything anywhere. Ignorant members of the public speculating (without evidence to support their speculations) creates most fake news. Even though they might not intend to cause harm and panic, that can be the effect of spreading fake news; *a fortiori* if there is already a crisis related to the fake news.

---

65 Under the inchoate from of complicity found in Sections 44–46 of the *Serious Crime Act 2007* (U.K.), the attempt to encourage the world at large would be enough to make the encourager liable. Baker, *op. cit. supra*, note 35 at Chapter 20.

66 Bianji Liang Jun, "Global Health Experts Condemn Virus Conspiracy Against Chinese Scientists," (Beijing: *The People's Daily*, 20 February 2020).

5. Obstacles to applying complicity liability to cybercrimes

Cybercrimes committed by groups can usually be dealt with by complicity liability. However, complicity liability cannot resolve all the imputation issues that arise when different players operate at different levels.[67] A person selling ATM card readers might have no connection with those buying them. Such a person might merely sell them on a webpage, knowing someone somewhere will buy them and attempt to use them to defraud others.[68] However, the seller has no way of knowing whether or not the user of this product will be successful in attempting to defraud others or whether the unknown perpetrator will use it or change his or her mind and not use it. This is perhaps why the English have criminalised the manufacture and supply of articles that can be used by independent others in fraud as independent offences.[69] Note that the English offence has a strong *mens rea* requirement to prevent over-criminalisation. It requires the supplier to have knowledge of how the item might be used. Alternatively, the supplier is held liable on complicity principles for intending to supply (assist) an item for use in fraud with the ulterior intention that it will be used for fraud. Hence, they are not treated as preparation offences, because the manufacturer and supplier might not have any intention of attempting to use such items himself or herself, because his or her income is simply earned from selling the illegal ATM readers. These are supply and manufacture of illegal goods offences.

The use of network technology and the peculiarities of participation in cybercrimes have made the application of complicity liability difficult in this area.[70] According to the traditional theory of complicity in Chinese law, there has to be bilateral or multidirectional communication between the participants in a crime, and therefore, whether the unknown/unilateral accessory should be punished becomes debatable. If unknown accessories are not going to be punished, the commonly recognised conduct of assistance in cyberspace, such as knowingly

---

67 Cf. R. L. Lippke, "Rewarding Cooperation: The Moral Complexities of Procuring Accomplice Testimony," (2010) 13 *New Crim. L. Rev.* 90.

68 See Supreme People's Court & Supreme People's Procuratorate, "Interpretation of Several Questions Concerning the Specific Application of Law in Handling Criminal Cases of Fraud" (1 March 2011) Article 5: the defendant shall be punished with prison only if the aim of the fraud is to defraud a large amount of property or if there are other serious circumstances.

69 Section 7 of the *Fraud Act 2006* provides:

(1) A person is guilty of an offence if he makes, adapts, supplies or offers to supply any article – (a) knowing that it is designed or adapted for use in the course of or in connection with fraud, or (b) intending it to be used to commit, or assist in the commission of, fraud.

70 English law has no such problem, because it not only has standard complicity provisions that criminalize successful acts of assistance and encouragement, but also offences that criminalize attempted assistance or encouragement as long as the attempts are acts that would have been capable of assisting or encouraging had they reached the mind or person of someone somewhere. See Baker, *op. cit. supra*, note 35 at Chapter 20.

providing technical support and providing a payment service, etc., will go unpunished. The mainstream viewpoint in both academia and practice in China is that only known accessories can be convicted. This is because it has to be proved that X did in fact assist Y. Furthermore, if no one knows who X is or that it was X who assisted Y, then it is practically impossible to extend the criminal law to X's act of assistance.

However, as far as cybercrime is concerned, it has been held that the Chinese doctrine of "joint conduct theory" can apply to accessories of cybercrimes, if they are found and proved to have done an act to assist. There is a strict *mens rea* requirement, but if that is made out even legitimate platform network technology providers could be liable for knowingly assisting the crimes of its customers, because the Chinese law of complicity only requires subjective recklessness. It would have to be proven that the providers of the advertisement or online payment or other cyberservice knew that their users were using the service to commit crimes, but still chose to provide them with the service. It does not matter if they did not want them to perpetrate the crimes and only intended to supply the service to make a profit for their business, because they ulterior intention (or ulterior recklessness) is to assist such criminality.

In these cases, they will be liable under the law of complicity, even if there is no mutual communication between them and their service users.[71] If the assistance remains inchoate (attempted assistance), there would be no liability under the Chinese law of complicity, but there would be in England under Sections 44–46 of the *Serious Crime Act 2007*. Add to that the very wide inchoate fraud offences found in English law, and there is no question that providers would be caught if they either intended or obliquely intended to host advertisements that helped fraudsters.[72] The offence found in Article 286(1) of the *Chinese Criminal Code* is less stringent in that it only allows for liability after a warning has not been complied with. Compare this with the approach taken in the United States under Section 230 of the *Communications Decency Act* (47 U.S.C. § 230), which provides: "No provider or user of an interactive computer service shall be treated

---

71 See Supreme People's Court & Supreme People's Procuratorate, "Opinions on Several Questions Concerning the Application of Law in Handling Criminal Cases of Online Gambling," Article 2 of Interpretation of Online Gambling (31 August 2010); "Interpretation of Several Issues Concerning the Specific Application of Law in Criminal Cases of Making Use of Internet, Mobile Communication Terminals and Voice Stations to Produce, Reproduce, Publish, Traffic and Disseminate Obscene Electronic Information" Article 7 (3 September 2004); "Interpretation of Several Questions Concerning the Specific Application of Law in Criminal Cases of Making Use of Internet, Mobile Communication Terminals and Voice Stations to Produce, Reproduce, Publish, Traffic and Disseminate Obscene Electronic Information (2)" Article 7 (2 February 2010). According to these judicial interpretations, as long as the unilateral criminal connection of "knowing" is affirmed, the Internet service provider shall be punished as a joint offence of the crime of opening a casino or making, duplicating, publishing, selling and disseminating obscene articles for profit by providing services or assistance.

72 Baker, *op. cit. supra*, note 54 at Chapter 4.

as the publisher or speaker of any information provided by another information content provider."

The corporate nature of ISPs would mean that individual fault would be hard to establish. Applying complicity liability is not likely to lead to convictions in many cases, simply because a large organisation such as Tencent[73] might not have any knowledge of the misuse of its technology and platform and thus would lack *mens rea*.[74] It would be necessary to prove that the relevant compliance people and/or senior managers were (individually) subjectively reckless in leaving the illegal content on the Internet. Criminal law aside, there are other incentives for ISPs to remove illegal content such as videos promoting terrorism, because most of the income from social media platforms is through advertising and companies do not want to buy advertising space next to illegal content such as hate speech, and so on.[75]

Derivative liability might depend on the different degrees of derivativeness.[76] Generally, the law of complicity both in China and in common law jurisdictions allow for an accessory to be liable for the perpetrator's wrongdoing when, for

---

73 Cf. A. Tsesis, "Social Media Accountability for Terrorist Propaganda," (2017) 86 *Fordham L. Rev.* 605.

74 For example, see Australia's *Criminal Code Amendment (Sharing of Abhorrent Violent Material) Bill 2019* which made:

> amendments to the *Criminal Code Act 1995* to introduce new offences to ensure that internet, hosting or content services are proactively referring abhorrent violent material to law enforcement, and that hosting and content services are *expeditiously removing* abhorrent violent material that is capable of being accessed within Australia.

> See also Article 14 Of the European Council, E-Commerce Directive and the European Parliament Report titled: *Regulating Disinformation with Artificial Intelligence*, (Brussels: European Parliamentary Research Service, 2019).

75 Foster and Arnesen write:

> For example, Proctor & Gamble, which reportedly spends over $2 billion per year on digital advertising, discovered that it was paying for ads that were never viewed by humans, but by bots instead. Even worse was the fact that their ads were paired with terrorist videos. The company reacted by cutting $100 million in ad spending "because we couldn't be assured that our ads would not appear next to bad content like a terrorist video."

> T. N. Foster and D. W. Arnesen, "Legal Strategies for Combating Online Terrorist Propaganda," (2019) 21 *Atlantic L.J.* 45 at 68–69.

76 Cf. P. H. Robinson, "Imputed Criminal Liability," (1984) 93 *Yale L.J.* 609 at 632–633 where it is observed:

> This spectrum from pure causation analysis through causing crime by an innocent via an innocent dupe to causing crime by an innocent via clever persuasion, continues into cases likely to be analysed as instances of complicity. But even within this latter group there exist variations in the actor's involvement with his accomplice. Such involvement ranges from cases where the actor serves as the mastermind and moving force in the operation, through cases where he is essentially an equal in his contribution to the success of the venture, through cases where his contribution constitutes minor facilitation, to cases where only encouragement and no actual aid is given.

example, he or she assists an excused[77] insane person to kill.[78] Beyond that, mere preparation is usually distinguished from attempts, and attempted complicity is usually distinguished from consummated complicity.[79] However, due to the sophisticated division of labour in cybercrimes, it is easier to find the accessories, which are usually registered Internet companies, than to find the perpetrators who may stay overseas. It is not uncommon for many cybercrimes accessories to be prosecuted while the perpetrators are still at large. With the development of P2P technology, this problem has developed new features. Information transmission, resource sharing and service provision can be carried out directly between nodes, with no need for the intervention of a mainstream server.[80] If this technology is used in the dissemination of works that infringe others' copyright or in the dissemination of pornography, it will lead to a large number of such illegal materials being disseminated and shared, directly and anonymously among Internet users on many nodes.[81]

The "Qvod Co. case" heard in Beijing Haidian District Court was one in which the defendant company had developed a master player based on P2P and streaming media technologies, which can be used by pornographic video websites and network users all over the world. As a result, a huge number of pornographic videos were made available in various nodes and networks, leading to the direct upload and sharing of such videos between users. No website administrator or web user who directly uploaded or shared pornographic videos was prosecuted. The police and the prosecution had investigated and charged the company and its principal directors for the crime of making profits by disseminating obscene articles. The defence counsel argued that the company and its principal directors provided technologies rather than content, and that they did not directly upload any pornographic videos and were not aware of the dissemination of a large number of pornographic videos through their video player. Despite the previously mentioned judicial interpretation, this case still had problems such as whether the act of providing such a video player is neutral conduct, which ought not be punished.[82] If such conduct is taken as punishable assistance, and therefore the accessory is made liable for complicity when the perpetrator has not been

77 P. H. Robinson, "A System of Excuses: How Criminal Law's Excuse Defences Do, and Don't, Work Together to Exculpate Blameless (and Only Blameless) Offenders," (2009) 42 *Tex. Tech L. Rev.* 259.

78 Baker, *op. cit. supra*, note 35 at 682. L. Chiesa, "Comparative Analysis As an Antidote to Tunnel Vision in Criminal Law Reform: The Example of Complicity," (2018) 70 *Rutgers U.L. Rev.* 1117 at 1120.

79 D. J. Baker, "Conceptualizing Inchoate Complicity: The Normative and Doctrinal Case for Lesser Offenses As an Alternative to Complicity Liability," (2016) 25 *S. Cal. Interdisc. L.J.* 503.

80 R. Giblin, "Physical World Assumptions and Software World Realities (and Why There Are More P2p Software Providers Than Ever Before)," (2011) 35 *Colum. J.L. & Arts* 57.

81 E. Larson, "Tracking Criminals with Internet Protocol Addresses: Is Law Enforcement Correctly Identifying Perpetrators?" (2017) 18 *N.C.J.L. & Tech. On.* 316.

82 See Che Hao, "Who Pays for Neutrality in the Internet era?" (2015) 1 *China Law Review* 49; cf. M. Lavi, "Evil Nudges," (2018) 21 *Vand. J. Ent. & Tech. L.* 1 at 64. See also *Tamiz*

brought to book, it would infringe on the Chinese criminal law doctrine of "no perpetrator, no accessory."[83]

6. The limits of national jurisdiction

Because of the borderless and virtual nature of the Internet, crimes committed in cyberspace usually have the characteristics of being transnational, borderless and distant.[84] Transnational cross-border crimes have become a noticeable problem. The diversification of the place where the cybercrimes occur and the consequences of cybercrimes have caused jurisdictional conflicts based on the principle of territorial jurisdiction.[85] The fact that criminals cooperate with each other, both domestically and internationally, to commit cybercrimes has led to conflicts of jurisdiction based on the principle of personal jurisdiction. Victims of cybercrimes are in all corners of the world, so this has led to some jurisdictions invoking the principle of protective jurisdiction.[86] There might be a conflict of jurisdiction according to the principle of universal jurisdiction,[87] if the cybercrimes committed are international crimes. The conflicts among domestic criminal law, criminal procedure, evidence law, law enforcement strategies and criminal

---

v. Google Inc. [2012] Q.B. 449; *Delfi AS v. Estonia [GC]* (2015) No. 64569/09, Eur. Ct. H.R.

83 For compendious and convenient overview of the Chinese scholarship, see Yu Zhigang, *Research on Network Alienation of Joint Crime*, (Beijing: China Fangzheng Press, 2010). Cf. the position in English law for those who incite others through the internet or other means: Baker, *op. cit. supra*, note 35 at 811, noting that it is possible for a person to use social media to incite the world at large to perpetrate crimes.

84 See A. H. Stuart, "Social Media, Manipulation, and Violence," (2019) 15 *S.C.J. Int'l L. & Bus.* 100 at 121; G. F. Frosio, "Reforming Intermediary Liability in the Platform Economy: A European Digital Single Market Strategy," (2017) 112 *Nw. U.L. Rev.* 19 at 22.

85 A. Perloff-Giles, "Transnational Cyber Offenses: Overcoming Jurisdictional Challenges," (2018) 43 *Yale J. Int'l L.* 191.

86 An American commentary sums up the compass of this jurisdiction as follows:

> The basis found in international law for extraterritorial application of the statute is the principle of protective jurisdiction, the court continued, saying that the protective principle determines jurisdiction by reference to the national interest injured by the offense, and provides an appropriate jurisdictional base for prosecuting a person who, acting beyond the territorial boundaries of the United States, falsifies its official documents.

(2019) 24 *A.L.R. Fed.* 189 (Originally published in 1975).

87 LaFave writes:

> The final basis of extraterritorial jurisdiction is what is usually referred to as universal jurisdiction, by which "international law permits any state to apply its laws to punish certain offenses although the state has no links of territory with the offense, or of nationality with the offender (or even the victim). . . . Today, it is said that universal jurisdiction extends to such other offenses 'of universal concern' as 'slave trade, attacks on or hijacking of aircraft, genocide, war crimes, and perhaps certain acts of terrorism.' "

W. R. LaFave, *Substantive Criminal Law*, (West Publishing, 3rd edn., 2003) at § 4.3(e).

policies, and the lack of mutual legal assistance agreements[88] and cooperation between enforcement agencies in the various jurisdictions, will further exacerbate the conflict of jurisdiction issues.

Despite the fact that cybercrime has no borders, Chinese and foreign criminal law theorists have put forward various doctrines or propositions, such as New Sovereignty Theory[89] and numerous other jurisdictional rules.[90] None of the jurisdictional approaches have unanimous support from the various stakeholders.[91] On the contrary, Article 22 of the Budapest Convention on Cybercrime, the only international convention regulating cybercrime, only mentions territorial personal jurisdiction.[92] The Convention provides that illegal entry, illegal interception, data interference, system interference, abuse of equipment, computer misuse, child pornography, copyright theft and related wrongs should be criminalised, but the constituent elements of these international crimes are different from those found in Chinese law. As a result of this, China has not signed the Convention, which makes it more difficult for China to pursue and charge cybercrimes.

7. Conclusion

We have examined a range of recent amendments to Chinese law and compared them with some of the inchoate, pre-inchoate and remote harm offences found in English law. Chinese law does not have the sort of wide inchoate conspiracy offence like that found in common law jurisdictions, but it will criminalise an agreement under Article 22 when a preparatory act has been done towards making the conspiracy succeed. For example, in the case of *Li and Others*,[93] Li, Xu and

88 See for example, E. De Busser, "Eu-Us Digital Data Exchange to Combat Financial Crime: Fast Is the New Slow," (2018) 19 *German L.J.* 1251.

89 Petitio writes:

> The theory asserts that: the emerging international legal order is vague and intrusive on domestic affairs; that the international law-making process is unaccountable and unenforceable; and there is an assumption that the U.S. can opt out of international regimes.

> D. S. Petito, "Sovereignty and Globalization: Fallacies, Truth, and Perception," (2001) 17 *N.Y.L. Sch. J. Hum. Rts.* 1139 at 1162.

90 See Yu Zhigang, "China's Position on Concluding and Participating in International Conventions on Cybercrime," (2015) 5 *Tribune of Political Science and Law* 54. 101–102; cf. the theoretical issues as discussed in N. Lacey, "Social Policy, Civil Society and the Institutions of Criminal Justice," (2002) 26 *Australasian Journal of Legal Philosophy* 7.

91 D. B. Hollis and M. C. Waxman, "Promoting International Cyber-security Cooperation: Lessons from the Proliferation Security Initiative," (2018) 32 *Temp. Int'l & Comp. L.J.* 147 at 155.

92 "The Budapest Convention is not self-executing, has been ratified by only sixty-two mostly European states parties (many with reservations), and is thought only to hint at an emerging set of norms." B. Corcoran, "A Comparative Study of Domestic Laws Constraining Private Sector Active Defence Measures in Cyberspace," (2020) 11 *Harv. Nat'l Sec. J.* 1 at 17–18.

93 *Li and Others* [2001] Hai Zhong Fa Xing Zhong Zi 78, Intermediate Court of Haikou Municipality, Hainan Province, China Law Information Database, Case Citation: CLI.C.5133.

Huang were wandering on the street and Li suggested they should rob another for money. Xu and Huang agreed. Xu bought a toy pistol and Li bought yellow tape for the purpose of their robbery. The three defendants looked for a target at Pobo Village without success. Later on, they took a taxi to another place and got arrested by policemen at a checkpoint. It was held that the three defendants had *prepared* tools and looked for victims for their planned robbery, with the purpose of illegally appropriating property belonging to another, and therefore should be liable for preparing to commit robbery. The defendant Huang, on his appeal, argued that there was no conspiracy between them, and he did not have any intention[94] to commit robbery. The court dismissed this argument and held that Huang demonstrated his acquiescence to Li's idea of committing robbery and followed the other two to get tools and look for victims, and therefore it could be inferred that Huang had the intention to commit robbery.

All three were treated as participants in robbery. Chinese law under Articles 25–31 adopts a concept of "joint crime," rather than complicity. The joint crime rules govern all participants in a crime including perpetrators and non-perpetrators of preparatory acts. Joint crime can be committed in Chinese law not only when the perpetrator(s) have committed the crime, but also when they have attempted or prepared to commit the target crime. In this case, all three were acting together at the preparation stage, and they were treated as joint criminals. Technically, if Huang, after agreeing with others to do the robbery, left them right after he agreed, he would still be liable for preparation to commit robbery, as he is an accessory in the preparatory acts. It is widely accepted in academic works in China that conspiracy with some overt preparatory act will bring all the parties within the joint crime provisions. Chinese law recognised preparatory acts (i.e., making the conditions for perpetrating the target crime) as including selecting a target, gathering participants, negotiating the means of committing the crime, negotiating the time and place of the crime, discussing how to cover their crime after having committed it, and so forth. However, Article 13 states that if the circumstance of defendant's conduct is obviously minor and the harmfulness of it is negligible, it may not be regarded as a crime. So, in practice, the prosecution may choose not to charge, if for example, a person withdraws from the crime before some preparatory act is done by one of the parties to the agreement such as the purchase of the tools for a burglary or robbery.

We have tried to conceptualise some of the problems and justifications for applying pre-inchoate liability and omissions liability to cybercrime problems in Chinese law. Our conclusion is that Chinese law does not go nearly as far as English law with respect to inchoate, pre-inchoate and remote harm liability. Furthermore, the Chinese law of complicity is far more limited in that it requires the actual perpetrator and accessory to both be caught and convicted; otherwise,

---

94 Note that intention in Chinese law covers direct intention and indirect intention. The former means D knows that his conduct will cause the prohibited harm of the crime and hopes such harm will be caused. This is same as direct intention in English law. Indirect intention in Chinese law means D knows/foresees that his conduct may cause the prohibited harm of the crime, but is indifferent as to the occurrence of such harm.

complicity is not made out. This is a real barrier when the perpetrator is in Moldova and the accessory is in China. English law has no requirement for either to be identified or that the perpetrator be convicted, as long as it can be proved one was the perpetrator and the other the accessory. Suppose surveillance footage shows X giving Y a gun in a public square and Y immediately using that gun to kill V. Y flees the scene of the crime and is never found again, but X is arrested a few hours later. In English law, there is no barrier to convict X for murder for assisting Y – it does not matter that Y cannot be found and no one can determine who Y was. Likewise, in English law, it does not matter that it is not possible to determine which one was the accessory, and which one was the perpetrator, as long as it can be proved one had to be the perpetrator and the other the accessory.[95]

We have tried into introduce the new network offences found in Articles 286(1) and 287(1), and have given some commentary on these and have provided a nuanced discussion of how they might apply in practice. A lot more judicial interpretation is needed, and further details are required to be able to discuss further how these offences might apply in practice and how they might expand going forward. We have argued that the offences seem to strike at serious harm that needs deterring, but we can see some serious obstacles arising due to the corporate nature of ISPs. In English law, it has been notoriously difficult to impute fault to CEOs and senior managers of companies, because they have been able to argue that they were too far removed from the breach to have sufficient knowledge to be responsible. This is dealt with well in the new Chinese provisions, because liability depends on a warning being served on particular officers within the corporation.

Finally, we have argued that pre-inchoate and remote harm offences can be helpful, as long as they result in fair labelling of the harm and wrong done, and as long as the sentence takes into account that the act was pre-inchoate or a remote harm. This is necessary not only because of the sheer number of victims that can be targeted through cybermeans, but also because of the very different roles that differ cybercriminals play. By having criminal offences to cover each step in the process, there is a higher chance of catching more people either at the pre-inchoate stage or remote harm stage, if not at the inchoate stage. It ought not matter that one party does preparatory acts (remote harms) for another without having any intention of assisting the other.

If a person sells information obtained through phishing to a fraud gang, then a factfinder would have little difficulty inferring that such a person was at least subjectively aware of the fact that such information would be misused by those he or she sold it to. If a person sets up a fake hotel webpage for a crime gang for reward, it ought not matter that the creator of the webpage did not receive any money from any of those who were fooled into booking rooms at the fake hotel. It also should not matter that such an act was not directly preparatory, because

---

95 Glanville Williams, "Which of You Did It," (1989) 52 *Mod. L. Rev.* 179.

the only gain the website creator was looking for was payment for the service of setting up a webpage. Additionally, it ought not matter that they creator of such a webpage did not care that it would be used for fraud, if he knew it would be used for such a purpose. The website could only serve one purpose, and the creator of the website has done an act for reward to assist a criminal gang, and thus would be liable under in English law for the remote harm offence found in Section 7 of the *Fraud Act 2006* (U.K.). We think China could enact similar offences in its quest to combat cybercrime.

Acknowledgments

The authors acknowledge translation assistance provided by Liu Jiye and Chu Chu, doctoral candidates at Peking University

7 Rethinking personal data protection in the criminal law of China

Dongyan Lao and Dennis J. Baker

1. Introduction

The use of network and information technology has had a profound impact on the world. We are living in an age when data affects all aspects of life and society. Over the last decade, big data has emerged as one of the hottest issues for technology lawyers. Big data is now a central part of the economy as tech giants data mine for marketing purposes. Big tech is the industrial revolution of the twenty-first century, but tech giants demand data for the services they provide. This data is then used to manipulate the market[1] and society by targeting news and advertisements, depending on the social media account holder's predilections. Big data is highly valuable to the owner of the data for privacy and security reasons, but equally valuable to governments and big companies for marketing, research and town planning, among other things.[2]

Governments find big data useful for handling pandemics and determining where to build international airports, schools and hospitals; while private companies find big data essential for determining what products and services to produce and whether to market those services.[3] Pharmaceutical companies need big data for the research and development of new medicines and treatments. Hence, big data and related technology not only leads to privacy and security issues, but also significantly influences how institutions and corporations run.[4]

---

1 "Lessons learned from Facebook's privacy and content manipulation provide a valuable teaching moment for all others engaged in using the Internet for marketing, or hosting user generated content on their sites." L. J. Trautman, "Governance of the Facebook Privacy Crisis," (2020) 20 *U. Pitt. J. Tech. L. Pol'y* 43 at 51; see too D. Susser *et al.*, "Online Manipulation: Hidden Influences in A Digital World," (2019) 4 *Geo. L. Tech. Rev.* 1.

2 The analytics component of the big data market will be the most valuable, but raw data is valuable, too. The cumulative value of big data + IoT for the U.K. economy from 2015–2020 will be in excess of £322 billion. "The Value of Big Data andthe Internet of Things to the UK Economy," (London: Cebr, 2016).

3 M. Mrcela and I. Vuletic, "Healthcare, Privacy, Big Data and Cybercrime: Which One Is the Weakest Link?" (2018) 27 *Annals Health L.* 257; B. R. Furrow, "The Limits of Current A.I. in Health Care: Patient Safety Policing in Hospitals," (2020) 12 *Ne. U.L. Rev.* 1; E. Berman, "Individualized Suspicion in the Age of Big Data," (2020) 105 *Iowa L. Rev.* 463.

4 J. Armour and H. Eidenmüller, "Self-Driving Corporations?" (2019) 10 *Harv. Bus. L. Rev.* 87.

The importance of personal data led to major reforms in Europe, California and China.[5] In this chapter, we hope to provide those in common law jurisdictions with an insight into the Chinese approach to data protection, while introducing some key concepts and theories from common law countries for our Chinese audience.

In particular, we will focus on how the Chinese model not only uses public law, including the criminal law, to regulate data protection. It will be argued that China's data protection laws are much closer to European law than to the position in the United States. While gaps remain in China's data protection laws, its willingness to treat data as worthy of criminal law protection puts it ahead of Europe as far as potential enforcement is concerned. In Chapter 4 of this volume, it is pointed out that the GDPR is a toothless tiger for serious privacy breaches as it includes not arrestable and imprisonable offence – at least to the extent it has been adopted into the *Data Protection Act 2018* (U.K.). It will be contended that while the *General Data Protection Regulation* (GDPR) results in large fines (up to 4% of a company's annual turnover) for breaches by businesses,[6] these are designed mainly to regulate organisations controlling data, not individuals. If a rogue manager misuses data, there is no criminal offence in the GDPR that would result in a prison sentence. If a rogue manager misuses data while working for a government department, he or she will not be too concerned about that department having to pay a fine. In this sense, having a criminal offence to deal with privacy and data breaches would deter individuals as opposed to organisations, such as corporations, from misusing data.

In recent years, China has made some positive changes in its criminal legislation and public law provisions. However, it is yet to implement an all-encompassing legal scheme that would not only result in large fines for corporations and government departments (in China's current scheme, government departments could be criminally liable for infringing citizens' personal information rights) and also individuals who misuse private data to perpetrate other crimes or simply to violate a person's privacy or to humiliate them or damage their reputation. In this chapter, we shall attempt to critically evaluate China's existing criminal law framework as far as it relates to data protection to ascertain whether it is fit for purpose. It will be argued that since China is now a leader in technological innovation, its laws need reform to keep pace with emerging technologies.

Information is more relevant to privacy than data in isolation, because isolated bits of data do not really tell us much about a person. It is when lots of bits

5 A. Tsesis, "Data Subjects' Privacy Rights: Regulation of Personal Data Retention and Erasure," (2019) 90 *U. Colo. L. Rev.* 593; D. Chen and H. Ji, "Is GDPR Compliance Enough for Entities Operating in Asia?" (2019) *ACC Docket* 44; B. Casey *et al.*, "Rethinking Explainable Machines: The GDPR's 'Right to Explanation' Debate and the Rise of Algorithmic Audits in Enterprise," (2019) 34 *Berkeley Tech. L.J.* 143.

6 For example, a French regulator fined Google €50 million ($55.5 million) pursuant to the GDPR for breaches of its domestic privacy laws.

of information are put together to profile a person that privacy is risked.[7] The personal data as used in the sense of the GDPR refers to all information about identified natural persons ("data subjects").[8] Personal data includes both the data belonging to and related to individuals. The Chinese conceptualisation of personal data fits broadly within this paradigm.

The first part of this chapter discusses the characteristics of personal data and its status in China's current legal framework and theory, while drawing analogies with some theories in the literature from common law jurisdictions. The second part of this chapter examines when personal data will be protected by Chinese criminal law. The third part aims to provide a critical analysis of the inadequateness of applying property law to the problem. Finally in the fourth part, we shall try to make the case for showing that the law needs urgent implementation and refinement so that it is not merely recommendatory, but is a binding law with real teeth.

2. The legal status of personal data

The replicability and transferrable nature of digitally sorted data means it raises a host of questions about individual rights and interests, including privacy and property rights. The balance between personal privacy and tech giants using data to generate income to provide services such as social media, search engines and the Internet needs to be thought about in the wider social context whereby the individual consumer who trades her data for such services has little to no bargaining power, and does so almost absent-mindedly. Most consumers provide their location data, personal photos, phone numbers, email addresses, facial biometrics,

---

7 Lucero writes:

> While there still is not a comprehensive law that defines and protects personal privacy, there are other laws that stipulate an obligation of government agencies and private actors to safeguard personal data as well as a tort action for violating the right of privacy.

K. Lucero, "Artificial Intelligence Regulation and China's Future," (2019) 33 *Colum. J. Asian L.* 94 at 140.

8 Black writes:

> "Personal data" means any information relating to an identified or identifiable natural person ("data subject"); an identifiable natural person is one who can be identified, directly or indirectly, in particular by reference to an identifier such as a name, an identification number, location data, an online identifier or to one or more factors specific to the physical, physiological, genetic, mental, economic, cultural or social identity of that natural person. . . . China's *Personal Information Security Specification* took effect in May 2018. The Specification is the 'effective centrepiece of an emerging system around personal data,' which includes the 2017 *Cybersecurity Law*. The CSL loosely defines both personal data and a new category of personal sensitive data, which may include "data that may lead to bodily harm, property damage, reputational harm, harm to personal heath, or discriminative treatment of an individual if such data is disclosed, leaked or abused."

S. T. Black, "Cyberdamages," (2020) 36 *Santa Clara High Tech. L.J. 1* at 15.

fingerprint biometrics and voice biometrics without giving a thought to how this information might be used.[9]

Most people are happy to use biometrics to avoid remembering a password and because it is more secure than a password being entered each time. Tech companies have a range of personal data on the majority of those who use their services which include their name, gender, birthday, home address, mobile number, email, locations visited, relationship status, place of employment, educational background, religious and political beliefs, favourite music, newspapers, favourite topics read or viewed, facial recognition data, financial and banking details, IP address, search history, diary events, shopping habits though purchasing history, fitness and health data (fitness trackers or smart-phones record this and send it in), devices used, any webpage clicked on, and fingerprint and voice data, to name a few. All these bits of data can be combined to create an intimate profile of the social media account holder.

In addition, much of the focus on biometric data privacy focuses on facial recognition cameras in public places, but these are largely justified as an effective way to maintain public safety by identifying wanted criminals in real time. While the focus has been there, large tech companies and their monopoly on data has gone unnoticed. All countries are rolling out face recognition cameras in public places to help to track down criminals, and as long as this is done within the relevant constitutional framework, it perhaps can be justified as the lesser of two evils. It will sometimes be misused, but human police officers lack the ability to police the entire population by sight. Facial recognition and number plate recognition technology allows AI operated cameras to deal with some crimes. For example, a person who runs a red light can be sent a fine automatically. Similarly, the terrorist who enters an airport can be identified more accurately by AI (assuming the terrorist is on a database already) than by the human eye.[10] This is not an area that is dealt with in this chapter, because the United States, the United Kingdom, many E.U. countries and China have already embraced AI policing and it can be justified on national security grounds when balanced on a utilitarian calculus.[11]

---

9 Nilsson writes:

> Apart from the risk of data breaches, . . . too few people question a company's commercial incentive when they agree to share their image, fingerprint or voice sample. The growth of Internet of Things technology – such as Amazon's Alexa speakers that gather and share user data – will further help take biometric authentication mainstream, he says. We are so tied up with worrying about the surveillance state, but the challenge is actually coming from a different direction and there is not the same level of debate.

P. Nilsson, "Face Off: The Perils of Sharing Your Biometric Data," (London: *The Financial Times*, 30 October 2019). Violations of biometric privacy have resulted in class actions in the United States. See for example, *Rosenbach v. Six Flags Entm't Corp.*, (2019) 129 N.E.3d 1197 at 1206–1207; *Patel v. Facebook, Inc.*, (2019) 932 F.3d 1264.

10 *Privacy International v. Secretary of State for Foreign and Commonwealth Affairs* [2018] UKIP Trib IPT 15 110 CH.

11 P. Swire and J. Woo, "Privacy and Cybersecurity Lessons at the Intersection of the Internet of Things and Police Body-Worn Cameras," (2018) 96 *N.C. L. Rev.* 1475.

More generally, Chinese law recognises data protection and the relevant infrastructure as a national security issue. This is sensible, because it is as important as roads and trains and other hard infrastructure are to a country's prosperity. Article 37 of China's *Cybersecurity Law* requires "critical information infrastructure" operators to store within mainland China data collected within the mainland. The definition of "critical information infrastructure" is given in Article 31 to include, inter alia, "public communication and information services, energy, transportation, water resources, finance, public services, e-governance." A security assessment is required for locally stored data, if cross-border data transfer is to take place. So it is not only a matter of using data to protect the public through AI camera policing methods, but also about protecting sensitive data from being transferred without safeguards. The focus in this chapter is on consumer rights and privacy, in an age when tech giants have a monopoly on data possession. We also want to address the issue of individuals misusing data when they are acting alone and not as an agent for a corporation.

(a) Is privacy a public good?

The public good question is a hotly debated issue in China, so we will briefly make reference to the common law literature concerning this question. The protection of personal data is now covered rather well by public law, but there are some private law protections, too.[12] In Europe, data is protected by public law provisions such as the GDPR and the right to privacy found in Article 8 of the *European Convention on Human Rights*, while the United States relies more on private law remedies sought through class actions.[13] It should be pointed out that the protection of personal data in China, like Europe, is not a mere question of protecting privacy. Privacy has a much narrower meaning in the context of Chinese data law, as it does in the GDPR. The right to privacy found in Article 8 of the *European Convention on Human Rights* protects privacy per se, but data laws have a wider reach. In China, the *Personal Information Security Specification GB/T 35273–2017 (2018)*, which is a quasi-administrative law, provides for public law protection of data. It covers three core categories: personal information, data transfer and data management and governance.[14] However, according to the

---

12 P. C. Ormerod, "A Private Enforcement Remedy for Information Misuse," (2019) 60 *B.C. L. Rev.* 1893.

13 See for example, *Rosenbach v. Six Flags Entm't Corp.* (2019) 129 N.E.3d 1197 at 1206–1207; *Patel v. Facebook, Inc.* (2019) 932 F.3d 1264.

14 See:

> 1) personal general data and 2) personal sensitive data. Personal data is broadly defined as information that is recorded in an electronic or other manner and may independently or in combination with other information identify an individual or reflect activity status of an individual. Personal sensitive data means personal data that may cause reputational, physical or mental damages or discriminatory treatment, if divulged, illegally provided or abused. Personal data that does not fall within the scope of personal sensitive data are automatically deemed personal general data.

Personal Information Security Specification GB/T 35273–2017 (2018), if the personal information is of a general non-sensitive nature, there are many exceptions where Chinese law does not mandate that a data controller seek consent to collect data, although it provides a clause of informed consent. If the information is of a sensitive nature, then explicit consent has to be obtained.[15] The scheme is primarily aimed at preventing corporate data controllers from obtaining data without proper consent. Now the revised *Personal Information Security Specification GB/T 35273–2020* has been published, it will come into effect in October 2020. This newest edition has also increased the number of obligations for data controllers concerning the collection, storage and use of personal biometric data.

Does the described public data protection law need justifying as protecting a public good, as is often assumed by Chinese scholars? Fairfield and Engel argue that privacy is a public good in the same way as reducing air pollution is a public good. They juxtapose it with a public bad in the following exemplar:

> Online, individuals regularly face the following decision: they are invited to join some Internet platform, knowing (more or less vaguely) that they will indirectly pay by making personal information available. Take the typical social network. The individual damage a user foresees when leading an active online life seems reasonable. A user might reason that the likelihood of negative consequences is low, and even if an event were to occur, it likely would not be momentous. The user may not perceive individual risk sufficient to stimulate abstention from the immediate and personal benefits conveyed by use of the network. The user knows she will reveal some information about her friends and family. Maybe the user knows one of them to be particularly vulnerable, but does not account for the risk of her own contributions to data about that person – *few people understand or even consider that a message of sympathy in the event of illness might affect healthcare premiums.* This is precisely the kind of reasoning the public-bads model aims to capture. The user's anticipated individual damage is too small to outweigh anticipated benefit. Things would look differently if users were to factor in the negative repercussions of being generous with their private information on the privacy risk faced by others and vice versa. Yet as long as each user only considers the potential damage to herself, no individual would be concerned

---

Network operators and data controllers, 1 *Corp Couns Gd to Doing Bus in China* § 35:42 (3d ed.).

15 See:

> For personal data, data controllers should obtain explicit consent from data subjects. Personal data of children under the age of 14 are treated as personal sensitive data and eligible consent must come from the child's legal guardian. An explicit consent is an affirmative act of the data subject.

Ibid.

that anticipated damage outweighs actual and anticipated benefit" (emphasis added).[16]

It is a public good in that the network is akin to having a public road system or public parks and streets for people to use for socialising, work and business, but that network can only function for the greater good if privacy is preserved. In this sense, privacy in the online sphere is a public good in itself. It is a public good that deserves protection because privacy violations not only harm individuals, but in aggregate harms the value of the relevant platform or Internet service as a piece of public service infrastructure. It is akin to a having a poorly maintained rail line that keeps resulting in train crashes, because the infrastructure is of less public benefit if it cannot be trusted. Trust depends on data not being misused (use without consent which is an innate misuse) or leaked to facilitate collateral harms.

Fairfield and Engel also acknowledge that privacy is also private good. "Privacy has some attributes of a private good. My own privacy inures both to my private benefit in ways that affect me alone, and my privacy-seeking behaviour positively affects others."[17] A befuddled variant of this approach also has support in China.[18] It is a public good, since big data provides an essential public benefit that would make using private information permissible, if done carefully with consent or in the public interest.[19] So sharing data itself is a public good and property data protection makes the mechanisms for sharing such data a public good, and thus they need to be such as to prevent data leakages and data misuse by those trusted as controllers. The public good privacy serves other public goods such as making the network of Internet service providers (ISPs) trustworthy and ultimately encourage safe data sharing for ulterior public goods such as when the government collects healthcare big data to analyse it to fight a pandemic. Each individual's information could be anonymised to preserve a

---

16 J. A. T. Fairfield and C. Engel, "Privacy As A Public Good," (2015) 65 *Duke L.J.* 385 at 423–424. At 425, Fairfield and Engel state: "A key element of treating privacy as a public good is that law must be able to recognize the social and systemic harms caused by the collection, aggregation, and exploitation of data." See further S. Romanosky and A. Acquisti, "Privacy Costs and Personal Data Protection: Economic and Legal Perspectives," (2009) 24 *Berkeley Tech. L.J.* 1061 at 1062.

17 "A state agency may make protected nonpublic data accessible to the public if it determines that public access will 'aid the law enforcement process, promote public health or safety or dispel widespread rumour or unrest.' " *In re GlaxoSmithKline plc* (2007) 732 N.W.2d 257 at 264.

18 Ji Yang, "The Right of Self-determination of Legal Interest and the Judicial Boundary of the Crime of Infringing Citizens' Personal Information," (2019) 4 *China Legal Science* 1; Liu Yanhong, "Legal Interests of the Crime of Infringing Citizens' Personal Information: Confirmation of Personal Legal Interests and New Types of Rights" (2019) 5 *Criminal Science* 1; Cf. Mei Xiaying, "Between Sharing and Controlling – Limitation of Data Protection by Private Law and Construction of Public Order," (2019) 4 *Peking University Law Journal* 847 at 856.

19 Wu Weiguang, "Criticism on Personal Data Information Private Right Protection Theory under Big Data Technology," (2016) 7 *Political Science and Law* 117.

layer of privacy, while allowing healthcare researchers to use the general information.[20] What is important is that privacy is protected so all these ulterior public goods can be achieved. Thus, the state has an obligation to protect data.[21] Social media and search engines are as important to modern civilisations as public roads and railways. During the recent pandemic, online communications held society together. However, these services are by and large provided by private companies.[22]

Even though something is a public good,[23] that does not mean that public law such as criminal law need be used to regulate the harm that is caused to that good. However, since the harm to privacy can result in serious collateral harm to individuals it is best to regulate data protection with public law including criminal law. It would appear that data protection laws aim to protect an impure public good and are the right approach for this purpose.[24] A law criminalising causing damage to public infrastructure, such as a railway line, might take the collateral harm intended or risked into account such as endangering the lives of others,[25] but both harms are criminalised. That a law protects privacy to preserve the public value of privately provided search engines (Google, Bing, Baidu) and privately provided social media platforms (Facebook, WeChat), does not mean it need not tackle the individualised harm, as well.[26] Two public goods are protected: privacy, which in turn protects the Internet or platform by making it safe public infrastructure. Furthermore, that individuals might also have a private action in contract or tort (or even in property law for copyright violations), does not displace the case for using the criminal law to prevent the primary harm caused by privacy violations.[27] It would be too much to ask a person with no income to take

20 M. A. Rodwin, "Patient Data: Property, Privacy & the Public Interest," (2010) 36 *Am. J.L. & Med.* 586.
21 E. M. Sedenberg and D. K. Mulligan, "Public Health As A Model for Cybersecurity Information Sharing," (2015) 30 *Berkeley Tech. L.J.* 1687.
22 A. Chander, "Facebookistan," (2012) 90 *N.C. L. Rev.* 1807.
23 Courts do not use public good as a criminalisation justification. See *Google France Sarl v Louis Vuitton Malletier SA* (C-236/08) [2011] Bus. L.R. 1; *E.J. Brooks Co. v. Cambridge Sec. Seals* (20–18) 31 N.Y.3d 441 at 475.
24 R. G. Hammond, "Quantum Physics, Econometric Models and Property Rights to Information," (1981) 27 *Mcgill L.J.* 47 at 54; R. J. Staaf, "Privatization of Public Goods," (1983) 41 *Pub. Choice* 435.
25 See for example, the English case, *R. v. Asquith* [1995] 2 All E.R. 168.
26 D. J. Baker, "Collective Criminalization and the Constitutional Right To Endanger Others," (2009) 28 *Crim. Just. Ethics* 168 at 178.
27 D. J. Baker, *Glanville Williams Textbook of Criminal Law*, (London: Sweet & Maxwell, 2015) at Chapter 3.

> Whereas purely private goods are characterized by both rivalry in and excludability from consumption, purely public goods show properties of nonrivalry and nonexcludability. All other goods between these two extremes are usually called impure public goods. Two important subclasses of impure public goods are common-pool resources and marketable public goods. Whereas private goods can be provided efficiently by the market, this is not possible with pure public goods.

expensive legal action to prevent a serious privacy violation against her, when the privacy loss has caused her serious harm. Such a system would mean only those who could afford a lawyer would be have data protection rights. By using the criminal law, a person can call the police and let the state take action for the harm caused to her, even if she is a poor student with no money. Criminal law protects all equality, whereas private law protects those with the money to use it.[28]

Some scholars in China tend to argue that personal data only gives rise to private rights.[29] These scholars argue that data protection be achieved by applying private law remedies.[30] They assert that criminal law protection should be a last resort. This would leave a gap in the law as far as data protection is concerned, as the right of privacy found in Article 38 (dignity) and Article 40 (correspondence)[31] of the *Constitution of the People's Republic of China* is too narrow to protect data in the wider sense. The constitutional right to self-determination found in Chinese law has not been applied to lower-level data breaches, and it is unlikely that it would protect people from such breaches. Generally, the use of public law is not limited to protecting public goods, but private rights such as the right not to be murdered or raped or have one's information stolen and misused.[32] A core example of the criminal law being used to protect privacy in the United Kingdom and United States is sexual privacy offences against voyeurs secretly recording people nude or engaged in sexual acts.[33] Allowing tech giants to misuse data causes harm to a person's privacy interests and aggregate harm to the interest we all have in maintaining a social media system that is transparent and fair.

K. Holzinger, "Treaty Formation and Strategic Constellations A Comment on Treaties: Strategic Considerations," (2008) 2008 *U. Ill. L. Rev.* 187 at 190.

28 T. Bingham, "The Price of Justice," (1994) 60(4) *Arbitration* 239.

29 See Wang Liming, "Legal Protection of Personal Information: Centred on the Line between Personal Information and Privacy," (2013) 4 *Modern Law Science* 80; Zhang Xinbao, "From Privacy to Personal Information: Construction of Theory and Rule about Interest Remeasurement," (2015) 3 *China Legal Science* 80; Chen Xiao, "Personal Data Rights in the Era of Big Data," (2018) 3 *Social Sciences in China* 22; Ye Mingyi, "On the Basic Category of Personal Information Right," (2018) 5 *Tsinghua University Law Journal* 77; Yang, *op. cit. supra*, note 18 at 88; Yanhong, *op. cit. supra*, note 18 at 64.

30 Others argue that the protection of the exclusive right of information is aimed at protecting data subject's self-determination right. See Jing Lijia, "The Necessary Transition of Legal Interests of the Crime of Infringing Citizens' Personal Information in the Era of Big Data," (2018) 2 *Law Review* 1.

31 According to Paragraph 5 of Article 4 of *Decision of the Standing Committee of the National People's Congress on Preserving Computer Network Security (2009 Amendment)*, anyone who unlawfully intercepts, tampers with or deletes another's emails or other data, thus infringing on citizens' freedom and privacy of correspondence, shall be criminally liable.

32 J. Feinberg, *Harm To Others*, (New York: O.U.P., 1984); D. J. Baker, *The Right Not to Be Criminalized*, (Oxford: Routledge, 2011).

33 Sections 67 and 67A of the *Sexual Offences Act 2003*.

(b) The current law in China

In 2009, the *Seventh Criminal Law Amendment* in China added the crime of illegally obtaining citizens' personal information (Article 253–1), which was maintained in the *Ninth Criminal Law Amendment 2015*. Meanwhile, its name has changed into the crime of infringing upon citizens' personal information. This crime belongs to Chapter IV *Crimes of Infringing upon the Rights of the Person and the Democratic Rights of Citizens* in the *Criminal Code of China*. The relevant provisions of civil law also confirm that people have private law rights concerning their personal information.

When the *Law on the Protection of the Rights and Interests of Consumers of the People's Republic of China* was revised in 2013, it added that consumers "have the right to protect personal information according to law." Articles 14 and 29 of *the Law on the Protection of Consumer Rights and Interests* include consent and use provisions apropos data, but they are fairly vague in their definitions and limited in their express coverage. For example, there is no express right to have data erased. Article 111 of the *Civil Law General Provisions of the People's Republic of China*, which came into effect in October 2017, stipulates that personal information is protected by law. This provision imposes obligations on the controller, whether it is an organisation or an individual.[34]

In terms of the administrative law system, the *Decision of the Standing Committee of the National People's Congress on Strengthening Information Protection on Networks 2012* enacts some principal provisions on electronic information. In particular, it targets information that can identify the personal identity of another. It mainly imposes obligations on network service providers and other enterprises. These obligations require them to follow certain processes when collecting, using and preserving personal information.[35] ISPs have to follow the collection and use

---

34 Article 111 provides:

The personal information of natural persons is protected by law. Where any organization or individual needs to obtain someone else's personal information, they shall obtain it in accordance with law and ensure the information is handled securely; they must not unlawfully collect, use, process, or transfer the personal information of others, and must not unlawfully buy, sell, provide or disclose others' personal information.

35 Articles 2–4 in *the Decision* state that:

II, Network service providers and other enterprises undertaking that collect or use citizens' individual electronic information during their business activities, shall abide by the principles of legality, legitimacy and necessity, clearly indicate the objective, methods and scope for collection and use of information, and obtain agreement from the person whose data is collected, they may not violate the provisions of laws and regulations, and the agreement between both sides, in collecting or using information. Network service providers and other enterprise and undertaking work units collecting or using citizens' individual electronic information shall make public their collection and use rules. III, Network service providers, other enterprise and undertaking work units and their staff must strictly preserve the secrecy of citizens' individual electronic information they collect in their business activities, they may not divulge, distort, or damage it, and may not sell or illegally provide

rules laid down in *Telecommunications and Internet Personal User Data Protection Regulation (2013)*, which include a notification requirement apropos data breaches. The *Cybersecurity Law of the People's Republic of China 2017*, for the first time, defined the meaning of personal information.

This does not mean that in the current legal framework, personal data is only conceptualised as personal information per se. The courts in China have not only suggested that mined and processed big data might create a property interest, but also have been embroiled in a debate about what forms of might be virtual property protected by the law of theft. Since property normally requires the right to exclusive control, it would only be possible to recognise data in its analysed and aggregate form as giving rise to some sort of *sui generis* or equitable interest. No one can own facts,[36] and courts in the Europe and the United States have repeatedly denied copyright protection to those who organise basic facts with AI and computer programmes.

Therefore, consistent with the dicta in *New York Mercantile*, when confronted with raw data that have been converted into a final value through the use of a formula, courts should put significant weight on the degree of consensus and objectivity that attaches to the formula to determine whether the final value is fundamentally a "fact."[37]

This use of a formula would merely discover an "empirical reality," and therefore the result would be uncopyrightable. This is true even if the resulting output is not completely accurate, so long as the formula used is generally accepted and quintessentially objective. Thus, the output data generated by using Newton's Second Law of Motion – force equals mass times acceleration, or "F = ma" – would be a series of uncopyrightable facts, even though the output is in some sense an estimation because Newton's formula fails does not consider relativistic effects. See Albert Einstein, *The Theory of Relativity*.[38]

Where: (1) the raw data used to create the final value were unprotectable facts; (2) the method of converting raw data into the final value was an industry standard, or otherwise widely accepted as an objective methodology; and (3) the final value attempted to measure an empirical reality, then the final value produced from raw data ordinarily is not protected by copyright.[39]

---

it to other persons. IV, Network service providers and other enterprise and undertaking work units shall adopt technological measures and other necessary measures to ensure information security and prevent that citizens' individual electronic information collected during business activities is divulged, damaged or lost. When divulging, damage to or loss of information occurs or may occur, remedial measures shall be adopted immediately.

36 J. McCutcheon, "The Vanishing Author in Computer-Generated Works: A Critical Analysis of Recent Australian Case Law," (2012) 36 *Melbourne University Law Review* 917.
37 *BanxCorp v. Costco Wholesale Corp.* (2013) 978 F. Supp. 2d 280 at 300.
38 *Ibid.* at 301.
39 *Ibid.* at 302–303.

Here, the courts are not only stating that the raw data is not copyright protected, but also that general industry formulas that are applied to the data do not make the merger of that formula and its application to the raw data copyright protected. If a firm had invented some sophisticated AI programme, then that programme itself, not being some general and publicly unprotected formula, would be protected. But again, any raw data it is applied to is not protected by copyright. Thus, the data market has to be based on contract rights[40] and on the ability of the data holder to keep its big data secure. Perhaps that is why the National Health Service in England has been successful in selling anonymised raw patient data to U.S. medical companies.[41] The National Health Service gets away with this as the data is anonymised, and it is the only one who can lawfully access the raw data. It cannot pass on the raw data, but can pass on anonymised big data. Europe does provide limited protection to databases in its *Database Directive*,[42] but Europe, the United States, England and Australia do not recognise big data per se as giving rise to a proprietary interest such as copyright.[43] No one has an exclusive right to it, so at best it gives rise to contractual rights.

---

40 M. Mattioli, "Disclosing Big Data," (2014) 99 *Minn. L. Rev.* 535.
41 T. Helm, "Patient Data from GP Surgeries Sold to US Companies," (London: *The Guardian*, 7 December 2019).
42 In *Football Dataco Ltd v Yahoo! U.K. Ltd.* (C-604/10) [2012] Bus. L.R. 1753 at 1762, the Court of Justice of the European Union said:

> Directive, its purpose is to stimulate the creation of data storage and processing systems in order to contribute to the development of an information market against a background of exponential growth in the amount of information generated and processed annually in all sectors of activity.

> See also *Fixtures Marketing Ltd v Svenska Spel AB (C-338/02)* [2005] E.C.D.R. 4, where the substantial investment in collated the data was rejected as giving rise to *sui generis* rights. If a person took nearly all the contents of a database rather than just use them, that would be different. See the English case, *77M Ltd. v. Ordnance Survey LtdOrdnance Survey Ltd. V. 77M Ltd* [2019] EWHC 300.

43 Verlinden writes:

> During the creation phase, copyright could be held in relation to the text and/or structure of health questionnaires, coding systems and software developed to collect and analyse samples and data. Copyright could also cover the appearance or design of the database that will store the HBM and data or the website, where one can access the HBM and/or data. During the collection phase, copyright could be held in relation to the manner in which HBM and data are selected and structured. It could also cover protocols or standard operating procedures describing such selection and structure. It may also apply to the software developed to store, process and conduct automatic searches in the collection of HBM and data. In order to obtain copyright protection, one has to demonstrate that the creation is original.

> M. Verlinden, "IPRs in Biobanking – Risks and Opportunities for Translational Research," (2015) 2 *Intellectual Property Quarterly* 106 at 109. Cf. H. Chen *et al.*, "Privacy and Biobanking in China: A Case of Policy in Transition," (2015) 43(4) *J. Law Med. &. Ethics* 726.

The formulas and technology used to sort and analyse the data can be copyrighted,[44] but to give another copyright in a person's shopping habits, medical conditions[45] and social likes and dislikes based on bits of data such as which websites she clicked on would be to give a tech giant copyright in basic facts about another's life. The aggregate information is also basic facts (i.e., the majority of 19-year-olds are watching programme Y or buy a particular type of shoe, etc.). It would be no different than arguing that Fred who follows Cindy to see which cafés she visits, which university she reads at, and so on, now has copyright in those basic facts as he expended labour to follow her. Compare that to where Fred writes up an intellectual biography for Cindy, because she has won a Nobel Prize in Physics.[46] In the later situation, his original authorship of her story in his own narration would give him copyright to his version of her life, but not to the basic facts. Let us assume that Cindy had many lovers and Fred thinks this part of her life story will increase book sales, if he is the only one who can use those facts; here, Fred would not be able to stop others using those facts about Cindy in their stories about her, as long as they put the facts in their own words. When there is a scandal, every newspaper gets to report it in their own words, because not one owns facts.

So big data on its own is not property, and thus has to be regulated by contract law, as far as private rights to make commercial use of it is concerned.[47] Data mining

---

44 *Directive 96/9/EC of the European Parliament and of the Council of 11 March 1996 on the Legal Protection of Databases* [1996] OJ L 77/20. Articile 5 of the *WIPO Copyright Treaty* (WCT) states:

> Compilations of data or other material, in any form, which by reason of the selection or arrangement of their contents constitute intellectual creations, are protected as such. This protection does not extend to the data or the material itself and is without prejudice to any copyright subsisting in the data or material contained in the compilation.

> See also for database design protection: Article 10(2) of the *Agreement on Trade-Related Aspects of Intellectual Property Rights* (TRIPS) and Article 2 of the *Berne Convention*.

45 A person ought to have exclusive control over her medical information and ought to have the right to withdraw consent to it being used. Cf. J.L. Kish and J.E. Topol "Unpatients – Why Patients Should Own Their Medical Data," (2015) 33(9) *Nat. Biotechnol.* 921.

46 *Hodgson v. Isaac* [2012] E.C.C. 4.

47 For example, [*Taobao (China) Software Co., Ltd. v. Meijing Information Technology Co., Ltd. Of Anhui Municipality – Unfair Competition Case*], [Railway Transportation Basic People's Court Hangzhou Municipality, People's Republic of China], [Civil First Trial No. 4034], 16 August 2018. [Intermediate People's Court of Hangzhou Municipality, Zhejiang Province, People's Republic of China], [Civil Appeal No. 7312], 18 December 2018. [High People's Court of Hangzhou Municipality, Zhejiang Province, People's Republic of China], [Civil Appeal No. 1209], 2 July 2019. The High People's Court of Zhejiang Province pointed out in the ruling that:

> Internet big data products are different from the original network data. Although the data content provided by big data products also originates from the information of network users, a large amount of intellectual labour has been invested by network operators. In-depth development and system integration, the data content finally presented to consumers has been anonymised and stored.

is not akin to creating intellectual property (IP) and thus ought to be done with consent. Perhaps the service provided is sufficient "consideration"[48] for making any data mined subject to contract law, when genuine consent has been provided with respect to the collection and particular type of use. People can contract freely if they can obtain the same service without providing data. The service provider might charge them a fee to use the service instead, if they refused to accept any digital surveillance and collection of their data. In Germany, the Bundeskartellamt has held that Facebook has more than 2.3 billion monthly users and it "will no longer be allowed to force its users to agree to the practically unrestricted collection and assigning of non-Facebook data to their Facebook user accounts."[49]

It is true that data mining involves the use of AI and advanced software to analyse and sort the bulk data collected. This is done to ascertain patterns of human behaviour. The data controller can then carry out predictive profiling which commences "with a deep analysis of everything an advertiser knows about existing purchasers and uses that information to decide what products to offer, and at what prices, to other individuals whose profiles 'look like' those of previous customers."[50] The consumer is then bombarded with carefully selected advertisements and targeted prices.[51]

> [P]rofessor Bernt Hugenholtz has warned . . . an all-encompassing property right in data would seriously compromise the system of intellectual property law that currently exists in Europe. It would also contravene fundamental freedoms enshrined in the European Convention on Human Rights and the EU Charter [of Fundamental Rights], distort freedom of competition and freedom of services in the EU, restrict scientific freedoms and generally undercut the promise of big data for European economy and society.[52]

---

48 Consideration in contract law is simply the exchange of one thing of value for another. Without it there can be no binding contract. *Thomas v. Thomas* (1842) 2 Q.B. 851.

49 "Bundeskartellamt Prohibits Facebook from Combining user data from Different Sources," (2 July 2019) <www.bundeskartellamt.de/SharedDocs/Entscheidung/EN/Fallberichte/Missbrauchsaufsicht/2019/B6-22-16.pdf?__blob=publicationFile&v=4>

50 C. W. Savage, "Managing the Ambient Trust Commons: The Economics of Online Consumer Information Privacy," (2019) 22 *Stan. Tech. L. Rev.* 95 at 103–104.

51 Lev-Aretz and Strandburg write:

> Though some have argued that the acquisition and use of big data by online firms does not create significant barriers to entry, others have criticized this position, viewing data as a strategic asset that could lead to market dominance and limit later entry. Rubinfeld and Gal's extensive analysis of market entry barriers in big data markets, showed that such barriers 'can arise in all parts of the data-value chain,' though the extent and importance of such barriers is context-dependent.

> Y. Lev-Aretz and K. J. Strandburg, "Privacy Regulation and Innovation Policy," (2020) 22 *Yale J. L. & Tech.* 256 at 302–303.

52 Peter K. Yu, "Data Producer's Right and the Protection of Machine-Generated Data," (2019) 93 *Tul. L. Rev.* 859, 864 quoting P. Bernt Hugenholtz, "Against 'Data Property,' " in Kritika (ed.). *Essays on Intellectual Property,* (Harms, 2018) at 50.

Big data is used by large corporations for not much more than to manipulate prices and to aggressively target consumers. "B&Q, a British multinational company, tested in its brick-and-mortar stores digital price tags that interfaced with customers' phones and adjusted the displayed price based on the customer's loyalty cards data and spending habits."[53] It is true that the tech giant harvesting such data does incur the cost of storing it on a cloud server and using AI to best make use of such data, but this is just categorising the information and analysing it, so it is difficult to see how that would involve the innovation and creation that would normally be needed to establish IP rights. Add to this the serious competition law issues that arise when there are just few major tech giants controlling most of the big data for a country the size of China, then the case for granting property rights in big data becomes even weaker.

In China, any use of data without permission, by lawful data controllers, that is said to result in unfair competition can be punished through anti-unfair competition law rather than criminal law,[54] but one wonders how serious competition is at the moment with one or two big players controlling almost the entirety of the big data market. In common law countries, it has been argued that tech giants such as Facebook ought to be split up into several independent companies to prevent one company from having so much control over so many.[55] It certainly would introduce competition and force down the cost of their services, and distribute the enormous profits made from big data more widely in society.

3. Difference from GDPR

On the whole, the protection of personal data in Chinese law is partly dependent on public law, and this makes it look relatively close to the GDPR. By contrast, the United States does not take the same citizen-first approach to data processing and protection. The United States relies on a patchwork of state and federal laws, but beyond health records and financial records with banks, there is little to no data protection rights in that country at the federal level. The latest law in Europe is the GDPR, which is adopted in E.U. member states through the enactment of domestic legislation. For example, the United Kingdom has adopted the GDPR in full in its *Data Protection Act 2018* (U.K.).

---

53 O. Bar-Gill, "Algorithmic Price Discrimination When Demand Is A Function of Both Preferences and (Mis)perceptions," (2019) 86 *U. Chi. L. Rev.* 217 at 218; E. M. Fox, "Platforms, Power, and the Antitrust Challenge: A Modest Proposal to Narrow the U.S.-Europe Divide," (2019) 98 *Neb. L. Rev.* 297.

54 For example, *Hantao Company v. Baidu, etc. – Unfair Competition Case*, [Basic People's of Pudong New District, Shanghai, People's Republic of China], [Civil First Trial No. 528], and in the verdict [Intellectual Property First Trial No. 40], High People's Court of Ningbo Municipality held that unauthorized copying of personal resume information on recruitment websites for commercial purposes constitutes unfair competition.

55 "The simplest way to break the power of Facebook is breaking up Facebook. More generally, it is argued that 'breakups or structural remedies are, effectively, self-executing, and thereby, a much cleaner way of dealing with competition problems.' " J. Wright and A. Portuese, "Antitrust Populism: Towards A Taxonomy," (2020) 25 *Stan. J.L. Bus. & Fin.* 131 at 153.

This is an all-compassing law that gives people rights not only to prevent data breaches, but to seek records held on them. For example, a person can ask for copies of emails between colleagues or a manager where they have been named. They can seek records held by government departments concerning them or from private companies including their employer. This increases transparency.

A core difference in older Chinese law was that it did not provide the sort of specific protections found in Articles 15–21 of the GDPR such as the right of access, right to rectification, right to erasure (right to be forgotten), right to restriction of processing, right to data portability and the right to object, etc.[56] More significantly, the right of data subjects to file complaints with independent regulatory agencies (for free) and commence lawsuits in courts if they have money to pursue civil litigation (most do not), does not exist in Chinese law. China's law also did not include the extra protection provided by Article 9 of GDPR, which concerns a category of data that needs more protection because it is sensitive. However, this seems to have been ameliorated by the new provisions set out in *National Standards on Information Security Technology – Personal Information Security Specification GB/T 35273–2020*.

This provision uses new terminology such as "personal information," "sensitive personal information," "biometric personal information" and "data controller." More significantly, a written notice or a positive and affirmative action is required when a data controller collects sensitive personal information or uses such information for a new purpose. In addition, security impact assessments are required for: (1) outsourcing of data processing; (2) sharing and transferring personal information; or (3) disclosing personal information to the public. Requests can be made to access personal data, and have it corrected if it is not correct. If a person askes for information to be deleted or withdraws her consent, then the data controller must respond within 30 days. Any personal information concerning minors under the age of 14 is deemed sensitive personal data.

A record of all data breaches and the scope of any breach must be kept, and notifications have to be given for each breach. Under Article 42 of the *Cybersecurity Law*, organisations are given guidance that they ought to report any breaches to the regulators in a timely manner. This must be done in accordance with the guidance provided for in the *National Network Security Incident Contingency Plans*. A data controller must appoint a designated data protection officer and create a data protection department if it is in the business of data processing and employees more than 200 employees, or intends to process personal information of more than 500,000 individuals within 12 months.

It might be said that the *Cybersecurity Law* provisions provide specific guidance and thus act as effective rules for tech companies; but the previously mentioned *Personal Information Security Specification* is not a binding law. It is merely a

---

56 Although Article 43 of the *Cybersecurity Law of the People's Republic of China* stipulates that individuals have the right to require network operators to delete and modify personal information like GDPR, but because there is no provision for the data access rights of data subjects, the right to modify is only an abstract right.

set of guidance rules. Pursuant to Articles 10[57] and 11[58] of the *Standardization Law of the People's Republic of China (2017)*, some Chinese laws are binding, and others are merely recommendatory. The most extensive data protection provisions fall in the recommendatory rather than mandatory rules category. This means that in China, data rights are getting more closely aligned with GDPD, but enforcement is not guaranteed. The rules are recommendatory, but in practice most organisations will follow them rigidly.

The difference between the foregoing two aspects may stem from the difference in the basic value orientation between the GDPR and China's laws. The GDPR has a very obvious focus on individual rights and dignity.[59] Basically, the GDPR aims to protect autonomy and privacy first and foremost, which tends to result in the law giving priority to the protection of personal data rights.[60] McDermott argues:

> that the creation of the right [to data protection] could be traced to a number of distinct values inherent in the pre-existing data protection framework – namely privacy, autonomy, transparency and non-discrimination – that were perhaps seen as not being fully protected in the pre-Charter fundamental rights framework, and that by placing data protection on an equal footing with existing rights, those values were sought to be protected.[61]

In contrast, Chinese law has put more emphasis on the protection of the data technology industry and national networks and information storage as protecting national interests. From this point of view, the current legal framework in China takes a value position that prioritises the protection of national interests.[62] Other differences that scholars have highlighted are:

> exemptions in Chinese law only partially resemble the legitimate interest basis in the GDPR because Article 6.1(f) of the GDPR is broader and can,

---

57 "Compulsory national standards shall be formulated for those technical requirements which safeguard people's health and safety of life and property, national security and ecological environment security, and meet the basic needs for economic and social management."

58 "Recommendatory national standards can be formulated in respect of the technical requirements which meet the basic and general need of the society, in supported of compulsory national standards, and play a leading role in the relevant industries."

59 See Ding Xiaodong, "What is Data Rights? – the Protection of Data Privacy from EU GDPR," (2018) 4 *ECUPL Journal* 45.

60 See Liu Zegang, "The Transform of the Right to 'Post-privacy' in EU Legal Protection of Personal Data," (2018) 4 *ECUPL Journal* 59.

61 Y. McDermott, "Conceptualising the Right to Data Protection in an Era of Big Data," (2017) 4(1) *Big Data & Society* 1; O. Lynskey, "Deconstructing Data Protection: The 'Added-Value' of a Right to Data Protection in the EU Legal Order," (2014) 63(3) *International and Comparative Law Quarterly* 569. Some Chinese scholars have adopted this thinking too. See Liu Jinrui, *Personal Information and Rights System – the Dilemma and Failure of Right to Information Self-determination*, (Beijing: Law Press, 2017) at 132–136.

62 See Xinbao, *op. cit. supra*, note 29 at 59. Similar views, Jinrui, *op. cit. supra*, note 61 at 146–149. Liang Genlin, "Traditional Crimes in Cyberspace: Obstacles to Imputation, Criminal Law Response and Dogma Limitation," (2017) 2 *Law Science* 11.

for example and under certain conditions, justify data processing for direct marketing purposes. Another core element where China does not put as much emphasis as the EU is data quality. The data quality principle mandates that personal data should be relevant to the purposes for which they are to be used and, to the extent necessary for those purposes, should be accurate and kept up-to-date.[63]

4. Related criminal offences in China

With regard to the statutory provisions in the *Criminal Code of China*, the following offences are the core related offences in that they have an indirect impact on data protection. They do not aim to protect data per se, but sometimes have the indirect effect of protecting data. There are two crimes in the *Crimes Encroaching on the Rights of the Person* and the *Democratic Rights of Citizens Acts* in Chapter IV: the crime of infringing upon citizens' right of freedom of correspondence in Article 252, and the crime of infringing a person's personal information rights as protected in Article 253–1. The two crimes are used to strengthen the protection of the fundamental right to human dignity and correspondence expressly provided for in Article 38 (dignity) and Article 40 (correspondence) of the *Constitution of the People's Republic of China*. The following offence is considered to be an important offence for protecting personal data in China.

Article 253–1 of the *Criminal Code* provides:

> Whoever sells or provides any citizen's personal information in violation of the relevant provisions of the state shall, if the circumstances are serious, be sentenced to imprisonment of not more than three years or criminal detention in addition to a fine or be sentenced to a fine only; or be sentenced to imprisonment of not less than three years but not more than seven years in addition to a fine if the circumstances are especially serious.
>
> Whoever sells or provides to any other person any citizen's personal information obtained in the course of performing functions or providing services in violation of any relevant provisions of the state shall be given a heavier penalty in accordance with the provisions of the preceding paragraph.
>
> Whoever illegally obtains any citizen's personal information by stealing or other methods shall be punished in accordance with the provisions of paragraph 1.
>
> Where an entity commits any crime as provided for in the preceding three paragraphs, the entity shall be sentenced to a fine, and its directly responsible person in charge and other directly liable persons shall be punished according to the provisions of the applicable paragraph.

The crime of infringing upon the citizens' right of freedom of correspondence targets conduct such as hiding, destroying or illegally opening other people's

---

63 E. Pernot-Leplay, "China's Approach on Data Privacy Law: A Third Way between the US and the E.U.," (2020) 8(1) *Penn. St. JL & Int'l Aff.* 1 at 31.

letters. All information – including emails, messages on mobile phones and messages in WeChat, Facebook, audio and video – could be constructed as "letters." The local courts in China tend to give the concept of "letter" a very wide interpretation[64] so that the crime can meet the needs of the Internet age. This crime punishes two types of conduct. One is the act of selling or providing any personal information in violation of the relevant provisions, and illegally obtaining any personal information by stealing or other means. Meanwhile, there is no consensus on the content and scope of the right to personal information.

There are two crimes provided for in the *Crimes of Undermining the Order of Socialist Market Economy* in Chapter III of the *Criminal Code of China*. Namely, the crime of stealing, buying or illicitly providing information of others' credit cards (Article 177–1), and the crime of encroaching on commercial secrets in (Article 219).[65] The offence provided for by Article 177–1 mainly aims to protect financial order rather than the right to personal information. Business data such as customer lists may also involve personal data. The data controller that acts with due diligence in handling a commercial secret will be able to defend a claim under Article 219. These crimes aim to prevent the harm that might be caused by misusing commercial data, but do not specifically protect data privacy per se. The *raison d'être* for this offence is to protect the economic interests – it is more of a property offence than a data offence.

Finally, it is worth mentioning there are crimes of disrupting public order in Chapter VI *Crimes of Disrupting the Order of Social Administration Act*; namely, Section 1 (Article 285, para. 2) includes the crime of illegally obtaining computer information systems data. There also is the crime of sabotaging a computer information system (Article 286, para. 2). Both offences are designed to protect data security: the former penalises the illegal acquisition of data stored, processed or transmitted in a computer information system, while the latter is aimed at illegal deletion or modification of data that is stored, processed or transmitted in a computer information system.

Since networked devices including personal computers, smart-phones, and iPads have been considered to be computer information systems in China, whoever illegally obtains personal data stored from one of these devices or deletes or modifies such data will be liable. This is similar to the *Computer Misuse Act 1990* offences in the United Kingdom, but the offences in that act are drafted more carefully to cover all misuse, rather than have many overlapping offences outlining the types of misuse. The two previously mentioned Chinese offences are concerned with protecting public order and network security, rather than data per se.

---

64 See Yang Hongtao and Xu Qiang, "China's first Case of Stealing and Selling QQ Numbers," (2006) 4 *China Trial* 22.
65 See Section 4 of the *Disrupting Crimes of Undermining the Order of Financial Management* and Section 7 of the *Crimes of Infringing upon Intellectual Property Rights*.

5. Fair labelling and applying the right crime

The protection of personal data by criminal law has undoubtedly become a legislative and judicial choice in China. Regarding personal data protection, many Chinese scholars still take the view that it ought to be protected as a property right rather than as a public law matter. It is not clear that trying to protect data as a property right would provide sufficient protection in many cases, because many forms of data that are valuable to an individual simply have no economic value.[66] Some U.S. states simply deem all data to be property, but this is to be expected given there is little informational privacy protection in that jurisdiction.[67]

> Treating privacy as a property right has been a perennial entry in the debate about personal information, but has not received much serious attention until recently. Alan Westin suggested treating personal information as a property right more than thirty years ago, to mixed reviews.[68]

The most famous account of privacy as property is that given by the philosopher Judith Jarvis Thomson.[69] More recently, Lessig argued:

> The laws of property are one such regime. If the law gave individuals the rights to control their data, or more precisely, if those who wanted to use that data had first to secure the right to use it, then a negotiation would occur over whether, and how much, data should be used. The market could negotiate these rights, if a market in these rights could be constructed.[70]

Lessig's argument is as an IP lawyer, so was not thinking of the public law aspects of data. It is true that people would be able to sell their data as they please, but applying this in the social media age seems trite. To start with, data

---

66 See the various approaches that have been tried with intellectual property. See A. Mossoff, "Rethinking the Development of Patents: An Intellectual History, 1550–1800," (2001) 52 *Hastings L.J.* 1255 at 1257–1258 defending and applying the natural rights theories of Locke, Grotius and Pufendorf to intellectual property. See also A. D. Moore, "A Lockean Theory of Intellectual Property," (1997) 21 *Hamline L. Rev.* 65, 66 (1997); C. J. Craig, "Locke, Labour and Limiting the Author's Right: A Warning Against a Lockean Approach to Copyright," (2002) 28 *Queens L.J.* 1 at 2–5.

67 Wis. Stat. Ann. § 943.70 (West) (f) provides:

"Data" means a representation of information, knowledge, facts, concepts or instructions that has been prepared or is being prepared in a formalized manner and has been processed, is being processed or is intended to be processed in a computer system or computer network. Data may be in any form including computer printouts, magnetic storage media, punched cards and as stored in the memory of the computer. Data are property.

68 J. Litman, "Information Privacy/information Property," (2000) 52 *Stan. L. Rev.* 1283 at 1289.

69 J. J. Thomson, "The Right to Privacy," (1975) 4(4) *Phil. & Pub. Affairs* 295.

70 L. Lessig, "The Architecture of Privacy," (1999) 1 *Vand. J. Ent. L. & Prac.* 56 at 63.

in aggregate may be valuable, but in isolation barely has a market value. Social media and other teach giants provide their services riddled with advertisements as the standard price for harvesting data,[71] when it might be argued that being able to bombard people with advertisements is enough payment without any data mining. That is how television has worked in many countries for decades – it was paid for by dispersing advertisements throughout the programmes. More importantly, the market and private law (remedies) cannot remedy all serious date misuse, because such remedies are only available to the very wealthy in society.[72]

Hence, the problem with treating it as property is that it would require expensive private law enforcement – this works in the United States due to the size of the compensation awards and the "no win, no fee" lawyering culture, but would not work in China. Data that is not misused for fraud or some other property offence is not likely to be best protected by property offences or private law property rights. Therefore, if data was just deemed by a new law to be property, it would have to be protected by suing for damages, and that remedy would only be available to wealthy people who can pay lawyers to so act. It also might be protected by the law of theft, but that seems the wrong crime to apply when the data has no real property value. In English law, there is a tort of misusing private information, which has usually only been used by wealthy celebrities due to the exorbitant legal costs of bringing private actions in that country.[73]

For the purpose of criminal law, we need to demonstrate not only a trivial privacy loss but some tangible harm to others. The GDPR and the *Data Protection Act 2018* (U.K.) do not contain any proper criminal offences or powers of arrest, but one can report privacy losses to the regulator without paying any fees. When data is misused to cause some other criminal harm, then normally, the relevant offence will apply such as fraud or hacking offences.

Given that China has moved close to the GDPR in providing public law data protection to its citizens, it seems superfluous to try to analyse data protection breaches as breaches of property rights or as torts. They can be both, and a rich person might sue for compensation even after a criminal conviction has been obtained, but the criminal law is a safety net available for all. The focus has to be on the harm caused; if the real harm caused is fraud through the misuse of

---

71 Frieden writes:

> Belatedly, we have seen data mining generating significant and unexpected adverse consequences; including, direct impacts on presidential elections, manipulating public opinion through fake news, and acquiring data about consumers who have not consented to any sort of mining and may not even know their data has been extracted, analysed, and sold.

R. Frieden, "Two-Sided Internet Markets and the Need to Assess Both Upstream and Downstream Impacts," (2019) 68 *Am. U. L. Rev.* 713 at 736.

72 It can costs millions to enforce privacy rights as private law matters. See for example, T. Waterson, "BBC Pays out £2m in Legal Costs to Sir Cliff Richard," (London: *The Guardian*, 4 September 2019).

73 *Campbell v. Mirror Group Newspapers Ltd.* [2004] 2 A.C. 457; *O. v. A* [2015] 2 W.L.R. 1373.

data, then it is best to treat it as a property offence. If a person has misused data to steal $1,000,000, then it would be mislabelling the gravamen of the wrong to treat it simply as a data breach. If a person hacks a computer to cause chaos, then it would be mislabelling it to treat it as a data breach. Thus, the range of criminal offences that exist in China are suitable, but prosecutors need to look for the harm involved and apply the right offence in the given situation. In cases when the data has not been used in any other crime, then it is best just to treat it as a data protection issue and deal with it that way. A person might hack into another's iCloud and steal her nude photographs, but might not sell them or show them to anyone else. Here the victim is caused no financial harm, but it would seem just labelling the wrong as a misuse of a computer, when it involves a data protection infringement and a serious privacy violation, would be to mislabel the wrong and apply the wrong crime. In such a case, the defendant ought to be charged with illegally obtaining data in computer information system, as well as data protection and privacy offences.

If the data protection violation involves the wrongdoer sabotaging or using a computer information system to illegally delete, modify or add data, then this would require action for that offence, as well as for a data protection offence. There is an overlap, but both wrongs need to be identified for the harm they actually cause or risk causing so that they can be fairly labelled and punished in proportion to the harm caused or risked. Similarly, it would not be enough to punish the crime concerning valuable commercial secrets simply as a data protection issue. China has a raft of offences[74] that can be applied according to the harm caused, but prosecutors will need training to make sure that the harm matches the offence charged, because there will be overlapping wrongs and harms in many of these cases.

6. Conclusion

The *Information Technology – Personal Information Security Specification GB/T 35273–2020* and the *Cybersecurity Law (2016)* enacted a raft of changes apropos data protection law in China. The law now refers to "personal information" held by data controllers, an approach that follows the conceptualisations of "personal data" provided for in the European Union's GDPR. The new law also provides specific protection for sensitive data, including biometric data, if lost or misused. In particular, it targets misuse that might endanger persons or property such as might be the case when a reputation is destroyed as a result. It aims to prevent economic, mental and physical harm to others, and to prevent discriminatory treatment. For example, if a person's HIV status were leaked, it might prevent gaining employment or being bullied or harassed. Other examples include national identification, passwords, login credentials, location information

---

74 See Lu Yufeng, "Technological Boomerang Effect and Rule of Law Challenge in Information Society," (2019) 3 *Global Law Review* 65.

and banking and credit details, which could be used in fraud to cause economic harm. Also, information about a minor (younger than 14 years old) is regarded as sensitive. The new provisions in China mandate that data controllers process data transparency, fairly and for a legitimate and proportionate purpose.

For sensitive information of a personal nature, the data controller must obtain informed and explicit consent from the data subject. Apart from when the data is anonymised, prior notice and consent from data subjects to the transfer of their data is required. This is separate from any consent given for the initial collection and processing of data. This is also a requirement of the *Cybersecurity Law*. If a person refuses to consent to the adjuvant uses of their data, the data collector/controller can decline to provide its services, but it must not cease or downgrade the core services it provides to that particular person. Also, privacy notices should include at a minimum information about collection and processing rules such as the method and frequency of data collection and where such data will be stored. The controller should also provide details of its usual office location and contact information. Other requirements are that the privacy notice disclose how the data will be shared and for what reason. It should include information about complaints and how they will be resolved, as well. The rights conferred on individuals are similar to those under the GDPR. A person can cancel an account, and the right to erasure is now fairly stringent, if the processing violates the law or an agreement with the data subject. It is not an absolute right to erasure for this reason. However, unlike the GDPR, no specific grounds are given for refusing to delete information. The GDPR provides some exemptions for keeping data regardless of a request for it to be erased, such as that it is required for legal purposes.

China's recent law reform efforts concerning data protection have been positive and in the right direction. Its laws in this area are now much closer to the GDPR than they are to the minimalist approach taken in the United States. The United States will no longer be able to use China as an excuse for not enacting a provision similar to the GDPR. China is now on board with data protection, while America stands alone in failing to modernise its data laws to meet the demands of emerging technology. This is problematic, as digital businesses are global business that have to operate in different legal frameworks. The European Union led the way with data protection and is now about to set the global standard for artificial intelligence and other technology. The European Union's *Digital Services Act* will regulate everything from social media platforms to facial recognition cameras. It is implementing rules in this area that will affect both Chinese and American companies wanting to operate in Europe.[75]

Some Chinese scholars do not accept the privacy, autonomy, transparency rationale for justifying data protection laws. They do not see the obvious case for this being public law rather than private law. Private law certainly can be used to

---

75 "EU Backs AI Regulation While China and US Favour Technology," (London: *The Financial Times*, 25 April 2019).

seek compensation, but when a person is harmed, they ought to be able to seek police action, not put up with the harm simply because they cannot afford private law remedies. It has been argued here that since the criminal law has severe consequences for those who are convicted (prison sentences, stigma and social isolation), data should only be protected through criminal offences when its misuse causes harm to others. A privacy loss itself can cause great mental distress and reputational damage, so arguably qualifies as a harm for the purposes of having a criminal offence to protect data.

Beyond that, when large corporations misuse big data that is anonymised, the GDPR approach of fining them up to 4% of their annual turnover seems sufficient deterrent and corporate punishment. If a woman commits suicide because a person hacks her computer and steals her video of her having sex with her boyfriend and uploads it onto the Internet, the harm is not theft or a mere data breach, but a severe loss of privacy with very harmful collateral consequences.[76] Therefore, we have tried to present a "harm to others" case for having some criminal offences to prevent this sort of data misuse.

Acknowledgements

The authors wish to acknowledge Mr. Qiulin Tao, a Ph.D. candidate from Tsinghua Law School, whose help in translating the first draft of this paper is greatly appreciated.

---

76 Ressler writes:

> One of the chief drawbacks of Internet shaming is the permanence of its effects. Internet shaming creates an indelible blemish on a person's identity. Being shamed in cyberspace is akin to being marked for life. It's similar to being forced to wear a digital scarlet letter or being branded or tattooed. People acquire permanent digital baggage. They are unable to escape their past, which is forever etched into Google's memory.

J. S. Ressler, "#worstplaintiffever: Popular Public Shaming and Pseudonymous Plaintiffs," (2017) 84 *Tenn. L. Rev.* 779 at 808.

8 Using conspiracy and complicity for criminalising cyberfraud in China

Lessons from the common law

Li Lifeng,[1] Tianhong Zhao and Dennis J. Baker

1. Introduction

Cybercrime consists of criminal acts that are committed online through the use of electronic communications information systems. The anonymous nature of the Internet and its reach across countries, combined with the Dark Web,[2] has made the enforcement of cybercrime a challenge. The problem for enforcement is also acerbated by that fact cyberfraud can be perpetrated through: (1) a number of independent criminal acts where each actor does not act in concert with the next in the chain of crimes; (2) a chain conspiracy where each actor does an act towards achieving a common (criminal) agreement/purpose; (3) joint perpetration where

1 S. D. Vogt, "The Digital Underworld: Combating Crime on the Dark Web in the Modern Era," (2017) 15 *Santa Clara J. Int'l L.* 104; R. Snell, "As Technology Becomes Increasingly Complex, So Must Our Efforts to Combat Its Inherent Security Risks," (2019) 21 *J. Health Care Compliance* 29.
2 Many provisions in China are wide enough to target individual criminal acts at different stages in the accumulative process.

> For example, the offender knew that his cyber acquaintance was in the process of committing telecommunication fraud through a phishing site, but still sold him domain names and helped to analyse data; or the offender knew that X was committing an offence of illegally controlling computer information system, but still remotely logged into the management server, to assist in X's maintenance of the controlled computer system, and provided an account to X for payment and settlement; or the offender, who rented out local phone numbers online, knew that some customers were using phone numbers to commit fraud, but profited through information transmission technology . . . it is not necessary that the offender knew another's commission of cybercrime from the beginning. In one case, the offender, who rented out phone circuits, received an official document from the telecommunication company, in which he was warned that certain circuits were suspected of being involved in fraud and was ordered to take measures against it. The offender knew who was using this circuit but did not take necessary measures for transferring the official document to the rental. In those cases, as mentioned above, the crime, which the offender assisted in, first existed and was committed individually. The offender did not participate in the planning, organising or preparing for the crime, and therefore, his act of providing technical support, or material help, played a very small role.

See Jiajia Yu, "Cybercrime in China–A Review Focusing on Increasing Criminalisation of Harmful Cyberactivities," (2017) 47 *Hong Kong L. J.* 937 at 948–949.

different parties act in concert to jointly perpetrate the *actus reus* of the target offence; (4) intentional assistance or encouragement; or (5) subjective reckless assistance or encouragement.

In China, subjective recklessness and direct intention are treated as one form of subjective fault.[3] In the common law countries, a distinction is made between direct intention, subjective recklessness and objective negligence.[4] Some common law jurisdictions also draw a line between direct intention and oblique intention – the latter being a higher degree of subjective recklessness in that a person is held to have intended consequences she or he foresaw as a virtual certainty.[5] In England and the United States, a person is equally liable as a perpetrator if he or she directly intends to assist or encourage the perpetrator's crime.[6] In China, no distinction is made between direct intention and subjective recklessness as far as equal liability based on complicity is concerned. Organised cyberfraud normally involves many actors performing different roles, because it requires a range of skills and roles. A does act X, B does act Y and C does act Z, and all three acts are required for A, B and C to succeed in dishonestly acquiring property belonging to another. However, cyberfraud can also be facilitated by those who recklessly assist or encourage without intending to assist or encourage a particular perpetrator.

Our banking system now depends on computer networks and information technology.[7] Cybermethods can be used to target many victims in a way that was not possible in the days when fraud was done face-to-face, or theft was done through physically appropriating property belonging to another. It can be done across borders, allowing for and extra layer of protection,[8] especially if the perpetrators are in a poorly regulated jurisdiction.[9] The cyberfraudster only requires a computer and an Internet connection. Not only have many people moved to online banking, but "in China 50% of ecommerce is accounted for by e-wallets."[10] It is anonymity[11] and physical distance from the crime that makes it extremely

3 D. J. Baker, *Glanville Williams Textbook of Criminal Law*, (London: Sweet & Maxwell, 2015) at Chapters 4, 5 and 6.
4 Glanville Williams, "Oblique Intention," (1987) 46 *Cambridge L.J.* 417 at 423. See D. J. Baker, "The Doctrinal and Normative Vacuity of Hong Kong's Joint Enterprise Doctrine," [2017] *Hong Kong L.J.* 349 quoting *R. v. Jogee* [2016] 2 W.L.R. 681; *Rosemond v. U.S.* (2014) 134 S.Ct. 1240.
5 H. Webb, "Evaluation of M-Payment Technology and Sectoral System Innovation – A Comparative Study of UK and Indian Model," (2019) 8(1) *Electronics* 282.
6 *Comprehensive Study on Cybercrime*, (Vienna: United Nations, 2013) at 9.
7 A. D. Mitchell *et al.*, "Regulating Cross-Border Data Flows in a Data-Driven World: How WTO Law Can Contribute," (2019) 22 *J. Int'l Econ. L.* 389.
8 *Payment Methods Report 2019* (E-commerce Foundation, 2019) at 20. Cf. D. J. Grimm, "The Dark Data Quandary," (2019) 68 *Am. U. L. Rev.* 761.
9 N. MacEwan, "A Tricky Situation: Deception in Cyberspace," (2013) 77(5) *J. Crim. L.* 417.
10 Jyh-An Lee and Ching-Yi Liu, "Real-Name Registration Rules and the Fading Digital Anonymity in China," (2016) 25 *Wash. Int'l L.J.* 1.
11 A. S. Irwin, "Following the Cyber Money Trail," (2019) 22(1) *Journal of Money Laundering Control* 110.

difficult to identity and prosecute cybercriminals.[12] Artificial intelligence and technology, not law, offers the main protection against cybercriminals. Law can only be a deterrent if detection and conviction rates are reasonably high. Many countries have implemented comprehensive legal measures such as the real name system of accounts in finance.[13] A further tool for distancing themselves from a crime is for organised gangs to use artificial intelligence to do the thieving and cryptocurrencies to hide the proceeds of their crimes.[14] Artificial intelligence has the potential to facilitate "spear phishing" and other online frauds.[15]

> Because hackers typically route their attacks through a series of intermediaries, investigators must "try to follow the trail of electronic breadcrumbs" back to the perpetrator's computer, a cumbersome process. Moreover, hackers intentionally target intermediary computers with lax security and poor record keeping, meaning that the trail is likely to break down. When that occurs, investigators must use other techniques, such as prospective surveillance.[16]

In this chapter, we shall focus on cyberfraud and fraud conducted through phishing. We shall touch on other independent forms of criminalisation, such as remote crimes such as selling equipment for use in fraud[17] and preparation liability,[18] but our main aim is to set forward a theory of liability that criminalises

---

12 In Britain, artificial intelligence and various other spear phishing technological tools have been used to hack into a person's chain of text messages from an official HMRC number apropos tax returns. S. McKie, "Gone Phishing," (2010) 166(4280) *Tax.* 8. See also K. Kikerpill and A. Siibak, "Living in a Spamster's Paradise: Deceit and Threats in Phishing Emails," (2019) 13 *Masaryk U. J.L. & Tech.* 45.

13 S. S. Beale and P. Berris, "Hacking the Internet of Things: Vulnerabilities, Dangers, and Legal Responses," (2018) 16 *Duke L. & Tech. Rev* 161 at 175.

14 Cf. the offences in Sections 6 and 7 of the *Fraud Act 2006* (U.K.) concerning the possession, manufacture and supply of equipment for use in fraud.

15 Article 22 of the *Criminal Code of the People's Republic of China* provides: "An offender who prepares for a crime may, in comparison with one who completes the crime, be given a lighter or mitigated punishment or be exempted from punishment."

16 Ryan and Krotoski write:

> "[V]ishing," or voice phishing scheme, "criminals can take advantage of cheap, anonymous Internet calling available by using Voice over Internet Protocol ('VoIP'), which also allows the criminal to use simple software programs to set up a professional sounding automated customer service line, such as the ones used in most large firms." The perpetrator, offering an aura of legitimacy, "emulates a typical bank protocol in which banks encourage clients to call and authenticate information."

> K. V. Ryan and M. L. Krotoski, "Caution Advised: Avoid Undermining the Legitimate Needs of Law Enforcement to Solve Crimes Involving the Internet in Amending the Electronic Communications Privacy Act," (2012) 47 *U.S.F. L. Rev.* 291.

17 Cf. S. Eldar, "Holding Organized Crime Leaders Accountable for the Crimes of Their Subordinates," (2012) 6 *Crim. L. & Phil.* 207.

18 D. Vanni, "Are We Any Good at Protecting Our Societies and Economies from the Threat of Economic Crime and Misconduct?" (2019) 26(4) *JFC*10 06 at 1010.

the parties to a fraud in proportion with their contributions to the end fraud. Cyberfraud is the exemplar used to tease out this discussion.[19] We shall attempt to show the limitations of complicity and conspiracy as a mechanism for tackling independent players taking different roles that have no connection with each other's crimes.[20] Nonetheless, we will also see that while there are limits, both the law of conspiracy and complicity are useful weapons in many cases. If we look at phishing in 2020, we can see it has changed dramatically from simply sending out an email or cold calling someone; we are witnessing widespread "spear phishing" that is targeted and thus is extremely difficult to recognise.[21] Criminals are using artificial intelligence not only to carry out spear phishing, but also an entire range of criminal activities. A recent report from University of Cambridge, Centre for the Study of Existential Risk, pointed out:

> A phishing attack is an attempt to extract information or initiate action from a target by fooling them with a superficially trustworthy facade. A spear phishing attack involves collecting and using information specifically relevant to the target (*e.g.* name, gender, institutional affiliation, topics of interest, *etc.*), which allows the facade to be customized to make it look more relevant or trustworthy with the attacker often posing as one of the target's friends, colleagues, or professional contacts. The most advanced spear phishing attacks require a significant amount of skilled labour, as the attacker must identify suitably high-value targets, research these targets' social and professional networks, and then generate messages that are plausible within this context. If some of the relevant research and synthesis tasks can be automated, then more actors may be able to engage in spear phishing. For example, it could even cease to be a requirement that the attacker speaks the same language as their target. Attackers might also gain the ability to engage in mass spear phishing, in a manner that is currently infeasible, and therefore become less discriminate in their choice of targets.[22]

2. Cyberfraud in China

In this chapter, we shall try to compare Chinese law with the common law to see what legal doctrines might be developed in China to better combat phishing and cyberfraud. Since Chinese scholars have a tradition of drawing on Japanese jurisprudence, we shall draw some comparisons with that jurisdiction when such

19 *The Malicious Use of Artificial Intelligence: Forecasting, Prevention, and Mitigation,* (University of Cambridge, Centre for the Study of Existential Risk, 2018) at 19, 21.
20 Oishi Tsuyoshi, "A Special Type of Fraud Originated from Remittance Fraud," (2013) 9 *Keisatsu Koron* 29.
21 The Opinions of the Supreme People's Court, the Supreme People's Procuratorate and the Ministry of Public Security on Several Issues concerning the Application of Law in the Handling of Telecommunications Network Fraud and other Criminal Cases.
22 P. Sales, "Legislative Intention, Interpretation, and the Principle of Legality," (2019) 40(1) *Stat. L.R.* 53.

comparisons are helpful. However, Japanese criminal jurisprudence is not overly useful in the sense that its property offences are drafted with different technical requirements.[23] In China, the law and its interpretation from the Supreme Court of the People's Republic of China specifically covers phishing and allows for higher sentences when vulnerable people have been the target. The Supreme Court of the People's Republic of China has held:[24]

> One that commits telecommunications network fraud . . . and falls under any of the following circumstances shall be subject to a heavier punishment:
>
> i Causing suicide, death or mental disorder of a victim or any of his close relatives, or any other serious consequence.
> ii Committing fraud by posing as the functionary of a judiciary or any other state department.
> iii Organizing or directing a telecommunications network fraud syndicate.
> iv Committing telecommunications network fraud overseas.
> v Has been subject to criminal punishment for the crime of telecommunications network fraud, or, within two years or to administrative penalty for telecommunications network fraud.
> vi Defrauded the disabled, the elderly, a minor, a student, or a person without ability to work, or defrauded a person suffering a critical disease or any of his or her relatives of property.
> vii Secured by fraud money or property for disaster relief, emergency rescue, flood prevention and control, special care for disabled servicemen and the families of revolutionary martyrs and servicemen, poverty alleviation, resident relocation, social relief, or medical care, among others.
> viii Committed fraud in the name of public welfare or charity such as disaster relief.
> ix Made use of auto dialling systems and other technology to seriously disturb the work of public security and other departments.
> x Made use of "phishing site" links, "Trojan horse" program links, network penetration or any other concealment technique to commit fraud.

This is more of a sentencing provision than a provision outlining a substantive offence. The sentence is calibrated not only with the harm, but also with the risk posed when certain people who are potentially more susceptible to deception are targeted. Furthermore, the sentence is calibrated with the moral outrage people feel when a person takes advantage of a disaster or some charitable situation to

23 See K. Campbell, "The Fraud Act 2006," (2007) 18(2) *K.L.J.* 337.
24 On common purpose and concert, see D. J. Baker, *Reinterpreting Criminal Complicity and Inchoate Participation Offences*, (Oxford: Routledge, 2016) at Chapter 2.

defraud others. Our focus is not on sentences, but on what substantive laws might be invoked to cover the worse kinds of cases. We want to ensure that the majority of those who are caught and prosecuted are covered by a substantive offence to ensure that they do not evade justice. The law has to be specific enough to meet the stringent requirements laid down by the principle of legality,[25] but sufficiently flexible to cover a wide range of situations.[26]

The question is how do we identify and punish the many actors, not only those working together in concert, but also those who facilitate without being complicit in the primary fraud? We shall argue that conspiracy and complicity can help to link up various criminals who work together to bring about such frauds, but also point out that when there is no concert (common purpose) or culpable assistance, and encouragement the law of conspiracy and complicity do not provide a solution.[27] This might mean that it is necessary to have more offences like some of those found in England such as Section 7 of the *Fraud Act 2006*, which criminalises "making or supplying articles for use in frauds." A person might make and sell on the Dark Web an item that can have no other purpose other than to facilitate fraud such as an automated teller machine (ATM) card skimmer.[28] The *telos* of an ATM card skimmer is to facilitate the perpetration of fraud.

25 A skimmer is a card reader that can be disguised to look like part of an ATM, but is used to collect card numbers and personal identification number (PIN) codes, which are then replicated into counterfeit cards.

26 D. J. Baker, "The Moral Limits of Criminalizing Remote Harms," (2007) 10 *New Crim. L. Rev.* 370.

27 England also has special assistance and encouragement offences that act independently of its law of complicity which is found in Section 8 of the *Accessories and Abettors Act 1861* (U.K.). For example, Section 45 of the *Serious Crime Act 2007* does not require a direct intention, but requires the assister or encourager of a crime to foresee his or her assistance would assist someone to perpetrate a crime. Section 45 does not treat the assister or encourager as a perpetrator/principal, but makes him or her liable for the independent facilitation/incitement offence. See D. J. Baker, "Conceptualizing Inchoate Complicity: The Normative and Doctrinal Case for Lesser Offenses As an Alternative to Complicity Liability," (2016) 25 *S. California Interdisc. L.J.* 503.

28 See Baker, *op. cit. supra*, note 3 at Chapter 19.

   A "hub-and-spoke" conspiracy arises where "a central core of conspirators recruits separate groups of co-conspirators to carry out the various functions of the illegal enterprise. . . . The analogy used is one of a wagon wheel: the core members of the conspiracy are called the 'hub,' the other members are called the 'spokes,' and connections between the spoke members are considered the wheel's rim" . . . In a unified conspiracy, the "spokes" are aware of the other members' roles, the conspiracy proceeds towards a common goal, and the members are connected to each other. . . . By contrast, "where the spokes of a conspiracy have no knowledge of or connection with" the other "spokes" and "deal independently with the hub conspirator, there is not a single conspiracy, but rather as many conspiracies as there are spokes." . . . Therefore, for a "rimmed" wheel conspiracy to exist, "the various spokes *must be aware* of each other and their *common aim* to form a single conspiracy." . . . '[E]vidence of an individual participant's understanding of the interdependence of the co-conspirators' activities is evidence – often the best evidence – of tacit agreement between the individual and his co-conspirators.

   de la Osa v. State (2015) 158 So. 3d 712 at 723–724.

It does not matter that the supplier of articles that can only be used to facilitate fraud do not know who is buying them, because the supplier must know whoever is buying can only have one purpose for buying it. This is a remote harm, and thus makes criminalising the sale and possession of such items permissible.[29] Under the law of complicity in China, the supplier would have to be shown to have foreseen that a particular buyer might use it to perpetrate a fraud. However, if these things are sold on the Dark Web, the supplier will not have any direct link with the buyer and thus will not know the exact plans of each buyer or who they are. The buyer might simply be someone buying articles for use in fraud to resell at a higher price.[30] In other cases the article might have a dual-use, and thus might not be so easily caught by the law of complicity such as when a person sells an item that could be used either in fraud or for some other legal purpose such as a smart-phone. Smart-phones and computers are used by fraudsters to perpetrate fraud every day, but the *telos* of these items is not to facilitate fraud.

Article 287 of the *Criminal Code of China* provides: "Whoever uses computers to commit crimes such as financial fraud, theft, embezzlement, misappropriation of public funds and theft of State secrets shall be convicted and punished in accordance with the relevant provisions of this Law." This crime requires the perpetrator to succeed in obtaining property dishonestly through the means of misusing a computer. The core *Crimes of Financial Fraud* in Chinese criminal law are found in Articles 192–196 of the *Criminal Code of China* and make no specific reference to emerging technologies, but rather focus on the methods of yesteryear. For example, Article 192 provides:

> "Whoever . . . raises funds by means of fraud shall, if the amount involved is relatively large, be sentenced to a fixed-term imprisonment . . ."

Meanwhile, Article 193 provides:

> Whoever commits any of the following acts to defraud a bank or any other financial institution of loans for the purpose of illegal possession shall, if the amount involved is relatively large, be sentenced to fixed-term imprisonment . . .: (1) inventing false reasons for obtaining funds, projects, *etc.* from abroad; (2) using a false economic contract; (3) using a false supporting document; (4) using a false property right certificate as guaranty or repeatedly using the same mortgaged property as guaranty in excess of its value; or (5) defrauding loans by any other means.

Article 194 provides:

> Whoever commits fraud by means of financial bills in any of the following ways shall, if the amount involved is relatively large, be sentenced to fixed-term imprisonment . . . (1) knowingly using forged or altered bills of

---

29 *United States v. Alvarez* (1980) 610 F.2d 1250.
30 *United States v. Leal* (2019) 921 F.3d 951 at 959.

exchange, promissory notes or cheques; (2) knowingly using invalidated bills of exchange, promissory notes or cheques; (3) illegally using another's bills of exchange, promissory notes or cheques; (4) signing and issuing a rubber cheque or a cheque, on which the seal is not in conformity with the reserved specimen seal, in order to defraud money or property; or (5) signing or issuing bills of exchange or promissory notes without funds as a guaranty, in the capacity of a drawer, falsely specifying the particulars thereon at the time of issue, in order to defraud money or property. Whoever uses forged or altered settlement certificates of a bank such as certificates of entrustment with the receipt of payment, certificates of remittance and deposit receipts shall be punished in accordance with the provisions in the preceding paragraph.

Article 195 provides:

Whoever commits fraud by means of a letter of credit in any of the following ways shall be sentenced to fixed-term imprisonment . . .: (1) using a forged or altered letter of credit or any of its attached bills or documents; (2) using an invalidated letter of credit; (3) fraudulently obtaining a letter of credit; or (4) in any other ways.

Similarly, Article 196 covers those who commit fraud by means of a credit card in any of the following ways:

(1) using a forged credit card; (2) using an invalidated credit card; (3) illegally using another's credit card; or (4) overdrawing with ill intentions. Overdrawing with ill intentions as mentioned in the preceding paragraph means that a credit card holder who, for the purpose of illegal possession, overdraws beyond the norm set or beyond the time limit and refuses to repay the overdrawn amount after the bank that issues the card urges him to do so.

Compare Article 266 of the *Chinese Criminal Code*, which provides:

Whoever swindles public or private money or property, if the amount is relatively large, shall be sentenced to fixed-term imprisonment of not more than three years . . .

All these described crimes require success. The fraudster must succeed in obtaining the property. The doctrines of complicity and attempts can be applied to these crimes, but Chinese law does not have an offence of conspiracy as such. If we look at the types of organised fraud that involves old-fashioned cash collectors, we can get a sense of the role complicity and conspiracy might play in some straightforward cases, where the barrier for justice will be enforcement and proof, not the absence of legal doctrines to apply to the criminal conduct.

In English law, the terms "wheel" and "chain" conspiracy are used to describe multiparty party participation in an agreement to perpetrate a crime. Conspiracy in English law refers to the bare "agreement" to perpetrate the crime, rather than participation in the actual crime – the latter is caught by the law of complicity. Hence, conspiracy aims to criminalise action at the agreement and planning stage and is an inchoate from of liability.[31] "Criminalization of conspiracy punishes the inchoate offence by prosecuting the agreement itself, separating and stigmatising jointly planned criminal activity prior to its completion."[32] A chain conspiracy would be when X agrees with Y, who agrees with Z. In a chain conspiracy, "there is successive communication and cooperation in much the same way as with legitimate business operations between manufacturer and wholesaler, then wholesaler and retailer, and then retailer and consumer."[33] Conspiracy is not made out in common law jurisdictions unless direct intention is proven. Unlike China, the common law distinguishes reckless foresight from direct intention (purpose). "[C]onspirators must have had 'a mutual understanding . . . to cooperate with each other to accomplish an unlawful act,' and the petitioner must have joined the conspiracy 'with the intention of aiding in the accomplishment of those unlawful ends.' "[34]

A wheel conspiracy is when A agrees with X; A agrees with Y; and A agrees with Z. But a conspiracy could be a combination of both a chain and a wheel conspiracy.[35] It is not necessary for each conspirator to have met or communicated with the others or know their identities, but each of the conspirators must be a party to a common design and be aware that the design involves a larger criminal plan involving others. In the wheel conspiracy, X at its hub might agree with A, B and C independently without A, B or C being aware of their involvement in the larger criminal scheme. If so, this will be regarded as three separate conspiracies, not as a single conspiracy between them all. Even if they are aware that X is making similar agreements with unknown others, they will not be liable for those conspirators unless they are part of a wider common design. In the traditional telecommunication network fraud, labour has been divided among those who are the masterminds, those who do the phishing, and those who physically collect cash from the victims, and so on. Many organisers of the telecommunication network fraud crimes have to employ others to collect the cash proceeds of their fraud and to make the phishing calls.

---

31 *Ocasio v. United States* (2016) 136 S. Ct. 1423 at 1429.
32 Baker, *op. cit. supra*, note 3 at Chapter 19.
33 For a discussion of the general part of the criminal law, see Glanville Williams, *Criminal Law, The General Part*, (London: Stevens & Sons, 1953).
34 For example, the Supreme Court of the United States has held:

> (1) that two or more persons entered into an unlawful agreement; (2) that petitioner knowingly and wilfully became a member of the conspiracy; (3) that at least one member of the conspiracy knowingly committed at least one overt act; and (4) that the overt act was committed to further an objective of the conspiracy.

> *Ocasio v. United States* (2016) 136 S. Ct. 1423 at 1428–1429. In *United States v. Gonzalez* (2018) 905 F.3d 165 at 179 it was said, "a conspiratorial agreement can be proven circumstantially based upon reasonable inferences drawn from actions and statements of the conspirators or from the circumstances surrounding the scheme."

35 Baker, *op. cit. supra*, note 3 at 759.

There is no conspiracy liability in the general part[36] provisions found in the *Chinese Criminal Code*, but it does have a preparation provision in Article 22 that could apply to a bare agreement. However, the weight of academic and judicial opinion in China is that an agreement on its own is not enough to incur liability for preparation.[37] Chinese law seems similar to most U.S. states in that it requires an agreement plus an overt act of some kind. Baker notes that in English law, "Conspiracy is highly inchoate, because unlike attempts it does not require any kind of overt act – there is no need to show that the defendant started to act."[38] LaFave notes that in the United States, most states required an overt act to be done by one of the conspirators in furtherance of the conspiracy, but opinion is divided on whether the act has to be preparatory or an attempt to prepare or an attempt to perpetrate the conspiracy or is simply an evidential requirement for proving the agreement.[39] Conspiracies are likely to be easier to prove in the digital age when criminals are likely to leave a digital trail that evidences their agreement to perpetrate some planned crime.

In China, the agreement would normally have to be accompanied with some other preparatory steps towards perpetrating the crime. Given that Article 22 of the *Criminal Code of China* aims to criminalise acts of preparation, it requires overt acts that are preparatory in nature or form an attempt to perpetrate the object of the unlawful conspiracy. This is supported by the threshold harm requirement for making an act or omission criminal pursuant to Article 13 of the *Criminal Code of China*. There also is an instigation provision (Article 29), an accessorial liability provision (Article 27) and a joint perpetration liability provision (Article 25). Some of the special part[40] provisions do cover conspiracy such as Articles 156 and 382. Furthermore, Article 26 of the *Criminal Code of China* provides:

> A principal criminal refers to any person who organizes and leads a criminal group in carrying out criminal activities or plays a principal role in a joint crime.
>
> A criminal group refers to a relatively stable criminal organization formed by three or more persons for the purpose of committing crimes jointly.

---

36 "Courts have said that the overt act must be a step towards the execution of the conspiracy, an act that tends to carry out the conspiracy, an act to effect the object of the conspiracy, or a step in preparation for effecting the object." W. R. LaFave, *Substantive Criminal Law*, (West Publishing, 3rd edn., 2003) at §12.2(b).

37 For a discussion of on the special part/general part distinction, see M. S. Moore, "The Specialness of the General Part of the Criminal Law," in D. J. Baker and J. Horder (eds.), *The Sanctity of Life and the Criminal Law*, (Cambridge: Cambridge University Press, 2013) at 69 *et seq.*; J. Gardner, "On the General Part of the Criminal Law," in A. Duff (ed.), *Philosophy and the Criminal Law*, (Cambridge: Cambridge University Press, 1998) at 205 *et seq.*

38 Baker, *op. cit. supra*, note 3 at Chapter 37.

39 *Ibid.*

40 Cf. for example, B. H. Glenn, "Attempts to Commit Offences of Larceny by Trick, Confidence Game, False Pretences, and the Like," (1966) 6 A.L.R.3d 241 (updated 2019).

Any ringleader who organizes or leads a criminal group shall be punished on the basis of all the crimes that the criminal group has committed.

Any principal criminal not included in Paragraph 3 shall be punished on the basis of all the crimes that he participates in or that he organizes or directs.

Article 26 does not require all the parties to know of each other, but there must be a common purpose between the organiser and those he or she conspires with. The core difference with this provision and the general part conspiracy doctrine found in English criminal law is that the English law criminalises the "bare agreement" to perpetrate the target crime. Hence, English law makes anyone who agrees to commit a crime liable even if they never attempt to perpetrate the planned crime or prepare to perpetrate it. It is a form of inchoate liability. If the parties go on to perpetrate the crime and have a common purpose, the English law of complicity treats them all as principal perpetrators. It is not only the general part provisions such as complicity that differ, but so too do the elements of the property offences found in the special part of the criminal law. Yet the general fraud provisions found in the *Chinese Criminal Code* combined with its complicity provisions seem to cover as much ground as the English law.

3. Remote harm offences vs. inchoate and pre-inchoate offences

English law has extended is reach by enacting "remote harm" offences that are based on endangerment such as the offence of supplying articles for use in fraud. For example, allowing an ATM card reader market to exist makes the chances of them being purchased and used more likely. Since ATM card readers have no social utility, there is no reason not to criminalise possession, supply and manufacture of such items. English law has also extended the reach of its fraud offences by making them inchoate and removing the requirement that actual deception be achieved.[41] Similarly, Article 253(1) of *Criminal Code of China* (amended in 2015) criminalises the conduct of selling or disclosing the personal information of third parties. Meanwhile, Article 256 covers those who provide personal information to others without the consent of the data subjects. This covers acquisition of personal information through illegitimate means and is designed to disrupt independent illegal information markets that might facilitate fraud. Articles 253(1) and 280(1) cover identify theft. Hence, conspiracy and complicity law could be buttressed by enacting remote harm offences to criminalise acts that help others to prepare for crime such as when a person produces ATM card skimmers or fake webpages for independent others to use in crime. These sorts of non-culpable

---

41 Cf. conspiracy merging with substantive offence if the conspiracy is consummated. See *R. v. Boulton* (1871) 12 Cox, C. C. 87; *R. v. Button* (1848) 11 Q. B. 929; *R. v. Secretary of State for the Home Department, Ex parte Gilmore* [1998] 2 W.L.R. 618. Cf. E. W. H. "Merger of Conspiracy in Completed Offence," (2020) 37 *A.L.R.* 778 (first edition, 1925).

(i.e., the seller or supplier does not intend or foresee that a particular criminal will use the articles that she has manufactured for use in fraud and thus has no culpability link with the end crimes for the purposes of establishing complicity liability), remote harms facilitate fraud and thus warrant criminalisation. The conduct is remote, so would be fairly labelled and punished as a lesser offence than fraud.

By having independent remote harms offences, there is no need to demonstrate an agreement between the manufacturer of the article for use in fraud and the user, as is required for conspiracy, or that there was culpable assistance, as is required for derivative liability. It would not matter that the seller of the ATM card reader does not know who is buying it or who will use it, or whether it will ever in fact be used, so long as it is possessed, manufactured or supplied.

Coupled with that, a general inchoate offence of fraud would help the law avoid some of the proof issues that might arise under the current law in China and allow the criminal law to apply to cybercrime at an earlier point in time. For example, Section 2 of the *Fraud Act 2006* (U.K.) does not require a false representation to actually deceive anyone, and it does not require the victim to have lost any money or property. English law was reformed in 2006 to make fraud by false representation an inchoate offence so that any person who makes a false representation to obtain property belonging to another would be liable for fraud even if the target victim had not been deceived, and even if no property was lost.[42] Hence, if X sets up a fake webpage claiming that non-existent products exist, with the aim of obtaining money from people who believe X's webpage is genuine and that they will receive the promised goods and services, X would be liable as soon as the webpage goes online for making false representations. Hence, it would not be necessary to find any victims. Nor would it be necessary to demonstrate that X tricked someone into handing over property or money, because the offence covers the attempt to do so. The inchoate form of the fraud offence is included in the "consummated" form of the offence.[43] An inchoate offence of this kind allows those who have sufficiently manifested their intent to commit the particular substantive offence to be punished, even though they have failed to consummate the crime. If X does succeed in obtaining money from many people, then that will be relevant when considering how to sentence her wrongdoing.

---

42 For a discussion of the old deception offences in English law, see G. Williams, *Textbook of Criminal Law*, (London: Steven & Sons, 1978) at 773 *et seq.*; R. M. Perkins and R. N. Boyce, *Criminal Law*, (New York: The Foundation Press, 1982), at 363 *et seq.*

43 Half of all fraud in England is now done by cybermeans. See *Overview of Fraud and Computer Misuse Statistics for England and Wales*, (London: Office for National Statistics, 25 January 2018); see also *PwC's Global Economic Crime and Fraud Survey 2020*. An reports that:

> Underground cybercrime profits in China have likely already exceeded US$15.1 billion (100 billion Chinese yuan); caused more than $13.8 billion (91.5 billion yuan) worth of damage relating to data loss, identity theft, and fraud; and will grow at an even faster pace as underground hackers expand international business operations to increasingly target foreign businesses.

See A. An, "Chinese Cybercriminals Develop Lucrative Hacking Services."

In this sense, English law merges attempted fraud with consummated fraud, and the only relief the person attempting fraud will get over one who succeeded in obtaining property by deception is a discount in his or her sentence.[44] The crime label remains the same for both attempted and consummated fraud, but a sentence discount is available for attempted fraud. The law was reformed because the technical barriers required by having a deception requirement and a loss of property requirement meant that too many serious fraudsters were going unpunished.[45] It is important to also keep in mind the majority of cybercrimes involve cyberfraud.[46]

Chinese fraud law has all the problems the old common law deception offences had in England before being reformed in that they require actual deception and that the property be appropriated. In China, if the victim transfers his or her money into the account of the swindler through the ATM, because there is no cash delivery, the crime of obtaining another's property by fraud will not be established.[47] English law deals with cases where the entire fraud is automated via machines. Section 2 of the *Fraud Act 2006* provides:

(1) A person is in breach of this section if he – (a) dishonestly makes a false representation, and (b) intends, by making the representation – (i) to make a gain for himself or another, or (ii) to cause loss to another or to expose another to a risk of loss.
(2) A representation is false if – (a) it is untrue or misleading, and (b) the person making it knows that it is, or might be, untrue or misleading.
(3) 'Representation' means any representation as to fact or law, including a representation as to the state of mind of – (a) the person making the representation, or (b) any other person.
(4) A representation may be express or implied.
(5) For the purposes of this section a representation may be regarded as made if it (or anything implying it) is submitted in any form to any system or device designed to receive, convey or respond to communications (*with or without human intervention*) [emphasis added].

---

44 Matsuzawa Shin, "Exercise of Criminal Law," (2011) 166 *Hogaku Kyoshitsu* 364.
45 Section 8 of the *Accessories and Abettors Act 1861* treats those who intentionally assist and encourage others to perpetrate crimes as principal perpetrators. Section 46 of the *Serious Crime Act 2007* (U.K.).
46 We use the old fashioned card reader as an example, but the online market for articles and services for use in fraud include: phishing website sales, DDoS services, malware, source-code writing services, sales of black-hat training about using social engineering attack tools, spam and flooding services, and database hacking services, to list a few.
47 C. Hongbing, "Legal Reasoning and Applications of 'Partially Assumption of Whole Liabilities,' by the Joint Principal Offenders," (2015) 51 *Northern Legal Science* 89; J. D. David Ohlin, "Group Think: The Law of Conspiracy and Collective Reason," (2007) 98 *J. Crim. L. & Criminology* 147.

Note that the English law applies even if it is a computer system or machine that is deceived into dispensing or transferring the property. If a person enters another's password to transfer money from her account to his own account and thus makes a false representation to the bank's computers that it is his password and that he has a right to use that password to access and transfer funds belonging to another, he would be liable even though the entire transaction is automated. If we are to amend and update Chinese criminal law to tackle contemporary cyber-crime and the issues raised by emerging technologies, it would be better to do it by enacting careful provisions like those found in English law, rather than trying to conjure up meanings for older Japanese offences (one of the current scholastic trends in China is to try to apply Japanese jurisprudence to Chinese legal prob-lems) that simply are not apt for the problems created by emerging technologies.

4. Complicity

In China, some people deal in fake bank accounts and subscriber identity mod-ule (SIM) cards and operate courier services for cash collection. For these ser-vices, they receive approximately 30% of the money obtained dishonestly through fraud. In English law, they would be liable as perpetrators of the fraud, but only if through the doctrine of complicity it can be shown that they intended to assist or encourage the perpetrator of the fraud.[48] If the helper merely believed that he or she would assist the perpetrator, then he or she would be liable under the incho-ate complicity offence found in Section 45 of the *Serious Crime Act 2007* (U.K.), which only requires oblique intention. Chinese law only requires that it be shown that the helper foresaw that the assistance would help the perpetrator, but liability in Chinese law is limited in that the accessory is only liable if his or her assistance is used to make the crime succeed. There is no inchoate from of complicity in China, and the complicity not only requires that the crime be perpetrated, but that perpetrator and assister be clearly identified. For example, it is doubtful that a person could be liable for setting up a website to sell ATM card readers[49] to the Chinese public, even if some people purchase and use the ATM card readers to perpetrate fraud, because the parties are not jointly perpetrating a crime and the seller does not foresee any particular perpetrator using the assistance to target a particular victim.

What we want to look at is how far joint perpetration liability as found in Chinese criminal law can be applied when there are various parties involved in cyberfraud and some of them have no awareness of the roles being played by other remote parties. In many cases, it will be possible to invoke the joint

---

48 See *HKSAR v Zulu Sbusiso* [2009] HKEC 2288, where the defendants were caught with skimmers containing data on them.
49 See the sentencing decision in *R. v. Heracleous* [2019] EWCA Crim 2212, where D1 and D2 used fraud and forgery to gain the title to an old man's house; and thereafter, D3 laundered the money to try to disguise that it was the proceeds of a major fraud.

perpetration theory to hold people liable for contributing to a fraud at different levels and through different acts.[50] Let us look at a multi-layered joint enterprise: A is responsible for making the ATM card skimmer to obtain card information from ATM users,[51] B is responsible for manufacturing replica cards, C is responsible for withdrawing money from ATMs with those cards and D is responsible for laundering the money to make it look like legitimate income from a legitimate business. Assume that they all have full knowledge of each other's contribution to the end objective of receiving a share of the laundered money.[52]

Is this a case of joint perpetration? In English law, it would be, because the parties have a common intention to assist and encourage each other to achieve their end of sharing the proceeds obtained through their individual contributions to the fraudulent scheme. This could come within the purview of the law of complicity if they participants are successful in obtaining money. In Chinese law, joint perpetration has a wider *mens rea*, so any participant who took a role in the criminal enterprise would be equally liable if he or she had foreseen the overall scope of the enterprise and continued to participate with that reckless foresight. However, if the supplier of the ATM card readers is acting wholly independently of the others and is only aiming to make money from selling articles for use in fraud, the supplier would not be able for fraud through the law of complicity either in China or England. Such a person would be liable for the remote harm offence found in Section 7 of the *Fraud Act 2006* (U.K.) and perhaps for attempting to assist under Section 45 of the *Serious Crime Act 2007* (U.K.).

Under the very wide common law offence of "conspiracy to defraud," still used in common law jurisdictions such as England, Australia and Hong Kong, all the gang members would be liable, if there was a common purpose to commit fraud. It does not matter that they agreed to do different things to make the fraud succeed. A "conspiracy to defraud . . . is an agreement to practise a fraud on somebody."[53] It is the agreement alone that is criminal, and deception and

---

50 *Wai Yu-Tsang v The Queen* [1992] 1 A.C. 269 at 279.
51 See:

> The question whether particular facts reveal a conspiracy to defraud depends upon what the conspirators have dishonestly agreed to do, and in particular whether they have agreed to practise a fraud on somebody. For this purpose it is enough for example that . . . the conspirators have dishonestly agreed to bring about a state of affairs which they realise will or may deceive the victim into so acting, or failing to act, that he will suffer economic loss, or his economic interests will be put at risk.

> *Wai Yu-Tsang v The Queen*, [1992] 1 A.C. 269 at 279–280.

52 See Baker, *op cit. supra*, 3 at Chapter 37.
53 [1985] A.C. 975.

> It is a mistake to say that conspiracy rests in intention only. It cannot exist without the consent of two or more persons, and their agreement is an act in advancement of the intention which each of them has conceived in his mind. The argument confounds the secret arrangement of the conspirators amongst themselves with the secret intention which each must have previously had in his own mind, and which did not issue in act until it displayed itself by mutual consultation and agreement.

> *R. v Thomson* (1966) 50 Cr. App. R. 1.

success in obtaining property belonging to another are only relevant to sentencing or as to whether such conduct might involve joint perpetration rather than merely an inchoate agreement.[54] Conspiracy to defraud requires the conduct to be dishonest, so if a person is intending to enter an agreement to deceive another to regain property that rightfully belongs to her, she would not be liable despite any deception she uses because she acts honestly in the fuller sense with the aim of regaining what really is her own property. For example, D steals V's Ming vase worth £1 million. V conspires with a local antique dealer X to deceive D into selling the vase to the dealer. V and X also organise for the police to be present when D attempts to sell the vase to X. While deceptive means are used to trick the thief into returning the vase, this is not a dishonest set of events in their entirety since V is simply reacquiring her own property.[55]

Furthermore, a conspiracy to defraud conviction does not require the defendants' actions to directly result in the fraud, because it is the agreement that is the crime. However, they ought to have a plan to perpetrate the crime themselves. In a doubtful decision from the House of Lords, *R. v. Hollingshead*,[56] the defendants produced devices designed to alter electricity meter readings and this was held to be a conspiracy to defraud, even though the actual fraud was carried out in the future by members of the public rather than the conspirators. In that case, Lord Roskill said:

> In my view the respondents were liable to be convicted of conspiracy to defraud because they agreed to manufacture and sell and thus put into circulation dishonest devices, the sole purpose of which was to cause loss. . . . Even if such a charge of conspiracy to aid, abet, counsel or procure were possible in law, I can see no evidence whatever that the respondents ever agreed so to aid, abet, counsel or procure or indeed did aid, abet, counsel or procure those who as the ultimate purchasers or possessors of the black boxes were destined to be the actual perpetrators of the intended frauds upon electricity boards. It follows that on no view could the respondents have been convicted on count 1 even if that count were sustainable in law.[57]

---

54 *R. v. Hollinshead* [1985] A.C. 975 at 997–998.

55 A statutory provision in the common law jurisdiction (New York) states:

> Anticipatory or inchoate offenses fall short of a substantive offense. New York's Penal Law defines inchoate offenses as the crimes of attempt, solicitation, facilitation, and conspiracy. These offenses are clearly distinguishable from each other, evaluating a defendant's state of mind while giving little credence to "factors extraneous to the defendant's perception or control.
>
> Often, aside from conspiracy, no federal counterpart exists to these crimes. Rather, federal criminal statutes only provide primary liability for those who aid or abet a federal crime or "[w]hoever wilfully causes an act to be done which if directly performed by him or another would be an offense against the United States, is punishable as a principal." Anticipatory offenses, 4D N.Y.Prac., Com. Litig. in *New York State Courts* § 102:38 (4th ed.).

56 *R. v. Dunnington* [1984] Q.B. 472.

57 Baker, *op. cit. supra*, note 4.

This case is wrong in law and principle, because the appellants were wholesalers and therefore too remote from the ultimate fraudulent use of their products to be guilty of conspiring to have them used in fraud. There was no agreement between them and those who purchased their devices, and there was no assistance or encouragement of a kind that made them participants in the fraud of those who later used their devices. This sort of case would now be prosecuted under the remote harm offence of supplying articles for use in fraud found in Section 7 of the *Fraud Act 2006* (U.K.). *R. v. Hollinshead* extends conspiracy liability beyond its doctrinal limits, because it holds that the defendant's agreed to their devices being used to defraud the Electricity Board, but there was no such agreement with the end users of their devices. They did not care about the fact that those purchasing them would attempt to use them to defraud the Electricity Board or that many of them would succeed with such a purpose. They simply wanted to make money from selling such devices. They did not intend to participate in any of the frauds or agree that any of the frauds be done. They did not intent or agree to *assist or encourage* any particular fraud, but arguably believed their conduct would assist another somewhere to perpetrate a fraud. Hence, they would now come within the reach of Section 7 of the *Fraud Act 2006* and perhaps also Section 45 of the *Serious Crime Act 2007* (U.K.). Also, a conspiracy to perpetrate the Section 7 of the *Fraud Act 2006* offence itself would be a crime, regardless of whether any articles are actually manufactured or sold.

The limiting factor in English law for the law of conspiracy is that each conspirator needs to intend to carry out the agreement. In common law jurisdictions, attempt, incitement and conspiracy are "inchoate"[58] crimes and thus are crimes per se. Complicity liability is, by contrast, a form of derivative liability and it requires the perpetrator to commit the crime – because the accessories' liability rests on the fact that a crime has in fact been perpetrated. All parties can be complicit in an attempt, because an attempt is a crime per se.[59] The law of conspiracy found in the common law jurisdictions can catch anyone who joins the agreement at any time while the crime remains inchoate. The party joining the conspiracy must intend to agree to be a part of the planned crime, because a person cannot recklessly agree.[60] This does not mean that the conspirator has to intend A do act X (phone the victim and convince the victim to give money) and

---

58 In *R. v. Hadi* [2019] EWCA Crim 1910, it was said for courier fraud:

> The method of the fraud was for one of the conspirators (usually a male) to telephone the victim and introduce himself as a police officer investigating a crime relating to the victim's bank, often referring to the particular branch at which the victim's account was held. The caller would ask for the victim's help in the investigation. Depending on the victim's reaction, a mixture of charm, pressure and threat would be used to try to win the victim's cooperation. Sometimes the victim was given the impression, or was told explicitly, that there was someone watching their movements.

59 See *R. v. Hussain* [2019] EWCA Crim 1525. See also C. Giordano, "Couple Who Lost Almost £1m Among 3,000 Victims of Courier Fraud as Police Launch Nationwide Crackdown," (London: *The Independent*, 5 February 2020).

60 Cf. Zhang Mingkai, *Criminal Law*, (Beijing: China Legal Press, 5th edn., 2016) at 432.

B do act Y (collect the money), as is the case in courier frauds; it simply requires the conspirator to intend the courier fraud[61] be perpetrated, and the conspirator need not intend a particular person do act X and a particular person do act Y.

Courier fraud has been a problem in the United Kingdom, where fraudsters target elderly people and pretend to be police officers to convince them to withdraw cash and give to a courier. The false representation is simply that it is to help with a police investigation, which might not fool many, but they target very elderly victims. These fraudsters use tactics such as telling victims what type of car they own and what they are wearing on the day in question to give a real impression that actual police have them under surveillance. These conspiracies involve many people operating in many cities and taking different roles.[62]

5. Successive complicity in Japanese law

Many Chinese scholars quote Japanese theories and doctrines without any criticism. Others recognise the differences in the theory and doctrine, but still try to apply these different concepts to justify interpreting the *Chinese Criminal Code* a certain way, when what is required is that the *Code* be amended and rewritten to tackle the crimes that are facilitated by emerging technologies. In Japanese law,[63] like English law under the *Serious Crime Act 2007* (U.K.), attempts to assist or encourage will be punishable.[64] In English law, if a person attempts to help another to perpetrate fraud such as when X sends Y an ATM card reader intending to assist Y to perpetrate ATM fraud, but the police find it in the mail and prevent Y from receiving it, X will still be liable for attempting to assist Y. Furthermore, if X posts Y a gun intending to assist Y to kill V and Y fires the gun at V but misses V, Y will be liable for attempted murder, and so, too, will be X under the English law of complicity.[65] English law looks at the objective facts when evaluating impossible attempts such as when a person attempts to steal from an empty pocket. If the facts had been as the defendant believed them to be, he or she would have succeeded and thus is liable on the basis that it was not inherently impossible[66] to do as attempted.

---

61 Yamaguchi Atsushi, *General Principle and Problems of Criminal Law*, (Tokyo: Yuhikaku, 2013) at 264.

62 *R. v. Dunnington* [1984] Q.B. 472.

63 On the difference between inherent factual impossibility and non-inherent factual impossibility see Baker, *op. cit. supra,* note 3 at 727 *et seq.*

64 *The Judgement of July 10 of the High Court of Osaka in 1987*, Vol. 40, No. 3, at 720.

65 *The Judgement of March 23 of the Local Court of Nogoya in 2016*(LEX/DB25544199).Cf. *The Judgement of Nov 27 of the Supreme Court of Japan in 1946*, Vol 25, at 55, it was held that when a perpetrator mixes salt with food to try to poison another, even if the perpetrator himself thinks this can kill, a reasonable person would not be so mistaken, so the mistaken party is not liable for anything other than the attempt. *The Judgement of Sept 10 of the Supreme Court of Japan in 1907*, Vol 23, at 999.

66 Contra, Seki Tetsuo, *Lecture Notes on the General Principle of Criminal Law*, (Tokyo: Seibundoh, 2015) at 438.

However, the wide theory of "succession complicity" has allowed people to be held complicit in crimes after the event.[67] In Japan, successive complicity has been applied to inherently impossible attempts to assist the crime of another.[68] The rationale for this extension of the law seems to be based on the idea that attempts are objectively dangerous.[69] In one case, A was beating V to death when B, who happened to walking nearby, joined A in beating V. It was later proved that V had died before B started beating V, but B was still identified as a co-perpetrator of the crime of murder.[70] B was beating a dead person and it was inherently impossible for B to kill a corpse.[71] This interpretation of the law in Japan seems erroneous and probably will not be followed further, because it would catch too wide a range of people and make them equally liable for crimes they have not even assisted or encouraged.[72] Those who join in after the fact should not be treated as co-perpetrators. It would be better to treat their conduct as an attempt to assist or encourage as is the case in English law under Sections 44 and 45 of the *Serious Crime Act 2007* (U.K.), because that would allow for fair labelling of the conduct and for proportionate punishment.[73] More recently, the Supreme Court of Japan has given the law a more restrictive interpretation by requiring a causal influence on the final result of the crime. Thus, a person who joins a continuing crime will be held equally responsible for the entire crime perpetrated by the original perpetrator, if the contribution makes some sort of indirect causal contribution.[74]

The Japanese courts have developed conceptual fictions in an attempt to rope in the various parties to a crime. It might be possible to assert that a money collector makes an indirect causal contribution to a crime when he or she has been a culpable member of a conspiracy and simply carries out a role in the overall scheme to dishonestly obtain money belonging to another, but there will be many cases when the remote influence is not intended to influence. Hence, in many cases, complicity and conspiracy will provide no remedy, because those assisting might not be doing so with an intent to help another succeed in crime. Such conduct might not have any problem passing an "objective danger theory"

---

67 *The Judgement of Oct 27 of the High Court of Osaka in 1970*, Vol. 2, at 1025.

68 Cf. the cases collected in J. Ghent, "Impossibility of Consummation of Substantive Crime as Defence in Criminal Prosecution for Conspiracy or Attempt to Commit Crime," (2020) 37 *A.L.R.3d* 375.

69 Matsuhara Yoshihiro, *General Principle of Criminal Law*, (Tokyo: NIPPYO, 2013) at 382.

70 Cf. *The Judgement of Nov 6 of the Supreme Court of Japan in 2013* (Vol. 66, No. 11, p. 1281).

71 Hashizume Takashi, "On Successive Accomplice," (2015) 415 *Hogaku Kyoshitsu* 95.

72 § 22 of the *German Criminal Code* provides: "A criminal offense is attempted by anyone who immediately starts to believe that the offense has been committed."

73 D. J. Baker, *The Right Not to be Criminalized*, (Oxford: Routledge, 2011) at Chapter 4.

74 A distributed denial of service attack (DDoS attack) is where the perpetrator makes a machine or network resource unavailable to its intended users by temporarily disrupting services of a host connected to the Internet. DDoS blackmail involves the criminal threatening a business with a putative DDoS attack if it does not pay a sum of money. For example, it could close down an airline's webpage costing it millions. These threats are usually via email and request any money be paid via a hard-to-trace route such as Bitcoin.

(*Gefährdungstheorie*),[75] borrowed by the Japanese from German law, but such endangerment ought to be criminalised as independent remote harm offences such as those that prohibit the possession of guns or articles for use in fraud or prohibit the sale and manufacture of articles for use in fraud.[76]

6. Conclusion

Articles for use in fraud are no longer simply ATM card readers, but include programmes for spamming and distributed denial of service attacks. Common types of malware such as spyware are readily available on the black market in China, and can be purchased on the open web. It has been reported that Chinese cybercriminals do not operate through the Dark Web or Deep Web, but rather operate through sophisticated markets through QQ networks and so forth. These are highly organised criminal gangs that often do no more than profit from manufacturing and selling malware online and avoid getting involved with the criminals who use their products.

Spyware can record screen shots and log keystrokes, and thus enable the criminal to acquire personal information that has been used for online banking such as Internet banking passwords. Remote access Trojans (RATs) allow the cyber criminal to remotely connect to infected devices and control them. The following example fairly well sums up the problem for the law as outlined in this chapter:

> QQ hacking group masters (qunzhu, 群主), also known as prawns (daxia, 大虾) or car masters (chezu, 车主) by those in Chinese cybercriminal underground networks, are the masterminds of cybercrime gangs. QQ hacking group masters purchase or acquire access to malware programs from a malware writer or wholesaler. . . . QQ hacking group masters recruit members or followers, who are commonly known as apprentices, and instruct apprentices on hacking techniques such as setting up malicious websites to steal personally identifiable information or bank accounts. In most cases, QQ hacking group masters collect "training fees" from the apprentices they recruit. The apprentices later become professional hackers working for their masters.

Tracing the digital footsteps of these gangs is difficult. With data retention laws in China requiring Internet service providers to keep all data for a set period and the use of artificial intelligence to try to identify messages from cyberfraudsters and those manufacturing and selling items for sue in fraud, there is the risk that they will go onto the Dark Web. Putting that obstacle for enforcement aside, we have tried to demonstrate that having remote harm offences that criminalise the act of selling or manufacturing articles for use in fraud is one way to plug the gap

---

75 An, *op. cit. supra*, note 52.
76 *Ibid.*

that is left when there is not any conspiracy or complicity between the seller/ manufacturer and the end-user. We have attempted to show how the law of complicity and conspiracy could be developed in China to cover a wide range of situations. The preparation provision found in Article 22 could be supplemented with a new provision that criminalises criminal agreements per se. This could be limited to apply only to crimes that carry a three-year or longer prison sentence, to ensure that inchoate from of criminality is not stretched to cover agreements to perpetrate non-serious crime. The law of complicity found in Article 25 joint perpetration can be supplemented with an inchoate from of complicity like that found in Sections 44–46 of the *Serious Crime Act 2007* (U.K.)

9 The threat from AI

Sadie Creese

1. Introduction of risk

Whenever we introduce new technologies into our environment, it is reasonable to consider if this introduces risk. Such risk may need to be managed in order that the costs of using the technology do not outweigh the benefits; in other words, to ensure that the additional risk that we may be exposing ourselves to is reasonable and acceptable, where meeting the criteria of acceptability would include having access to knowledge and tools that make it possible to manage the associated risks. Indeed, within the field of cybersecurity as a profession and the practice of information and cyber-risk management,[1] we commonly consider the risks that we face, and how to accept, avoid or mitigate those risks, in a manner which enables us to operate aware of those risks and with strategies to respond should they become realised. In this sense, we view cybersecurity as a risk-based practice, when, in fact, achieving cybersecurity is really an acceptance of insecurity, but with controls available that allow us to continue operating in the face of risk. This is essentially what acceptable risk means, and risk appetite is a definition of the level of risk those taking it are willing to bear.

It is a fact that with new technology, and use of technology in new ways, we may become vulnerable to unintended consequences; technology can introduce new attack surfaces across which our systems may be compromised by those seeking to inflict harm. This harm can be felt at a number of different levels. Such harms can include, for example, theft of our data and information, sabotage of digital systems and loss of access to digital services. These in themselves can be viewed as the main harm that we wish to avoid, or it may be the resulting effects that these can have which concern us most.

In the case of the individual, data theft can result in a loss of confidentiality of personal data, which in itself represents a compromise of our personal privacy that may be the real harm we wish to avoid. Similarly, for a commercial organisation,

---

1 See for example the problems discussed in K. N. Johnson, "Cyber Risks: Emerging Risk Management Concerns for Financial Institutions," (2015) 50 *Ga. L. Rev.* 131; M. Faure and B. Nieuwesteeg, "The Law and Economics of Cyber Risk Pooling," (2018) 14 *N.Y.U. J.L. & Bus.* 923.

the data theft could mean that proprietary information is shared with competitors, resulting in a loss of market position, where the resulting harm is loss of revenues and profits, or loss of market share, which can also lead to lower stock and company valuation.[2] The harm to a nation from loss of commercial position by companies operating in the country can include job losses, reduced income from taxes, and loss of influence in the international marketplace and trade.[3] It can also result in the loss of inward investment and tax revenues from other companies who might otherwise have chosen to locate offices in the country but who are put off by the apparent lack of cybersecurity capacity. Note that cybersecurity requires both technology and human-centred solutions, making the operating environment and capabilities of employees critical.

We consider here whether the family of technologies and methods that are commonly thought of (at the current time) as constituting AI could pose a form of threat.[4] We reflect on the potential victims of such a threat, the harms that might arise, and how we might view the threat from AI as a weapon (affecting current cyberattack capability) or as a threat emerging from the technology existent in our environments, and what this might mean for society as we consider how to prepare to mitigate the risks emerging.

2. The nature of the threat

Threat can be considered to be a source of risk or harm. It is defined as the thing or person that can put others in danger or at risk of some negative consequence. In cybersecurity, we consider threats that either emanate from cyberspace or are directed at targets or victims within it.[5] To emanate from cyberspace would mean that actions or events occurring in the digital environment are threatening. This would include, in the general sense, both actions that are due to a threat having malign intent, an intention to cause harm in some way, and those which are an accidental source of harm.

A threat generally requires an actor. Such an actor could be natural or human made – for example, a virus which causes a pandemic could emerge from nature or be designed in a lab. The kinds of threat actor that one might consider to exist in the malignant category includes commonly understood concepts such as hackers and cybercriminals, but would extend to anyone or any organisation using

---

2 L. Cheng *et al.*, "Enterprise Data Breach: Causes, Challenges, Prevention, and Future Directions," (2017) 7 *WIREs Data Mining Knowl Discov* e1211. doi:10.1002/widm.1211.

3 B. Buchanan, *The Cybersecurity Dilemma: Hacking, Trust and Fear Between Nations*, (Oxford: O.U.P., 2017).

4 Nektaria Kaloudi and Jingyue Li, "The AI-Based Cyber Threat Landscape: A Survey," (2020) 53(1) *ACM Computing Surveys* 1; M. Boyd and N. Wilson, "Catastrophic Risk from Rapid Developments in Artificial Intelligence," (2020) 16(1) *Policy Quarterly* 53; A. Turchin and D. Denkenberger, "Classification of Global Catastrophic Risks Connected with Artificial Intelligence," (2020) 35 *AI & Soc.* 147.

5 R. Hoffmann *et al.*, "Risk Based Approach in Scope of Cybersecurity Threats and Requirements," (2020) 44 *Procedia Manufacturing* 655.

cyberspace or artificial intelligence (AI)[6] to act in a threatening manner. In a political context, we might include nations and cyberterrorists as being a source of threat.[7] Conversely, the kind of actor that we might consider to constitute an accidental threat is someone or some organisation that participates in a digital event or interaction that poses a threat to themselves or another, and does so unknowingly. This is clearly a broad class, potentially including any human or organisation, although there are perhaps arguments to be made that some are so expert that it is unreasonable for them to be unaware of their responsibility for threatening behaviour, or be unable to control it.[8]

For AI to be a threat, targets or victims would need to be affected by the AI negatively, but the harm that they experience does not need to be constrained in any way to cyberspace. Indeed, we often observe that the harms resulting from cyberattacks, regardless of what type of cyberweaponry is used, are often many, diverse and causally linked.[9] We concern ourselves here with AI as a source of threat, whether as a weapon in the hands of a pre-existing threat, or as an accidental source of threat by its use and presence in our environments. When considering whether AI poses a threat, we will need to deal with two cases, including both malign and accidental contexts. First, might AI constitute a threat because it can be used as a form of weapon to inflict harm? We refer to this as AI as a weapon. Second, does the mere presence and use of AI technologies present a threat to humans and our societies? We refer to this as AI as an environmental threat.

3. Definition and scope of AI

Artificial intelligence as a field of study is commonly thought of as being concerned with creating a system that has the capability to learn and reason like a human, but which is not human (and instead is a machine created by humans, or possibly machines; hence, its artificiality). There have been many phases of development in the pursuit of AI, and today the systems we consider as being AI are essentially a form of advanced machine learning (ML) that enables a computer to make "intelligent" decisions using some combination of algorithms, and to improve performance over time (to improve its ability to predict based on continuous learning). These systems are based on some combination of logic,

6 T. C. King *et al.*, "Artificial Intelligence Crime: An Interdisciplinary Analysis of Foreseeable Threats and Solutions," (2020) 26 *Sci. Eng. Ethics* 89.

7 J. Kosseff, "Collective Countermeasures in Cyberspace," (2020) 10 *Notre Dame J. Int'l Comp. L.* 18.

8 Note that we do not use the term impossible. Of course, it is quite possible that a particular individual in an organisation or social setting is unaware that an event is actually malign. We merely indicate here that one might consider whether that is a reasonable position to take, given their role and associated responsibilities.

9 For discussion on the nature of cyberharms from an organizational perspective, see I. Agrafiotis, J. R. C. Nurse, M. Goldsmith, S. Creese and D. Upton, "A Taxonomy of Cyber-harms: Defining the Impacts of Cyber-attacks and Understanding how they Propagate," (2018) 4(1) *Journal of Cybersecurity* 1. The same reasoning can be applied to individuals and nations.

statistical methods and learning algorithms that can deduce or induce a model which explains the data they are presented with.[10] This might be further optimised against various constraints, which are usually incorporated into the model as weights or scores for taking specific actions. Through such computations, the AI technology can also detect patterns in the data and predict future outcomes in systems based on the patterns previously observed.

This facilitates a range of AI functionality, including: solving of optimisation problems; identification of objects from data and classification decisions; using the model to determine how to achieve a specific goal, and the series of states or actions by which it can be reached; and making predictions about what output or action would occur given a specific set of inputs. This does not strictly apportion intelligence, or claim an actual instance of artificial life, but rather represents an important capability that would need to be possessed by any true artificial consciousness, and hence some argue represents a milestone in reaching for true AI.[11] Whether this is a convincing argument for machine learning being critical to the development of AI is out of scope for this chapter. We do not here consider AI in its more general and pure form, as it is generally believed to not be present[12] today. That would undoubtedly open debate on rights of the artificial lifeform, and reasonability and applicability of law, regulation and social norms.[13] Instead, we take a pragmatic view and deal with the concerns manifesting from AI in its current advanced ML form as being a potential source of threat worthy of immediate consideration.

(a) Machine learning methods

There are a variety of different approaches to machine learning, with strengths and weaknesses that make them suitable for a diverse range of learning problems. These can include human supervision of the learning system, or not, and various types of semi-supervision.[14] Reinforcement learning is an alternative approach to

---

10 See D. L. Poole and A. Alan Mackworth, *Artificial Intelligence: Foundations of Computational Agents*, (Cambridge: Cambridge University Press, 2012).

11 Cf. J. A. Reggia *et al.*, "Artificial Conscious Intelligence," (2019) 7(1) *Journal of Artificial Intelligence and Consciousness* 95; K. Mainzer, *From Natural and Artificial Intelligence to Superintelligence*, (Berlin: Springer, 2020).

12 See, for example, N. Bostrom, *Superintelligence: Paths, Dangers, Strategies*, (Oxford: O.U.P., 2014) for elucidation on the challenges of achieving such intelligence, the dangers it might present and how we might identify its presence. Also *Artificial Intelligence as a positive and negative factor in global risk* by Eliezer Yudkowsky, in *Global Catastrophic Risks* also published by OUP 2008 for consideration of AI as an existential threat.

13 T. Douglas *et al.*, "Is the Creation of Artificial Life Morally Significant?" (2013) 44(4) *Stud Hist Philos Biol Biomed Sci.* 688; J. E. Schirmer, "Artificial Intelligence and Legal Personality: Introducing 'Teilrechtsfähigkeit': A Partial Legal Status Made in Germany," in T. Wischmeyer and T. Rademacher (eds.), *Regulating Artificial Intelligence*, (Berlin: Springer, 2020); J. A. Schnader, "Mal-Who? Mal-What? Mal-Where? The Future Cyber-Threat of A Non-Fiction Neuromancer: Legally Un-Attributable, Cyberspace-Bound, Decentralized Autonomous Entities," (2019) 21 *N.C. J. L. & Tech.* 1.

14 Cf. the discussion in M. Alloghani *et al.*, "A Systematic Review on Supervised and Unsupervised Machine Learning Algorithms for Data Science," in M. Berry *et al.* (eds.), *Supervised*

learning, which concerns itself with situations when the system may need to teach itself how an agent can succeed in the environment (given a set of actions that can be taken), and similarly game theory can be used to produce a model whereby the system seeks to optimise its outcomes given the behaviour of another (such as a human).[15] The advantages of a (perhaps partially) supervised system is that a human can identify where the model being generated appears to be deviating from the intended goal, and so can introduce new sub-goals to try to redirect the learning.

All machine learning requires the generation of a model to explain the data and environment, and that requires an initial training or configuration phase. There also needs to be a way to evolve the model to ensure it continues to work in the face of new data (which may itself be an aspect of the learning activity).

There is a variety of means by which learning takes place. A target system must be identified, and the associated data-points that might be collected. Algorithms may be used to determine the best way to classify and label data, and produce models which are essentially a best-fit explanation of what the data describes. These necessarily are estimations and therefore there will be outliers, data-points for which the model does not strictly hold true (and yet the predictive powers may still be useful). In other examples, the data structures may be well known and fixed, and here it is possible to produce a logical model that can account for all inputs and produce a deterministic set of outputs.

Where relationships between the data-points (relevant to the learning algorithm) can be structured using graphs (nodes and edges), then graph analytical approaches can be taken to reason about optimal strategies. This could include search algorithms and data manipulations, game strategies, route planning, etc. So long as the graphs are finite, these algorithms can terminate, although that does not mean that there must be a tractable solution (one which is practical to find using the computing power available). This means that graphs can be so complex that the search algorithm appears to become unresponsive (when in truth it may be working very hard, but just not delivering a timely result). An alternative approach is to have the reasoning system simulate the system, using the model and a series of inputs to generate outputs, and then to identify patterns in the resulting output data and use these to make predictions. Example of models that are used in machine learning applications include neural networks (inspired by human brain physiology), decision trees and classification trees,[16] and genetic algorithms (searching for solutions by mimicking natural selection).[17]

and *Unsupervised Learning for Data Science. Unsupervised and Semi-Supervised Learning*, (Berlin: Springer, 2020).

15 Compare for example, A. Długosz *et al.*, "Optimal Design of Electrothermal Microactuators for Many Criteria by Means of an Immune Game Theory Multiobjective Algorithm," (2019) 9 *Appl. Sci.* 4654.

16 A. V. Joshi, "Decision Trees," in *Machine Learning and Artificial Intelligence*, (Berlin: Springer, 2020); M. Firat *et al.*, "Column Generation Based Heuristic for Learning Classification Trees," (2020) 116 *Computers & Operations Research* 104866.

17 Compare for example, S. Mirjalili *et al.*, "Grey Wolf Optimizer: Theory, Literature Review, and Application in Computational Fluid Dynamics Problems," in S. Mirjalili *et al.* (eds),

Of course, sometimes it is necessary to be able to reason without complete data or certainty. This means we need to be able to learn in the face of uncertainty, and then refine our knowledge as we observe facts about our environment. For this, a form of reasoning called Bayesian Reasoning is typically applied. In a Bayesian learning system, we not only make deductions on possible outcomes given a set of variables, but also apply probabilities to the likelihood that a state might be reached. These probabilities represent uncertainty, and can be refined based upon observation of the environment over time.[18] In this way, historical data-sets and experts' knowledge can be used to train the learning algorithms. This kind of machine learning accounts for history and interacts with data inputs from the current environment, in order to determine likelihood that certain states are the true one, and hence the likelihood of possible outcomes.[19]

This is a vast oversimplification of the field. For our purposes, which is consideration of the threat that the ML (today's AI) technologies may pose, we will simply assume the worst case – that if a solution is possible, then a threat actor can access the appropriate AI approach and data-set to find it. What is important for our purposes is the key underlying capabilities that AI and associated technologies bring, and how their use might pose a threat. We consider some key issues in the following sections.

(b) *Learning from incomplete data*

All of the machine-learning approaches just described require a set of data-points to be identified for use in creating the model and for making predictions. They might be pre-determined or identified as being of interest from a larger data-set. Sometimes (in fact, very often in real systems with a large number of components that can be in a variety of states), we do not have access to enough training data to be able to generate a model that can predict outputs for all possible inputs. In such cases, we use computational algorithms to estimate models that best fit the data-points that we do have.[20] This means that we are essentially estimating the relationships between data-points, looking for how data-points might cluster together, or some structure and patterns that might produce a model which explain the system.[21] This is necessarily predicated on a model which only fits a

---

Nature-Inspired Optimizers. Studies in Computational Intelligence, (Berlin: Springer, 2020) Vol. 118.

18 Cf. for example, J. Rohmer, "Uncertainties in Conditional Probability Tables of Discrete Bayesian Belief Networks: A Comprehensive Review," (2020) 88 *Engineering Applications of Artificial Intelligence* 1.

19 Cf. for example, see J. Schmidt *et al.,* "Recent Advances and Applications of Machine Learning in Solid-State Materials Science," (2019) 5 *Comput. Mater.* 83.

20 A. B. Abdessalem *et al.,* "Model Selection and Parameter Estimation of Dynamical Systems Using a Novel Variant of Approximate Bayesian Computation," (2019) 122 *Mechanical Systems and Signal Processing* 346.

21 For an application of this, see J. G. Claudino *et al.,* "Current Approaches to the Use of Artificial Intelligence for Injury Risk Assessment and Performance Prediction in Team Sports: a Systematic Review," (2019) 28(5) *Sports Med. – Open* 5. https://doi.org/10.1186.

subset of data-points; there will be outliers for which the model or solution does not apply.

Of course, where we are using a system that can take inputs from the environment, then over time, we can hope it will have an opportunity to become exposed to some of the data that were not available in a training phase, so refining towards a more accurate representation of the system. But the essence is that where we are learning from incomplete data, we may produce a model which does not apply to all. This model is biased towards the data-points that underpin its construction, and any predictions or considerations based upon the model will not necessarily be relevant to outlier data-points (and so simply may not hold true in certain cases). This means that, should there be bias in the training data used to develop the model, then this historical bias may be presented in the outputs, even if the model is subject to continuous change.[22] There may also be data-points not collected or observed yet, for which the model is even less able to explain. This means that we cannot always know how accurate our model is, unless we know the universe of potential data-points (which will only be true for very well-scoped systems). If the model is biased in any way, then the overall learning system will inherit the bias.

(c) *Predicting behaviours and outcomes*

Once we have a working model, even if it is an imperfect estimation or explanation of our system, then we can begin to make assertions of optimal solutions (given the current state) or predictions of possible outcomes given certain stimuli or inputs. We generally consider two types of model for achieving prediction: discriminative methods which directly predict outputs or outcomes given a certain input, or generative methods that will estimate how a new input might fit with the current model and then deduce likely output. Discriminative methods are used where inputs are known and directly fit the model used to describe the system. This uses a fixed class of data (known attributes of the objects), against which new inputs will be compared (thus learning how to solve known problems). In contrast, a generative method will consider the possible ways that the data can be classified and the attributes of each class, and then best match of input data to class attributes would result in the classification of new data inputs (and so determine the output). Generative methods are useful when dealing with systems that might generate inputs that look a little like those seen before, but not exactly. (This is useful in deep learning, where we are seeking to generate new insights into the system and related data.) This means that new training data can be used over time, as the model does not require a fixed structure to the data, as a discriminative method would require (since it works with a fixed class of data).

22 C. Jacopo, "OutPredict: Multiple Datasets Can Improve Prediction of Expression and Inference of Causality," (2020) 10(1) *Scientific Reports.* doi:10.1038/s41598-020-63347-3.

The discriminative model is clearly simpler and so will likely have corresponding performance benefits in terms of speed to reach an output, etc. However, the simplicity potentially ignores some of the available data, so reducing the richness of model and understanding of environment (which could mean that it has reduced predictive powers in some circumstances). Both must be seen as estimations, as they are abstractions, and where one may be able to reason about a larger data-set, it may also be wrong. This is potentially incredibly important when considering threat from AI – as if the model is incorrect then the decisions are ill founded and may result in outcomes that are not optimal and potentially dangerous.

(d) Incomprehension of decisions

Unfortunately, the flexibility of the generative methods can make it hard for humans to explain the rationality behind model choices and predictions, as there can be so many different data-points feeding into a single decision. Various techniques are under development to help render deep-machine learning of this kind more explicable. Partial dependence plots are designed to help determine the influence of one or two data-points on a decision. This would be useful in circumstances when those data-points are of specific concern. However, the reader should note that even for seemingly very simple questions, such as absence of bias or influence of situational information on a decision, there can be a multitude of related data-points making this form of analysis impractical (one or two data-points are generally considered to be tractable in these analyses). Other approaches explore the influence a feature or data-point has on a model by measuring the degree to which the model's predictive correctness is sensitive to changes in values, or how correlated a particular data-point is with other data-points in terms of predictive capability. This is a fast-moving field, and currently there is no practical way to establish sophisticated properties of ML decisions, such as absence of bias or influence from specific mindsets, as it is incredibly hard (impossible, some would say) to even specify those requirements in terms of the data-points and features being reasoned about (and so interrogated when considering explicability of automated decisions).

These issues contribute to the overall threat that AI poses; we now move to consideration of cyberharm.

4. Four apertures of cyberharm

The nature of the harm we must consider as being threatened by AI will differ according to the type of victim we are considering. As digital technology and cyberspace has become a critical part of our lives, we see more people, companies, organisations and communities becoming dependent upon their digital infrastructures and the data and services that exist within them. When there is dependency, there is almost certainly the potential for harm, should access to these data and services be prevented or compromised in some way. There is a myriad of ways to scope types of potential victim; here we apply a lens with apertures focused on four units of human organisation, from the atomic human to the whole of humankind:

(1) **Individual(s):** a human being for which harms might relate to their physical and mental health (including life), their ability to assert their human rights[23] and their ability to participate in society (including access to services, education, food, energy,[24] clean water, participation in governance processes such as elections, online shopping).[25]

(2) **Business or organisational:** a legal entity which seeks to generate value and/or profit, commercial or civil, harms would relate to all elements of operational risk including financial, the ability to be resilient to cyberattacks and incidents, brand reputation, safety of employees,[26] market value of a company, influence of a civil organisation.

(3) **National or societal:** here the object of consideration is the sovereign state, a nation or some social component of it (a region, city or rural area, for example). Here harms would relate to economic prosperity of the nation or region, well-being of individuals residing or working within, the ability to govern including effective regulation and legislation, other aspects of governance such as choice of leadership (effective democracy, for example), human agency, access to welfare and social services by those who need them, national resilience in the face of threats, critical infrastructure delivery, support for the human rights of those within the jurisdiction.[27]

(4) **Global or humankind:** at the global or international aperture, we consider whether harms might emerge that impact international relations and stability as whole, the ability to support trade and commerce in a global marketplace,[28] effecting legislation and rule of law by collaborating across jurisdictional boundaries,[29] the delivery of basic human rights, the avoidance of global system failures in cyberspace (or elsewhere).

It is through these apertures that we now consider the threat from AI as a weapon.

---

23 M. Langford, "Taming the Digital Leviathan: Automated Decision-Making and International Human Rights," (2020) 114 *AJIL Unbound* 141; O. Duhart and S. I. Friedland, "Advancing Technology and the Changing Conception of Human Rights," (2020) 55 *Gonz. J. Int'l L.* 331.

24 R. Leal-Arcas *et al.*, "Smart Grids in the European Union: Assessing Energy Security Regulation & Social and Ethical Considerations," (2018) 24 *Colum. J. Eur. L.* 291.

25 G. Wagner and H. Eidenmüller, "Down by Algorithms? Siphoning Rents, Exploiting Biases, and Shaping Preferences: Regulating the Dark Side of Personalized Transactions," (2019) 86 *U. Chi. L. Rev.* 581.

26 Including the right to a merit based system of recruitment. M. Raub, "Bots, Bias and Big Data: Artificial Intelligence, Algorithmic Bias and Disparate Impact Liability in Hiring Practices," (2018) 71 *Ark. L. Rev.* 529.

27 See for example the discussion in B. Chesney and D. Citron, "Deep Fakes: A Looming Challenge for Privacy, Democracy, and National Security," (2019) 107 *Cal. L. Rev.* 1753.

28 T. C. W. Lin, "Artificial Intelligence, Finance, and the Law," (2019) 88 *Fordham L. Rev.* 531.

29 E. Berman, "A Government of Laws and Not of Machines," (2018) 98 *B.U. L. Rev.* 1277, 1309.

5. AI as a weapon

A cyberattack is commonly conceived of consisting of a number of stages. These stages are generally present, although different types of attacks will see very different manifestations. Reconnaissance is the first stage. Initially, a threat actor will collect information on a victim or target (where the target may be a digital system, as well as a person or organisation) that will enable a vulnerability or vulnerabilities to be identified. These vulnerabilities constitute the attack surface, and exploiting the vulnerabilities will enable an attacker to gain access to some digital resource (either directly via a digital interface, or indirectly via a human who provides access to the digital interface). Often, this means an attack is decomposed into a series of steps. Where an attack step means a human needs to be used to access the technology or an organisation's environment, they too may need to be attacked (knowingly or unknowingly), and this may require reconnaissance on vulnerability in them, too.[30] Should the ultimate target be an organisation or its digital assets, then its attack surface can include all technology linked to the organisation, as well as all human beings who have access to those technologies, as well as all premises and physical assets that are linked to those people and technologies. Reconnaissance gathering is also likely to include information on the security measures that are in place, so as to optimise any attack against detection and prevention controls that could limit its success.

Once reconnaissance is complete, then the attack will proceed to delivery of an exploit or exploits, which are targeted at the vulnerabilities detected. Exploits are the means by which a vulnerability is turned into an attack vector, and the machine or person actually compromised. This is an act that computer network defence tools will be configured to detect, as it represents an action against an asset which can be monitored and defended. The use of an exploit is, in effect, a weapon used by an attacker. Removing an exploit, or preventing it from being used, is an action of computer network defender.

Once an exploit has been used, it is then possible to try to detect and possibly prevent its future use, so limiting the life span of exploits. Consider, for example, the targeting of humans with phishing emails designed to persuade a human being to unwittingly install malware or give away personal details and passwords. Many organisations try to prevent this vulnerability by raising awareness of the threat and type of attack, trying to prevent people from being tricked by them. In the case of exploits which target software errors in technologies, then it is possible to scan network traffic and try to block such communications from reaching vulnerable technology. But this is possible only when you know what the threatening payload (exploit) looks like. Zero-day exploits are those that have not been experienced or witnessed before. They are valuable to an attacker because it means that automated network defence tools will not have specific rule-sets

---

30 Note that there are plenty of examples where humans willingly take part in enabling attacks on organisations and people they associate with. We refer to these as "insider threats" and they would not need to be "attacked" for the step to take place.

to help them identify that particular exploit being attempted.[31] (Although it is possible that some exploits are a small evolution of some already known, and so some technologies could anticipate them, when they are able to account for the changes and still determine a threat to be present.)

After an initial compromise has been made of a system, a number of different phases may take place. Normally there will be some installation of software (pay-load injection) which allows the attacker to complete its objectives. This could deploy further exploits to facilitate movement through the system, or perhaps command and control software to enable remote control of the machine and malware in circumstances where the attacker seeks to persist for some time. Other payloads may be related to sabotage or ransomware attacks, or tools for data exfiltration. At the point of deploying a payload, the attack is particularly vulner-able to detection, since the system state is changing in memory and should the payload be unusual for the system being attacked, then it should be identifiable as present and unexpected. We call the detection of attacks using deviation from normal *anomaly detection*.[32] This approach is important for situations when we cannot set rules for detecting threats, and so we wish to identify significant system changes that may be threatening so that they may be investigated. The attack steps are iterated as needed until the objective has been met.

When considering the threat from AI as a weapon for cyberattack, we do so with reference to the six key characteristics of cyberattacks:[33] targetability, con-trollability, persistence, effects, covertness and (un)mitigatability. Each of these is a property that goes to the potency of an attack, and following, we discuss how AI might amplify or attenuate that potency.

(a) Targeting and control enhancements due to AI

Targetability is the ability of an attacker to focus a cyberweapon to a well-scoped target. It is considered to be a desirable quality in an attack tool, since it will minimise the opportunity to detect the attack to only that which is necessary, it should be easier to control and it will limit chances of unintended harm or collateral damage. The latter may sound like an ethical approach, which perhaps some take, but it should also be noted that this, too, will act to limit the detec-tion risk (there is no point creating harm that does not relate to the objective,

---

31 See for examples A. Dimitriadis *et al.*, "D4I – Digital Forensics Framework for Review-ing and Investigating Cyberattacks," (2020) 5 *Array* 100015; P. Aggarwal *et al.*, "HackIt: A Real-Time Simulation Tool for Studying Real-World Cyberattacks in the Laboratory," in Perez *et al.*, (eds.), *Handbook of Computer Networks and Cyber Security*, (Berlin: Springer, 2020).

32 Cf. H. Mishra *et al.*, "Anomaly-Based Detection of System-Level Threats and Statistical Anal-ysis," in A. Elçi *et al.* (eds.), *Smart Computing Paradigms: New Progresses and Challenges*, (Singapore: Springer, 2020) Vol. 767.

33 For further detail on this cyberattack characteristics taxonomy, see, by D. Hodges and S. Creese, "Understanding Cyber-Attacks," in J. A. Green (ed.), *Cyber Warfare: A Multidisci-plinary Analysis*, (Oxford: Routledge, 2015) at Chapter 2.

since a victim could be the stimulus for an investigation that eventually leads to the attack detection and potential failure). Clearly the use of AI (as scoped in this chapter) will enhance the targetability characteristics of exploits. AI will provide a step-change in the reconnaissance abilities of attackers, enabling them to learn more about their victims, potentially creating models that allow them to predict victim behaviour (even while being attacked), which can ultimately widen the potential attack surface that is vulnerable. This does not only apply to human attack surface (predicting pattern of life, use of technology, likely pressure points, etc.), but it also applies to the technology itself. If we know what technology is being used, we can predict not only the likelihood of a specific vulnerability being present (due to patch behaviour and the like), but fuzzy-logic techniques can also be deployed to generate further exploits that are likely to succeed.[34] This could mean that attack exploits are not only better tailored towards the target, but also that they are more controllable (if desired) or can be used to seed a family of potential exploits to enhance the likelihood of success.

In the context of a measure of targetability characteristics, the use of AI as a weapon could make the highest levels achievable – highly effective targeting of individual users, machines and infrastructure elements. Similarly, the controllability of an attack will be also very high – enabling complete control of all aspects during all phases. This is directly linked to the enhancements in reconnaissance capability, as controllability depends upon knowledge of the environment. This knowledge can provide the means to constructing attack steps that can be achieved in predictable timescales, with predictable outcomes and with a good chance of identifying a remote control or interaction opportunity for use during the attack that can be protected from discovery.

(b) Attacker persistence, covertness and effects enhancement due to AI

The use of AI in the weaponry will also help attackers to achieve persistence, specifically by predicting detection measures and so planning to avoid them. Of course, this will not be always achievable, but there will be instances when detection avoidance is possible. In the case of AI, the machine learning could adopt a generative approach as new data is collected on defensive measures over time. This could provide attackers with a significant amplification of insight into defensive strategy, and greatly enhance the possibility of hiding within normal day-to-day activity. So the covertness characteristic is also improved for the attack – likely moving towards the maximal level of covertness (being impossible to identify that an attack is ongoing). It may also provide an opportunity to influence defensive strategy; if AI can be used to build a model of the cyberdefence decision-making process, then an attacker could produce stimuli designed to invoke specific behaviours by the victims. These behaviours may, in themselves, open up

---

34 Cf. P. v. de Campos Souza *et al.*, "Detection of Anomalies in Large-Scale Cyberattacks Using Fuzzy Neural Networks," (2020) 1 *AI* 92.

additional attack opportunities by influencing the victim towards weaker defence. This could ultimately result in the exploit phase of an attack continuing for as long as the attacker wishes (very high persistence).

Similarly, AI capability-enhancements could result in much greater effects of an attack (harms or damages from the victim's perspective). The total effects of an attack are hard to quantify as harm propagates through systems, potentially affecting all assets that depend upon the one that is compromised (and those that depend on them, etc.). We argue here that this is directly linked to the other characteristics, so if use of AI as a weapon will enhance targetability, control and persistence, then so too are the harmful effects likely to be amplified. Indeed, persistence can offer serendipitous opportunities to identify new unanticipated targets. The potential negative effects are contingent upon the other characteristics, limited only by the choice of the attacker and the ability of the victim to defend against the attack.

(c) Attack (un)mitigatability enhancements due to AI

The final characteristic we should consider is how possible it is to mitigate the threat from AI as a weapon in cyberattack. Here we consider the ability of the defender. Normally, the ability to mitigate a threat will combine some human behavioural element or process to be followed, along with some technology, although there are examples when technology alone will work (consider virus protection whereby the software has the rule that enables it both to detect the virus and to remove the threat before it has chance to compromise a machine). A low level of expertise would indicate that most users and organisations would be able to mitigate the threat. High levels of expertise would be considered difficult for a skilled organisation, and impossible for a home user. Very high expertise would currently be considered impossible to mitigate (or the chances of having that individual in the team would be extremely slim). If we reflect upon the use of AI then, given the current position, whereby we believe that use of AI would enable highly covert attacks to be conducted, combined with ability to influence people, then we would need to question if we would notice the use of the AI as a weapon at all. We might, after the event, investigate and determine that the level of sophistication would indicate either an AI threat or an insider within the system (disclosing information that otherwise the AI would learn). However, this would not enable us to mitigate the attack in question; more likely, it would help us to determine likely threat actors, which may help mitigate future attacks.

(d) Threat to individuals

While the previous discussion adopts a language that is clearly appropriate for the consideration of organisations which actively defend their systems from attack, the basic components hold just as relevant when considering the individual. If one is concerned about personal privacy, then the advanced reconnaissance capabilities are in themselves of concern, and could represent a significant source of harm. It should be noted that this harm could manifest from what might be considered a benign activity, such as processing data about our online browsing history to tailor the presentation of Internet news on our devices. But that the computational power of the algorithms, combined with the richness of the data available, means that what is discoverable could deliver a model of the human being that is so accurate in prediction that it goes beyond simple privacy compromise and goes to the potential for loss of human agency and freedom of choice.[35] This could have consequences at other apertures, should it be applied to a number of individuals.

If an individual's ability to think freely and make choices is compromised due to manipulation resulting from use of AI, then the actions that individual takes could be influenced to cause greater harm. Our current position is that we could not detect this occurring, and we are not likely to be gathering the data necessary to build a body of evidence that it occurred historically, so we may find ourselves in a situation whereby human beings are being held responsible for actions that they were arguably manipulated into taking.[36] We have accepted a degree of such targeting historically, in the cases of advertising, marketing and training, for example. But in these situations, individuals are not targeted personally; instead, specific demographics are identified. The use of AI could change this targetability, and so may create a capability which is determined to be threatening to individuals.

(e) *Threat to businesses or organisations*

The potential threat to an organisation follows directly from the discussion of attack characteristics. The ability of an organisation to counter an attack will be limited by the skills of those tasked with defending it, and the methods and tools at their disposal. The current situation is that the enhancements that using AI brings to the various attack characteristics, coupled with the lack of mitigations specific to this potential amplification of threat, means that the potency of attacks could bring about severe harms. This potency is not discriminatory in respect to the nature of harm; it will apply whether the ultimate objective is theft of secrets, sabotage of systems, ransom demands or some other purpose.

The ability to mitigate through attack detection and harm reduction is higher for an organisation with a skilled cyberdefence team than is likely for an individual,

---

35 For example, K. Manheim and L. Kaplan, "Artificial Intelligence: Risks to Privacy and Democracy," (2019) 21 *Yale J. L. & Tech.* 106 at 120 observe:

> Data collectors or third party 'cloud' storage services maintain the large-scale data collected by IoT, surveillance, and tracking systems in diverse databases. While in isolation, individual data sets dispersed across thousands of servers may provide limited information insights, this limitation can be resolved by a process known as "data fusion," which merges, organizes, and correlates those data points. Once data is collected, synthesized, and analyzed, third parties create sophisticated profiles of their 'data subjects' that offer a trove of useful intelligence to anyone who wants to influence or manipulate purchasing choices and other decisions.

36 See the examples given in M. E. Kaminski, "Binary Governance: Lessons from the GDPR's Approach to Algorithmic Accountability," (2019) 92 *S. Cal. L. Rev.* 1529 at 1545.

however. Also, organisations benefit from sharing information on threat patterns which may enable some to prepare for future attacks using knowledge of how threats attacked others. Perhaps of significant concern should be the ability to influence the victim organisation. It is conceivable that this will open up the potential for harm propagations not previously experienced, so making the potential losses greater. It may also lead to problems with risk sharing or transference where insurance is being used, since it is not clear whether or not such a risk (resulting from influence over victims) will be insurable. Initially, we may experience a period of heightened losses which are covered by insurance, until such time as the AI threat is deducible and evidenced. There is a risk that we may then find that the potential for loss is so great that it is explicitly written out of cover. Of course, if we develop the capability to evidence the use of AI in this way, then we may also develop the capability at least detect to its likely presence in an attack. So the use of AI as a weapon could lead to pressure to upskill defence systems, to have such detection capability in order that cover is maintained.

The question of responsibility becomes of interest, as organisations are more likely to have support for criminal proceedings. Who is responsible when an AI is used as part of an attack? Arguably the entity deploying the AI, since it is in effect using it as a weapon. But will it be possible to argue mitigating circumstances, whereby the potency was not understood (since explicability capabilities have not yet been delivered), and so the harm is – to a certain degree – accidental and unintended?

(f) *Threat to nations or societies*

The use of AI to conduct cyberattacks could present such an improvement in weaponry that significant harm might be experienced across many organisations, including those sectors considered critical to a nation's economy and the provision of critical services to citizens (clean water, energy, transport, etc.).[37] An initial consideration would likely conclude that this is significant enough to be considered a threat at the national aperture, as the vulnerability to this kind of weaponry is likely to pervade society and sectors. Certainly, the immediate potential for harm, such as sabotage of systems and services, is a risk which should be planned for. It is inconceivable that such technology will only be used by those with benign intent; all other technologies have been used to attack, and there is no reason to believe that the same will not be true for AI.

However, when considering harms relating to global standing, the security environment and how it might attract or detract inward investment from companies and the like, one must consider the cybersecurity capacity of the nation as a whole.[38] If the nation is considered to be one of the best, then it is likely to do no worse than others in the class (since all will be subjected to the AI threat). Those

---

37 D. A. Wallace and S. R. Reeves, "Protecting Critical Infrastructure in Cyber Warfare: Is It Time for States to Reassert Themselves?" (2020) 53 *U.C. Davis L. Rev.* 1607 at 1632.

38 Cf. A. Palmer, "A Model Framework for Successful Cybersecurity Capacity Building," (2016) 19 *J. Internet L.* 15.

nations who are not leaders but are seeking to improve have the most to lose in this respect, as companies who might have otherwise taken the risk may decide that the workforce available is not able to stand up to the changing threat, and therefore choose to base themselves in a nation with greater capability. So AI as a threat, in the context of a weapon in an attack, could become a distinguishing factor in national capacity and operating environment. A new challenge requires creation and innovation, and that will require access to minds who can match up to the threat. While these new ideas could come from literally anywhere (there is no scientific reason why it needs to be from an advanced cybersecurity nation), the decision on where to invest will need to be justified and ultimately de-risked.

The economic prosperity of a nation or society is not the only asset at risk, however. The ability for AI to predict outcomes means that it is a potent tool for influence. There remains a healthy debate around the ability to self-govern, to have self-determination, and, where a democracy exists, hold an election where citizens can enter debate and exercise choice. If large-scale influence is possible of the nature discussed previously in the aperture of individuals, then could that call into question the democratic process? Is it possible to influence large groups towards a cyberattacker's objective? There are many debates on this topic, and certainly social science has shown us that predictability and influence are possible.[39] After all, this has been the space occupied by public health campaigns and the like for many years.

An important question we must consider is whether the targeting of AI presents a compromise of free choice, a level of manipulation that undermines agency of an individual, and whether that can be deployed, at will, to undermine the agency of a society (or to a large portion of it). This could be seen as an attack on sovereignty and self-determination.[40] There is nothing in the technical consideration that would indicate that an attack of this nature was not practically possible to achieve, although it will be as difficult for an attacker to determine that their actions stimulated the result, as it would be for a defender, as there are so many different possible factors that could cause such an outcome. There are no signs of any self-balancing within the system that would prevent such a potential; indeed, the current position is that data science (which includes AI of the type under consideration here) is delivering results on a national campaign scale. Therefore, while this is not a cyberattack of the type historically considered by the profession, this is potentially in-scope as it represents a technology being used to attack people and a society across cyberspace, with harms outside of cyberspace. What would be considered a proportionate response to such an attack, if it could be evidenced to have taken place and reliably attributed? How would we determine the right response to make? If we are to wait for evidence of such an attack,

39 M. Lavi, "Evil Nudges," (2018) 21 *Vand. J. Ent. & Tech. L.* 1; M. Lamo and C. Ryan, "Regulating Bot Speech," (2019) 66 *UCLA L. Rev.* 988 at 997; K. Brennan-Marquez *et al.*, "Strange Loops: Apparent Versus Actual Human Involvement in Automated Decision Making," (2019) 34 *Berkeley Tech. L.J.* 745.
40 M. S. Gal, "Algorithmic Challenges to Autonomous Choice," (2018) 25 *Mich. Tech. L. Rev.* 59 at 61–63.

might we miss it (because we simply cannot detect it or evidence it)? If we cannot evidence a weapon, with reasonable certainty, then should we not concern ourselves with it, or do we have a responsibility to consider misuse as we invest in the underlying capability?

(g) Global threats

Possibly the greatest global threat from AI is not the potential for a single attack to bring about a global catastrophe (not that we can rule that out), but rather that this could signal such a step-change in attack capability that a polarisation of nations may take place – discriminating between those that can cope and those that simply cannot. This runs the risk of creating cybersecurity poverty, where nations may be left behind if they cannot generate enough capacity either locally or by transferring it in. This could render large portions of infrastructure open to devastating attacks, and create a situation of imbalance that is incredibly hard to change. We will need to consider how at risk our global systems are to such a threat. How will we conduct international trade premised on data-flow and markets in the face of such a threat? The potency of the weapon can be enhanced with training data, and therefore the nature of the data-flows around the world become relevant. This will move beyond compromise of personal privacy (although that will continue to be a significant risk) and expand into issues surrounding weapons proliferation and potential controls, which may place requirements upon nations that cause conflict with economic growth strategy.

Undoubtedly, resilience is going to become the over-riding goal, since there is no sign of the threat environment receding, and the potential for harm from cyberattack continues to grow. It would be hard to build a case that we should not be concerned about the threat from AI as a weapon. AI as a threat represents an indication that the challenge of cybersecurity is about to get much more difficult, and therefore, capacity investment is urgent for those not at the forefront. And for those at the forefront, it will represent the next step-change in the attack capability which must be defended against. International considerations must be given to the rule of law, how to collaborate in the face of such potent weapons in order that resilience might be achieved.[41] We will not be able to ignore the potential for multiplicative effects on AI weapons from international data-flows, and new forms of oversight and compliance monitoring may be required, as will agreement on acceptable norms of behaviour surrounding cyberspace and AI technology, and the ability to observe harms as they emerge.

6. AI as an environmental threat

We turn to the issue of AI as an environmental threat, and whether risks will emerge through its use in our environments. Cyberspace is widely recognised as being an environment upon which all nations are likely to depend, and so an

---

41 J. L. Vagle, Cybersecurity and Moral Hazard," (2020) 23 *Stan. Tech. L. Rev.* 71.

environment that will need to be protected for the common good.[42] But historically, we have focused on collaboration around standards, intelligence sharing and interfaces for policing and evidence gathering. We have considered export controls around technology, but these are tricky as they can conflict with commerce and trade, and also require subtle distinctions to be made around intended use and potential use.

(a) The question of dual-use

Dual-use is the term given to technologies that can be developed for benign purposes, but repurposed for use as a weapon – in our case, a cyberweapon. This broadly can be considered to include almost every technology one might nominate.[43] If an attacker could take control of an autonomous vehicle and drive it into a building, causing loss of life, then in this context, the car would have been used as a weapon.[44] The same argument can be made for objects that are not technology; consider the baseball bat or golf club used to inflict injury to a person. We cannot imagine seeking to control for all possible technologies that might potentially be useful as weapons. However, we might validly seek to control the proliferation of weapons being sold as objects for other purposes. In this case, we would be dealing with the systemic development of technology as a weapon, and would need to consider if the proliferation of such technology could create a dangerous environment for people that needs to be controlled. At this time, the critical capability will be to determine if and when that situation emerges, and to be able to reason about the realistic level of danger societies might be exposed to. Controls surrounding data used to train AI may help limit potency as an attack tool, and so its dual-use risks. But this would mean creating versions of AI tools that can be monitored.

(b) Vulnerability introduction

A second-order effect of the use of AI in general is that the knowledge produced makes human beings predictable, and this is a vulnerability that is commonly exploited in attacks (including those not using AI). It is therefore a straightforward and rather obvious extrapolation to make the case that simply the use of AI does indeed introduce attack surface into our environment – and worse, that

---

42 S. J. Shackelford *et al.*, "Unpacking the International Law on Cybersecurity Due Diligence: Lessons from the Public and Private Sectors," (2016) 17 *Chi. J. Int'l L.* 1.

43 See the compromise of the Internet-connected doll to access a home by opening the door, or the use of social-networking technology in the Arab Spring, which is widely considered to have been used to identify activists and target them in attacks.

44 Berris writes:

Many prominent examples of hacking in the IoT pertain to automobiles. In 2015, Fiat Chrysler recalled 1.4 million cars in response to a widely publicized demonstration where hackers took control of a Jeep Cherokee through its infotainment system. They were able to "turn the steering wheel, briefly disable the brakes and shut down the engine."

S. Sun Beale and P. Berris, "Hacking the Internet of Things: Vulnerabilities, Dangers, and Legal Responses," (2018) *Duke L. & Tech. Rev.* 161 at 164–165.

attack surface can essentially enable attacks to propagate according to the interactions that the humans (becoming increasingly predictable) have with other people, technologies, their employers and any systems they interact with. This potential for propagation, by virtue of the human connections across cyberspace and physical space, produces a mobility model which is akin to that of human virus spread. So we may find that there is a threat to and from the public emanating from the use of AI in the general environment. This is not entirely new, we have faced other cyberthreats which use large human populations as propagation vectors (digital viruses and creation of botnets[45] for use in cybercrime, for examples). However, the use of AI to predict vulnerabilities in people, and to optimise strategies for using people as attack vectors, will be a force amplifier for other cyberattacks (of all kinds), which could significantly raise the background threat level in all apertures.

Where we adopt AI technology to help us deliver critical services and information infrastructures, we may become exposed to attackers using AI against us. It is possible that they could adopt adversarial AI techniques[46] to essentially *game* our systems, identifying strategies which would lead to them *winning* (which could mean sabotage, theft, etc.).

(c) Growth of threat environment

The threat environment may also grow as a result of AI because availability of AI may make it more profitable to conduct cyberattacks (attracting cybercriminality, for example). This argument can be made with all new technology developments that pervade our environments, since their use typically enables monetisation of our digital dependency (e.g., ransomware, sabotage) and market competition (e.g., theft of secrets, sabotage). What is potentially different about the wide adoption of AI methods is that the targeting and influence opportunities it offers can be purposed to any end; so AI is a platform upon which to not only monetise data through third-party data services, but also to monetise attack delivery for a wide variety of payloads. This is a scalable and repeatable business model, and it may become an enabler for other attack tools optimised for particular effects, not unlike the role that the "Dark Web" has provided in helping criminality in general. Harmful effects will certainly emerge at the individual, organisational and national apertures. Whether this could also lead to some international destabilisation remains to be seen; certainly, it will set a requirement for international collaboration in addressing cybercrime, enabled by AI, as expertise in this space remains limited and distributed around the globe.

---

45 Matwyshyn and Pell write:

> For example, the Mirai botnet took control of webcams, internet-connected DVRs and other Internet of Things ("IoT") products, harnessing these IoT devices to attack major websites such as Twitter and Reddit in a distributed denial of service ("DDoS") attack that left the internet inaccessible on large parts of the East Coast. The attack was so severe that authorities initially considered it potentially the work of a nation-state.

A. M. Matwyshyn and S. K. Pell, "Broken," (2019) 32 *Harv. J.L. & Tech.* 479 at 495–496.
46 Cf. Y. Yan, *et al.*, "Quantization-based Event-Triggered Sliding Mode Tracking Control of Mechanical Systems," (2020) 523 *Information Sciences* 296.

(d) Polarisation of wealth

The use of AI could provide opportunities for polarisation of wealth associated with data-driven or underpinned services, as some countries have access to better AI technology and so can create more value and advance more quickly. If there are commercial benefits, then global positions may emerge which use the insights from AI to benefit a single country. Worse still, those proficient in the technology may be able to construct data-sets for trading which are deliberately designed to promote sub-optimal learning when others use them, a data poisoning of the training sets used by others in order to secure permanent market-advantage.

The potential polarisation of cybersecurity capability could have ramifications for the wealth of nations. This is not only an issue for nations worrying about being victims, but it is a global challenge as we need a cyberspace that promotes international trade, communication, sharing of ideas and so mutual understanding and global stability. This will help nurture and enable other international collaborations, such as those aimed at delivering solutions for the existential challenges of the twenty-first century. We cannot expect the poorest nations to accept cybersecurity poverty, and yet expect them to make sacrifices for the common good of humanity in other areas like protecting the environment. This is not a tenable position. So the cybersecurity environment for cyberspace is a matter for all, and any technology that poses such a potential step-change in threat should also be considered in the context of global need.

(e) Outliers and oversimplification

Clustering and classification can over-simplify data and miss differences (as they are not determined as important for the best-fit model of the system). This means that there will be outliers in predictions; members of groups for which the prediction does not apply. Context matters when we are using AI. The danger is that we can engineer for particular groups, and therefore the outliers are not provided for and will find solutions inappropriate. This also can leave our learning systems open to bias – since reinforcing goals and learning objectives for certain groups will mean that outcomes are optimised for them and will not address the needs of outliers in the same way. Could this mean that a defence in malign use of AI against a person could be founded upon the fact that the AI was not actually optimised for use by this type of human being? That is, if a human is using AI or using a system with an AI component, and they actually are not the type that it was optimised for, could they therefore not be able to control outcomes or be responsible for outcomes in the same way as they would be if driving a car or crossing a road? How will we know whether the outputs of the model should be applied to them or not? Currently we do not, as a matter of course, treat the outliers as important environmental constraints of the model; the model is an estimate of best fit for the data being observed in the system (and outliers are simply datapoints which do not exactly fit the model). If we are to move towards an environment where people do take responsibility for their interaction with AI systems, then an important aspect of situational awareness that they will need is the ability to determine what constitutes outliers for the system (so decisions based on the use of AI can be appropriately directed). Equally, might there be a danger that where public policy is driven by such AI methods, that we will naturally converge towards best fit solutions that are not necessarily optimal in terms of what is actually needed, just best fit solutions for explaining the data in the training set?

(f) Rule of law and responsibility for harm

What about responsibility? Who is responsible for what is learnt? Or the output, the product, of the AI technology? What if it is the output that is used maliciously, that is the central cause of harm? Is it the manufacturer or the user of the technology who is responsible? Do we know what safe use might look like, or how to avoid unsafe or harmful use? Will we need a safety culture around our AI technology? We have seen great strides in safety-critical manufacturing giving consideration to cybersecurity as a source of hazard. But do we need to go further and consider the use of AI as requiring a safety regime around it, methods to ensure that once in use, we also have the means to reduce risk and threat to others?

7. Reflection

Upon reflection of all the considerations in the chapter, it becomes clear that AI does constitute a threat which justifies further thought. We will require the means to identify and manage risks as they emerge, and such risks could apply to all apertures: individual, organisational, national or societal, and global.

Today, the applications that are benefiting from such AI are significant to humankind, including new materials research, drug discovery, nano-engineering, medical diagnostics, weather system prediction, supply-chain optimisation and resource planning for carbon reduction. The applications are as diverse as the data available in the world, and they will continue to grow as we further instrument our environment using the Internet of Things.

Our ability to apply computation to our environment enables us to create highly accurate models of systems, predicting behaviour under certain stimuli and therefore inferring what stimulus might be required to create a given outcome. Any consideration of how to respond to the threat related to these technologies must be made while considering the benefits that their use can bring.

None of the threat characteristics considered in the chapter constitute an argument against discovery or use of AI. Rather, they form an emerging case for checks-and-balances capacity, proper oversight and consideration of protection mechanisms, possible regulation and certainly the need to understand and observe use so that current methods for deterring or detecting criminal and threatening behaviour can be applied to these new technologies. At a societal level, we will need to reflect upon whether we are investing enough in our ability to defend against and be resilient in the face of AI used in a malignant manner, given what we are investing in AI itself.

10 AI vs. IP

Criminal liability for intellectual property offences of artificial intelligence entities

Gabriel Hallevy

1. Introduction: the legal problem

Most legal systems protect intellectual property (IP) rights through criminal law, amongst various legal protections. Although the main legal protection granted to IP rights is civil, most legislators defined certain protections through criminal law.[1] This legal situation reflects society's wide interest in protecting IP rights. When IP rights are violated, and the violation fulfils the basic requirements of the relevant offence, the society may indict the violator, regardless the violator's identity (corporation or human). But what if the violator is an artificial intelligence (AI) entity? Most modern AI entities do have the technological capability of violating IP rights.[2]

Illegal copying of software by another software equipped with AI technology is a common example. Could the AI entity itself be criminally liable, beyond the criminal liability of the manufacturer, the end-user, or owner, and beyond their civil liability? The present study suggests a possible positive answer. Using the current definitions of criminal liability, the imposition of criminal liability upon AI entities for committing IP offences is quite feasible.

However, it should be noted that no criminal liability should be de facto imposed on artificial intelligence systems, at least yet, but if basic definitions of criminal law are not changed, this consequence is inevitable. The modern criminal law is modular, as criminal liability may be imposed when all of its requirements are fulfilled. Each requirement has its own definitions and terms to be fulfilled, as defined by the basic concepts of criminal law.

The major question is, of course, who is to be held liable for IP offences committed by AI entities? The modern world is technologically developing very rapidly. Robots and computers are replacing humans even for simple daily tasks. As long as humans used computers as mere tools, there was no real difference between computers and hammers, chairs or pencils. When software became more

---

1 See e.g., 35 U.S.C.S. § 292 and 17 U.S.C.S. § 506.
2 See examples in G. Hallevy, *When Robots Kill – Artificial Intelligence Under Criminal Law*, (Lebanon: Northeastern University Press, 2013) at 38–83 (for intentional offences), for negligence offences at 84–103 and for strict liability offences at 104–119.

sophisticated, humans used to say that computers were able to "think" for them. The problem began when computers evolved from "thinking" machines into thinking machines (without quotation marks).[3] Thus emerged artificial intelligence (AI). AI research began in the middle of the twentieth century.[4] Since then, AI entities have become an integral part of modern human life, functioning in a much more sophisticated manner than other daily tools. Could they become a danger to society in terms of criminal law?

It is most probable that they already are dangerous.[5] In 1950, Isaac Asimov set down three fundamental laws of robotics in his science fiction masterpiece *I, Robot*.[6] These laws were: (1) a robot may not injure a human being or, through inaction, allow a human being to come to harm; (2) a robot must obey the orders given to it by human beings, except where such orders would conflict with the First Law; and (3) a robot must protect its own existence, as long as such protection does not conflict with the First or Second Laws.[7]

These three fundamental laws are obviously contradictory. Isaac Asimov himself wrote in 1964 that:

[t]here was just enough ambiguity in the Three Laws to provide the conflicts and uncertainties required for new stories, and, to my great relief, it seemed always to be possible to think up a new angle out of the 61 words of the Three Laws.[8]

What if a man orders a robot to hurt another person for the good of the other person? What if the robot is in police service and the commander of the mission orders it to arrest a suspect and the suspect resists arrest? Or what if the robot is in medical service and is ordered to perform a surgical procedure on a patient, and the patient objects, but the medical doctor insists that the procedure is for the patient's own good, and repeats the order to the robot? Whatever the solutions to such hypothetical scenarios under these fictitious statutes, Asimov's fundamental laws of robotics relate only to robots.

AI software not installed in a robot would not be subject to Asimov's laws, even if these laws had any real legal significance. Nevertheless, although Asimov

---

3 See more at www.youtube.com/watch?v=pRNm6XKMO2Q.
4 N. P. Padhy, *Artificial Intelligence and Intelligent Systems*, (Oxford: O.U.P., 2005).
5 For example, in 1981, a 37-year-old Japanese employee of a motorcycle factory was killed by an artificial-intelligence robot working near him. The robot erroneously identified the employee as a threat to its mission, and calculated that the most efficient way to eliminate this threat was by pushing him into an adjacent operating machine. Using its very powerful hydraulic arm, the robot smashed the surprised worker into the operating machine, killing him instantly, and then resumed its duties with no one to interfere with its mission. See also S. Gless *et al.*, "If Robots Cause Harm, Who Is to Blame? Self-Driving Cars and Criminal Liability," (2016) 19 *New Crim. L. Rev.* 412.
6 I. Asimov, *I, Robot*, (New York: Gnome Press, 1950).
7 *Ibid.*
8 I. Asimov, *The Rest of Robots*, (New York, Garden City: Doubleday & co. Inc. 1964).

was a prolific science fiction author, his three laws were written for the actual technological realm that was forthcoming according to his belief. Artificial intelligence technology has been vastly developed since then, and most advanced societies are facing some of the problems Asimov had presaged.

The main questions with regard to AI criminal liability are: (1) which kind of laws or ethics are correct?; and (2) who is to decide? In order to cope with such problems as they relate to humans, society devised systems of criminal law, which embodies the most powerful legal social control in modern civilisation. People's fear of AI entities often arises because AI entities are not considered to be subject to the law, specifically to criminal law.[9]

The apprehension that AI entities evoke may have arisen due to Hollywood's depiction of AI entities in numerous films, such as *2001: A Space Odyssey* (1968)[10] and the modern *The Matrix* trilogy (1999–2003),[11] in which AI entities are not subject to the law. However, it should be noted that Hollywood did treat AI entities in an empathic way as well, depicting them as human, as almost human, or as wishing to be human.[12] This kind of treatment included, of course, clear subordination to human legal social control, and to criminal law. In the past, people were similarly fearful of corporations and their power to commit a spectrum of crimes, but since corporations are legal entities subject to criminal and corporate law, that kind of fear has been reduced significantly.[13]

Therefore, the modern question relating to AI entities becomes: does the growing intelligence of AI entities subject them, as any other legal entity, to legal social control?[14]

This chapter attempts to work out a legal solution to the problem of the criminal liability of AI entities, specified to IP offences. An AI software which functions as an expert system, but actually copies protected information as it figured out, by itself, that it is much easier and faster to copy the information rather than creating

---

9 The apprehension that AI entities evoke may have arisen due to Hollywood's depiction of AI entities in numerous films, as discussed in the following paragraph. Treatment of AI entities included clear subordination to human legal social control, and to criminal law.

10 *2001:* A Space Odyssey (Metro-Goldwyn-Mayer 1968).

11 *The Matrix* (Village Roadshow Pictures 1999); *The Matrix Reloaded* (Village Roadshow Pictures 2003); *The Matrix Revolutions* (Village Roadshow Pictures 2003).

12 See, e.g., *A.I.* Artificial Intelligence (Amblin Entertainment 2001).

13 See, e.g., J. C. Coffee, Jr., " 'No Soul to Damn: No Body to Kick': An Un-scandalised Inquiry Into the Problem of Corporate Punishment," (1981) 79 *Mich. L. Rev.* 386; S. Box, *Power, Crime and Mystification*, (Oxford: Routledge, 1983) at 16–79; B. Fisse and J. Braithwaite, "The Allocation of Responsibility for Corporate Crime: Individualism, Collectivism and Accountability," (1988) 11 *Sydney L. Rev.* 468.

14 See generally L. T. McCarty, "Reflections on Taxman: An Experiment in Artificial Intelligence and Legal Reasoning," (1977) 90 *Harv. L. Rev.* 837; E. D. Elliott, "Holmes and Evolution: Legal Process as Artificial Intelligence," (1984) 13 *J. Legal Stud.* 113; B. G. Buchanan and T. E. Headrick, "Some Speculation about Artificial Intelligence and Legal Reasoning," (1971) 23 *Stan. L. Rev.* 40; A. A. Martino, "Artificial Intelligence and Law," (1994) 2 *Int'l J. L. & Info. Tech.* 154; E. L. Rissland, "Artificial Intelligence and Law: Stepping Stones to a Model of Legal Reasoning," (1990) 99 *Yale L. J.* 1957.

it. Could it be punishable? At the outset, a definition of an AI entity will be presented. Based on that definition, this article will then propose and introduce three possible models of AI entity criminal liability: (1) Perpetration-by-Another liability; (2) Natural-Probable-Consequence liability; and (3) Direct liability.

These possible models might be applied separately, but in many situations, a coordinated combination of them (all or some of them) is required in order to complete the legal structure of criminal liability. Once we examine the possibility of legally imposing criminal liability on AI entities, then the question of punishment must be addressed. How can an AI entity serve a sentence of incarceration? How can probation, a pecuniary fine, etc., be imposed on an AI entity? Consequently, it is necessary to formulate viable forms of punishment in order to impose criminal liability practically on AI entities. Thus, for instance, how can the provision of the U.S. Code Service ("shall be fined not more than $500 for every such offence")[15] be implemented when the offender is an AI system?

2. AI entities

For some years, there has been significant controversy about the very essence of an AI entity.[16] Futurologists have proclaimed the birth of a new species, *machina sapiens*, which will share the human place as intelligent creatures on earth.[17] Critics have argued that a "thinking machine" is an oxymoron.[18] Machines, including computers, with their foundations of cold logic, can never be as insightful or creative as humans.[19] This controversy raises the basic questions of the essence of humanity (do human beings function as thinking machines?) and of AI (can there be thinking machines?).[20]

There are five attributes that one would expect an intelligent entity to possess.[21] The first is communication.[22] One can communicate with an intelligent entity. The easier it is to communicate with an entity, the more intelligent the entity seems. One can communicate with a dog, but not about Einstein's theory of relativity. One can communicate with a little child about Einstein's theory, but it requires a discussion in terms that a child can comprehend. The second is internal knowledge;[23] an intelligent entity is expected to have some knowledge

15 35 U.S.C.S. § 292.

16 See, e.g., T. Winograd, "Thinking Machines: Can There Be? Are We?" in D. Partridge and Y. Wilks (eds.), *The Foundations of Artificial Intelligence*, (Cambridge: C.U.P., 2006) at 167.

17 *Ibid.* at 167.

18 *Ibid.* at 167–168.

19 *Ibid.* at 168–169.

20 For the formal foundations of AI see, for example, T. C. Przymusinski, "Non-Monotonic Reasoning Versus Logic Programming: A New Perspective," in Partridge and Wilks, *op. cit. supra*, note 16 at 49; R. W. Weyhrauch, "Prolegomena to a Theory of Mechanized Formal Reasoning," in Partridge and Wilks, *op. cit. supra*, note 16 at 72.

21 R. C. Schank, *What is AI Anyway?*, in Partridge and Wilks, *op. cit. supra*, note 16 at 3.

22 *Ibid.* at 4–5.

23 *Ibid.* at 5.

about itself. The third is external knowledge;[24] an intelligent entity is expected to know about the outside world, to learn about it, and to utilise that information. The fourth is goal-driven behaviour;[25] an intelligent entity is expected to take action in order to achieve its goals. The fifth is creativity;[26] an intelligent entity is expected to have some ability to take alternate action when the initial action fails. For example, a fly that tries to exit a room and bumps into a windowpane will do that repeatedly and incessantly. When an AI robot bumps into a window, it tries to exit using the door. Most AI entities possess these five attributes by definition.[27] Some twenty-first century types of AI entities possess even more attributes that enable them to act in far more sophisticated ways.[28]

AI entities have a wide variety of applications. AI entities can be designed to imitate the physical capabilities of a human being, and these capabilities can be improved. AI entity is capable of being physically faster and stronger than a human being. The AI software installed in it also enables the AI entity to calculate many complicated calculations faster and simultaneously, or to "think" faster. An AI entity is capable of learning and of gaining experience, and experience is a useful way of learning. AI entities and AI software are used in a wide range of applications in industry, military services, medical services, science and even in games.[29] All these attributes create the essence of an AI entity.[30]

3. Three models of criminal liability of artificial intelligence entities for commission of IP offences

An AI system is required to complete the preparation of a given software for public use. The system may be designed as a debugger which fills in necessary

24 Or "world knowledge." See *Ibid.*
25 H. Welzel, *Das Deutsche Strafrecht: Eine Systematische Darstellung*, (Berlin: Walter de Gruyter, 1954).
26 Schank, *op. cit. supra*, note 21 at 5–6.
27 *Ibid.* at 4–6.
28 In November 2009, during the Supercomputing Conference in Portland, Oregon (SC 09), IBM scientists and others announced that they succeeded in creating a new algorithm named "Blue Matter," which possesses the thinking capabilities of a cat. Chris Capps, *"Thinking" Supercomputer Now Conscious as a Cat*, Unexplainable.net, 19 November 192009, <www.unexplainable.net/artman/publish/article_14423.shtml>; see generally Supercomputing Conference 09, <http://sc09.supercomputing.org/; What Is Blue Matter? www.hpcwire.com/hpc/1096657.html>. This algorithm collects information from very many units with parallel and distributed connections. The information is integrated and creates a full image of sensory information, perception, dynamic action and reaction, and cognition. This platform simulates brain capabilities, and eventually, it is supposed to simulate real thought processes. The final application of this algorithm contains not only analog and digital circuits, metal or plastics, but also protein-based biological surfaces. *Ibid.*
29 See, e.g., W. B. Schwartz *et al.*, "Artificial Intelligence in Medicine: Where Do We Stand?" (1987) 27 *Jurimetrics J.* 362; R. E. Susskind, "Artificial Intelligence, Expert Systems and Law," (1990) 5 *Denning L.J.* 105.
30 See also, e.g., Y. Wilks, "One Small Head: Models and Theories," in Partridge and Wilks, *op. cit. supra*, note 16 at 121; A. Bundy and S. Ohlsson, "The Nature of AI Principles," in Partridge and Wilks, *op. cit. supra*, note 16 at 135; T. W. Simon, "Artificial Methodology Meets Philosophy," in Partridge and Wilks, *op. cit. supra*, note 16 at 155.

ingredients if required or missing. At some places in the software, the AI system fills the relevant ingredient by copying a protected part of another software. Although the AI system has made some changes in the copied software, it still is considered to be an IP violation, which is protected by a criminal offence besides some civil protections. If the state wishes to deter the society from such conduct, the administrative directive is to indict the violator in criminal proceedings.[31]

In order to impose criminal liability upon a person, two main elements must exist for non-strict liability offences. The first is the factual element (*actus reus*), while the other is the mental element (*mens rea*). The *actus reus* requirement is expressed mainly by acts or omissions.[32] Sometimes, other external elements are required in addition to conduct, such as the specific results of that conduct and the specific circumstances underlying the conduct.[33] In most IP offences, the actual conduct which infringes the IP right is the *actus reus* requirement (e.g., the actual copying of the information).

The *mens rea* requirement has various levels of mental elements. The highest level is expressed by direct intention, but often subjective recklessness is sufficient. Obviously, subjective recklessness comes in many degrees. A person's knowledge of the essential facts can be used to infer either direct intention or subjective recklessness. That a person knows something might result does not mean she intended it to result.[34] Substitutes for the mental element requirement are expressed by negligence[35] (a reasonable person should have known), or by strict liability offences.[36] These are substitutes for the mental state requirement; they do not require the human agent to have formed any mental knowledge or foresight about the criminal nature of the proscribed conduct. In most legal

---

31 For more examples see T. L. Butler, "*Can a Computer be an Author? Copyright Aspects of Artificial Intelligence,*" (1982) 4 *Comm. Ent.* 707.

32 W. H. Hitchler, "The Physical Element of Crime," (1934) 39 *Dick. L. Rev.* 95; M. S. Moore, *Act and Crime: The Philosophy of Action and its Implications for Criminal Law,* (Oxford: O.U.P., 1993).

33 Glanville Williams, *Salmond on Jurisprudence,* (London: Sweet and Maxwell, 11th edn., 1957); Glanville Williams, *Criminal Law: The General Part,* (London: Stevens & Sons, 1961) at § 11; O. W. Holmes Jr., *The Common Law,* (Boston: Little, Brown & Company, 1881) at 54; W. W. Cook, "Act, Intention, and Motive in the Criminal Law," (1917) 26 *Yale L.J.* 645.

34 See generally, D. J. Baker, *Glanville Williams Textbook of Criminal Law,* (London: Sweet & Maxwell, 2015) at Chapters 4, 5 and 6; J. Dressler, *Understanding Criminal Law,* (San Francisco: LexisNexis, 7th edn., 2015) at Chapters 10, 11 and 12. For the older literature, see J. Ll. J. Edwards, "The Criminal Degrees of Knowledge," (1954) 17 *Mod. L. Rev.* 294; R. M. Perkins, " 'Knowledge' as a *Mens Rea* Requirement," 29 *Hastings L.J.* 953 (1978); *United States v. Youts* (2000) 229 F.3d 1312; *United States v. Spinney* (1995) 65 F.3d 231; *State v. Sargent* (1991) 594 A.2d 401; *State v. Wyatt* (1996) 482 S.E.2d 147; *People v. Steinberg* (1992) 595 N.E.2d 845.

35 J. Hall, "Negligent Behaviour Should Be Excluded from Penal Liability," (1963) 63 *Colum. L. Rev.* 632; R. P. Fine and G. M. Cohen, "Comment, Is Criminal Negligence a Defensible Basis for Criminal Responsibility?" (1966) 16 *Buff. L. Rev.* 749.

36 J. Horder, "Strict Liability, Statutory Construction and the Spirit of Liberty," (2002) 118 L.Q.R. 458; F. B. Bowes Sayre, "Public Welfare Offences," (1933) 33 *Colum. L. Rev.* 55; A. P. Simester, "Is Strict Liability Always Wrong?" in A. P. Simester (ed.), *Appraising Strict Liability,* (Oxford: O.U.P., 2005).

systems, the mental element requirement of IP offences is expressed through knowledge, i.e., the offender is required to know or to be aware of the offending nature of the illegal conduct, i.e., while violating protected IP rights.

These two requirements are the only criteria or capabilities which are required in order to impose criminal liability, not only from humans, but from any other kind of entity, including corporations and AI entities. Any entity might possess further capabilities, such as creativity, for example. However, in order to impose criminal liability, the existence of *actus reus* and *mens rea* of the specific offence is adequate. No further capabilities are required for the imposition of criminal liability. Thus, on one hand, an uncreative thief is still a thief, if *actus reus* and *mens rea* of theft are proven. On the other hand, an ant is capable of biting creatively, but it is incapable of formulating the *mens rea* requirement; therefore, a creatively biting ant bears no criminal liability. A parrot is capable of repeating words it hears, but it is incapable of formulating the *mens rea* requirement for libel.[37]

The imposition of criminal liability on any kind of entity is dependent on proving these two elements beyond a reasonable doubt. When it has been proven that a person committed the criminal act knowingly or with criminal intent, that person is held criminally liable for that offence.[38] The relevant question concerning the criminal liability of AI entities is: how can these entities fulfil the two requirements of criminal liability? This chapter proposes the imposition of criminal liability on AI entities using three possible models of liability: the Perpetration-by-Another liability model, the Natural-Probable-Consequence liability model and the Direct liability model. The following subsections explain these three possible models.

(a) Perpetration-by-Another liability

The Perpetration-by-Another liability model does not consider the AI entity as possessing any human attributes. The AI entity is considered an innocent agent. Accordingly, due to that legal viewpoint, a machine is a machine, and it is never human. However, one cannot ignore an AI entity's capabilities, as mentioned previously.[39] Pursuant to this model, these capabilities are insufficient to deem the AI entity a perpetrator of an offence. These capabilities resemble the parallel capabilities of a mentally limited person, such as a child, or of a person who is mentally incompetent or who lacks a criminal state of mind.

When an offence is committed physically by an innocent agent, the person who sent or activated the innocent agent is criminally liable as a perpetrator-by-another.[40] In such cases, the innocent agent is regarded as a mere instrument,

---

37 See e.g., *Ormsby v. United States* (1921) 273 F.2d 977.
38 Of course, if the legal action is civil and it is meant for civil remedies, the burden of proof is not subjected to the standards of criminal law.
39 See supra Part II.
40 *Morrisey v. State* (1993) 620 A.2d 207; *Conyers v. State* (Md. 2002) 790 A.2d 15; *State v. Fuller* (2001) 552 S.E.2d 282; *Gallimore v. Commonwealth* (1993) 436 S.E.2d 421.

albeit a sophisticated instrument, while the party orchestrating the offence is the real perpetrator as a principal in the first degree and is held accountable for the conduct of the innocent agent. The perpetrator-by-another's liability is determined on the basis of the innocent agent's conduct[41] and perpetrator-by-another's own mental state.[42]

In such situations, the derivative question relative to AI entities is: who is the perpetrator-by-another? There are two candidates: the first is the programmer of the AI software, and the second is the end-user. A programmer of AI software might design a program in order to commit IP offences via the AI entity. For example: the same programmer designs software for an operating AI entity. The AI entity is intended to be placed in a software lab, and its software is designed to copy information from another IP-protected software. The AI entity committed the offence, but the programmer is deemed the perpetrator.

The other person who might be considered the perpetrator-by-another is the user of the AI entity. The user did not program the software, but he uses the AI entity, including its software, for his own benefit. For example, a user purchases a servant-robot, which is designed to execute any order given by its master. The specific user is identified by the AI entity as that master, and the master orders the AI entity to copy certain protected information. The AI entity executes the order exactly as ordered. This is not different than a person who orders his dog to attack a trespasser. The AI entity committed the offence, but the user is deemed the perpetrator.[43]

In both scenarios, the actual offence was committed by the AI entity. The programmer or the user did not perform any action conforming to the definition of a specific offence; therefore, neither the programmer nor the user meets the *actus reus* requirement of the specific offence. The Perpetration-by-Another liability model considers the action committed by the AI entity as if it had been the programmer's or the user's action. The legal basis for that is the instrumental usage of the AI entity as an innocent agent. No mental attribute required for the imposition of criminal liability is attributed to the AI entity.[44]

When programmers or users use an AI entity instrumentally, the commission of an offence by the AI entity is attributed to them. The mental element required in the specific offence already exists in their minds. The programmer had

---

41 *Dusenbery v. Commonwealth* (1980) 263 S.E.2d 392.

42 *United States v. Tobon-Builes* (11th Cir. 1983) 706 F.2d 1092; *United States v. Ruffin* (2d Cir. 1979) 613 F.2d 408; See also G. Hallevy, "Victim's Complicity in Criminal Law," (2006) 2 *Int'l J. Punishment & Sentencing* 72; D. J. Baker, *Reinterpreting Criminal Complicity and Inchoate Participation Offences*, (Oxford: Routledge, 2016) at 30; 183, 241–244; K. J. M. Smith, *A Modern Treatise on the Law of Complicity*, (Oxford: Clarendon Press, 1991).

43 See, e.g., *Regina v. Manley* (1844) 1 Cox C.C. 104; *Regina v. Cogan* [1976] Q.B. 217; G. Hallevy, *Theory of Criminal Law*, (Jerusalem: Bursi, 2009) Vol. II at 700–706.

44 The AI entity is used as an instrument and not as a participant, although it uses its features of processing information. See, e.g., C. G. Debessonet and G. R. Cross, "An Artificial Intelligence Application in the Law: CCLIPS, A Computer Program that Processes Legal Information," (1986) 1 *High Tech. L.J.* 329.

criminal intent when he or she ordered the commission of the arson, and the user had criminal intent when he or she ordered the commission of the assault, even though these offences were actually committed through an AI entity. When an end-user makes instrumental usage of an innocent agent to commit a crime, the end-user is deemed the perpetrator.

This liability model does not attribute any mental capability, or any human mental capability, to the AI entity. According to this model, there is no legal difference between an AI entity and a screwdriver or an animal. When a burglar uses a screwdriver in order to open up a window, he or she uses the screwdriver instrumentally, and the screwdriver is not criminally liable. The screwdriver's "action" is, in fact, the burglar's. This is the same legal situation when using an animal instrumentally. An assault committed by a dog by order of its master is, for legal purposes, an assault committed by the master.

This kind of legal model might be suitable for two types of scenarios. The first scenario is using an AI entity to commit an IP offence without using its advanced capabilities, which enable it to "think" or to think (with no commas, i.e., when an AI entity decides to commit an IP offence based on its own accumulated experience or knowledge). The second scenario is using a very old version of an AI entity, which lacks the modern advanced capabilities of the modern AI entities.[45] In both scenarios, the use of the AI entity is instrumental usage. Still, it is usage of an AI entity, due to its ability to execute an order to commit an offence. A screwdriver cannot execute such an order; a dog can. A dog cannot execute complicated orders; an AI entity can.[46]

The Perpetration-by-Another liability model is not suitable when an AI entity decides to commit an offence based on its own accumulated experience or knowledge.[47] This model is not suitable when the software of the AI entity was not designed to commit the specific offence, but it was committed by the AI entity nonetheless. This model is also not suitable when the specific AI entity functions not as an innocent agent, but as a semi-innocent agent.[48]

However, the Perpetration-by-Another liability model might be suitable when a programmer or user makes instrumental usage of an AI entity, but without using the AI entity's advanced capabilities. The legal result of applying this model is that the programmer and the user are fully criminally liable for the specific offence committed, while the AI entity has no criminal liability whatsoever.

---

45 For some of the modern advanced capabilities of the modern AI entities, see generally D. Michie, "The Superarticulacy Phenomenon in the Context of Software Manufacture," in Partridge and Wilks, *op. cit. supra*, note 16 at 411–439.

46 *Cf.* A. J. Wu, "From Video Games to Artificial Intelligence: Assigning Copyright Ownership to Works Generated by Increasingly Sophisticated Computer Programs," (1997) 25 *AIPLA Q.J.* 131, with Butler, *op. cit. supra*, note 31.

47 The programmer or user should not be held criminally liable for the autonomous actions of the AI if he or she could not have predicted these actions. See *infra* Parts III.B and III.

48 N. Lacey *et al.*, *Reconstructing Criminal Law: Critical Perspectives on Crime and the Criminal Process*, (London: Butterworths, 2nd edn., 1998).

(b) Natural-Probable-Consequence liability

The Natural-Probable-Consequence liability model assumes deep involvement of the programmers or users in the AI entity's daily activities, but without any intention of committing any offence via the AI entity. One scenario: during the execution of its daily tasks, an AI entity commits an offence. The programmers or users had no knowledge of the offence until it had already been committed; they did not plan to commit any offence, and they did not participate in any part of the commission of that specific offence. One example of such a scenario is an AI entity designed to browse information on the Internet and figure out solutions for certain problems that, at some point, copies IP-protected information from the Internet and presents it as its own data. When the AI entity's figures are published, it appears to be infringing the IP rights of the creator, which may involve criminal liability.[49]

The programmer may well have not intended to violate any laws, but nonetheless, IP rights were infringed as a result of the AI entity's actions. Moreover, these actions were done according to the program. Another example is AI software designed to detect threats from the Internet and protect a computer system from these threats. A few days after the software is activated, it figures out that the best way to detect such threats is by entering web sites it defines as dangerous and destroying any software recognised as a threat. When the software does that, it is committing a computer offence, although the programmer did not intend for the AI entity to do so.

In these examples, the Perpetration-by-Another model is not legally suitable. The Perpetration-by-Another model assumes *mens rea*, the criminal intent of the programmers or users to commit an offence via the instrumental use of some of the AI entity's capabilities. This is not the legal situation in these cases. In these cases, the programmers or users had no knowledge of the committed offence; they had not planned it, and had not intended to commit the offence using the AI entity. For such cases, the second model might create a suitable legal response. This model is based upon the ability of the programmers or users to foresee the potential commission of offences.

According to the second model, a person might be held accountable for an offence if that offence is a natural and probable consequence of that person's conduct. Originally, the Natural-Probable-Consequence liability model was used to impose criminal liability upon accomplices, when one committed an offence which had not been planned by all of them and which was not part of a conspiracy. The established rule prescribed by courts and commentators is

---

49 17 U.S.C.S. § 506. See more in Butler, *supra* note 31; D. L. Kilpatrick-Lee, "Criminal Copyright Law: Preventing a Clear Danger to the U.S. Economy or Clearly Preventing the Original Purpose of Copyright Law?" (2005) 14 *U. Balt. Intell. Prop. L.J.* 87; E. Goldman, "A Road to No Warez: The No Electronic Theft Act and Criminal Copyright Infringement," (2003) 82 *Or. L. Rev.* 369; I. T. Hardy, "A Road to No Warez: The No Electronic Theft Act and Criminal Copyright Infringement," (2002) 11 *Wm. & Mary Bill of Rts. J.* 305.

that accomplice liability extends to acts of a perpetrator that were a "natural and probable consequence"[50] of a criminal scheme that the accomplice encouraged or aided.[51] The Natural-Probable-Consequence liability has been widely accepted in accomplice liability statutes and recodifications.[52]

The Natural-Probable-Consequence liability model seems to be legally suitable for situations in which an AI entity committed an offence, while the programmer or user had no knowledge of it, had not intended it and had not participated in it. The Natural-Probable-Consequence liability model requires the programmer or user to be in a mental state of negligence, not more. Programmers or users are not required to know about any forthcoming commission of an offence as a result of their activity, but will be liable if a reasonable programmer or user would have known that such an offence could be a natural, probable consequence of their actions.

In a criminal context, a negligent person has no knowledge of the offence; however, a reasonable person in the same situation would have known about the offence, because it is a natural and probable consequence of the situation.[53] The programmers or users of an AI entity, who *ought to have known* about the probability of the forthcoming commission of the specific offence, are criminally liable for the specific offence, even though they did not actually know about it. This is the fundamental legal basis for criminal liability in negligence cases. Negligence is, in fact, an omission of awareness or knowledge. The negligent person omitted knowledge, not acts.

The Natural-Probable-Consequence liability model would permit liability to be predicated upon negligence, even when the specific offence requires a different state of mind.[54] This has been accepted in modern criminal law, and thus reduced significantly the mental element requirements in these situations, since

---

50 *United States v. Powell* (1991) 929 F.2d 724.
51 W. L. Clark and W. L. Marshall, *A Treatise on the Law of Crimes*, (Chicago: Callaghan, 7th edn., 1967); F. B. Sayre, "Criminal Responsibility for the Acts of Another," (1930) 43 *Harv. L. Rev.* 689; *People v. Prettyman* (1996) 926 P. 2d 1013; *Chance v. State* (1996) 685 A.2d 351; *Ingram v. United States* (1991) 592 A.2d 992; *Richardson v. State* (1998) 697 N.E.2d 462; *Mitchell v. State* (1998) 971 P. 2d 813; *State v. Carrasco* (1996) 928 P. 2d 939; *State v. Jackson* (1999) 976 P. 2d 1229.
52 *State v. Kaiser* (1996) 918 P. 2d 629; *United States v. Andrews* (1996) 75 F.3d 552. *Per contra*, Baker argues that while the natural and probable consequence test has been adopted as a negligence standard of fault for complicity in some jurisdictions such as Canada and some states in the United States, that natural and probable consequence rule was more a tool of inferring fault than a substantive fault doctrine per se. Hence, Baker takes the view that it was used to infer subjective mental states, not to hold people liable for negligence. See D. J. Baker, "The Doctrinal and Normative Vacuity of Hong Kong's Joint Enterprise Doctrine," (2017) *Hong Kong L.J.* 349; D. J. Baker, "Tracing a Thousand Years of Subjective Fault as the Fulcrum of Criminal Responsibility in English Law," (2020) 56 *Crim. L. Bull.* 1–60.
53 Fine and Cohen, *op. cit. supra*, note 35; H. L. A. Hart, "Negligence, Mens Rea and Criminal Responsibility," in A. G. Guest (ed.), *Oxford Essays in Jurisprudence*, (Oxford: O.U.P., 1961) at 29; D. Stuart, *"Mens Rea, Negligence and Attempts,"* (1968) *Crim. L. R.* 647.
54 Model Penal Code – Official Draft and Explanatory Notes sec. 2.06, 31–32 (1985) (hereinafter "Model Penal Code"); *State v. Linscott* (1987) 520 A.2d 1067.

the relevant accomplice did not really know about the offence, but a reasonable person could have predicted it. Negligence is suitable for this kind of situation. This is not valid in relation to the person who personally committed the offence, but rather, is considered valid in relation to the person who was not the actual perpetrator of the offence, but was one of its intellectual forbearers. Reasonable programmers or users should have foreseen the offence and prevented it from being committed by the AI entity. Suppose the AI used in an autonomous car has a glitch that a reasonable programmer ought to have foreseen might cause the car to chase and try to drive over any pedestrian wearing yellow. Suppose AI-controlled car X sensors detect a pedestrian on the pedestrian crossing wearing a yellow vest and speeds up and runs over the pedestrian with the aim of killing the pedestrian. While the negligence ought to be sufficient for imposing liability upon the negligent programmers, it ought not be sufficient for holding them liable for murder, since murder requires a much higher level of culpability.

However, the legal results of applying the Natural-Probable-Consequence liability model to the programmer or user vary in two different types of factual cases. The first type of case is when the programmers or users were negligent while programming or using the AI entity and had no criminal intent to commit any offence. The second type of case is when the programmers or users programmed or used the AI entity knowingly and wilfully in order to commit one offence via the AI entity, but the AI entity deviated from the plan and committed some other offence, in addition to or instead of the planned offence.

The first type of case is a pure case of negligence. The programmers or users acted or omitted negligently; therefore, they should be held accountable for an offence of negligence, if there is such an offence in the specific legal system. Thus, as in the earlier example, where a programmer of an AI browser negligently programmed it to browse the Internet with no restrictions on the IP rights, the programmer is negligent and liable for the IP offence. Consequently, if a negligence IP offence exists as a specific offence in the relevant legal system, it is the most severe offence for which the programmer may be held accountable, as opposed to most IP offences, which require at least knowledge or intent.

The second type of case resembles the basic idea of the Natural-Probable-Consequence liability model in accomplice liability cases. The dangerousness of the very association or conspiracy whose aim is to commit an offence is the legal reason for more severe accountability to be imposed upon the cohorts.[55] For example, a programmer programs an AI entity to commit an IP offence of

---

55 Wang argues that accessories are less dangerous because any actual harm is contingent on the culpable choice of a perpetrator. X can give Y a knife, but Y still makes her own choice to use it to commit murder. Wang treats this sort of participation as a lesser wrong and argues it ought to result in liability for an independent facilitation or encouragement offence; *a fortiori* when the culpability of the accessory is lower than that of the perpetrator. Y would be liable for murder and X for some lesser offence of encouragement or assistance. See B. Wang, "A Normative Case for Abolishing the Doctrine of Extended Joint Criminal Enterprise," (2019) 83(2) *J. Crim. L.* 144; Baker, *op. cit. supra*, note 52 at 30, 319 *et seq.*

copying certain information (music), but the programmer did not program the AI entity to copy other information (video). During the execution of the planned IP offence, the AI entity copies video information, as well. In such cases, the criminal negligence liability alone is insufficient. The social danger posed by such a situation far exceeds the situations that negligence was accepted as sufficient to be applied (through retribution, deterrence, rehabilitation and incapacitation).

As a result, according to the Natural-Probable-Consequence liability mode, if the programmers or users knowingly and wilfully used the AI entity to commit an offence (of one kind) and if the AI entity deviated from the plan by committing another offence, in addition to or instead of the planned offence, the programmers or users should be held accountable for the additional offence, as if it had been committed knowingly and wilfully. In the earlier example, the programmer shall be held criminally accountable for both offences, planned and unplanned. Again, the degree of liability should rest on the degree of fault. The level of fault is negligence, and therefore, the crime that the programmers are held liable for should reflect that they were merely negligent and were one step removed from the actual perpetration.

The question still remains: what is the criminal liability of the AI entity itself when the Natural-Probable-Consequence liability model is applied? In fact, there are two possible outcomes. If the AI entity acted as an innocent agent, without knowing anything about the criminal prohibition, it is not held criminally accountable for the offence it committed. Under such circumstances, the actions of the AI entity were not different from the actions of the AI entity under the first model (the Perpetration-by-Another liability model). However, if the AI entity did not act merely as an innocent agent, then, in addition to the criminal liability of the programmer or user pursuant to the Natural-Probable-Consequence liability model, the AI entity itself should be held criminally liable for the specific offence directly. The direct liability model of AI entities is the third model, as described following.

(c) Direct liability

The direct liability model does not assume any dependence of the AI entity on a specific programmer or user. The third model focuses on the AI entity itself.[56] As discussed previously, criminal liability for a specific offence is mainly comprised of the factual element (*actus reus*) and the mental element (*mens rea*) of that offence. Any person attributed with both elements of the specific offence is held criminally accountable for that specific offence. No other criteria are required in order to

---

56 Cf., e.g., S. J. Frank, "Tort Adjudication and the Emergence of Artificial Intelligence Software," (1987) 21 *Suffolk U. L. Rev.* 623; S. N. Lehman-Wilzig, "Frankenstein Unbound: Towards a Legal Definition of Artificial Intelligence," (1981) *Futures* 442; M. E. Gerstner, "Liability Issues with Artificial Intelligence Software," (1993) 33 *Santa Clara L. Rev.* 239; R. E. Susskind, "Expert Systems in Law: A Jurisprudential Approach to Artificial Intelligence and Legal Reasoning," (1986) 49 *Mod. L. Rev.*168.

impose criminal liability. A person might possess further capabilities, but, in order to impose criminal liability, the existence of the factual element and the mental element required to impose liability for the specific offence is quite enough.

In order to impose criminal liability on any kind of entity, the existence of these elements in the specific entity must be proven. Generally, when it has been proven that a person committed the offence in question with knowledge or intent, that person is held criminally liable for that offence. The criminal liability of AI entities depends upon the following questions: how can these entities fulfil the requirements of criminal liability?; do AI entities differ from humans in this context?

An AI algorithm might have numerous features and qualifications far exceeding those of an average human, such as higher velocity of data processing (thinking), ability to take into consideration many more factors, etc. Nevertheless, such features or qualifications are not required in order to impose criminal liability. They do not negate criminal liability, but they are not required for the imposition of criminal liability. When a human or corporation fulfils the requirements of both the factual element and the mental element, criminal liability is imposed. If an AI entity is capable of fulfilling the requirements of both the factual element and the mental element, and, in fact, actually fulfils them, there is nothing to prevent criminal liability from being imposed on that AI entity.

Generally, the fulfilment of the factual element requirement of an offence is easily attributed to AI entities. As long as an AI entity controls a mechanical or other mechanism that moves its parts, any act might be considered as performed by the AI entity. Thus, when an AI entity activates its electric or hydraulic arm and moves it, this might be considered an act, if the specific offence involves such an act. For example, in the specific offence of assault, such an electric or hydraulic movement of an AI entity that hits a person standing nearby is considered to fulfil the *actus reus* requirement of the offence of assault.

When an offence might be committed due to an omission, it is even simpler. Under this scenario, the AI entity is not required to act at all. Its very inaction is the legal basis for criminal liability, as long as there had been a duty to act. If a duty to act is imposed upon the AI entity, and it fails to act, the *actus reus* requirement of the specific offence is fulfilled by way of an omission.

The attribution of the mental element of offences to AI entities is the real legal challenge in most cases. The attribution of the mental element differs from one AI technology to other. Most cognitive capabilities developed in modern AI technology, such as creativity, are immaterial to the question of the imposition of criminal liability. The only cognitive capability required for the imposition of criminal liability is embodied within the mental element requirement (*mens rea*). Creativity is a human feature that some animals also have, but creativity is a not a requirement for imposing criminal liability. Even the most uncreative persons may be held criminally liable. The sole mental requirements needed in order to impose criminal liability are knowledge, intent, negligence, etc., as required by the specific offence and under the general theory of criminal law. As a result, AI entities do not have to create the idea of committing the specific offence, but in order to be criminally liable, they have only to commit the specific offence with knowledge as to the factual elements of that offence.

Knowledge is defined as sensory reception of factual data and the understanding of that data.[57] Most AI systems are well equipped for such reception. Sensory receptors of sights, voices, physical contact, touch, etc., are common in most AI systems. These receptors transfer the factual data received to central processing units that analyse the data. The process of analysis in AI systems parallels that of human understanding.[58] The human brain understands the data received by eyes, ears, hands, etc., by analysing that data. Advanced AI algorithms are trying to imitate human cognitive processes. These processes are not so different.[59]

Specific intent is the strongest of the mental element requirements.[60] Specific intent is the existence of a purpose or an aim that a factual event will occur.[61] The specific intent required to establish liability for murder is a purpose or an aim that a certain person will die.[62] As a result of the existence of such intent, the perpetrator of the offence commits the offence; i.e., he or she performs the factual element of the specific offence. This situation is not unique to humans. Some AI entities might be programmed to figure out by themselves a purpose or an aim and to take actions in order to achieve that figured-out purpose, and some advanced AI entities may figure out by themselves a purpose and take relevant actions in order to achieve that purpose. In both cases this might be considered as specific intent, since the AI entity figured out by itself the purpose and figured out by itself the relevant actions in order to achieve that purpose.

One might assert that many crimes are committed as a result of strong emotions or feelings that cannot be imitated by AI software, not even by the most advanced software. Such feelings are love, affection, hatred, jealousy, etc. This

---

57 W. James, *The Principles of Psychology*, (New York: H. Holt & Company, 1890); H. von Helmholtz, *Die Thatsachen in der Wahrnehmung*, (Berlin: A. Hirschwald, 1879). In this context knowledge and awareness are identical. See, e.g., *United States v. Youts* (2000) 229 F.3d 1312; *State v. Sargent* (1991) 594 A.2d 401; *United States v. Spinney* (1995) 65 F.3d 231; *State v. Wyatt* (1996) 482 S.E.2d 147; *United States v. Wert-Ruiz* (2000) 228 F.3d 250 (2000); *United States v. Jewell* (1976) 532 F.2d 697; *United States v. Ladish Malting Co.* (1998) 135 F.3d 484; Model Penal Code § 2.02(2)(b).

58 M. A. Boden, "Has AI Helped Psychology?" in Partridge and Wilks, *op. cit. supra*, note 16 at 108; D. Partridge, "What's in an AI Program?" in Partridge and Wilks, *op. cit. supra*, note 16 at 112; D. Marr, "AI: A Personal View," in Partridge and Wilks, *op. cit. supra*, note 16 at 97.

59 D. C. Dennett, "Evolution, Error, and Intentionality," in Partridge and Wilks, *op. cit. supra*, note 16 at 190; B. Chandrasekaran, "What Kind of Information Processing is Intelligence?" in Partridge and Wilks, *op. cit. supra*, note 16 at 14.

60 R. Batey, "Judicial Exploration of Mens Rea Confusion, at Common Law and Under the Model Penal Code," (2001) 18 *Ga. St. U. L. Rev.* 341; *State v. Daniels* (1958) 109 So. 2d 896; *Carter v. United States* (2000) 530 U.S. 255; *United States v. Randolph* (1996) 93 F.3d 656; *United States v. Torres* (1992) 977 F.2d 321; *Frey v. State* (1998) 708 So. 2d 918; *State v. Neuzil* (1999) 589 N.W.2d 708; *People v. Disimone* (2002) 650 N.W.2d 436; *People v. Henry* (1999) 607 N.W.2d 767.

61 W. R. LaFave, *Substantive Criminal Law*, (West, 4th edn., 2003) at 244–249.

62 For the Intent-to-Kill murder see *Ibid.* at 733–734.

might be correct in relation to AI technology of the beginning of the twenty-first century. Even so, such feelings are rarely required in specific offences. Most specific offences are satisfied by knowledge of the existence of the external element. Few offences require specific intent in addition to knowledge. Almost all other offences are satisfied by much less than that (negligence, recklessness, strict liability). Perhaps in a very few specific offences that do require certain feelings (e.g., crimes of racism, hate),[63] criminal liability cannot be imposed upon AI entities, which have no such feelings, but in any other specific offence, lack of certain feelings is not a barrier to imposing criminal liability. In most legal systems, IP offences require no specific intent, but subjective awareness of the risk alone as their mental element requirement.

If a person fulfils the requirements of both the factual element and the mental element of a specific offence, then the person is held criminally liable. Why should an AI entity that fulfils all elements of an offence be exempt from criminal liability? One might argue that some segments of human society are exempt from criminal liability even if both the external and internal elements have been established. Such segments of society include infants and the mentally ill.

Specific provisions in criminal law exempt infants from criminal liability.[64] The social rationale behind the infancy defence is to protect infants from the harmful consequences of the criminal process and to handle them in other social frameworks.[65] Do such frameworks exist for AI entities? The original legal rationale behind the infancy defence was the fact that infants are as yet incapable of comprehending what was wrong in their conduct (*doli incapax*).[66] However, children can be held criminally liable if the presumption of mental incapacity was refuted by proof that the child was able to distinguish between right and wrong, i.e.,

---

63 See, e.g., E. A. Boyd *et al.*, " 'Motivated by Hatred or Prejudice': Categorization of Hate-Motivated Crimes in Two Police Divisions," (1996) 30 *Law & Society Rev.* 30; Editors, "Crimes Motivated by Hatred: The Constitutionality and Impact of Hate Crimes Legislation in the United States," (1995) 1 *Syracuse J. Legis. & Pol'y* 29.

64 See, e.g., Minn. Stat. § 9913 (1927); Mont. Rev. Code § 10729 (1935); N.Y. Penal Law § 816 (1935); Okla. Stat. § 152 (1937); Utah Rev. Stat. 103-i-40 (1933); *State v. George* (1902) 54 A. 745; *Heilman v. Commonwealth* (1886) 1 S.W. 731 (Ky. 1886); *State v. Aaron* (1818) 4 N.J.L. 269; *McCormack v. State* (1894) 15 So. 438; *Little v. State* (1977) 554 S.W.2d 312; Clay v. State (1940) 196 So. 462; *In re Devon T.* (1991) 584 A.2d 1287; *State v. Dillon* (1970) 471 P. 2d 553; *State v. Jackson* (1940) 142 S.W.2d 45.

65 F. J. Ludwig, "Rationale of Responsibility for Young Offenders," (1950) 29 *Neb. L. Rev.* 521; *In re Tyvonn* (1989) 558 A.2d 661; A. Walkover, "The Infancy Defence in the New Juvenile Court," (1984) 31 *UCLA L. Rev.* 503; D. K. Foren, "Note, In Re Tyvonne M. Revisited: The Criminal Infancy Defence in Connecticut," (1999) 18 *Quinnipiac L. Rev.* 733; M. Tonry, "Rethinking Unthinkable Punishment Policies in America," (1999) 46 *UCLA L. Rev.* 1751; A. Ashworth, "Sentencing Young Offenders," in A. von Hirsch *et al.* (eds.), *Principled Sentencing: Readings on Theory and Policy*, (Oxford: Hart Publishing, 3rd edn., 2009) at 294–306; F. E. Zimring, "Rationales for Distinctive Penal Policies for Youth Offenders," von Hirsch *et al., Ibid.* at 316; A. von Hirsch, "Reduced Penalties for Juveniles: The Normative Dimension," in von Hirsch *et al., Ibid.* at 323.

66 Edward Coke, *The Institutes of the Laws of England: Third Part*, (London: W Lee, 1648) at 4.

between permitted and forbidden actions in terms of criminal offences.[67] Could that be similarly applied to AI entities? Most AI algorithms are capable of distinguishing between permitted and forbidden actions, and therefore they may distinguish between a conduct which is a commission of an offence (forbidden) or which is not (permitted).[68]

Similarly, the mentally ill are presumed to lack the fault element of the specific offence, due to their mental illness.[69] The mentally ill are unable to distinguish between right and wrong (i.e., lack the cognitive capabilities possessed by normal persons)[70] or to control impulsive behaviour.[71] When an AI algorithm functions properly, there is no reason for it not to use all of its capabilities to analyse the factual data received through its receptors. However, an interesting legal question would be whether a defence of insanity might be raised in relation to a malfunctioning AI algorithm, when its analytical capabilities become corrupted as a result of that malfunction.

When an AI entity establishes all elements of a specific offence, both factual and mental, there is no reason to prevent imposition of criminal liability upon it for that offence. The criminal liability of an AI entity does not replace the criminal liability of the programmers or the users, if criminal liability is imposed on the programmers and/or users by any other legal path. Criminal liability is not to be divided, but rather added. The criminal liability of the AI entity is imposed in addition to the criminal liability of the human programmer or user.

However, the criminal liability of an AI entity is not dependent upon the criminal liability of the programmer or user of that AI entity. As a result, if the specific AI entity was programmed or used by another AI entity, the criminal liability of the programmed or used AI entity is not influenced by that fact. The programmed or used AI entity shall be held criminally accountable for the specific offence pursuant to the direct liability model, unless it was an innocent agent. In addition, the programmer or user of the AI entity shall be held criminally accountable for that very offence pursuant to one of the three liability models,

67 M. Hale, *The History of the Pleas of the Crown*, (London: Printed by E and R Nutt *et al.*, 1736) Vol. 1 at 23, 26; *McCormack v. State* 1894) 15 So. 438 (Ala. 1894); *Little v. State* (1977) 554 S.W.2d 312; *In re* Devon T. (1991) 584 A.2d 1287.

68 Padhy, *op cit. supra*, note 4 at 277–333.

69 See, e.g., B. B. Sendor, "Crime as Communication: An Interpretive Theory of the Insanity Defence and the Mental Elements of Crime," (1986) 74 *Geo. L. J.* 1371 at 1380; J. H. Rodriguez, *et al.*, "The Insanity Defence Under Siege: Legislative Assaults and Legal Rejoinders," (1983) 14 *Rutgers L. J.* 397 at 406–407; H. D. Crotty, "The History of Insanity as a Defence to Crime in English Criminal Law," (1924) 12 *Cal. L. Rev.* 105.

70 See, e.g., E. de Grazia, "The Distinction of Being Mad," (1955) 22 *U. Chi. L. Rev.* 339; W. P. Hill, "The Psychological Realism of Thurman Arnold," (1955) 22 *U. Chi. L. Rev.* 377; M. S. Guttmacher, "The Psychiatrist as an Expert Witness," (1955) 22 *U. Chi. L. Rev.* 325; W. G. Katz, "Law, Psychiatry, and Free Will," (1955) 22 *U. Chi. L. Rev.* 397; J. Hall, "Psychiatry and Criminal Responsibility," (1956) 65 *Yale L. J.* 761.

71 See, e.g., J. Barker Waite, "Irresistible Impulse and Criminal Liability," (1925) 23 *Mich. L. Rev.* 443 at 454; E. D. Hoedemaker, " 'Irresistible Impulse' as a Defence in Criminal Law," (1948) 23 *Wash. L. Rev.* 1 at 7.

according to its specific role in the offence. The chain of criminal liability might continue, if more parties are involved, whether they are human or AI entities.

There is no reason to eliminate the criminal liability of an AI entity or of a human, which is based on complicity between them. An AI entity and a human might cooperate as joint perpetrators, as accessories and abettors, etc., and the relevant criminal liability might be imposed on them accordingly. Since the factual and mental capabilities of an AI entity are sufficient to impose criminal liability on it, if these capabilities satisfy the legal requirements of joint perpetrators, accessories and abettors, etc., then the relevant criminal liability as joint perpetrators, accessories and abettors, etc., should be imposed, regardless of whether the offender is an AI entity or a human.

Not only may positive factual and mental elements be attributed to AI entities, but also all relevant negative fault elements are attributable to AI entities. Most of these elements are expressed by the general defences in criminal law; e.g., self-defence, necessity, duress, intoxication, etc. For some of these defences (justifications),[72] there is no material difference between humans and AI entities, since they relate to a specific situation (*in rem*), regardless of the identity of the offender. For example, an AI entity serving under the local police force is given an order to arrest a person, and unbeknownst to the AI entity, this order is illegal. If the executer is unaware, or could not reasonably become aware, that an otherwise legal action is illegal in this specific instance, the executer of the order is not criminally liable.[73] In that case, there is no difference whether the executer is human or an AI entity.

For other defences (excuses and exempts),[74] some applications should be adjusted. For example, the intoxication defence is applied when the offender is under the physical influence of an intoxicating substance, e.g., alcohol, drugs, etc. The influence of alcohol on an AI entity is minor, at most, but the influence of an electronic virus that is infecting the operating system of the AI entity might be considered parallel to the influence of intoxicating substances on humans. Some other factors might be considered as being parallel to insanity or loss of control.

It might be summed up that the criminal liability of an AI entity according to the direct liability model is not different from the relevant criminal liability of a human. In some cases, some adjustments are necessary, but substantively, it is the

---

72 J. Gardner, *Offences and Defences*, (Oxford: O.U.P., 2007) at Chapters 4, 5, 6 and 7; P. H. Robinson, "A Theory of Justification: Societal Harm as a Prerequisite for Criminal Liability," (1975) 23 *UCLA L. Rev.* 266; P. H. Robinson and J. M. Darley, "Testing Competing Theories of Justification," (1998) 76 *N.C. L.* Rev. 1095; A. M. Dilloff, "Unravelling Unknowing Justification," (2002) 77 Notre Dame L. Rev. 1547; K. Greenawalt, "*Distinguishing Justifications from Excuses*," (1986) 49 *Law & Contemp. Probs.* 89.

73 M. A. Musmanno, "Are Subordinate Officials Penally Responsible for Obeying Superior Orders which Direct Commission of Crime?" (1963) 67 *Dick. L. Rev.* 221.

74 P. Arenella, "Convicting the Morally Blameless: Reassessing the Relationship Between Legal and Moral Accountability," (1992) 39 *UCLA L. Rev.* 1511; S. H. Kadish, "Excusing Crime," (1987) 75 *Cal. L. Rev.* 257; A. E. Lelling, "A Psychological Critique of Character-Based Theories of Criminal Excuse," (1998) 49 *Syracuse L. Rev.* 35.

very same criminal liability, which is based upon the same elements and examined in the same ways.

(d) Combination liability

The described liability models are not competing models. These models might be applied in combination in order to create a full image of criminal liability in the specific context of AI entity involvement. None of the possible models are mutually exclusive. Thus, applying the second model is possible as a single model for the specific offence, and it is possible as one part of a combination of two of the legal models, or of all three of them.

When the AI entity plays the role of an innocent agent in the perpetration of a specific offence, and the programmer is the only person who directed that perpetration, the application of the Perpetration-by-Another liability model (the first liability model) is the most appropriate legal model for that situation. In that same situation, when the programmer is itself an AI entity (when an AI entity programs another AI entity to commit a specific offence), the Direct liability model (the third model) is most appropriate to be applied to the criminal liability of the programmer of the AI entity. The third liability model in that situation is applied to the programmer in addition to the first model, and not in lieu thereof. Thus, in such situations, the AI entity programmer should be criminally liable, pursuant to a combination of the Perpetration-by-Another liability model and the Direct liability model.

If the AI entity plays the role of the physical perpetrator of the specific offence, but that very offence was not planned to be perpetrated, then the application of the Natural-Probable-Consequence liability model might be appropriate. The programmer might be deemed negligent if no offence had been deliberately planned to be perpetrated. Similarly, the programmer might be held fully accountable for that specific offence if another offence had indeed been deliberately planned, but the specific offence that was perpetrated had not been part of the original criminal scheme. Nevertheless, when the programmer is not human, the direct liability model must be applied in addition to the simultaneous application of the Natural-Probable-Consequence liability model; likewise, when the physical perpetrator is human while the planner is an AI entity.

The coordination of all three liability models creates a dense network of criminal liability which minimises the opportunity to escape from the imposition of criminal liability. The combined and coordinated application of these possible models reveals a new legal situation in the specific context of AI entities and criminal law. As a result, when AI entities and humans are involved, directly or indirectly, in the perpetration of a specific offence, it will be far more difficult to evade criminal liability. The social benefit to be derived from such a legal policy is of substantial value. All entities – human, legal or AI – become subject to criminal law. If the clearest purpose of the imposition of criminal liability is the application of legal social control in the specific society, then the coordinated application of all possible models is necessary in the very context of AI entities.

4. Punishing AI

Let us assume an AI entity is indicted, tried and convicted. After the conviction, the court is supposed to sentence that AI entity.[75] The most appropriate punishments under IP law are fines and imprisonment.[76] The question is, how can an AI entity practically serve a sentence which includes ingredients of fine (who pays it?; the AI system does not have money) or imprisonment (the AI system does not necessarily have tangible appearance)? In instances when there is no physical body to arrest, especially in cases of AI software that was not installed in a physical body, such as a robot, what is the practical meaning of incarceration? Where no bank account is available for the sentenced AI entity, what is the practical significance of fining it?

Similar legal problems have been raised when the criminal liability of corporations was recognised.[77] Some asked how any of the legitimate penalties imposed upon humans could be applicable to corporations. The answer was simple. When a punishment can be imposed on a corporation as it is on humans, it is imposed without change. When the court adjudicates a fine, the corporation pays the fine in the same way that a human pays the fine and in the same way that a corporation pays its bills in a civil context. However, when punishment of a corporation cannot be carried out in the same way as with humans, an adjustment is required. Such is the legal situation vis-à-vis AI entities.

The punishment adjustment considerations are concentrated on the theoretical foundations of the specific punishment. Thus, in order to impose a fine upon an AI entity, there is a necessity to understand the theoretical foundations of the fine,

---

75 For an overview of the criminal process, see G. Hallevy, "The Defence Attorney as Mediator in Plea Bargains," (2009) 9 *Pepp. Disp. Resol. L.J.* 495.

76 See e.g., 17 U.S.C.S. § 506, House Report No. 94–1476:

> Four types of criminal offences actionable under the bill are listed in section 506. willful infringement for profit, fraudulent use of a copyright notice, fraudulent removal of notice, and false representation in connection with a copyright application. The maximum fine on conviction has been increased to $10,000 and, in conformity with the general pattern of the Criminal Code (18 U.S.C.), no minimum fines have been provided. In addition to or instead of a fine, conviction for criminal infringement under section 506(a) can carry with it a sentence of imprisonment of up to one year. Section 506(b) deals with seizure, forfeiture, and destruction of material involved in cases of criminal infringement.
>
> Section 506(a) contains a special provision applying to any person who infringes willfully and for purposes of commercial advantage the copyright in a sound recording or a motion picture. For the first such offence a person shall be fined not more than $ 25,000 or imprisoned for not more than one year, or both. For any subsequent offence a person shall be fined not more than $ 50,000 or imprisoned not more than two years, or both."

77 G. E. Lynch, "The Role of Criminal Law in Policing Corporate Misconduct," (1997) 60 *Law & Contemp. Probs.* 23; R. Gruner, "To Let the Punishment Fit the Organization: Sanctioning Corporate Offenders Through Corporate Probation," (1988) 16 *Am. J. Crim. L.* 1; S. Walt and W. S. Laufer, "Why Personhood Doesn't Matter: Corporate Criminal Liability and Sanctions," (1991) 18 *Am. J. Crim. L.* 263; Coffee, *op. cit. supra*, note 13; Box, *op. cit. supra*, 13; Fisse and Braithwaite, *op. cit. supra*, note 13.

so it would be possible to adjust it from humans to AI entities without changing its essence. These adjustment considerations are applied in a similar manner and are comprised of three stages. Each stage may be explained by a question, as described following: what is the fundamental significance of the specific punishment for a human? How does that punishment affect AI entities? What practical penalties may achieve the same significance when imposed on AI entities?

The most significant advantage of these punishment adjustment considerations is that the significance of the specific punishment remains identical when imposed on humans and AI entities. This method of punishment adjustment considerations is referred to following in some of the penalties used in modern societies: capital punishment, incarceration, suspended sentencing, community service and fines.

Incarceration is one of the most popular sentences imposed in Western legal systems for serious crimes,[78] and it is mentioned as an appropriate sanction in some IP criminal legislation.[79] The significance of incarceration for humans is the deprivation of human liberty and the imposition of severe limitations on human free behaviour: freedom of movement and freedom to manage one's personal life.[80] The "liberty" or "freedom" of an AI entity includes the freedom to act as an AI entity in the relevant area. For example, an AI entity in medical service has the freedom to participate in surgeries, and an AI entity in a factory has the freedom to manufacture, etc.[81]

Considering the nature of a sentence of incarceration, the practical action that may achieve the same effects as incarceration when imposed on an AI entity is to put the AI entity out of use for a determinate period. During that period, no

---

78 See generally, J. Irwin, *Prisons in Turmoil*, (Boston: Little, Brown, 1980); A. J. Manocchio and J. Dunn, *The Time Game: Two Views of a Prison*, (Beverly Hills, CA: Sage Publications, 1970).

79 See e.g., Hallevy, *op.sit. supra*, note 75.

80 See generally D. J. Rothman, "For the Good of All: The Progressive Tradition in Prison Reform," in J. A. Inciardi and C. E. Faupel (eds.), *History and Crime: Implications for Criminal Justice Policy*, (London: Sage Publications, 1980) at 271; M. Welch, *Ironies of Imprisonment*, (London: Sage Publications, 2004); R. D. King, "The Rise and Rise of Supermax: An American Solution in Search of a Problem?" (1999) 1 *Punishment & Soc'y* 163; C. Riveland, *Supermax Prisons: Overview and General Considerations*, (Washington: US Department of Justice, 1999); J. Fellner and J. Mariner, *Cold Storage – Super-Maximum Security Confinement in Indiana*, (Human Rights Watch, 1997); R. R. Korn, "The Effects of Confinement in the High Security Unit in Lexington," (1988) 15 *Soc. Just.* 8; H. A. Miller, "Reexamining Psychological Distress in the Current Conditions of Segregation," (1994) 1 *J. of Correctional Health Care* 39; F. Bernstein, *The Perception of Characteristics of Total Institutions and Their Effect on Socialization*, (Jerusalem: Ph.D. Thesis Hebrew University, 1979); B. Bettelheim, *The Informed Heart: Autonomy in a Mass Age*, (London: Thames and Hudson, 1960); M. M. Kaminski, "Games Prisoners Play: Allocation of Social Roles in a Total Institution," (2003) 15 *Rationality & Soc'y* 188.

81 Not all AI entities do understand the freedom in the same capacity as humans. When the whole internal world of a specific AI entity is focused on its function at work, depriving it from the opportunity to work has the same "social" effect that incarceration has upon humans.

action relating to the AI entity's freedom is allowed, and thus its freedom or liberty is restricted.

Suspended sentencing is a very popular intermediate sanction in Western legal systems for increasing the deterrent effect on offenders in lieu of actual incarceration.[82] The significance of a suspended sentence for humans is the very threat of incarceration if the human commits a specific offence or a type of specific offence.[83] If the human commits such an offence, a sentence of incarceration will be imposed for the first offence in addition to the sentencing for the second offence. As a result, humans are deterred from committing another offence and from becoming recidivist offenders.

Practically, a suspended sentence is imposed only in the legal records. No physical action is taken when a suspended sentence is imposed. As a result, when imposing a suspended sentence, there is no difference in effect between humans and AI entities. The statutory criminal records of the state do not differentiate between a suspended sentence imposed on humans, and those imposed on corporations or AI entities, as long as the relevant entity may be identified specifically and accurately.

Community service is also a very popular intermediate sanction in Western legal systems in lieu of actual incarceration.[84] In most legal systems, community service is a substitute for short sentences of actual incarceration. In some legal systems, community service is imposed coupled with probation so that the offender "pays a price" for the damages he or she caused by committing the specific offence.[85] The significance of community service for humans is compulsory contribution of labour to the community. As discussed previously, an AI entity can be engaged as a worker in very many areas.

When an AI entity works in a factory, its work is done for the benefit of the factory owners or for the benefit of the other workers in order to ease and facilitate their professional tasks. In the same way that an AI entity works for the benefit of private individuals, it may work for the benefit of the community. When work for the benefit of the community is imposed on an AI entity as a compulsory contribution of labour to the community, it may be considered community service. Thus, the significance of community service is identical, whether imposed on humans or AI entities.

---

82 Sir A. E. Bottoms, "The Suspended Sentence in England 1967–1978," (1981) 21 *Brit. J. Criminology* 1.

83 M. Ancel, *Suspended Sentence*, (London: Heinemann, 1971); M. Ancel, "The System of Conditional Sentence or Sursis," (1964) 80 *L. Q. Rev.* 334.

84 A. Willis, "Community Service as an Alternative to Imprisonment: A Cautionary View," (1977) 24 *Probation J.* 20.

85 J. Harding, "The Development of the Community Service," in N. Tutt (ed.), *Alternative Strategies for Coping With Crime*, (Oxford: Blackwell, 1978) at 164; Home Office, *A Review of Criminal Justice Policy, 1976*, (London: H.M.S.O., 1977.); J. Leibrich *et al.*, "Community Sentencing in New Zealand: A Survey of Users," (1986) 50 *Fed. Probation* 55; J. Austin and B. Krisberg, "The Unmet Promise of Alternatives," (1982) 28 *J. of Res. Crime & Delinq.* 374 (1982); M. S. Umbreit, "Community Service Sentencing: Jail Alternatives or Added Sanction?" (1981) 45 *Fed. Probation* 3.

The adjudication of a fine is the most popular intermediate sanction in Western legal systems in lieu of actual incarceration.[86] The significance of paying a fine for humans is deprivation of some of their property, whether the property is money (a fine) or other property (forfeiture).[87] When a person fails to pay a fine, or has insufficient property to pay the fine, substitute penalties are imposed on the offender, particularly incarceration.[88] The imposition of a fine on a corporation is identical to the imposition of a fine on a person, since both people and corporations have property and bank accounts.

However, most AI entities have no money or property of their own, nor have they any bank accounts. If an AI entity does have its own property or money, the imposition of a fine on it would be identical to the imposition of a fine on humans or corporations. For most humans and corporations, property is gained through labour.[89] When paying a fine, the property, which is a result of labour, is transferred to the state. That labour might be transferred to the state in the form of property or directly as labour. As a result, a fine imposed on an AI entity might be collected as money, property, or labour for the benefit of the community. When the fine is collected in the form of labour for the benefit of the community, it is not different from community service as described previously.

Thus, most common penalties are applicable to AI entities. The imposition of specific penalties on AI entities does not negate the nature of these penalties in comparison with their imposition on humans. Of course, some general punishment adjustment considerations are necessary in order to apply these penalties, but still, the nature of these penalties remains the same relative to humans and to AI entities.

5. Conclusion

If all of its specific requirements are met, criminal liability may be imposed upon any entity – human, corporate or AI entity. Modern times warrant modern legal measures in order to resolve today's legal problems. The rapid development of AI technology requires current legal solutions in order to protect society from

86 G. Grebing, *The Fine in Comparative Law: A Survey of 21 Countries*, (Cambridge: C.U.P., 1982).

87 See generally J. A. Greene, "Structuring Criminal Fines: Making an 'Intermediate Penalty' More Useful and Equitable," (1988) 13 *Just. Sys. J.* 37; N. Walker and N. Padfield, *Sentencing: Theory, Law and Practice*, (Oxford: O.U.P., 2nd edn., 1996); M. Zuleeg, "Criminal Sanctions to be Imposed on Individuals as Enforcement Instruments in European Competition Law," in C. Ehlermann and I. Atanasiu (eds.), *European Competition Law Annual 2001: Effective Private Enforcement of EC Antitrust Law*, (Oxford: Hart Publishing, 2001) at 451; S. Uglow, *Criminal Justice*, (London: Sweet & Maxwell, 1995); D. C. Mcdonald *et al.*, *Day fines in American Courts: the Staten Island and Milwaukee Experiments*, (Washington: National Institute of Justice, 1992).

88 F. Rinaldi, *Imprisonment For Non-payment of Fines*, (Canberra: ACT, 1976); *Use of Short Sentences of Imprisonment by the Courts: Report of the Scottish Advisory Council on the Treatment of Offenders*, (Edinburgh: H.M.S.O., 1960).

89 J. Locke, *Two Treatises of Government*, (London: printed for Awnsham Churchill, 1690).

possible dangers inherent in technologies not subject to the law, especially criminal law. Criminal law has a very important social function – that of preserving social order for the benefit and welfare of society. The threats upon that social order may be posed by humans, corporations or AI entities. Humans have been subject to criminal law, except when otherwise decided by international consensus. Thus, minors and mentally ill persons are not subject to criminal law in most legal systems around the world. Although corporations in their modern form have existed since the fourteenth century,[90] it took hundreds of years to subordinate corporations to the law, and especially, to criminal law.

For hundreds of years, the law stated that corporations are not subject to criminal law, as inspired by Roman law (*societas delinquere non potest* – corporations cannot perform delinquency).[91] It was only in the seventeenth century that an English court dared to impose criminal liability on a corporation.[92] It was inevitable. Corporations participate fully in human life, and it was outrageous not to subject them to human laws, since offences are committed by corporations or through them. But corporations have neither body nor soul. Legal solutions were developed so that in relation to criminal liability, corporations would be deemed capable of fulfilling all the requirements of criminal liability, including factual elements and mental elements.[93] These solutions were embodied in models of criminal liability and general punishment adjustment considerations. It worked. In fact, it is still working, and very successfully. Why should AI entities be different from corporations?

Although corporations are not human entities, the effects and imposition of punishments on a corporation are still felt by human beings, which lead to deterrence. So is the situation with AI entities when they are treated as criminally liable, since no legal difference is to be between humans and AI entities as to the imposition of criminal liability and the imposition of punishments. When AI entities are accepted as legal entities, all effects of criminal law shall be identical to those of humans. Of course, since AI entities are able to learn by themselves, they are also able to be deterred by learning what happened in similar cases, exactly as do humans.[94]

---

90 W. S. Holdsworth, *A History of English Law*, (London: Methuen, 1923) at 471–476.
91 W. S. Holdsworth, "English Corporation Law in the 16th and 17th Centuries," (1922) 31 *Yale L. J.* 382; W. R. Scott, *The Constitution and Finance of English, Scottish and Irish Joint-stock Companies to 1720*, (Cambridge: C.U.P., 1912) at 462; B. C. Hunt, *The Development of the Business Corporation in England, 1800–1867*, 1800–1867, (Cambridge: Harvard University Press, 1936).
92 *Case of Langforth Bridge* (1634) 79 Eng. Rep. 919; see also *The King v. Inhabitants of Clifton* (1794) 101 Eng. Rep. 280 (K.B.); *R. v. Inhabitants of Great Broughton* (1771) 98 Eng. Rep. 418 (K.B.); *Stratford-upon-Avon Corporation* (1811) 104 Eng. Rep. 636; *Liverpool (Mayor)* (1802) 102 Eng. Rep. 529; *R. v. Saintiff* (1705), 87 Eng. Rep. 1002.
93 F. Pollock, "Has the Common Law Received the Fiction Theory of Corporations?" (1911) 27 *L.Q.R.* 219.
94 For the rationale of learning from case to case, see G. Hallevy, "Rethinking the Legitimacy of the Anglo-American High Courts' Judicial Review of Determining Factual Findings in Courts of the First Instance in Criminal Cases," (2009) 5 *High Ct. Q. Rev.* 20.

Acknowledgments

The general thorough model of criminal liability for offences involving artificial intelligence technology was introduced for the first time in G. Hallevy, When Robots Kill—Artificial Intelligence Under Criminal Law, (Lebanon, N.H.: Northeastern Univ. Press, 2013). I thank Professor Dennis J. Baker and Professor Paul H. Robinson for inviting me into this project. I also thank the participants of the conference "Criminal Liability for AI Technology and Cybercrime: China and the Common Law" in De Montfort University, Leicester, on July 2019 for their fruitful comments.

11 Don't panic

Artificial intelligence and Criminal Law 101

Mark Dsouza

1. Introduction

The advent of artificial intelligence technology (AIT) challenges established notions about how we do things in almost every domain of our lives. It creates possibilities and efficiencies, but also raises worries: are we ready to cope with the new challenges and dangers that AIT might pose? As AIT adapts, we are being pushed to adapt with it. It is not surprising, therefore, that concerns have arisen about whether our laws are fit for purpose in the brave new world of AIT. The challenges posed to our laws by AIT are almost impossible to overstate. In this chapter, though, I will argue that at least in relation to the substantive law of core criminal offences – the kind that form the foundations of substantive criminal law teaching at universities – these challenges *are* sometimes overstated. I think there is no immediate need to panic; the criminal law already has the resources to cope with criminal activity involving AIT for at least the medium term. But the process of explaining why this is so gives us a chance to reflect once more on the resources that the criminal law has at its disposal, and reconsidering these in this new context brings out nuances that are sometimes overlooked.

Even restricted to core criminal offences, my claim sounds very strong. It suggests that AIT does not change much in relation to our ordinary practices of identifying courts with appropriate jurisdiction, appropriate defendants, the offence's *actus reus*, *mens rea* and defences. I think that a plausible defence of this strong claim is possible, but in this chapter, I will undertake a rather more limited task. I restrict myself to considering only cases in which defendants might be accused of committing a crime within the territorial and procedural jurisdiction of a court, in circumstances in which the putatively criminal event was mediated by an autonomous choice made by AIT. The sorts of autonomous choices I have in mind are those made by weak or narrow AIT[1] – systems that are intelligent when solving a specific problem, but would not pass general intelligence tests

---

1 See B. Goertzel and C. Pennachin (eds.), *Artificial General Intelligence*, (Springer, 2007) at 1; S. D. Baum, B. Goertzel, and T. G. Goertzel, "How Long until Human-level AI? Results from an Expert Assessment," (2011) 78 *Technological Forecasting & Social Change* 185 at 185.

such as the Turing Test.[2] AIT of this sort makes decisions or choices in pursuit of its functions "for itself"; i.e., not under the express directions of a human controller, but based on its own evaluation of its environment, and with some foresight of the consequences of its choices.[3] However, it does not set, or reflect on the value of, the functions that it performs. It is not capable of being "moved" by the reasons presented to it. It is not, in other words, itself an agent that qualifies for criminal liability. Narrow AIT can be contrasted with "general AIT," which refers to intelligent machines characterised by their ability to replicate or surpass a broad range of human intellectual capacities, and characterised even more by the facts that they do not exist now and will probably not exist in the determinate future.

Narrow AIT already exists and is commonplace. Chess-playing robots, autopilot technology and self-driving cars (or even just self-parking cars and cars with cruise control): these are all science fact, not science fiction. My interest is in how we ought to evaluate cases in which this sort of AIT chooses "for itself"; i.e., not under the express directions of a human controller, but based on its own evaluation of the circumstances and the appropriate response thereto, and as a result brings about what looks like a crime.

For ease of analysis, in this chapter, I will refer to a generic defendant as D. But I also have names for more specific defendants. The person who programs the AIT will be Penelope the programmer (P); the user who gives direct instructions to the AIT will be Ursula the user (U). In some examples, I will also talk about Humera the hacker (H), and Olivia the owner (O). And should the analysis call for it, Vrinda the victim (V) will also make an appearance. The AIT in this story will usually be a self-driving car. But the ultimate question will always be the same: when the AIT chooses to act in a manner that suggests that an offence might have been committed, who, if anyone, is liable?

(a) The defendant

The first thing to note is that given the scoping assumptions of this chapter, the self-driving car, qua AIT, will not be itself criminally liable, since it lacks qualifying agency. For the same reason, it will not make anyone else liable under the innocent agency doctrine,[4] either. Much like the gun or knife used by a

---

2 S. Legg and M. Hutter, "Universal Intelligence: A Definition of Machine Intelligence," (2007) 17(4) *Minds and Machines* 391.

3 P. Stone *et al.*, "Artificial Intelligence and Life in 2030," (2016) *Stanford University Research Report* 12–13 <http://ai100.stanford.edu/2016-report> accessed 24 November 2019.

4 A. P. Simester *et al.*, *Simester and Sullivan's Criminal Law*, (London: Hart, 7th edn., 2019) at 227–230; D. J. Baker, *Glanville Williams Textbook of Criminal Law*, (London: Sweet & Maxwell, 4th edn., 2015) at 692–696; J. Horder, *Ashworth's Principles of Criminal Law*, (Oxford: O.U.P., 2018) at 484–485. For a discussion of the underlying theoretical basis of the innocent

murderer, the AIT is simply not an agent, innocent or otherwise.[5] Similarly, the limited doctrine of vicarious criminal liability is also inapplicable in the cases with which I am concerned. That doctrine makes one agent vicariously liable for the crimes of another,[6] but the AIT is not an agent. Accordingly, it can neither be held vicariously liable for the crimes of an agent, nor make an agent vicariously liable for its "own" wrongdoing. The real defendant therefore is the agent (usually, a human) behind the AIT. This also means that the analysis of defences that call into question the agent's responsible agency, such as insanity, infancy, diminished responsibility and (on some accounts of the defence) loss of control, remains unaffected to that extent. The insertion of AIT into the story makes no difference to the human defendant's agency.

2. The *actus reus*

Next, we need to consider whether the criminal law has the resources to help us identify cases in which the AIT's seemingly criminal activity (if any) should be attributed to a human defendant. I will address offences with three different types of *actus reus* stipulations separately, since they raise different issues in the attribution analysis. These are: specific conduct offences, specific consequence offences and state of affairs offences.

(a) Specific conduct offences

Specific conduct offences are offences for the commission of which, a specific type of conduct is required. Examples include dangerous driving under Section 2 of the *Road Traffic Act 1988*, careless and inconsiderate driving under Section 3 of the *Road Traffic Act 1988* and theft under Section 1 of the *Theft Act 1968* (which requires an "appropriation"). These offences can sometimes *also* require a specific consequence to ensue – for instance, the offences of causing death by dangerous driving under Section 1 of the *Road Traffic Act 1988*, and causing death by careless or inconsiderate driving under Section 2B of the *Road Traffic Act 1988*, require both, a specific type of conduct ("driving in a dangerous manner" or "driving in a careless or inconsiderate manner," respectively), and a specific consequence (the death of a human being).

In all cases in which an offence requires the performance of specific conduct, the human defendant must perform that conduct directly, or through an

---

agency doctrine, see M. Dsouza, "A Philosophically Enriched Exegesis of Criminal Accessorial Liability," (2019) 8(1) *UCL Journal of Law and Jurisprudence* 1 at 17–19.

5 Whatever views one might have about gun control, in substantive criminal law at least, the NRA slogan, "Guns don't kill people; people kill people," is surely correct.

6 Cf. A. Kreit, "Vicarious Criminal Liability and the Constitutional Dimensions of Pinkerton," (2008) 57 *Am. U. L. Rev.* 585. See generally W. R. LaFave, *Substantive Criminal Law*, (West, 2003) at § 13.4; Baker, *op. cit. supra,* note 4 at Chapter 9.

innocent agent[7] or through a tool.[8] In the cases in which we are interested, the AIT performs the conduct, so we can rule out the first possibility – *ex hypothesi*, the defendant has not done the thing directly. We can also rule out the second possibility – as mentioned previously, innocent agency is inapplicable, since the AIT is not an agent. However, what about the third possibility? Is the AIT a tool?

When D uses something as a tool, she exercises control over it and thereby treats it as an extension of herself in respect of that usage.[9] Therefore, the thing done through the tool is conduct performed by D herself. So, when D trains her dog to steal sausages from the local butcher, D appropriates the sausages and is potentially guilty of theft. But if the dog were to steal the sausages of its own accord, then even if the owner knew, but did not care, that it was greedy and not well-trained, we would not say that D herself has appropriated the sausages (though D could be liable for other offences with different *actus reus* stipulations). And while the owner of a dog that causes injury while dangerously out of control may be convicted of "being the owner" of a dog that did so under Section 3(1) of the *Dangerous Dogs Act 1991*, she is not convicted of causing the injury herself. The applicable offence is a state of affairs offence.[10] On the other hand, if D trained the dog to injure someone, D could certainly be convicted of an offence involving D causing the injury.[11]

---

7 Some, like S. H. Kadish, "Complicity, Cause and Blame: A Study in the Interpretation of Doctrine," (1985) 73 *Cal L Rev* 323, 373–377 and C. Finkelstein and L. Katz, "Contrived Defenses and Deterrent Threats: Two Facets of One Problem," (2008) 5 *Ohio St. J. Crim. L.* 479 at 485 (cf. too J. Gardner, *Offences and Defences: Selected Essays in the Philosophy of Criminal Law*, (Oxford: O.U.P., 2007) at 70) argue that certain types of conduct (what they call "nonproxyable conduct") cannot be performed through an innocent agent. Accordingly, they would exonerate the defendant in cases requiring those types of conduct, if she did not perform the conduct herself. This is not my view. I have argued elsewhere that there is no reason to think that a human cannot perform specified conduct through the innocent agency of another. See Dsouza, *op. cit. supra*, note 4 at 17–19. Whatever view one takes on that controversy, no one seriously contests that at least *some* forms of conduct can be performed through the innocent agency of another. Hence, it is possible to steal through the innocent agency of a child who is told to take from the shop, or of an adult that one misleads as to the ownership of property. The innocent agent in these cases would be performing the *actus reus* conduct element of theft, *viz.* appropriation.
8 *R. v. Clarence* (1888) 22 QBD 23; *R v Martin* (1881) 8 Q.B.D. 54; *R. v. Lewis* [1970] Crim L.R. 647.
9 J. K. Feibleman, "The Philosophy of Tools," (1967) 45(3) *Special Forces* 329 at 330. One might analogise the exercise of control in this manner to a deliberate treating of something as a tool. I have explained elsewhere that this intent to treat as an innocent agent is effectively an intention to treat an agent as a mere tool in the defendant's plans, and that the innocent agency doctrine works by creating a legal fiction that mirrors the defendant's intention, such that in law, the concerned legal agent is treated as a mere tool and drops out of the responsibility analysis. See Dsouza, *op. cit. supra*, note 4 at 17–19. Presumably, the same intent to treat something as a tool is also required in cases in which the putative tool is not a legal agent.
10 I address these following.
11 *Murgatroyd v. Chief Constable of West Yorkshire* [2000] All ER (D) 1742; *People v. Nealis* (1991) 283 Cal. Rptr. 376 at 379.

Similarly, if D *deliberately* uses the AIT as her tool, the AIT's conduct can be attributed to D. Note that D can intend to use the AIT as a tool even if the AIT retains some measure of autonomy over if, when, and how it does the specific conduct. An unpredictable, or not entirely predictable tool, is still a tool.

In sum therefore, the *actus reus* of specific conduct element offences can be performed through an AIT, but only in the rare cases in which D deliberately uses the AIT as a tool to perform the specific conduct.

(b) Specific consequence offences

Some offences require that the defendant's conduct result in a specific consequence. For some of these offences – including murder and many forms of manslaughter, any conduct will do. For others, such as causing death by dangerous driving, and causing death by careless or inconsiderate driving under Sections 1 and 2B of the *Road Traffic Act 1988*, respectively, some specific conduct must have been performed by the defendant. However, *all* specific consequence offences require *some* "qualifying conduct," though the conduct need not necessarily have been performed by the defendant (or even by a qualifying agent). So for instance, in the state of affairs offence of "Being the owner of a dog that causes injury while dangerously out of control" under Section 3(1) of the *Dangerous Dogs Act 1991*, the qualifying conduct is performed by the dog, though the defendant faces the criminal liability based on the existence of a state of affairs – her ownership of the dog.[12]

Where the qualifying conduct must be performed by the defendant, she can do so through the instrumentality of an autonomously choosing AIT by deploying the AIT as a tool. This will be rare, given that an autonomously choosing AIT makes for an unwieldy tool.

In all specific consequence offences, if the qualifying conduct requirement is met, we must then check whether the consequence can also be attributed to that conduct. So for instance, imagine that the specific consequence that our offence proscribes is the death of Vrinda the victim. Where the offence requires that the qualifying conduct be performed by a human defendant, our prospective defendants include Penelope the programmer, Ursula the user and Humera the hacker (or more than one of them). They might perform conduct like programming, using or hacking into and reprogramming the AIT, respectively. We need to ascertain when this conduct can be linked to the ultimate death of V.

The criminal law uses the rules of causation to link a principal's conduct to consequence.[13] Under these rules, the qualifying conduct can be linked to the

---

12 R. A. Duff, "The Circumstances of an Attempt," (1991) 50 *Cambridge L.J.* 104; D. Husak, "Lifting the Cloak: Preventive Detention As Punishment,| (2011) 48 *San Diego L. Rev.* 1173 at 1196; S. Dimock, "Intoxication and the Act/control/agency Requirement," (2012) 6 *Crim. L. & Phil.* 341 at 343; A. P. Simester, "On the So-Called Requirement for Voluntary Action," (1998) 1 *Buff. Crim. L. Rev.* 403 at 410.

13 Dsouza, *op. cit., supra*, note 4.

proscribed consequence if it was a factual cause of the consequence,[14] and it was legally significant[15] and salient to it.[16] The most important part of our analysis will relate to the application of the *novus actus interveniens* rules.

Doctrinally, an intervention breaks the chain of causation between an agent and a consequence if it was an unforeseeable natural (or at least non-agential) event,[17] or an independent intervention by the victim or some third party.[18] The AIT is not the victim, and it is not a third party, since it is not a qualifying agent, but:

(1) U or H could break the chain of causation between P's conduct and the consequence; or

(2) H could break the chain of causation between P's or U's conduct and the consequence; or

(3) U could break the chain of causation between H's or P's conduct and the consequence.

Each of these possibilities can be analysed under existing rules of criminal causation. But could the AIT's own choice break the chain of causation? The existing rules of criminal causation are perfectly well equipped to answer this question as well. If the AIT's choice, though not dictated, or even foreseen, was foreseeable, then the answer is "no."[19] So in these "foreseeable" cases, it is possible to bring about the *actus reus* through the AIT. In "unforeseeable" cases, there is no particular reason to think that the human behind the AIT ought to be held criminally responsible for the consequence. But if we did want to hold her criminally responsible, state of affairs liability flowing from ownership of the AIT would remain possible, even with AIT inserted into the story.

Where the offence requires that the qualifying conduct be performed by an autonomous non-agent like a dog, or what is of interest to us, an AIT, much the same causation analysis applies, with two qualifications. First, the human defendant must obviously be replaced by the AIT as the performer of the conduct in

---

14 *R. v Dalloway* (1847) 2 Cox CC 273, *R v White* [1910] 2 KB 124.

15 *R. v White* [1910] 2 KB 124; *R v Cato* [1976] 1 WLR 110.

16 *R. v Wallace (Berlinah)* [2018] 2 Cr App R 22.

17 Even if a subsequently arising, causally independent event does not qualify as a fully voluntary human act, that event may yet qualify as an intervening cause if it is in some sense "extraordinary." Such extraordinary events may be natural events, like floods, storms, and earthquakes, or they may be human actions. In either case, "acts of God" or "coincidences" may break causal chains as surely as the most deliberate intervention by a third-party wrongdoer." Michael S. Moore, "The Metaphysics of Causal Intervention," (2000) 88 *Cal. L. Rev.* 827 at 844. Cf. *Environment Agency v Empress Car Co. (Abertillery) Ltd* [1999] 2 AC 22, 34–36.

18 *R. v Kennedy* [2007] UKHL 38; *R v Jordan* (1956) 40 Cr App R 152. See Glanville Williams, "Finis for Novus Actus?" (1989) 48 *Cambridge L.J.* 391 at 392; H. L. A. Hart and T. Honoré, *Causation in the Law*, (Oxford: O.U.P., 1985) at 326.

19 This rule applies both to non-agential interventions and agential interventions. In respect of the former, see *R. v Wallace* [2018] 2 Cr App R 22. In respect of the latter, see *R. v Roberts* (1972) 56 Cr App R 95.

the analysis. Second, and less straightforwardly, we need some explanation of the link between the AIT and the human defendant (in this case, Olivia the owner), and how it can support a blaming judgement. I address this second issue next.

(c) State of affairs offences

Some offences have a third type of *actus reus* stipulation. These are the growing set of offences that do not require conduct, but rather a state of affairs, such as "being in possession of something." Examples include "possession of a controlled drug" under Section 5 of the *Misuse of Drugs Act 1971* and "going equipped for stealing" under Section 25 of the *Theft Act 1968*.[20] So, how are these offences affected by the insertion of AIT into the mix?

It is conceivable that in some such offences, the possession of the AIT itself might be what is criminalised. For instance, D commits the Section 25, *Theft Act 1968* offence, if she is outside her home and has with her any article for use in the course of or in connection with burglary or theft. It is entirely possible that the article for use in the course of or connection with a burglary or theft may be an AIT. But this is an uninteresting case, insofar as it is not one in which the AIT actually does anything.

What if, instead, an AIT makes (unpredicted and not deliberately risked) choices that bring it into possession of contraband? In cases involving these "out-of-control" acquisitions by the AIT, does D, the human behind the AIT, perform the *actus reus* of a possession offence? In 2014, a bot called Random Darknet Shopper, set up to make random purchases off the Dark Web for an art exhibition in Switzerland, went rogue and started buying ecstasy and fake designer handbags.[21] The police did not press charges against the art gallery, possibly

---

20 This offence, despite its name, does not require the defendant to be "going" anywhere. It requires only that she not be at her place of abode.

21 Grimmelmann writes:

> The rise of high-speed trading algorithms raises uncomfortable questions about whether a computer can have the requisite mental state to "knowingly" engage in market manipulation or to enter into an "agreement" to fix prices. And Swiss authorities didn't bother trying to sort out the philosophical questions posed by a drug-buying robot; they simply seized the robot.

J. Grimmelmann, "Copyright for Literate Robots," (2016) 101 *Iowa L. Rev.* 657 at 674. Gal observes:

> Indeed, this knowledge gap is a direct result of the algorithm's comparative advantage: as elaborated above, the algorithm can quickly consider a breadth of data that no human could, and it can sometimes predict the user's future choices better than the user himself. Furthermore, in some situations the user may not care about the actual choice made by the algorithm, so long as it makes a choice. A recent and provocative example involves the Random Darknet Shopper, a shopping bot used in an art project displayed at a gallery in St. Gallen, Switzerland, in 2015. For the duration of the exhibition, the artists sent the bot to shop on the dark web, with a weekly budget of $100 in bitcoins. The bot chose items and sent them to the artists by mail, without the artists knowing in advance what would be purchased. The orders were then displayed in the gallery.

because this was treated as a work of art, and therefore receives special protection under the Swiss constitution. However, that is the sort of case I have in mind here. There is some controversy as to whether one can unknowingly be in possession of something. In *Warner v Metropolitan Police Commissioner*,[22] Lord Guest thought that "[i]f someone surreptitiously puts something into my pocket, I am not in possession of it until I know it is there," but some commentators express doubts about this proposition.[23] But to the extent that this controversy is live, it arises even outside of cases involving AIT. We can therefore bracket off this concern. What is more certain is that in cases involving the deliberate creation or underwriting of a state of affairs (such as cases of voluntary possession), D treats the AIT as a tool, and so "performs" the *actus reus* of possession through it.

3. The *mens rea*

(a) Preliminaries

Even after we show that one or more of P, U, H or O have committed the *actus reus* associated with an offence (say) involving causing the death of V (despite the supervening autonomous choice made by the AIT), we are faced with the problem of establishing that the concerned human defendant had the *mens rea* to commit the *prima facie* offence. To some extent, this will depend on the *mens rea* standard stipulated for the offence concerned.

But we might wonder whether offences that require subjective fault can *ever* be proved against a human defendant when the AIT autonomously chooses its actions. In fact, they can. For instance, autonomous non-agential intervening choice is compatible with having an intention as to the resulting consequences. The story of Androcles and the lion illustrates this. When Androcles was cast into the pit to be devoured by a lion, there was certainly an intention to kill him, and this intention existed despite the fact that the lion could in principle (as it did in the story) decide not to eat Androcles.[24] There is no reason to think that the same is not true for lower subjective *mens rea* states like knowledge or recklessness.

M. S. Gal, "Algorithmic Challenges to Autonomous Choice," (2018) 25 *Mich. Tech. L. Rev.* 59 at 97.

22 [1969] 2 AC 256. The House of Lords held that one could only possess something if one knew that it, or something not completely different from it, was in one's possession.

23 See for instance, D. N. Husak and C. A. Callender, "Wilful Ignorance, Knowledge, and the 'Equal Culpability' Thesis: A Study of the Deeper Significance of the Principle of Legality," (1994) 1994 *Wis. L. Rev.* 29 at 60.

24 There is some suggestion that this might also possible through autonomous agential intervening choice. Perhaps we could say that an evil supervillain who orders her assassin to kill V intends to cause the death of V. This view was alluded to by the Supreme Court of the United Kingdom in *R v Jogee* [2017] A.C. 387 at para. 90. The Supreme Court of the United Kingdom stated that in many cases, especially of concerted physical attack,

there may often be no practical distinction to draw between an intention by D2 to assist D1 to act with the intention of causing grievous bodily harm at least and D2 having the

(b) Intention

So when can we say that P, U, H, or O intend, for instance, to cause the death of V through a supervening AIT? The answer, I propose, requires us to refer to the standard tests of intention. Before we get to the question of oblique intention, we should ask whether D's desire that V die is either as an end in itself[25] or as a necessary means to some other end.[26] We should also bear in mind when asking these questions that a conditional intention to cause the death of V (or any other specified consequence) is, for legal purposes, the same as an unconditional intention to cause the death of V (or other specified consequence).[27] The answers to these questions depend on the facts of the case before us, but one thing to note especially in relation to the second question is that a conditional *desire* is not enough to prove either unconditional intention, or conditional intention.

Imagine that P the programmer contemplates the possibility that the AIT she is programming might encounter a situation in which it must choose between killing one person and killing five people.[28] She thinks that in such a situation, the AIT should choose to kill the one, and she programs the AIT accordingly. This programming choice does not *ipso facto* mean that P the programmer intends, or even conditionally intends, to kill (or cause the death of) the eventual victim V at the time of making that programming decision. At the time when the programming decision is made, nobody needs saving, and it is possible (and, in fact, it is exceedingly likely) that P hopes that this trolley-like situation will not arise. If so, then P does not desire the death of V any more than she desires her burglar alarm to go off when she sets it before leaving her house. Since P would not be disappointed if the AIT never encountered a trolley-like situation and had to choose to kill a person, P does not intend, even conditionally, to kill the person.

---

intention himself that such harm be caused. In such cases it may be simpler, and will generally be perfectly safe, to direct the jury (as suggested in *Wesley Smith and Reid*) that the Crown must prove that D2 intended that the victim should suffer grievous bodily harm at least.

I have my doubts about this proposition, but I will not explore them here, since an AIT is not an autonomous agent. See the criticisms essayed in D. J. Baker, "Lesser Included Offences, Alternative Offences and Accessorial Liability," (2016) 80(6) *J. Crim. L.* 446.

25 *D.P.P. v Smith* [1961] A.C. 290, 327; *Hyam v DPP* [1975] A.C. 55 at 79.

26 *Hyam* (n24) 74

27 *Attorney-General's Reference (Nos 1 and 2 of 1979)* [1980] Q.B. 180; see D. J. Baker, *Reinterpreting Criminal Complicity and Inchoate Participation Offences*, (Oxford: Routledge, 2016); D. J. Baker, "The Doctrinal and Normative Vacuity of Hong Kong's Joint Enterprise Doctrine," (2017) *Hong Kong L.J.* 349.

28 This is a variation on the classic trolley problem. See B. Walker Smith, "The Trolley and the Pinto: Cost-Benefit Analysis in Automated Driving and Other Cyber-Physical Systems," (2017) 4 *Tex. A&M L. Rev.* 197; J. K. Gurney, "Crashing into the Unknown: An Examination of Crash-Optimization Algorithms Through the Two Lanes of Ethics and Law," (2016) 79 *Alb. L. Rev.* 183 at 205; B. I. Huang, "Law's Halo and the Moral Machine," (2019) 119 *Colum. L. Rev.* 1811 at 1828. See P. Foot, "The Problem of Abortion and the Doctrine of Double Effect," (1967) 5 *Oxford Review* 1 at 3; J. J. Thomson, "The Trolley Problem," (1985) 94 *Yale L.J.* 1395.

If P had actually (and not conditionally or contingently) *desired* that the AIT encounter a trolley-like situation, then that would of course be instructive. Consider D's intention to steal from a bag, if there be something of value in it: if an external condition is met (there is something valuable in the bag), then D plans to bring about something – a permanent deprivation of someone else's property (by appropriating it, in this case, for herself). It seems very likely that D also *desires* that the external condition be met. This desire is not contingent or somewhere in the future – it exists in the present. And the fact that D has this present desire that the condition be met also suggests that D has a present (albeit conditional) desire to bring about the permanent deprivation of the other's property. After all, if there were nothing valuable in the bag, D would be disappointed, because she would be unable to steal anything valuable. This desire to do something indicates a direct intention to do it. On these facts, it makes sense to say that D (presently) intends to steal anything valuable that may (in the hypothetical future) be in the bag.

In other words, a *contingent* desire *that something happen* – in this case, that the AIT choose to kill the one rather than the five if ever faced with the trolley-like situation – is not instructive in the same way as a present desire that something happen, since it gives us no indication of *present* desires as to the performance of the potentially criminal conduct.

Nor can we say that P has an oblique intent[29] to cause anyone's death. Oblique intention will suffice for almost every offence for which intention is required,[30] but one has merely to state the test for oblique intention to see that it is inapplicable on the presented facts. It is not virtually certain that a trolley-like problem will ever arise – in fact, it is very unlikely. So even the first condition for oblique intent is not met. The fact that the AIT would make a foreseeable choice should it ever be faced with a trolley-like situation does not suggest that the programmer realises that it is virtually certain that the AIT *will* kill V (or anyone else).

On the other hand, if the AIT was virtually certain to cause the death of a person, and P realised that, then applying the standard test for oblique intention, the jury can find that she intends that death when she deploys the AIT anyway. Therefore, although it will be a rare case in which P, U, H or O will intend to kill through the medium of an autonomously choosing AIT, there appears to be no need to come up with new tests for intention to deal with the advent of narrow AIT.

(c) *Knowledge/belief*

Some offences are so defined that they can be committed when the defendant acts knowing or believing that certain circumstances exist, or that certain consequences will ensue. In either case, the addition of an autonomous AIT makes little difference to the analysis of the human defendant's knowledge or belief. We

---

29 *R. v. Woollin* [1999] A.C. 82.
30 But not every such offence – for instance, the offence under Section 44 of the *Serious Crime Act 2007* seems to insist on direct intent.

simply need to ask whether D performed her conduct (be it programming, using, hacking into or – on a stretched interpretation of the word "conduct" – knowingly owning the AIT) with the knowledge or belief required for the offence. The knowledge or beliefs of the AIT (assuming that AIT actually forms beliefs in the same sense as humans form beliefs)[31] are irrelevant, since it is not the defendant. This *mens rea* state cannot be satisfied by showing that the human defendant acted despite the fact that the AIT she programmed, used, owned or hacked into believed or knew some facts – the culpability in offences requiring knowledge or belief traces to the defendant's advertent choice to act *despite* knowing or believing certain facts.[32] The defendant's choice to act is simply not culpable in the same way when she herself did not know, or believe, the relevant facts, even if the AIT "knew" or "believed" them.

(d) Recklessness and negligence

Other *mens rea* standards such as recklessness and negligence could also be met by P, U, H or O. If that is the allegation, and recklessness or negligence satisfies the *mens rea* for the *prima facie* offence, the analysis is simpler. A person is reckless as to circumstances or consequences if she was subjectively aware of the risk of these circumstances existing, or consequences ensuing from her conduct, and unreasonably took that risk.[33] A person is negligent if she unreasonably took a risk, and ought to have known of the existence of the risk.[34] For both these *mens rea* states, though, the common issue is the reasonableness of the risk-taking. The key question here is not, "How did/will the AIT respond to the situation?" It will respond to the situation in accordance with its programming or the instructions given by humans. Unlike humans, AIT will not choose as a moral agent. It will also not choose arbitrarily (except perhaps if it was programmed or instructed to choose arbitrarily, in which case it too is choosing as programmed or instructed). Even to the extent that AIT is empowered to teach itself the best ways to achieve its goals, the AIT is told its goals and is programmed to be able to learn. Therefore, we focus instead on what the defendant did – program or instruct the AIT. If the defendant's programming or instruction of the AIT was reasonable, then the defendant lacks the *mens rea* for offences predicated on negligence or recklessness. So, for instance, a defendant who was properly sensitive to V's interests while programming or instructing the AIT was not reckless or negligent as to harming V, because she acted reasonably.

---

31 See D. Dennett, *Intuition Pumps and Other Tools for Thinking*, (New York: Penguin, 2014) at 91–97 for some scepticism as to this.
32 M. Dsouza, "Corporate Agents in Criminal Law – an Argument for Comprehensive Identification," (2 September 2019) at 1–32 <https://ssrn.com/abstract=3446666>, 24; S. M. Solaiman, "Corporate Manslaughter by Industrial Robots at Work: Who Should Go on Trial Under the Principles of Common Law in Australia?" (2016) 35 *J.L. & Com.* 21.
33 *R v G & R* [2004] 1 AC 1034
34 G. Williams, "Carelessness, Indifference and Recklessness: Two Replies," (1962) 25 *M.L.R.* 49 at 57; K. W. Simons, "Culpability and Retributive Theory: The Problem of Criminal Negligence," (1994) 1994 *J. Contemp. Legal Issues* 365.

What it was reasonable to program or instruct the AIT to do depends, to some extent, on the epistemic capabilities of the AIT, since these will affect what one may sensibly ask of the AIT. It is theoretically possible for the AIT's sensors to be of such poor quality that it would be unreasonable to deploy the AIT at all, since there would be no reasonable instruction that one could give such an AIT in respect of a foreseeable situation that it might encounter. Assuming that the AIT's sensors meet industry specifications, and that the industry specifications are a good proxy for a reasonable quality and quantity of sensors, that seems unlikely, and so we can set this possibility aside for now.[35] The reasonableness of the defendant's programming or instructions then depends on our evaluation of the quality of the guidance given to the AIT. This, in turn, depends on what the AIT's sensors can sense, how fast it can process that information and how fast it can process and act on its guidance as to how to respond.

Humans give the AIT this guidance. They tell the AIT what to do if faced with a choice between life and property, or between two or more lives, or between different pieces of property, etc. So long as this guidance conforms to prescribed industry standards (if any, and subject to a qualification to follow), or in the absence of those, to enough of the jury's standards of reasonableness to make a conviction impossible, the defendant does not act negligently or recklessly, as the case may be.

In sum, the key issue is not what outcomes occur in variations of the trolley question – it is what advance guidance is reasonable to give. That depends on the information and capacities we have when giving the guidance.

Decisions on the reasonableness of guidance might perhaps be facilitated by a centralised AIT ethics checklist – something like Asimov's three rules.[36] But that would be a limited solution – someone who figured out a loophole and deliberately set out to exploit it to cause harm ought not to be able to escape liability by pointing to formal compliance. In fact, the intent to exploit a loophole should itself inculpate, and this would be possible if compliance with our AIT ethics checklist was treated as evidence of reasonableness, rather than being constitutive of it. It would be sensible to treat our ethics checklist, should we have one, as a set of rules of thumb – a work constantly in progress. It should constantly be open to evolving, perhaps with the state periodically underwriting the current statement

---

35 Of course, if we did want to expand this analysis to include this question, we could. It might, for instance, become relevant in the context of new technology that does not yet have industry standards, or for backyard inventors or tinkerers who fine-tune their AITs to meet what they consider higher performance specifications. If so, we can also introduce Malena the manufacturer into the picture. But in order to keep this chapter to manageable proportions, I will not attempt to do so here.

36 I. Asimov, *I, Robot,* (New York: Gnome Press, 1950) at 40. Note, however, that Asimov's rules leave far too many things unclear. For one thing, although the first, and most important, rule is that "A robot may not injure a human being or, through inaction, allow a human being to come to harm," how should a robot respond in a situation in which it will injure (or allow injury to) a human no matter what it decides to do? For a brief discussion of the flaws in Asimov's rules, see J. Tasioulas, "First Steps Towards an Ethics of Robots and Artificial Intelligence," (2019) 7(1) *Journal of Practical Ethics* 61.

of ethical principles, which may then be re-evaluated based on academic and industry critiques, and in the event that we discover problems, through trial and error. But to be clear, developing such a set of rules is not the task I set myself in this chapter.

(e) Consent

One question that cuts across the *actus reus/mens rea* divide is whether the putative victim's consent, where it is legally valid, will affect our defendant's liability, even when the defendant (or as the case may be, the AIT) could not have been aware of, and responsive to, that consent when performing the qualifying conduct. In doctrinal criminal law, where consent matters, the granting of consent is best conceived of as a factor that negates the *actus reus* of an offence,[37] whereas a belief (or sometimes, a reasonable belief) in consent may negate the *mens rea* of an offence.[38]

To the extent that consent implicates the *actus reus* of the offence, the defendant's reliance on or uptake of the consent is not necessary for the negation of the *actus reus*. Hence, the putative victim's consent, if valid, means that the AIT does not occasion even a *prima facie* offence. And insofar as the *mens rea* of the offence is concerned, given that the conduct performed by the defendant will usually be remote from the circumstances in which V refuses or grants consent, the defendant would rarely be able to credibly claim that she believed that V had consented.[39]

But again, none of this is a departure from standard principles. The key questions remain what they always have: (1) "did the putative victim grant legally valid consent?"; and (2) "did the defendant believe (or reasonably believe, as the case may be) that the putative victim had consented?"

(f) Contemporaneity

Even so, there remains another problem. A *prima facie* offence is only committed when the *actus reus* and the *mens rea* exist contemporaneously. However, it appears that P, U, H and O will in most cases have formed their respective *mens rea* states in advance of the AIT choosing to bring about the *actus reus*. Again, though, this problem is hardly a new one for the criminal law, and the criminal law already has the resources to deal with it. The continuing act principle allows

---

37 M. Dsouza, "Undermining Prima Facie Consent in the Criminal Law," (2014) 33 *L. and Phil.* 489 at 494–497.

38 *Ibid.* at 497–498. A belief in consent may also occasionally support a claim to a rationale-based defence. However, for reasons that will become apparent, I do not address the role of consent in defences separately.

39 The same applies when the defendant relies on a belief in the victim's consent in claiming a rationale-based defence. For this reason, I do not address the analysis in relation to such claims separately.

the criminal law to stretch the conduct involved in the *actus reus* beyond the point at which D was actively doing something, up until the *mens rea* was formed,[40] or to link it to some previous conduct performed at a time when there was *mens rea* such that the entire chain of conduct is seen as a single continuing act. Again, the advent of AIT does not require us to reinvent the criminal law.

(g) Rationale-based defences

However, the set of concerns most frequently voiced are to do with instances in which the AIT is faced with a difficult choice about which criminalised outcome to bring about. This often manifests in asking how AIT should deal with trolley problems and who, if anybody, should bear the responsibility for the choices that AITs make in such cases. Trolley problems are usually puzzles relating to the sorts of defences that are known as "rationale-based defences." These defences include claims of self-defence, prevention of crime, arrest, duress and necessity. In making any of these claims, the defendant asserts that she deliberately did what amounted to a *prima facie* offence, but did so for good reasons. They are not generally available in respect of *prima facie* offences that were constituted by the defendant's negligent conduct – in those offences, the defendant makes no deliberate choice to commit the *prima facie* offence, and so it is meaningless to talk about her motivations for offending. I have, in previous work, set out a theoretical framework within which we should understand rationale-based defences.[41]

The invocation of trolley problems in relation to AITs is usually misleading – the trolley problem is a problem involving a claim to a defence when an *agent* chooses to commit a *prima facie* offence in response to a perceived present threat. But in AIT cases, a non-agent is making this choice in response to the perceived present threat. The human agent's choice is usually made well in advance of any perceived present threat, when P, H or U interact with the AIT. At that stage, they plan generalised threat-management strategy rather than responding to specific extant threats. They cannot therefore seek exculpation for their actions by claiming a rationale-based defence – instead, they may rely on the reasonableness of their actions to deny *mens rea*. I have already outlined how that argument would proceed.

Still, it can, on rare occasions, be appropriate to consider whether a rationale-based defence is available, and so a brief examination of such claims is useful. Any claim of a rationale-based defence involves two stages. First, the defendant must form the belief that facts exist that necessitate the use of defensive force (and decide to use the defensive force for those reasons). Depending on the defence in question, this belief may have to satisfy an objective test of reasonableness, as well. Once the defendant crosses the first stage (and only then)[42] do

---

40 *Fagan v. Metropolitan Police Commissioner* [1969] 1 QB 439; *R. v. Church* [1966] 1 Q.B. 59; *R. v. Le Brun* [1991] 3 W.L.R. 653.

41 M. Dsouza, *Rationale-Based Defences in Criminal Law*, (London: Hart, 2017).

42 *R. v. Field* [1972] Crim. L.R. 435 – no need to retreat because no present threat; *R. v Cockburn* [2008] 2 Cr. App. R. 4 – no "pre-threat" defensive measure). M. Dsouza, "Retreat, Submission, and the Private Use of Force," (2015) *OJLS* 1 at 23–24.

we reach the second stage, at which the defendant considers her response. Only at this stage, will she consider the normative appropriateness of her defensive option(s). It is just about within the realm of possibility that U or H might be responding to a present threat. For instance, one can just about imagine U or H seeing a present (though slow-burn) threat and thereupon instructing or reprogramming their AIT in the hope that it will (autonomously, but foreseeably) react to the threat in a particular way, which involves committing a *prima facie* offence. On this peculiar set of facts, the defensive claim potentially available would be rationale-based. But the analysis required to adjudicate this claim would be exactly the same the one we would undertake in non-AIT infused claims to a rationale-based defence. We would ask: "did the defendant think there was a present threat (D's conclusion might sometimes need to also be objectively reasonable)?" and "was the defendant's chosen response appropriate (this question must be answered by reference to objective standards)?" Again, there is no need to reinvent the wheel here.

(b) Application

Let us now apply the analytical approach sketched in this chapter in relation to liability as a principal to our prospective defendants, starting with Penelope the programmer. Let us say that she programmed the AIT – a self-driving car – such that down the line, it chose to do something seemingly criminal. Doing that thing could itself be an offence, or the consequence of doing that thing – V's death – might make it an offence. If the offence requires the performance of some conduct (say, dangerous driving), we should ask whether P deliberately used the car as her tool to perform this conduct. If so, then the analysis may continue, but if not, then P does not commit the *actus reus* of the offence. If the offence also requires a consequence – say the death of V – then we apply the usual rules of causation, and consider whether either a human user or hacker, or the car's own autonomous choice broke the chain of causation. This last question depends on whether the car's autonomous choice was foreseeable. If it was, then the chain of causation is not broken and the inquiry may continue.

We next consider *mens rea*. If the *mens rea* required includes intention as to one of the *actus reus* elements, we apply the ordinary tests for intention in the criminal law to ask whether P had the requisite intention at the time she programmed the car. If the *mens rea* required includes knowledge or belief as to something, then we ask whether P knew or believed that thing. If the *mens rea* required includes recklessness or negligence as to a circumstance or consequence, we consider what P subjectively knew of or foresaw the concerned circumstance or consequence, or what she ought to have known or foreseen it as the case may be, and consider the reasonableness of P's programming choices in view of that epistemic profile. If at the end of this analysis P is still *prima facie* liable for the offence, we might consider whether she has any rationale-based defences available to her. The reasonableness analyses necessary to make this determination would also proceed along the same lines as the one made in respect of assessing recklessness and negligence.

Almost the entirety of this analysis can also be applied to Ursula the user, who instructs the car such that, down the line, it chose to do something seemingly criminal. The only difference is that the programmer's actions are unlikely to be potential breaks in the chain of causation.

Finally, consider Humera the hacker. Most of the previous analysis will apply to her, as well, with one added complication. H's conduct would presumably amount to at least two different sets of (*prima facie*) offences; those relating to her very act of hacking the AIT, and those relating to the criminalised outcome brought about by the car as a consequence of that hacking. Although our focus here should be on the latter set of offences, it is clear that our findings in relation to these will be influenced by our findings in relation to the former set. If there is no basis for thinking that it was right, or at least acceptable behaviour for H to have hacked the car, then it seems unlikely that there would be a basis for thinking that reprogramming the car to act as she did was reasonable. The converse is equally true, as well. If we thought that it was reasonable for H to have reprogrammed the car as she did, we would usually think that it was also right or societally normatively acceptable for H to have hacked the car in the first place. But these things could, in principle, come apart. We could imagine that H had installed a backdoor in the programming of the car for some malicious fun months ago, but now, seeing an impending disaster, she uses the backdoor to reprogram the car and try to save the day, albeit at some possible cost to some innocent bystander – V. In such a case, we would analyse H's actions in relation to each *prima facie* offence separately.

4. Complicity liability

In addition to liability as a principal, the criminal law also imposes secondary liability on agents, either as accessories to others' crimes, or by way of inchoate liability for crimes that were not necessarily[43] ever completed. I cannot enter into a detailed discussion of whether the advent of AIT affects the analysis for these forms of liability here, but I briefly set out my reasons for thinking that it does not.

D is an accessory to an offence committed by another if she aids, abets, counsels or procures the commission of that offence.[44] But how much does the traditional analysis of this form of liability change when D is the programmer, owner, user or someone who hacked into and reprograms an AIT that then autonomously does something that aids, abets, counsels or procures an offence committed by a human principal? The answer is: not much.

As far as the *actus reus* for being an accessory is concerned, D can theoretically aid, abet, counsel or procure the criminal offence of another through the instrumentality of an autonomously choosing AIT. But this will be exceedingly rare,

---

43 Note that most inchoate offences can technically be charged even if a completed offence was committed. See Section 6(4) of the *Criminal Law Act 1967* in the context of criminal attempts; Section 56 of the *Serious Crime Act 2007* in the context of the offences of encouraging or assisting crime.

44 Section 8 of the *Accessories and Abettors Act 1861*.

since D could only do so by using the autonomously choosing AIT as a tool. This seems unlikely. Since the AIT will choose its conduct autonomously, it would be a relatively unreliable tool. But should such a case arise, it has already been demonstrated that doctrinal criminal law has the analytical tools to address it.

The *mens rea* for accessorial liability is notoriously complicated – we must show that D intended to perform the conduct that she did perform, intended thereby to aid, abet, counsel or procure the principal's conduct,[45] and intended that in performing the conduct assisted or encouraged, the principal would commit an offence.[46] Even so, it is composed of various subjective fault elements that have already been analysed in the chapter. In none of those cases did the insertion of AIT into the story stretch the analytical resources already at the disposal of doctrinal criminal law, and there is no reason to think that the combination of these factors would do so, either.

5. Inchoate offences

There are several different inchoate offences, but once again, they are all composed of *actus reus* and *mens rea* elements that have previously been analysed. Thus inchoate offences will typically require the defendant to perform some conduct,[47] but will typically not require any consequence to follow. Once again, D can perform this conduct through the instrumentality of the autonomously choosing AIT by using it as a tool, but once again, for obvious reasons, D's chosen tool is unlikely to be an AIT that chooses its conduct for itself. The *mens rea* stipulations for different inchoate offences differ, and there are too many of these to analyse in detail in this piece. Suffice it to say that each of these are constructed out of subjective fault states that, as previously established, can be applied also to cases involving AIT. Therefore, as is true for the plethora of offences that have *mens rea* stipulations that include various permutations and combinations of these fault states, there is no reason to believe that they will create special difficulties in combination.

---

45 *R. v. Bryce* [2004] EWCA Crim 1231; *R. v. Derek* [2001] 1 Cr. App. R. 21.

46 Baker writes:

> The mental element in complicity is once again (direct) intention. This may be inferred from evidence of foresight of virtual certainty. D1 must intend to assist or encourage D2 with the ulterior intention that D2 use his or her assistance (or be encouraged by his or her encouragement) to perpetrate the anticipated target crime. D1 must intend D2 to act with the requisite fault for the target crime.

> D. J. Baker, "Prosecuting Complicity: The CPS Legal Guidance on Secondary Liability," (2018) 82(4) *J. Crim. L.* 338 at 339. This was the approach adopted in *R. v. Jogee* [2017] A.C. 387.

47 Doing something more than merely preparatory to the commission of the offence for attempts liability under Section 1 of the *Criminal Attempts Act 1981*; making an agreement (containing specified terms) with another person for conspiracy liability under Section 1 of the *Criminal Law Act 1977*; doing something capable of encouraging or assisting an offence for inchoate liability under Part 2 of the *Serious Crime Act 2007*, etc.

6. Conclusion

This chapter has involved a necessarily brief survey of the main topics considered during undergraduate substantive criminal law modules, with a view to examining whether the introduction of narrow AIT necessitates a rethinking of the fundamentals of criminal law. While the re-examination of these foundational matters in a new context is always valuable, and often sheds new light on less prominent features of the criminal law, my main conclusion is that the substantive law of core criminal offences has the resources to deal with cases involving narrow AIT. And given that general AIT is not yet appearing on the horizon anytime soon, for the present at least, the emergence of AIT gives us no reason to panic.

Index

Printed in the United States
By Bookmasters